Looking Backward, Moving Forward

Also by Richard G. Hovannisian

Armenia on the Road to Independence

The Republic of Armenia (4 volumes)

The Armenian Image in History and Literature

The Armenian People from Ancient to Modern Times (2 volumes)

Enlightenment and Diaspora: The Armenian and Jewish Cases

The Armenian Genocide in Perspective

The Armenian Genocide: History, Politics, Ethics

Remembrance and Denial: The Case of the Armenian Genocide

Islam's Understanding of Itself

Ethics in Islam

Poetry and Mysticism in Islam: The Heritage of Rumi

The Thousand and One Nights in Arabic Literature and Society

The Persian Presence in Islam

Religion and Culture in Medieval Islam

Armenian Van/Vaspurakan

Armenian Baghesh/Bitlis and Taron/Mush

Armenian Tsopk/Kharpert

Confronting the Armenian Genocide

Looking Backward, Moving Forward

Richard G. Hovannisian
editor

Transaction Publishers
New Brunswick (U.S.A.) and London (U.K.)

This book is printed on acid-free paper that meets the American National Standard for Permanence of Paper for Printed Library Materials.

Library of Congress Catalog Number: 2002073266
ISBN: 0-7658-0196-5 (cloth); 0-7658-0519-7 (paper)
Printed in the United States of America

Library of Congress Cataloging-in-Publication Data

Looking backward, moving forward : confronting the Armenian Genocide / edited by Richard G. Hovannisian.

p. cm.

Includes bibliographical references and index.

ISBN 0-7658-0196-5 (cloth : alk. paper)—ISBN 0-7658-0519-7 (pbk. : alk. paper)

1. Armenian massacres, 1915-1923. 2. Armenians—Turkey—History. 3. Genocide—Turkey. 4. Turkey—History—20th century. 5. Armenia—History—1901- I. Hovannisian, Richard G.

DS195.5 .L66 2003
956.6'2015—dc21 2002073266

Contents

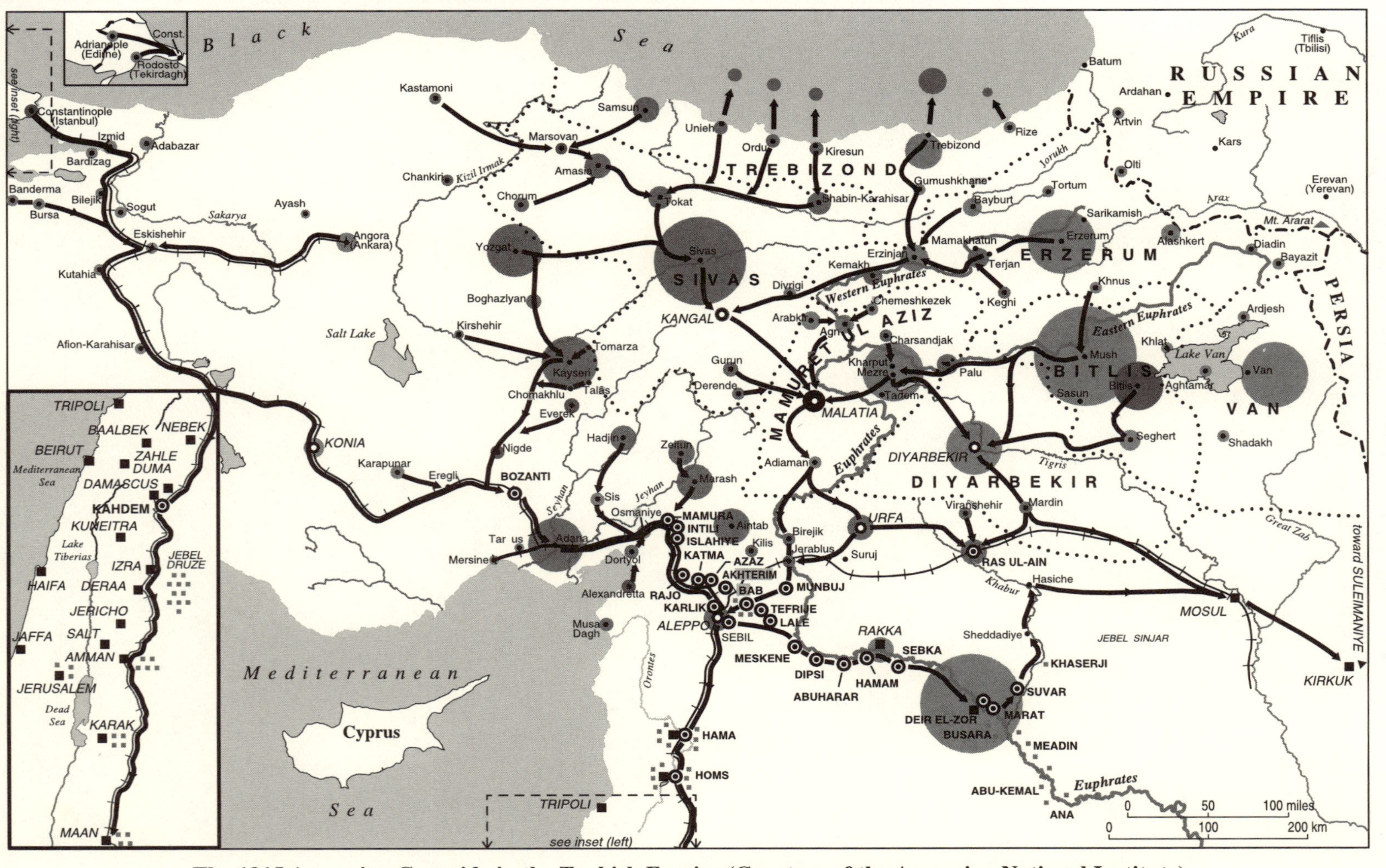

The 1915 Armenian Genocide in the Turkish Empire (Courtesy of the Armenian National Institute)

1

Introduction: Confronting the Armenian Genocide

Richard G. Hovannisian

The Armenian Genocide, like the Holocaust and mass killings in Cambodia, the Balkans, and many parts of Africa, has passed into a previous century and even a previous millennium. The question naturally arises, why remember? Why remember in a world so heavily laden with a legacy of unbridled violence, especially with the unprecedented instruments of annihilation made possible through the technological advances of the twentieth century? Why is it that after the passage of many years collective memory stirs deep passions both among the descendants of the victims and of the perpetrators? These questions apply all the more so to the genocides and genocidal massacres that have not been formally acknowledged, that have been denied by the perpetrator regime, often with the tacit support of world economic, political, and military partners.

The decimation of the Herero people at the hands of imperial Germany and its colonists in the first decade of the twentieth century, the destruction of the Armenian people in the very cradle of their civilization in the second decade, the calamitous losses of the Ukrainians and other victims of the Stalinist revolution and purges in the third decade, the genocides perpetrated under the cover of a world war in the fourth decade, have been followed by so many cases of mass murder that they cannot all be listed. The horrendous executions of urban dwellers, Buddhist monks, and minorities in Cambodia, the mutual slaughter in the Balkans and central Africa, the plight of the southern Sudan, the assault on the identity of the Kurdish people, and the intentional elimination of native groups from forests and jungles as hindrances to economic development constitute only a partial record of the century and, in some cases, the process still continues.

The case of the Holocaust stands alone in the bloody record of the twentieth century. In all other cases, there has not been full recognition of the crime or open acceptance of guilt by the perpetrator side. Nor have these violations of the fundamental right to life yet been contextualized within the historical consciousness of humankind. The ultimate goal of denial is to prevent the crime from becoming a part of permanent collective memory. To this end no efforts are spared, ranging from the allocation of financial and intellectual resources for propagandistic purposes to economic and military blackmail. In the case of the Armenian Genocide, there is a long trail of multileveled denial by the perpetrator side to suppress memory and in so doing to expunge the historical record.

The failure of absolute denial has led to more devious and sinister forms through rationalization; that is, explanations and excuses for what occurred, and through relativization; that is, attempts to obscure the intent and scope of the crime by placing it within the context of general human suffering during wartime. Third parties, whether individuals, groups, or governments, are often complicit in the denial because of their own perceived interests, be they economic, political, military, or geostrategic. And, as the perpetrator side is often powerful and in control of a state machinery, it becomes all the more difficult for the victims and victim groups to thwart the designs of the deniers.

Yet memory persists and collective memory shapes the identity of both the victim and the perpetrator sides. Armenians the world over realize that it is essential to face the future openly and freely, that the preservation of the small existing Armenian republic is vital to their own self-preservation, and that throughout history their people have recovered and advanced, not through dwelling morbidly or fatalistically on the past, but by reviving and rebuilding. It was the creative talents of the Armenian people that allowed them to persevere through centuries of oppressive foreign rule and in circumstances of great adversity. But the Genocide of 1915 dealt such a forceful blow that this time it thrust most survivors beyond their native lands into a diasporan existence. Armenians feel deeply that they cannot fully overcome that blow until it is acknowledged through acts of contrition and redemption. Hence, in some ways they are imprisoned by the past and their liberation is dependent on actions of the perpetrator side.

In the Republic of Turkey a monolithic state narrative of the "events" of 1915 gripped the country for decades, directing the whole of society to accept a construction of history that no other government, including those that have tacitly or directly assisted in the cover up, believes to be the truth. The narrative has cast Turkey into an incessantly defensive and self-delusional stance, producing a deeply colored view of the world and its own history. In recent years, however, there have emerged Turkish voices, both inside and beyond the borders of the country, that are calling for a reassessment of the facts and striking out on a path that might free their people and their country from the psychological harm of denial. Hence, with the turn of a new century, new hope is also kindled.

This volume considers how the Armenian Genocide may be contextualized from a temporal distance of nearly a century. The theme itself implies that the issue remains current, that it has not disappeared down a memory hole, that it cries out for an answer and a solution. The contributors seek to restate and clarify the historical record, to understand the developments that led to the genocide, to examine the legal and international ramifications, to suggest new directions in education, literature, and historiography, to pose the harm of denial against the need for healing and conciliation, and to assess the role of historical memory in the foreign policy of the small post-Soviet Armenian republic that neighbors the large, powerful Turkish state that incorporates most of the lands on which the Armenian people once lived.

Most chapters in this volume have grown out of an international conference held at the University of California, Los Angeles, in April 2000, on the occasion of the eighty-fifth anniversary of the Armenian Genocide. The conference, titled "The Armenian Genocide and Historical Memory: Challenge of the Twenty-First Century," was organized by UCLA's Armenian Educational Foundation Chair in Modern Armenian History, currently held by the editor of this volume. Three additional chapters on a contemporary agenda for the prevention of genocide, on the determinants of the Armenian Genocide, and on the discourse and periodization of Turkish historiography enhance the volume and take the place of three conference papers that do not appear in this publication. The views and findings presented are, of course, those of the individual authors and, as is often the case, may not necessarily be shared in full by the editor.

In his introductory essay, Gijs M. de Vries places the Armenian Genocide and its recognition within the context of the history of efforts to prevent and punish the crime of genocide, which he labels "the darkest word in the human language." As a state minister of the Netherlands and a human rights activist, he has been directly involved in assessing the work of the international tribunals created at the close of the twentieth century on war crimes and crimes against humanity. He outlines recent trends towards achieving the original intent of the U.N. Genocide Convention and considers the role of national legislatures and international organizations, such as the European Union, in gaining universal recognition of the Armenian Genocide and other crimes against humanity.

The twelve chapters that follow that opening essay may be divided into clusters of four. The first cluster focuses on and interprets the historical record. In a thought-provoking analysis, Donald Bloxham analyzes the polarization in the Ottoman Empire which gave rise to the Young Turk movement and its incumbent nationalism. He places into historical context the incremental victimization of the Armenian people culminating in the genocide. The coup d'état of the extreme wing of the Young Turk party in 1913, after the Ottoman defeat in the first Balkan War, placed in power the forces of exclusive nationalism, and the initial military setbacks in the first months of World War I set in motion the plan of elimination of the Armenian population. Simon Payaslian examines U.S. policies and actions during the genocide. These were linked closely with domestic issues and presidential politics in a country that was desperately trying to avoid being drawn into the European war. Hence, a clear and consistent distinction was maintained between humanitarian pleading and intercession and political-military intervention in the affairs of the Ottoman Empire and its Young Turk regime, and this distinction was maintained even after the rupture of United States-Ottoman relations in April 1917.

Vahram Shemmassian studies the plight of Armenian survivors of the genocide and their final expulsion by the victorious forces of the new Turkish state headed by Mustafa Kemal (Ataturk). Assistance to the dispossessed was one of the undertakings of the League of

Nations and of dedicated figures such as the American missionary and Near East Relief volunteer Emma Cushman and the Danish humanitarian, Karen Jeppe, who holds a special place of honor in Armenian memory. The calculations and actions of the British and French governments, the mandatory regimes in the Arab provinces where the exiles sought refuge, are integral to this story. Richard Hovannisian presents the sweet and bitter memories of the last generation of Armenians to have been born in the Ottoman Empire. Based on the more than 800 oral history interviews that have been collected at UCLA under his direction, he contrasts descriptions of a simple, happy, protected, almost idyllic childhood with those of abrupt and total disruption, bewilderment, and continuing trauma.

The second cluster of chapters deals with the Armenian Genocide in the context of international law, literature, and education. Steven Jacobs has discovered in the extensive papers of Raphael Lemkin, father of the Genocide Convention and originator of the term "genocide," clear evidence that Lemkin regarded the Armenian deportations and massacres as a clear-cut case of genocide. Aside from Lemkin's own autobiography, two manuscripts in his collection deal specifically with this issue. Joe Verhoeven places the Armenian Genocide within the context of current international law and tribunals treating crimes against humanity. Although he finds that most existing legal remedies can no longer be applied to the Armenian case because the actual perpetrators no longer are living, he finds a strong argument for alternate moral action as demonstrated in various forms of extralegal remedies that are currently being extended to individuals and groups victimized during World War II.

Rubina Peroomian demonstrates how literature is a highly effective way of conveying the totality and enormity of genocide. Using examples of the writings both by descendents of survivors and by non-Armenians, she maintains that the temporal distancing from the event itself does not diminish the impact but rather allows for a contextualization and a sensitivity that makes literature all the more powerful as an instrument of memory and mission. Joyce Apsel sees the role of education as critical in learning about the scourge of genocide and its prevention. She assesses the state of Armenian studies in the United States and shares her firsthand classroom experience on ways to integrate the Armenian Genocide into the broader curriculum.

The third cluster of chapters concentrates on historiography and denial of the Armenian Genocide, the price paid both by the victim and the perpetrator side, and the current political dimensions. Fatma Müge Göçek, in a critical essay, analyzes the characteristics of the three major phases in the Turkish historiography of the Armenian deportations and massacres. Making extensive use of memoir literature and state-sponsored publications, she shows how the narrative of events has been constructed, before pointing to a recent positive trend that can make strong strides if properly nurtured through measures helping to create a democratic civil society in Turkey. Henry Theriault turns to the pain and trauma caused by persistent denial of the Armenian Genocide and argues that the hallowed principle of freedom of speech is not without limits and qualifications. That principle, he argues, is not intended to allow intentional harm and suffering in the way that denial of genocide does. Denial of the Armenian Genocide, therefore, should be prohibited by law, just as a number of countries have done in the case of the Holocaust.

Ervin Staub underscores the importance of healing. Based on years of study and more recent field work, he maintains that people have fundamental psychological needs to feel secure from physical and psychological harm, to have a positive view of self and surroundings, and to be connected to other human beings. This is not possible, however, so long as victims or victim groups are denied recognition of their suffering. Acknowledgment brings rapid, if not amazing, healing, and it is the responsibility of third parties not only to recognize the crime themselves but also to encourage the perpetrator side to come to terms with its past. Finally, Raffi Hovannisian examines the state of Armenian-Turkish relations since the emergence of a new Armenian republic in 1991. As the first foreign minister of that precarious, landlocked state, he was involved in attempts to reach a normalization of relations with the Republic of Turkey, only to find that his government and all subsequent Armenian governments have come up against a set of Turkish preconditions revolving around repudiation of any claim, present or future, pertaining to the Armenian Genocide. The Armenian government, he maintains, must coordinate and master a spectrum of activities to safeguard the state and its citizenry while at the same time affirming the historical record as an uncompromised national value.

This is the fourth volume on the Armenian Genocide that this editor has prepared. The first of these, *The Armenian Genocide in Perspective*, also published by Transaction Publishers, grew out of an international conference on the Holocaust and Genocide, held in Tel Aviv in June 1982. The conference was a watershed not only because it was the first major international gathering that considered all genocides, but also because it was torpedoed by the Turkish government. When it was learned that there would be a handful of papers that dealt with the Armenian Genocide, Ankara applied such strong pressure on the Israeli government and the sponsoring institutions, including Tel Aviv University and Yad Vashem's Institute for Holocaust Research, that they felt constrained to withdraw their support. Jewish lives, it was stated, were at risk. The conference, though crippled, nonetheless proceeded with an intensified sense of mission. That blatant act of interference has been repeated many times since, but such disruptions have not halted in-depth studies and a growing understanding of the Armenian Genocide, its antecedents, perpetration, and aftermath.

Since 1982, scores of documented studies, memoirs, and literary, dramatic, and artistic works on the Armenian Genocide have appeared. *The Armenian Genocide in Perspective* was primarily descriptive for the purpose of making the genocide known to a broader public through a multidisciplinary factual approach. Now, however, there are hundreds of volumes that deal with the "darkest word in the human language"—and the impossible choiceless choices that accompany that word. Much more evidence, of course, remains to be gathered, hopefully with the assistance of a new generation of conscientious Turkish scholars, but the state of cutting-edge scholarship has progressed beyond descriptive narrative to insightful interpretation and analysis. It is hoped that the essays in *Looking Backward, Moving Forward: Confronting the Armenian Genocide* may serve as a modest contribution toward integrating the lessons and legacy of this unrequited crime into the collective human record—into collective human memory.

2

Genocide: An Agenda for Action

Gijs M. de Vries

Genocide: the darkest word in the human language. Yet how can any word even begin to address the immeasurable suffering inflicted on so many people? How to convey the intensity of the horrors that lie behind the statistics? How to honor the dignity of each individual man, woman, and child crushed in a wave of criminal madness so devastating that it has repeatedly claimed hundreds of thousands, even millions of lives?

Genocide is a crime so enormous and so heartrending that it seems to defy understanding. Yet understand it we must. If mankind is to confront this ultimate evil, we must harness our sense of shame and dismay and seek to understand its causes and manifestations. Without understanding there will be no effective strategy to prevent genocide. In terms of its gruesome potential for violence and human suffering, genocide is among the foremost political issues of our time. Prevention of genocide must rank as a top priority of states and international organizations. Here, I shall focus on the role of international law and diplomacy in the prevention of genocide.

In response to the Holocaust, the 1948 United Nations Genocide Convention defined genocide as "acts committed with the intent to destroy, in whole or in part, a national, ethnical, racial or religious group, as such." The definition has proved to be controversial and difficult to apply, legally as well as politically. More inclusive definitions have been offered, embracing, for example, the concept of "cultural genocide," but the text of the Convention still stands. It raises some difficult questions. At what level of human suffering does wholesale slaughter turn into genocide? Does the extermination of an ethnic group by members of that same group constitute genocide? At what point does a campaign to eliminate physically political opponents provide evidence of the intent to destroy an ethnic group "as such"? Fortunately, through the painstaking work of the international criminal tribunals for Rwanda and the former Yugoslavia, some of these questions are now being addressed in jurisprudence.

The International Criminal Tribunal for Rwanda (ICTR), established by the United Nations in Arusha, Tanzania, has achieved some impressive results. For the first time since World War II, an international tribunal has convicted someone for genocide. For the first time, rape has been defined as a component of genocide. The ICTR has convicted some high officials, including former prime minister Jean Kambanda. Other key political and military leaders are in custody. Regrettably, progress in bringing the killers to justice has been unacceptably slow. As the International Crisis Group has argued, the ICTR needs more resources and better oversight.

The International Criminal Tribunal for the former Yugoslavia (ICTY), based in The Hague, has also broken important new ground, for example in defining sexual offenses as a crime against humanity. We have come a long way since Nuremberg, when not a single prosecution dealt with rape. In the first international conviction for genocide in Europe since World War II, the ICTY found former general Radislav Krstic guilty of the murder of thousands of Bosnian Muslims.

The establishment of the International Criminal Court is the most important step in the struggle for human rights since the adoption of the Universal Declaration in 1948. The ICC's importance is threefold. First, it will help bring to justice those accused of war crimes, crimes against humanity, and genocide. No longer will those who murdered a single person be more likely to stand trial than those responsible for the genocide of millions. Second, as a permanent, independent court, the ICC will act as a deterrent to those contemplating such crimes. Its jurisdiction will not be contingent on political expediency. No future Idi Amin or Pol Pot will be immune from prosecution. Third, the ICC will promote reconciliation. By focusing criminal responsibility on individuals, not states or groups, and by bringing perpetrators to justice, the court will help break the cycle of revenge that so often perpetuates ethnic conflict. The ICC is an essential instrument to counteract the negative stereotyping conducive to large-scale violence. Of course, the ICC cannot by itself put an end to injustice and war. Much will still depend on the willingness of governments to prevent and punish the most serious crimes of concern to the international community. Whatever the case, the ICC represents a victory of accountability over impunity.

In 2001 the U.S. House of Representatives voted in favor of a bill that would require cutting off military aid to most countries that ratify the ICC treaty unless they pledge never to surrender an American to the Court. This legislation, which never reached the office of the president, would also authorize the government to use force to rescue Americans—including those held in the Netherlands, where the ICC will be based. I very much hope that a review of current policies will enable the United States to overcome its inhibitions and join its friends and allies in support for the Court.

In regard to bringing *génocidaires* and war criminals to justice, mention should be made of the impending creation of an international criminal tribunal for Sierra Leone. Another important development is the application, notably by Belgium, of the principle of universal jurisdiction in the prosecution of genocide and other grave breaches of international law. One in five Cambodians, an estimated 1.7 million people, died of starvation, disease, or execution during the terror unleashed by the Khmer Rouge from 1975 to 1979. Longstanding efforts to bring to justice those responsible for the "killing fields" have yet to produce results. In August 2001, King Norodom Sihanouk and the Constitutional Council of Cambodia approved a law on the framework for setting up a tribunal to try the former Khmer Rouge leaders. This, however, would not be an international tribunal modeled after the ones on Rwanda and Yugoslavia. It seems only persons "who are most responsible" would face trial, so many mid-level Khmer Rouge functionaries might walk free. King Sihanouk has already pardoned Heng Sary, Pol Pot's foreign minister, for genocide. The United Nations may find that Cambodia's latest proposals do not meet the necessary standards.

In view of China's insistence that it would veto any Security Council resolution creating a United Nations tribunal for Cambodia, however, it is also clear that some form of compromise may be the only way to bring the perpetrators of the Cambodian Genocide finally to justice. An impressive amount of incriminating evidence has already come to light, thanks to the courageous and painstaking work of the

Cambodian Documentation Center in Phnom Penh and the research recently carried out by the War Crimes Research Office of American University, led by Professor Diane Orentlicher. The assistance provided by these *amici curiae* and the groundbreaking jurisprudence of the two U.N. Tribunals in The Hague will prove instrumental in providing a measure of accountability for the crimes committed by Pol Pot and his henchmen.

No threats of a veto have marred the Security Council's deliberations about the creation of a tribunal for Sierra Leone. In August 2001, the Council requested Secretary General Kofi Annan to propose a blueprint for such a tribunal. The Security Council has stopped short, however, of agreeing to Annan's request for mandatory financing—it will be up to the individual U.N. member states.

The 1949 Geneva conventions relative to the protection of civilian populations and the treatment of prisoners of war give any ratifying nation the right to prosecute crimes against humanity and war crimes committed anywhere in the world. It is generally accepted that universal jurisdiction also applies to genocide. Belgium has assumed a leading role in applying this important principle. In 1993 it gave local courts jurisdiction over violations of the Geneva Convention regardless of where they occurred and irrespective of the nationality of victims and indictees. In 1999 the law was extended to violations of the Genocide Convention. In June of 2001, a Belgian court wrote history by convicting, under its 1993 law, four Rwandan citizens of crimes against humanity for their role in the 1994 Rwandan Genocide. This is unlikely to be the last case of its kind, for several more complaints are pending. Even Israeli Prime Minister Ariel Sharon faced indictment in Belgium over the 1982 massacre of Palestinian civilians in the Sabra and Shatila refugee camps in Beirut by Israel's Christian militia allies.

It is a moot point whether diplomatic immunity should take precedence over alleged violations of human rights. In 2000, Belgium issued a warrant to arrest the Congolese Foreign Affairs Minister Abdulaye Yerodia during his visit to Belgium, which prompted Congo to issue a complaint to the International Court of Justice. Denmark recently took the opposite view in a dispute over the nomination of Carmi Gillon as Israeli ambassador to Denmark. Mr. Gillon, a former head of the Israeli security service Shin Bet, has admitted authorizing the torture of Arab suspects. The Danish government averted a diplomatic row with Israel by ruling that diplomatic immunity under the 1961 Vienna Convention on Diplomatic Relations ranks higher than the United Nations convention against torture.

Without resorting to universal jurisdiction, other countries have begun to face up to atrocities committed on their own territory. In Guatemala, for instance, criminal investigations have been launched against former presidents Romeo Lucas Garcia and Efrain Rios Montt. They have been accused of committing genocide against the Maya population during a period of Guatemala's civil war, from 1978 to 1983.

Nor are investigations of genocide limited to cases in contemporary history. In recent years, the European Parliament, the parliaments of Cyprus, Greece, and Italy, the Vatican, and the senates of Russia and Belgium, have all recognized that the Armenians were subjected to genocide in the Ottoman Empire. In January 2001, the French parliament went a step further. Overriding the objections of the president and the prime minister, it adopted a bill recognizing the Armenian Genocide of 1915. Turkey, which has long insisted no genocide ever happened, reacted by recalling its ambassador for consultations and by canceling a $200 million contract for a military intelligence satellite awarded to Alcatel, as well as many other projects amounting to hundreds of millions of dollars. The Speaker of the U.S. House of Representatives, Dennis Hastert, in the year 2000 year agreed to withdraw a resolution recognizing the Armenian Genocide only after a personal intervention by President William Clinton, who argued the resolution, should it be adopted—as looked certain—would undermine U.S. national interests.

In March 2000, 126 Holocaust scholars, holders of academic chairs, and directors of Holocaust research and studies centers signed a statement (subsequently published in the *New York Times*, June 9, 2000) affirming that the Armenian Genocide during World War I is "an incontestable historical fact" and urging the governments of Western democracies to recognize it as such. It would, of course, be particularly important for the government and parliament of Turkey finally to come to terms with this dark chapter in Ottoman history. As the signatories indicated, to recognize the Armenian Genocide would provide an invaluable impetus to the process of the democratization of Turkey.

As these examples indicate, there is a growing willingness to face up, legally and politically, to the horrors of our recent past. And yet, the obligations of international law notwithstanding, genocide and crimes against humanity have ravaged Cambodia, the former Yugoslavia, and Africa's Great Lakes region. Indeed, it was the failure of the international community to avert these atrocities, including the massacre of Muslims at Srebrenica, that gave rise to the creation of the ICTR, the ICTY, and the ICC.

There are some crucial facts we now know about the events in Rwanda. Thanks to Alison DesForges and her colleagues, we know that the genocide was not the inevitable result of inscrutable ethnic rivalries, to which conflicts in Africa have so often been ascribed, but the intended outcome of a carefully planned campaign by political elites. We know that governments the world over were fully aware of what was happening. On January 11, 1994, three months before the genocide began, the commander of the U.N. peacekeeping forces in Rwanda, General Romeo Dallaire, sent his now famous "genocide fax" to U.N. Headquarters in New York. It was never brought to the attention of the Secretary General. We know that the U.S. government, at the height of the killings, telephoned the Hutu leadership to ask for restraint. Everybody realized what was going on, but nobody cared enough to act. We know now that the worst of the killings could have been prevented.

A modest force of 5,000 troops, sent to Rwanda sometime between April 7 and 21, 1994, could have significantly altered the outcome of the conflict. Yet nothing was done. The Belgian government, shocked by the death of ten of its U.N. peacekeepers, lobbied for a scaling back of the U.N. forces in Rwanda. The Clinton Administration, one year after its humiliating withdrawal from Somalia, told its civil servants not to refer to the Rwandan bloodbath as genocide for fear this would compel the United States to intervene, which might not have enhanced the president's domestic popularity. The rest of the world stood by while 800,000 human beings were shot, strangled, beaten, burned, and hacked to death.

"Never again" it was pledged in 1948, when the Genocide Convention was adopted and at countless ceremonies to commemorate the Holocaust. "Never again"—how hollow do these words ring in light of the international non-response to the genocides in Rwanda and elsewhere. To our lasting shame, we have allowed the unprecedented to become a precedent. Did the international community learn its lesson? Are leading powers more prepared today to exert the necessary pressure on states where grave breaches of human rights occur? What about Sudan? United States Secretary of State Colin Powell has said that there is "perhaps no greater tragedy on the face of the earth" than Sudan. In the summer of 2001, a genocide warning was issued by the U.S. Holocaust Memorial Museum's Committee on Conscience. The government of Sudan, the committee stated, is engaged in a divide-to-destroy strategy of pitting ethnic groups against each other, with enormous loss of life. It uses mass starvation as a weapon of destruction; it bombs hospitals, schools, and other civilian targets; and it tolerates enslavement of women and children. How will the world react to developments in Sudan, now that the Sudanese government has become a much-valued ally in the U.S.-led coalition against terrorism following the attacks of September 11, 2001?

What about Chechnya? "I don't want to irritate the authorities, but what is happening is practically genocide," declared Ruslan Khasbulatov, the head of the former Congress of Peoples' Deputies in Moscow. As is usual in a civil war, atrocities have been committed on both sides, but there can be no question about the brutality with which the Russian military operate against Chechen civilians. At least 30,000 civilians have lost their lives. Villages and residential neighborhoods have been subjected to indiscriminate shelling and "ethnic cleansing"; torture, extrajudicial killing, looting, and rape are distressingly common. Attempts by the Organization for Security and Cooperation in Europe (OSCE) and the U.N. to send observers have been blocked. The response of the international community to these blatant violations of the Geneva conventions has been ambiguous and ineffective. On the positive side, the U.N. Human Rights Commission in 2001 deplored the disproportionate use of force by Russia in Chechnya—the first time a member of the Security Council has been censured by the commission. The Council of Europe's Committee for the Prevention of Torture has criticized Russia's blocking of inquiries. But in January of 2001, the Council of Europe's Parliamentary Assembly voted to reinstate the Russian delegation, whose voting rights it had suspended only eight months earlier in protest over the human rights abuses in Chechnya. Neither the United States nor the European Union appears willing to drag President Vladimir Putin over the coals for the human rights violations committed under his authority, particularly in view of Chechen rebels' close association with the Al Qaeda network and Putin's support for President Bush's war on terrorism.

The burgeoning of international law in the past fifty years has been impressive. Universal human rights standards have been codified, expanded, and refined; the authority of international law has been considerably enhanced. Today, every U.N. member state is a party to one or more of the six major human rights treaties, and 80 percent have ratified four or more. Yet, as events have borne out time and again, to define behavior as criminal under international law is not in itself sufficient to prevent savagery. So far the deterrent effect of international human rights law has been limited.

Lessons

For human rights to be respected, international law must be backed up by the exercise of power, be it political, military, or economic. To paraphrase Pascal: power without justice constitutes tyranny; justice without power amounts to impotence. The 1648 Treaty of Westphalia marked the emergence of a system of sovereign states. It was a system dominated by the search for an often elusive balance of power. Spinoza wrote in 1677: "Whereas freedom or inner strength are the virtues of the individual, a state knows no other value than its own security." Sovereign states continue to form the dominant actors in the global system, but the principles that govern their behavior no longer exclusively reflect the precepts of power. A paradigm shift has been introduced by the Universal Declaration of Human Rights and subsequent human rights law. In René Cassin's words, for the first time "the individual becomes a subject of international law both in respect of his life and his liberty." The great challenge of our generation is to create an international order that protects the dignity and hence the rights of humankind.

It is often argued that criminal proceedings against suspected war criminals could undermine political efforts at strengthening peace and democracy. Peace, in other words, should take precedence over justice. The events in Belgrade in the summer of 2000 offer strong evidence to the contrary. With Milosevic in The Hague largely because of U.S. pressure, Yugoslavia did not collapse. Indeed, the 1995 Dayton accord was signed notwithstanding the fact that all leaders in the Bosnian conflict were explicitly denied immunity from prosecution for war crimes. There is an important lesson to be learned from these episodes: the search for justice does not necessarily hinder the quest for peace and democratic rebuilding in war-torn nations.

For power to be harnessed in support of justice, member states must enable the United Nations to do its job. Acting under Chapter VII of the U.N. Charter, the Security Council may authorize military intervention in case of a threat to international peace and security. There is, as yet, no explicit legal basis for U.N.-authorized intervention in domestic conflicts, let alone for intervention without the agreement of the Security Council ("humanitarian intervention"). In recent years, however, the Security Council has occasionally resorted to an extensive interpretation of Article 39, authorizing foreign military intervention to end or prevent atrocities in Somalia (1992) and Rwanda and Haïti (1994). Efforts should continue to refine the rules of engagement for international intervention in cases of grave breaches of humanitarian law.

Military intervention, of course, is not the only instrument the international community can use to prevent or limit human-made disasters. Pressure can be brought to bear through a variety of means, including condemnation by governments and international organizations, suspension or expulsion from international bodies, withdrawal of international funding, "smart" economic sanctions such as the freezing of accounts, and so forth.

How can we tell which instruments will be most effective in preventing or ending cases of war crimes, crimes against humanity, and genocide—cases which in practice often overlap and between which, in an emergency, it may not be easy to distinguish? Recent academic research into the causes of genocide and other forms of mass violence has yielded significant results. Historical analysis shows a correlation between the nature of a political regime and the occurrence of genocide. The less authoritarian a regime, and the more human rights and civil liberties are being respected, the less likely is it for genocide to occur.

Professors Barbara Harff and Ted Gurr have analyzed the factors most closely related to genocide and other forms of mass violence: a ruling elite representing a politically significant minority and expounding an exclusivist ideology; autocratic rule; previous state failure; and low trade openness. Warning signs of possible genocide include the scapegoating, demonizing, or dehumanizing of segments of the population. The prevalence of hate speech in official discourse or in the media is a particularly significant portent of violence. And when political leaders seek to annihilate freedom of expression and critical judgment by burning books, as happened in Germany in 1933 and again in Cambodia under Pol Pot, the world must be prepared for the worst. As yet, however, no single set of indicators of the potential for genocide has been agreed upon.

Better use could be made of the reports and findings generated by the human rights mechanisms of the United Nations. Human rights violations such as extrajudicial or arbitrary executions can be powerful indicators of the potential for genocide. The previous U.S. administration has set up an Atrocities Prevention Interagency Working Group as part of a genocide early warning system. The European Union has established a Policy Planning and Early Warning Unit. The U.N. has a Framework Team for Early Warning. These efforts must be linked together. Non-Governmental Organizations (NGO), such as the Forum on Early Warning and Early Response (FEWER) and the European Platform for Conflict Prevention and Transformation (EPCPT), also have an important role to play. As Kofi Annan has argued: "The international community must summon the will to use this information to act in time." We need to weld a global coalition against genocide.

Initiatives

Let me indicate a number of initiatives such a coalition should deploy.

—Human rights training of security forces should be included in the good governance programs agreed upon by international donors with recipient countries. Security sector reform should be an integral part of development policy. Police officers must understand that torture is a crime against humanity—an illegal act even when committed during an emergency. The military must know that, should a war crime be ordered, their duty lies in disobedience.

—Domestic and international programs in human rights training, particularly for journalists, should be supported. We need the media to show the human face of the individuals trapped in the depths of the horror that crimes such as genocide represent. We need to break the veil of anonymity. It is equally important to focus international assistance on investment in systems of education that honor the values of critical thinking and of moral clarity. Let us work until every student knows and understands the directive found on the flyleaf of Bertrand Russell's family Bible: "Thou shalt not follow a multitude to do evil."

—International efforts are needed to enforce the laws of war. Three areas are of particular importance: eradicating anti-personnel mines, curbing the proliferation of small arms, and eliminating the use of child soldiers. The Ottawa Convention on Antipersonnel Mines (1997) prohibits the production, stockpiling, transfer, and use of anti-personnel mines. It further obliges states to clear mines they have laid and to make provisions for victims of mines. Regrettably, major mine producing countries such as China, India, Pakistan, Russia, and the United States have not signed the Ottawa Convention. Diplomatic efforts to enlist these states should be intensified.

—Small arms are major contributors to human suffering. They are, as Chris Patten has argued, "the poor man's weapon of mass destruction." During the past decade, small arms have been responsible for 90 percent of the casualties of conflict, claiming more than 3 million victims, two-thirds of them civilian. About half of the estimated 500 million small arms in the world are illegal. A U.N. conference in July 2001 called on governments to make manufacturers mark small arms so illegally trafficked weapons can be traced. The United States blocked a similar appeal to consider legal restrictions on ownership of small arms and managed to delete a recommendation to withhold arms from non-state actors, arguing that U.S. foreign policy options such as helping to overthrow oppressive regimes should not be compromised. In contrast, the member states of the European Union adopted a code of conduct on arms exports in 1998 which limits sales only to legitimate governments. While the United States has supported verification mechanisms for the control of nuclear and chemical weapons, it has steadily obstructed similar measures to curb the spread of small arms. On the positive side, actions have been taken toward post-conflict disarmament. In Cambodia, for example, the EU is involved in a major effort to assist in drafting new legislation, collecting arms, improving storage facilities, and destroying surplus stocks.

—In societies emerging from conflict, former combatants must be disarmed, demobilized, and helped to find jobs. The U.N. conference on combating illicit small arms offered several useful first measures in this direction, but much remains to be done. An NGO coalition involved in preparing the conference, the International Action Network on Small Arms (IANSA), could play an important role in keeping the issue on the agenda, creating an internationally-recognized system for marking weapons so that they can be traced.

—Diplomatic efforts should be intensified to eliminate the use of child soldiers. According to U.N. estimates, in 1995-96 alone, 250,000 children were serving either in government armies or in opposition forces. The Statute of the International Criminal Court lists as a war crime conscription or enlistment of children under the age of fifteen or their active use in hostilities. To thrust children into combat is to rob them of their youth, their education, and their future. Today's child soldiers may well grow up only to become tomorrow's war criminals.

—In many parts of the world, government has become a criminal enterprise. Throughout Africa, wars are being waged for profit. In the Democratic Republic of Congo, Rwanda, Angola, and elsewhere, commercial interests of warring factions and their leaders perpetuate violent conflict. The international community must step up its efforts to stop these merchants of evil. Financial sanctions need to be refined. Trade in minerals and other valuables should be cleaned up, as is being done with respect to diamonds. Where the difference between war and crime gets blurred, war crimes may not be far off.

—The U.N. human rights system needs strengthening. Member states should speed up ratification of the Statute of the ICC. They should also work for the universal ratification of the Genocide Convention. To date, 127 countries have ratified, meaning that around one-third of the member states have not yet done so. States harboring suspects indicted by the ICTR and the ICTY should arrest these fugitives and hand them over to the tribunals.

—The fight against poverty must be pushed up the global agenda. One quarter of the earth's population, 1.4 billion people, live in extreme poverty, with 800 million of them severely malnourished. Their social and economic rights deserve as much respect as their civil and political rights. As a matter of priority, care must be taken that sufficient financial resources are put at the disposal of the United Nations. Securing adequate financing remains a critical challenge to guarantee the effectiveness of the U.N. system for the protection of human rights and human welfare.

—The Pinochet case has established that sovereign immunity can no longer be invoked against former heads of state charged with crimes against humanity. If immunity of current heads of state is not to imply impunity for heinous crimes, is there not a case for amending the Vienna Convention so as to restrict the operation of immunity? This would bring the law with respect to crimes against humanity in line with Article IV of the Genocide Convention, which already extends punishment to constitutionally responsible rulers.

—The United Nations Commission on Human Rights has proposed a set of principles to assist victims of human rights violations, including the right to reparations and the right of relatives to know the fate of missing persons. How can a post-conflict process of healing and reconciliation begin unless families and friends are able to establish what happened to their loved ones? As part of postwar rehabilitation efforts, therefore, international aid must be provided to assist in the search for missing people, to exhume mass graves, and to identify human remains.

—Public and private donors should work together to support academic research on genocide. There is much more to be done to learn about the causes of genocide and to deepen our understanding about effective strategies of prevention, reconciliation, and rehabilitation. The Task Force for International Cooperation on Holocaust Education, Remembrance and Research, set up in 1998 at the initiative of Sweden, has an important role to play. I am pleased to note that, in April 2001, the government of the Netherlands agreed to create and fund for a period of ten years a Center for Holocaust and Genocide Studies.

This brief discussion of desirable initiatives is not, of course, comprehensive. Moreover, I am only too aware that each of the steps is politically controversial and will be difficult to implement. I am convinced, however, that these initiatives would make a significant contribution to reducing the likelihood of genocide. Taken together, they would represent genuine progress in fulfilling the commitment embodied in Article 1 of the Genocide Convention—not only to punish but also to prevent the crime of genocide. Together, they constitute an agenda for action.

There is much about genocide we do not yet understand. To work against it may seem a daunting, perhaps presumptuous endeavor. One thing we do know, however: not to seek to understand genocide, and not to oppose it, would constitute complicity in evil. Evil requires us to choose sides, and to engage ourselves. Elie Wiesel has effectively expressed this imperative: "In every area of human creativity, indifference is the enemy. Indifference of evil is worse than evil." Let us heed this warning. Let us make a difference.

3

Determinants of the Armenian Genocide

Donald Bloxham

Despite growing scholarly consensus on the *fact* of the Armenian Genocide, widespread divergence of opinion remains on the circumstances in which it developed. As in the historiography of the Nazi "final solution of the Jewish question," issues of when and why (and even if) a decision was made to destroy the Ottoman Armenian community during World War I still divide academics. Some historians choose to place the genocide in a continuum of Armenian victimization beginning with the 1894-96 massacres of about 100,000 Armenians during the reign of Sultan Abdul-Hamid II (1876-1908/09). Some also emphasize the character of Muslim-Christian relations in the "Turkish-Armenian polarization." The weight of scholarly opinion is perhaps on the side of the view that a chauvinistic "Young Turk" nationalism developing between 1908 and 1915 was the primary determinant in the genocide, while accepting the significance of the 1894-96 massacres in illustrating the precarious position of the Armenians in Ottoman society by the late nineteenth century. Even accepting the shorter timeframe, there is still no unanimity on exactly how an ideology of exclusivist nationalism was translated into the most extreme practice conceivable. Was, for instance, the wartime decision to deport Armenians an inevitable consequence of the policy of the empire's rulers in the years prior to the war? Or conversely, did such a decision emerge unpredicted out of a combination of factors unique to the circumstances of war?

The first section of this essay seeks to suggest the continuities and distinct contrasts within Turkish-Armenian relations in the nineteenth century and up to 1914. It puts those relations in the wider contexts of inter-imperial politics (the "Eastern Question"), socioeconomic developments in the Ottoman Empire, and the important role of nationalist ideology in the Near East and its surrounding regions from the nineteenth century onward. The aim is to provide something of a synthesis of existing knowledge, though it is also unavoidably layered with my own interpretations, some of which will not meet with universal agreement. The second section provides a breakdown of the events of the war period itself, without offering a full "answer" to why the genocide was perpetrated. It will raise questions for further research. Again, however, the breakdown may illustrate certain problems with some existing interpretations in the development of the Catastrophe—the *Aghet*.

Ideology and Circumstance

Full agreement has still to be established about the precise nature of the ideology of the Ittihad ve Terakki (Committee of Union and Progress; CUP), the ruling party that led the Ottoman state into the genocide of the Armenians and the forcible deportation of other ethnic groups during World War I. The Young Turk revolution of 1908 was a bid to preserve the moribund empire through radical reform and thus as an important by-product to undermine arguments for secession of the different subject nationalities. It was clearly not born out of a desire for reform for the sake of non-Muslim groups, and its rhetoric of equality did not imply devolution of power to such groups. The growing, exclusive Turkish nationalism identified by Şükrü Hanioğu among the Young Turks in opposition to Sultan Abdul-Hamid II still seems to have been informed by the notion of the Muslim community as the *millet-i hakime*, the dominant "nation," and as such foresaw, at least in some Young Turk rhetoric, the coexistence of Muslims under a modernizing Turkish hegemony.[1] Either way, it was not conducive to genuine Muslim-Christian pluralism, particularly after a split in the ranks between Young Turk nationalists and liberals in 1902.[2]

The trajectory of Turkish nationalism was influenced by the neocolonial subordination that inspired the Chinese Boxer Rebellion at the turn of the century—a movement that also turned on native Christians. Donald Quataert describes the establishment of the Public Debt Administration in 1881 as "perhaps the landmark event of late Ottoman history." It meant transfer of control of fiscal policy to the European powers in order that they might secure repayments of their reckless loans to the Ottomans, while simultaneously gaining security for future loans that would in turn further European economic and, consequently, political influence.[3] This external domination compounded the ongoing territorial decline of the Ottoman Empire, as its European provinces strained under centrifugal nationalism and then broke away.[4] And if nationalist secession from the empire generally relied on great power sponsorship when it was in the interests of one or more of those powers, then the empire was only maintained out of self-interest, particularly of Great Britain, but also of France and later an increasingly competitive German empire.[5] Therefore the Turkish-Armenian polarization that culminated in the genocide did not occur in isolation. Inter-communal social and economic relations cannot be divorced from the state of international relations, the erosion of the Ottoman Empire, and the issue of Turkish/Muslim sovereignty.

Collaboration between Armenian groups and the Young Turks from 1896, though calling for Muslim-Christian solidarity and condemning the massacres of 1894-96, did not mean a complete mutual identification of goals.[6] The Young Turks were formed from an echelon of bureaucrats and soldiers dissatisfied with the way that the empire was being run, notably in the face of the accelerating erosion of its territories.[7] Many of these men had been exposed to Western intellectual trends in their secular, Europeanized training institutions, notably the Harbiye military academy and the Tibbiye military medical school.[8] Very significantly, "social Darwinism" was also absorbed in a half-digested manner through contact with then-current Western intellectual movements.[9] This sort of Manichaean thinking acquired an immediacy in the years of imperial decline. Equally important, many of the CUP leaders hailed from the peripheries of the empire and were thus particularly sensitized to its diminution and had a special vested interest in its maintenance.[10] A redistribution of power in favor of themselves and a more efficient and vigorous defense of the Ottoman construct and the "national" interest group to which they allied themselves was their goal, and it was increasingly influenced by pragmatism as much as a set of ideological precepts.[11]

In this sense, "Ittihadism," inasmuch as we can precisely define the phenomenon,[12] was only the latest of a series of Ottoman "solutions" to the challenges posed to the antiquated empire by the other powers since the eighteenth century and to the related extension of incompatible Western ideas of nationalism into a theocratic empire. It was preceded by the pan-Islamic policy of the last significant sultan, Abdul-Hamid II. This sought to galvanize the empire's Muslims into a more coherent political community at the expense of Muslim-Christian relations. He had permitted and encouraged the 1894-96 massacres as a means of ethnic "punishment" for a community he feared might follow in the path of Balkan separatism—though the Armenian "revolutionary" parties established from outside the empire from the late 1880s were primarily seeking only reforms for their Anatolian kin.[13]

Abdul-Hamid's policies can only be comprehended if we consider the results, in turn, of foregoing attempts in the middle decades of the nineteenth century to modernize the state along French lines. This, too, was part of a broader narrative of bringing the empire "up to speed" to compete within a burgeoning international system in which the more efficient armies, industries, and administrations of the more coherent European societies, informed by the Enlightenment and scientific advancement, gave them colossal competitive advantages over the Ottomans.[14] Reforming the eastern provinces was particularly important since in the Russo-Turkish War of 1828-29 the tsarist armies had quite illustrated what a tenuous control the Ottomans had over this region.

The ensuing *Tanzimat* period (circa 1839-76) brought with it the theoretical introduction of inter-religious equality as well as promises of greater social justice and economic and administrative reform. Yet it actually contained the seeds of the destruction of the previous order, in which society had been regimented along strictly religious lines, in a stable if unequal form, with Jews and the different Christian confessional groups developing at various periods their own internally self-administering *millet*. Beyond urban centers, the Tanzimat did not bring the envisaged reforms in the eastern provinces, resulting instead in dislocation and no little chaos, in large part because of non-implementation of the reforms by local Muslim officials. It even resulted in a worsening of the condition of parts of the peasantry, since new government officials in what were now the redrawn provinces (*vilayet*s) of eastern Anatolia effectively doubled the burden of taxes, which many were still paying to the previously established local authorities and tribal chieftains.[15]

The Ottoman attempts at centralization and reform were accom-panied by a forcible assault against the powerful Kurdish emirs who enjoyed great de facto authority in the eastern provinces and against other local potentates. Centralization and modernization would indeed be a rationale in the anti-Kurdish policies pursued by Republican Turkey from 1925 (and were certainly one motivation for the Kurdish deportations of 1916-17). In the shorter term, it contributed to a deterioration of relations between Turks and Kurds but also between both groups and Armenians as the delicate, hierarchical balance between Christians and Muslims was upset. Various institutionalized abuses of Armenians, which had always been present as Muslims exploited their religiously-determined hegemony over the Christians, now intensified as the former perceived the Armenians—no longer under even their nominal "protection"—to be the beneficiaries of the reforms that were so threatening to the prescribed order.[16]

One important developmental impact of the Tanzimat in this direction was the opening of the empire not just to greater European economic penetration but also to Western missionaries and their schools. This complemented and channeled an Armenian cultural renaissance begun early in the nineteenth century in which a modernized vernacular and proto-national literature had started to provide a social glue for the disparate Armenian communities.[17] The large number of Armenians attending mission schools learned something of social emancipation and developed different interpretations of how to achieve it,[18] while the increasing number of children of the bourgeoisie educated in Europe gained firsthand experience of Enlightenment benefits and brought back more concrete notions of modern nationhood. In this epoch of social re-imagining, Christians led the way among the peoples of the Ottoman Empire, and Armenians among the peoples in the Asiatic provinces.[19] They were led in turn, however, by a politicized vanguard often living cosmopolitan, urban lives far removed from the eastern provinces—and in the case of the vastly influential intellectual developments stemming from Russian Armenia, even outside the empire altogether—yet harking back to it as the ancestral home of their people. For the Armenians, over the course of the nineteenth century—to simplify considerably—the religious millet system metamorphosed into a situation of proto-nations, influenced by elite-sponsored community formation and the promise, if not the reality, of greater emancipation. This shift was reflected in the reorganization of the Armenian millet through the Armenian "Statutes" or "National Constitution" of 1863.[20]

The majority of the Ottoman Armenian population, the peasantry on the historic Armenian Plateau in eastern Anatolia, were surely primarily concerned with their own grinding poverty and were joined in their plight by Kurdish and Turkish peasants. From the mid-century, these Armenians also began to suffer more pronouncedly at the hands of their neighbors as their lands were appropriated in little more than legalized theft by sedentarizing Kurds and also allocated to Muslim refugees (*muhajirs*) fleeing from Russia from the 1850s and from the Balkans between 1878 and 1913.[21] The policy was centrally enforced upon Abdul-Hamid's accession and was not reversed by the Ittihadists despite protestations to the contrary.[22]

If many Armenians began to experience a sense of "relative deprivation" as their hopes and aspirations were raised well above the reality of the reforms, the same was true for Ottoman Muslims who saw some Christians benefiting from the changes. [23] A powerful stereotype of Armenians began to emerge based on relative Armenian socioeconomic success in certain quarters, as Armenian social visibility increased. This stereotype was founded on urban professionals, merchants, moneylenders, and middlemen, the rural traders, as well as on certain regions and elements of the agricultural economy, notably in Cilicia.[24] Furthermore, Armenian success was associated with foreign influences, based in part on the Armenian importation of Western technologies.[25] Finally, the prominence of Armenians as agents and brokers for European interests and the extension to individual Armenians of the extraterritorial privileges enjoyed by citizens of the great powers living in Turkey seemed to confirm a picture of Christians not pulling together with the Muslim population in the interests of the state on whose territory they dwelled.[26]

The importance of maintaining the social cohesion and territorial integrity of Anatolia was growing ever greater for the ruling Osmanlis, as Ottoman territory in Europe was being claimed by Balkan nationalists. Whereas the European provinces of Rumelia had traditionally been regarded as the center of gravity of the empire, the late nineteenth century saw Turkish intellectuals looking more and more to the east, retrospectively reformulating those regions as the seedbed of the Turkish people, and the center for its future renewal.[27] Thus, portentously, on the veil of the twentieth century Turks had come to envisage areas with major Armenian and Kurdish populations as their own spiritual "heartland."

Almost immediately upon the Ittihadist ascension to power in 1908 the empire that they were attempting to maintain took another major knock as Bosnia-Herzegovina was annexed by the Austro-Hungarian Empire, Bulgaria declared its independence, and Crete united with Greece. Armenian political leaders might have been awakened to the limited prospects for genuine reform under the new government when in the spring of 1909 between 10,000 and 20,000 Armenians were murdered in the Adana region of Cilicia against the backdrop of an anti-Ittihadist insurgency by liberals and Islamists. Ittihadist forces were implicated in the massacre, and some popular participation seems to have been the result of economic-based jealousies.[28] The events of 1908 and particularly the quashing of the countercoup in 1909 saw further distancing of the Ittihadists from the liberals. A law on political associations now prohibited the formation of organizations with non-Turkish national aims.[29] Measures of enforced cultural Turkification, revolving particularly around language use, were introduced during 1910 and 1911.[30]

The losses of 1908 gave impetus to the idea of a new "national economy"—a centrally controlled and independent system.[31] For many Turks, this implied removal of Christian economic influence alongside nullification of the concessions to foreign powers and their subjects—the Capitulations. The year 1909 saw abortive moves to impose trade boycotts against the Ottoman Greeks, as part of a general strategy suggested for use also against Armenians by Young Turk radicals even before the 1908 revolution. The rationale in the Armenian case was to increase the number of Muslim artisans and merchants at the expense of the Christians.[32] The development of a Turkish middle class was specified in Ittihadist policy in 1914, at the climax of a period of de facto economic warfare between Ottoman Greeks and Muslims. This was concluded in favor of the Muslims in 1913-14 and 1915-16 by a combination of population engineering and economic appropriation, using boycotts, murders, terrorization, and then deportation of the western Anatolian Greek population, which was cast as increasingly suspect by its ties to mainland Greece.[33] This practice bears comparison with the Nazi policy of "Aryanization"—a device based on a reorganization of economic resources in favor of "ethnically-desirable" citizens and therefore of the ethnically-defined state itself. It was far more costly in terms of life than the Nazi practice, however, for at least a million Greeks left western Anatolia with a substantial death toll.[34] Thus, a "new Turkish bourgeoisie" was to be brought into being, complementing the move towards an Islamicized peasantry in the eastern provinces and offering the two vital elements that would contribute to a modernized, Muslim-Turkic national economy in Asia Minor.[35]

The development of Ottoman population policy was punctuated by the military conflicts of the empire, as the Russo-Turkish War of 1828-29 and the subsequent Crimean War had shown. Abdul-Hamid's ascension to the throne in 1876 after the Bulgarian uprising and resulting Turkish atrocities signified the end of the Tanzimat period. It was shortly followed by another Russo-Turkish war. These conflicts precipitated a greater mass movement of Muslim refugees into Anatolia, while the Turkish defeat in the eastern provinces left the fate of the region in the balance. The Anatolian provinces of Van and Erzerum were returned to Ottoman control only at the behest of the British, who wished to retain the balance of power in the Near East by bolstering Turkey against Russian expansion, but Tsar Alexander was able to retain a part of the territories his armies had conquered in the Caucasus, namely Kars, Ardahan, and Batum.

The negotiated peace at Berlin in mid-1878, supplanting the victor's peace in the Russian-Turkish treaty of San Stefano, saw British lip service paid to the future well-being of the Armenians in the eastern vilayets. It stipulated reforms for these provinces without providing enforcement. This "internationalization" of the Armenian Question was important both in encouraging Armenian pressure for reform and in sparking Turkish suspicion about Armenian loyalty vis-à-vis the ever-increasing influence of external powers. The failure of the European powers to enforce the reform clauses led to the formation of Armenian "revolutionary" societies from the 1880s onwards, compromising the traditional authority of the ecclesiastical hierarchy. These parties owed much to radical Russian Armenian influences and pursued their interpretation of Ottoman Armenian "national" interest without much recourse to the security of ordinary Armenians. The latter, while suffering the many inequities of Ottoman rule in its decades of decline, also suffered in the reprisals brought down by the sometimes violent and reckless policies of the revolutionaries. Meanwhile, the existence of the revolutionaries meant two things: "by entering into an armed dynamic with the state while projecting themselves as a national movement, they provided an open invitation for Abdul-Hamid to portray *all* Armenians as a monolithic fifth column"; and "by peaking [in the 1890s] without any genuine military capability to carry out their agenda, they not only stymied their own mobilization, but left the Armenian population weakened."[36]

At Berlin, if Great Britain made inflammatory but insincere gestures towards the Armenians, the interests of the Kurds, the other of the two largest population groups in eastern Anatolia, were ignored entirely. This helped to pave the way for Abdul-Hamid's exploitation of Kurdish resentment in his pan-Islamic policy, as embodied in the later formation of the irregular Kurdish *Hamidiye* regiments that contributed so much to the 1894-96 massacres. It also further severed bonds of common Kurdish-Christian opposition to Turkish rule.[37] Equally portentous, if Russia had proposed a degree of Armenian local self-governance and the protection from Circassians and Kurds in the eastern provinces, Britain's plan to maintain the region under Turkish sovereignty through reforms that included the formation of ethnographically-concentrated administrative regions continued to spur Armenian hopes. Perhaps, it was suggested, this might include the movement of the Turkish element westward. Abdul-Hamid, reminded of the continued vulnerability of the eastern provinces and fearing the potential of nationalism among his subject peoples, employed precisely the contrary policy as he began to remodel the region in the image that he perceived was required to maintain it for the Ottoman Empire.[38]

It is no accident that this period saw the beginning of a statistical battle between the Sublime Porte and Armenian spokesmen, the first trying to establish the numerical supremacy of Muslims and the second of Christians, mainly Armenian, in the region.[39] These proportions were shifting with the settlement of Muslim refugees from the Balkans and the Caucasus, which taken together formed the bulk of an inflow of millions from 1783 to 1914.[40] In the reverse direction, the Armenian population declined through flight to the Russian Empire in the nineteenth century, especially after the withdrawal of the Russian armies in 1829 and 1878 and the turmoil accompanying the massacre of 1894-96 and 1909.[41] At the beginning of 1915, there were around 2 million Armenians in the empire, concentrated primarily in the eastern vilayets and secondarily in Cilicia, with a very large population in Constantinople and smaller groupings dotted throughout western Anatolia, particularly in urban centers.

Concern for statistical proportions remained, in theory at least, in the genesis of the mass deportations of Word War I, and they have remained paramount in the misrepresentation by successive post-war Turkish governments of the number of Armenians that dwelled in the empire. The Ittihadists' demographic deliberations of 1913-14 and the pattern of muhajir settlement over the preceding generations owed a conceptual debt to a practice of population transfer (*sürgün*) that had been employed in the empire since the fourteenth century. Originally a method of importing Muslim colonists into conquered regions, the practice of sürgün had developed over time to incorporate punitive deportations of religious and other groups.[42] Eastern Anatolia witnessed both manifestations of this practice, first as a recipient of a sort of internal Ottoman colonization by "desirable" groups, then as a site of ethnic cleansing of the "undesirable," during which colonization continued as Muslim refugees were relocated into vacant Armenian dwellings.

The first Balkan War in 1912-13 accelerated the influx of refugees into Anatolia as the remaining key Rumelian lands and even the Muslim region of Albania were torn away. In their viciousness the wars allowed for what would now be called "ethnic cleansing" of Christians and Muslims by each side respectively and also further exacerbated ethnic tensions in Asia Minor and the eastern provinces. Like those before them, the Muslim refugees provided an anti-Christian constituency from which the government made appointments to local administrative posts and that went on to form a large part of the gendarmerie that would figure prominently in slaughtering Armenians during World War I.[43] As the Balkan War cast Muslim-Christian relations into the sharpest of relief, with widespread Christian draft evasion and Ottoman Bulgarian and Greek soldiers, though not Armenians, swapping sides to fight alongside their ethno-religious brethren, the Ittihadists also sanctioned the deportation of small groups of Christians from the vicinity of military communications routes.[44] A further coup in January 1913 in the context of Turkish defeats reestablished in power the Committee of Union and Progress, which had been voted out of office, and made it into a one-party dictatorship under the triumvirate of Talaat, Enver, and Jemal, guided behind the scenes by the Ittihadist central committee—a triumph for the "activists" within the Young Turk ranks.[45] The feeble Ottoman performance in the first Balkan War reinforced their view about the necessity of relying in the future on Muslim forces bound by Islamic prerogatives.[46]

The Balkan War, it is generally agreed, signified the death of any vestiges of Ittihadist pluralism.[47] Taner Akçam has revealed a highly significant aspect of this development in his detailed exploration of Ittihadist thinking about the demographic restructuring of Anatolia in the aftermath of the fiasco in 1912-13. His reading of the memoirs of leading Ittihadists also concludes that shortly after Enver's appointment as minister of war in January 1914, a series of secret meetings were held to discuss the cleansing of Anatolia of its non-Muslim "tumors" in a plan of "homogenization." Implementation of this plan, it might be argued, began with the harassing and dispossessing the Greeks of Anatolia, and Akçam suggests that the relocation of Armenians to the deserts of Syria and Iraq was also already envisaged.[48] We do know that at this time, owing to their links with mainland Greece and their concentration in western Anatolia, the Ottoman Greeks were probably more "suspect" to the Ittihadists than were the Armenians, although Armenians also suffered in the economic boycotts.

The closing of the Balkan War saw the resurrected vision of externally enforced reform in the eastern vilayets. A reform plan, which was ultimately negotiated between Russia and Germany, the imperial powers with the greatest interests in the Asiatic provinces, was promoted with self-interested Russian support by the supreme patriarch, the Catholicos of All Armenians, whose Holy See was at Echmiadzin in Russian Armenia.[49] Significantly, the Russian foreign ministry began applying pressure at precisely the time that Turkey was induced to recognize the new frontiers with Bulgaria. The final Armenian reform package, signed in February 1914 by the Russian chargé d'affaires in Constantinople and the Sublime Porte, provided for two European inspectors-general to oversee the reforms, including the prohibition of further encroachments by muhajirs and greater security of Armenian life and property. Point twenty of the plan also stipulated reforms for Armenians in Cilicia. In its obvious benefit to Christians, this development ran directly counter to the ongoing trend of Ittihadist policy in the region—whatever the promises to Armenian representatives—and indeed to the trend of Ottoman policy since the mid-nineteenth century. Its ignoring of the Kurds meant that the Ittihadists could drive the wedge yet deeper between Kurds and Armenians, which would ramify in the participation of certain Kurdish tribes in the genocide.

For the Ittihadists, as a number of bitter threats of revenge then and subsequently show, the imposition of the plan by a Christian power for Christians was the strongest of confirmations of the inherent incompatibility of an Armenian presence in the "heartland" of the empire and of the danger that this presence posed to Turkish sovereignty in the region.[50] These fears seemed only to be confirmed by Russian pronouncements.[51] We may speculate on the basis of chronological simultaneity that any designs in embryo for "cleansing" Anatolia of Armenians before World War I were strengthened in reaction to the reform plan that was soon to be introduced. On the Turkish entrance into the war, the reform plan was annulled alongside the Public Debt Administration and that other prime symbol of Ottoman degradation at the hands of the powers, the Capitulations.[52]

The Turkish entry into the European conflict, against the better judgment of some Ittihadists, bespeaks a do-or-die effort to eradicate external influences in the empire. It was also an attempt to reinvigorate the empire by incorporating Turkic populations to the north and east at the expense of Russia (and even Great Britain), thus further accentuating the radical change that had occurred in its ethnic profile with Muslim immigration and the loss of huge Balkan Christian populations. The sense of victimhood and embattlement in light of the Balkan wars and the encroachments of the European powers and of the threat posed by the Christian "tumors," however incongruous it may seem in the light of the Armenian Genocide, is vital in understanding the way that extreme violence could be legitimated in "solving" the problems of the empire. The Austrian ambassador to the Sublime Porte in 1914 perceived the Ittihadist entry into the world war as rolling into one all the facets of the so-called Eastern Question: "the Egyptian, the Armenian, the question of the Straits, of Constantinople, indeed the very question of the partition of the Turkish Empire."[53]

War and Genocide

The attempt to reshape internally what was left of the Ottoman Empire was the other side of the coin of protecting the frontiers against further external incursion. The strand of social Darwinism in Ittihadism and its emulating of central and eastern European nationalism meant that reformulating a would-be modern Turkish state, "to streamline, make homogeneous, organise people to be uniform in some sense...[to] compete, survive and develop,"[54] required that this uniformity be determined ethnically. The Armenians and Greeks were not the only non-Turkish minority to suffer during World War I, and their fates may not be divorced from the broader context. Assyrian (especially Nestorian) Christians in western Persia, Diarbekir, Van, and Bitlis provinces (particularly in their strongholds in the Hakkiari highlands) were massacred alongside Armenians in 1915, although they were not subject to the same systematic destruction as the Armenian communities.[55] Various Kurdish, Arab, and even Jewish (Zionist) groups were also expelled and/or deported on suspicion of nationalist agitation.

A strong case can be made that the Ottoman Armenians had nothing more to hope for from the Ittihadists upon the recall of the European inspectors provided for in the reform plan of February 1914. Nevertheless, it remains a matter for debate whether the course and extremity of their fate in 1915 was determined before the outbreak of war in 1914. Prior to the act of genocide, a series of lesser measures were introduced, such as searches for arms among Armenian communities from the declaration of war through the onset of the genocide in April 1915. These have been interpreted as preparatory stages for the genocide. A different interpretation might be that they were the actions of an Ittihadist regime that had inherited Abdul-Hamid's paranoia and that was acutely conscious of the potential of even small revolutionary groups, inasmuch as they themselves had overturned the Hamidian order with a comparatively small number of insurgents.[56] In this atmosphere, murderous, indiscriminate arms searches that encompassed whole communities and went well beyond the members of the Armenian political organizations served both as a means of reassuring the regime by emasculating those communities and preempting by terror any form of anti-government action.

The Turkish nationalist line has, of course, been that Armenians, unbidden by Turkish policy, brought deportations upon themselves by wartime treachery. This is patently incorrect given the preexisting trajectory of Ittihadist nationalism. The fact is that some Ottoman Armenians, and more from beyond Turkey's borders, did pursue a rebellious agenda during World War I, in pursuit of what was being denied them under Turkish rule and in some cases in continuance of earlier revolutionary practices. Naturally, the Armenian majority, as in any population, remained inactive and uninvolved. As in the past, most ordinary Armenians were deeply apprehensive about the behavior of some of their compatriots. Questions remaining to be fully resolved concern whether the actions of a small minority did contribute to exacerbating Turkish policy or whether, as many scholars of the genocide would argue, they provided a pretext for the enactment of a preconceived policy.

In more general historical terms, it is clear that Ittihadism was shaped in relation and reaction to other nationalisms,[57] of which Armenian nationalism was only one, but also that Ittihadism developed a particularly extreme and intolerant coloring that was by no means predetermined. Just as the worsening plight of the empire had demanded more and more extreme measures to sustain it internally, the Ittihadists, believing the Asiatic provinces to be threatened on all sides by Christian powers, now ordered the deportation of the Armenians. In the perception of the Ittihadists, the empire was also threatened from the inside by the continued presence of the ethnically and religiously "different" Armenian population. In that scenario, chauvinist Turkish policies resulted in a self-fulfilling prophecy of Armenian disaffection that, in circular fashion, helped to catalyze further radicalization of Ittihadist actions, including massacres as collective "reprisals" and "preemptive reprisals" against the entire Armenian population and the wartime acceleration of the longer process of ethnic "homogenization."[58] Yet, as this interpretation continues, general deportation and massacre were instituted because—and only because—of the preexisting cognitive picture that the Ittihadists had of all Armenians as anomalous and disloyal by virtue of their very *ethnic identity*.

The primary weapons of genocide were the mass deportations to the southern desert regions ordered from May onwards and the massacres that accompanied those expulsions. Together, these accounted for some 800,000 Armenian deaths. The survival chances of the deportees were dependent on the origin and route of deportation, with massacre manifested primarily in the eastern vilayets.[59] Further mass death resulted among the approximately 870,000 remaining deportees from starvation, privation, exposure, and disease in the deserts. In 1916 surviving Armenians congregated in what were effectively open-air concentration camps towards the end of the deportation routes and were subjected again to extensive massacres.[60]

Conversions to Islam were also an intrinsic part of the process of destroying the Armenian community. The process should not be interpreted, however, as fundamentally a religious one. Indiscriminate forced conversions were less of a factor than they had been in earlier pogroms, and indeed new evidence shows that the Ittihadists proceeded to deport even those who they deemed had converted only out of necessity.[61] The convertees numbered perhaps between 5 and 10 percent of the Ottoman Armenians. The majority were children and women of childbearing age who were brought into Muslim households and had their names changed by way of absorption into the new national community. It has been posited that this was as much a part of the process of genocide as the direct killing, for, in accordance with the United Nations definition, forced conversion is included in the methods pursuant to an "intent to destroy" a racial, national, ethnic, or religious group "as such."[62]

Since the murder or dislocation of every last Armenian was not central to this scheme, it was not inconsistent that small populations survived in pockets across the empire, isolated and traumatized, even after further waves of deportation. According to a United Nations report, up to 400,000 Armenians survived in the empire until the end of the war, with a particular concentration in Constantinople, from which there were only selective deportations of the leadership and sojourners from the provinces. Some 350,000 refugees were beyond the boundaries of Anatolia, not including those who had fled to the Caucasus during wartime. In the aftermath of further flight caused by the postwar withdrawal of the French garrisons in Cilicia, the defeat of the Greek forces in 1921-22 (which also saw the massive expulsion and flight of Ottoman Greeks), and new pogroms at the hands of the Kemalists, the number of Armenians by 1922 had dwindled to between 110,000 and 150,000, not including the "multitude" of women and children enslaved and "assimilated" by Muslim families.

Many who fled found their way by some route to the Caucasian Armenian republic around Erevan, while others remained in Mesopotamia and Syria. All left behind property, which was appropriated by Muslims and the state, thereby completing the wholesale pillage that had been such an intrinsic part of the genocide and the process of "capital transfer" from one ethnic group to another.[63] Those Armenians remaining in Turkey outside Constantinople reportedly were largely Catholics and Protestants, who to a certain extent had been shielded by foreign intervention and were perhaps considered not only confessionally, but also "politically" separate from the majority Armenian Apostolic community.[64] By 1935, two years after the beginning of Hitler's persecutions in Europe, the number of Armenian refugees was still more than twice as great as that of Jewish and political refugees from Germany.[65]

Retrospectively, the development of Ittihadist policy towards the Armenians can be divided into a number of broad time-phases. These should not be taken as a definitive guide, for every historian might schematize this complex period somewhat differently. Rather, the suggestions should be taken as a plea, and perhaps a signpost, for further research. The main case still to be proven categorically is whether Ittihadist policy had an inherent and irresistible logic pushing towards the point at which the Armenians were to be destroyed as a collectivity or whether the spread and intensification of that policy were the expressions of escalation or radicalization over time in 1914-15.

The argument that the extirpation of the Armenians was broadly decided upon before the war—an argument that might be buttressed by findings about Turkish demographic thinking in 1914—requires further substantiation to address two facts. The deportations were not enacted immediately after the outbreak of war nor at the time of the first major Ottoman military campaign from eastern Anatolia into the Caucasus in December 1914. Conversely, it is clear that discriminatory practices and outright murder of large numbers of Armenians had already taken place before the end of 1914.

The first time-phase actually precedes the Turkish declaration of war and can be dated from August 1914, the date of the secret Ittihadist military pact with Imperial Germany and the expansion of the European conflict. This period was marked by the beginning of ruthless war requisitioning, in which the Ottoman Christian communities were disproportionately targeted, perhaps in an indirect continuation of the practice of economic dispossession.[66] Approaches were also made from both the Turkish and the Russian sides to different national groups in the Caucasus and eastern Anatolia in preparation for any declaration of hostilities between the two empires. The Ittihadists sought primarily to agitate among the Muslim communities of the Caucasus and Persia, but they also tried unsuccessfully to persuade the Ottoman Armenians through the party Dashnaktsutiun to influence the Russian Armenians to revolt against the tsar in the event of war. The Russian Armenians rallied to the Russian flag. The majority were assigned to regular service on the European front, but the Russian command also agreed to the formation of irregular volunteer battalions made up of a number of Ottoman Armenians. These battalions served useful military functions, both as guides in terrain that they knew well and as a committed fighting force.[67] The best-known illustration of their combat value was their role in helping to thwart the major Turkish offensive into the Caucasus at the turn of 1914-15. Enver Pasha's debacle in the Sarikamish campaign cost some 80,000 casualties and the initiative on the Caucasus front.

The Ittihadists soon claimed that these battalions served as *agents-provocateurs* among the Ottoman Armenians for the Russian cause. The Central Powers knew that the Russian authorities in the Caucasus had made overtures to the Ottoman Armenians, trying to lure them with false promises of postwar autonomy. Armenian desertion from Ottoman military ranks and cases of defection over the Caucasus border seemed to give substance to Turkish fears.[68] It is possible to correlate quite closely the *loci* of activities of these volunteer battalions with the *loci* of massacres in the early war months by the standard-bearers of Ottoman irregular warfare, the *Teshkilat-i Mahsusa* or "Special Organization." From November onward, the Special Organization seems to have targeted areas in the Caucasus and Persia whence the Armenian volunteers operated and also those settlements left exposed by the tactical withdrawals of the Russia forces and volunteer units.[69] Further research is needed to contextualize the history of actions taken by the Special Organization within the subsequent history of deportation in order to analyze precisely the decision-making process behind the expansion of the massacres and the relationship, if any, to the operations of the Armenian volunteer battalions.

It is instructive to consider that though the Special Organization may not have begun as a genocidal instrument as such, its irregular nature was highly significant. James Reid has observed the potential for irregulars not subject to military norms to resort to massacre and abrogation of the rules of war.[70] The actions of the Kurdish Hamidiye regiments in 1894-96 provide the obvious historical illustration that such practices were not only to be expected but were explicitly prompted by the Ottoman authorities. The murderous potential of irregular forces was only increased by the incorporation of specially-released violent criminals and extreme ethnic nationalists to fight with the Special Organization in the ethnically-mixed border regions of the Caucasus and Persian Azerbaijan. The "usefulness" of such forces in World War I was in part predicted by the German geopolitical theorist Max Oppenheim in 1914. He noted that the Circassians, Chechens, and Muslim Georgians who had fled from Russia during the previous half century "have repeatedly had to endure severe conflict with the old-established peoples" and then added: "The survivors have maintained a warlike spirit," and many "retain connections and influence in their Russian home...almost all are well-armed." They could, Oppenheim maintained, easily provide an experienced and "fanatical" force to help in the reinvasion of their Caucasus home.[71]

Indeed, the Muslim communities from the Caucasus and the Balkans had often received harsh treatment at the hands of Christian regimes. The Circassians in particular had been subjected in the 1860s to a program of forced expulsion, deportation, and massacre by the Russian government, resulting in anything up to 1,500,000 deaths.[72] These irregular elements, coming from brutalized communities, could shift more easily than most from their original function of guerrilla warfare and stimulate ethnic-based insurgencies over enemy lines[73] to unofficial assaults on "suspect" Armenian settlements, and then from June 1915 onward to full-scale massacre of deportation trains, once they had received leeway and authorization to do so.[74] Their use by the Ittihadist regime is indicative of the utter lack of concern from the very beginning of the war, even before the genocide, for the safety of Armenians.

In focusing on the role of irregular forces, however, and acknowledging the civilian "political" influence on them of leaders such as Ittihadist central committee member Behaeddin Shakir, we must not overlook the fact that the Special Organization was a military subunit, albeit an undisciplined one.[75] The regular military played a fulsome role in mass murder, and the army leadership was involved in pushing for deportations, as attested to, if he is to be believed, by Talaat himself.[76] Indeed, Enver represented the blurring of "political" and "military" functions in this "nationalist war" and personified military ruthlessness, as did his brother-in-law Jevdet, who also combined military and civilian offices in the crucial province of Van. Enver had firsthand experience both as a Turkish officer fighting Balkan Christian nationalist irregulars (*komitaji*s) and as an irregular himself, in clashes in which no quarter had been asked or given.[77]

The opening of hostilities in World War I was accompanied in November 1914 by a declaration of *Jihad*, or Holy War, by the Sheikh-ul-Islam (the highest religious authority and a member of the Ottoman cabinet until 1917). This marks the beginning of a second time-phase in my periodization and the first to feature carefully planned and supervised mass violence. The declaration of Jihad, a corruption of the Quranic prescription, was generally ineffective in stimulating uprisings of foreign Muslim populations against the "infidel" rule of Russia and Great Britain or even in galvanizing the different Muslim communities of the Ottoman Empire.[78] Nevertheless, the policy is a further illustration of the exclusion of Ottoman Christians from the "universe of obligation," and it undoubtedly facilitated the participation of many individuals in atrocities against Christians.[79]

The intensification of anti-Armenian sentiment after the Turkish defeat at the battle of Sarikamish at the turn of 1914-15 suggests the opening of a third stage in my periodization. For some scholars it marked the decisive moment.[80] Ittihadist radicals in provincial posts began to call for "revenge" against Armenians, as for instance in Erzerum and Diarbekir.[81] The atmosphere of suspicion arising from that and the other engagements of the Armenian volunteer battalions also influenced the disarmament of Armenian military conscripts in February 1915.

Contrary to popular belief, the Armenian military conscripts were not systematically murdered immediately upon their assignment to labor battalions but rather during the course of the general Armenian deportations themselves. This discriminatory practice was based upon a preexisting chauvinism and mistrust of non-Muslim troops. It did, however, also initially serve a practical purpose in terms of labor required for the war effort.[82] Though it may not have been a planned prelude to genocide, this discriminatory "security" measure was massively attritional by the very nature of the conditions and the tasks that the Armenian soldiers had to perform. Thus, before April 24, 1915, a German observer could report on a conversation with Enver that "because the shortage of means of transport and the poor roads jeopardize the supply of the Caucasus army, Enver has assigned 50,000 bearers [*Träger*] in furtherance of the task! None of the German officers here will maintain that he...expected this outcome of Turkish mobilization. But equally few of us wish to know the terrible toll of victims [*ungeheuren Opfer*] he has thereby inflicted on the land."[83] When the genocide began, the disarmed, enfeebled soldiers of the work battalions were easy prey for Ottoman regulars and irregulars.

The month of March 1915 brought yet further intensification of anti-Armenian sentiment, and one important scholar identifies the middle of the month as the point of departure of the genocide.[84] From March 5 onwards the outer forts of the Dardanelles were under assault by a growing Anglo-French naval presence. At the other end of the empire, Jevdet Bey had been defeated in Persia. Turkish suspicion about Ottoman Armenian links to the Entente powers resulted both in a mooted plan for deporting the Armenians of Constantinople and its western Anatolian hinterlands at the time of the Dardanelles assault[85] and the authorization of extended powers to Behaeddin Shakir and the Special Organization to fight the "inner enemy" in the eastern vilayets.[86] The period also saw the dispatching of radical Ittihadist emissaries to the provinces and the replacement of some moderate officials by more radical ones.[87]

This period, up until the time of the famous Van uprising beginning on April 20, was characterized by brutal regionalized policies in different parts of the empire. Thus, while the Special Organization and the military were expanding the scope of their killing in the eastern border regions, with particular intensity in the east of the Van province, localized disturbances caused by deserters and some smaller scale Armenian nationalist agitation in Zeitun in Cilicia were met from the beginning of April with deportations both to the south and to the northwest to the vicinity of the salt lake near Konia. At this stage, these did not entail the massacre of the deportees, though many would die because of the harsh conditions.[88]

The Van uprising was a response to the increasing brutality of Turkish action in the region. Returning from unsuccessful campaign-

ing in Persia, the governor, Jevdet Bey, drove the Van Arme
self-defense by unleashing massacres in the outlying settleme
the first hint of serious trouble in the province.[89] Nevertheless,
Ittihadists presented the events as a planned Armenian insurgency,
not least because it fatally diverted Turkish troops from the ongoing conflict in Persia.[90] The rising also coincided with the gathering of British and French forces in the Mediterranean in preparation for troop landings on the Dardanelles at the tip of the Gallipoli peninsula, which occurred on April 25. From April 24 also, the ongoing deportations from Zeitun were now directed southwards toward the desert regions.[91]

An important immediate catalyst for the introduction of the general deportations from the eastern provinces seems to have been provided by the Turkish retreat from Van and its occupation on May 16 by Russian troops preceded by an Armenian volunteer battalion. Exaggerated reports of the number of Muslims killed during and after the uprising were soon put into circulation. A general Russian advance into Anatolia was anticipated over the spring and summer, and in its face deportations were ordered from that second half of May from Erzerum, the province neighboring Van.

A number of studies of the regional unfolding of the destruction process are in existence,[92] but full analysis of the development and dynamics of the deportations is lacking, and it remains difficult to establish many of the deportation routes beyond the major ones.[93] Shortly after the Erzerum deportation orders, the expulsions spread westward and southward in quick succession in June and July, through the province of Sivas, including Shabin-Karahisar (where there had been an Armenian uprising in mid-June), the province of Mamuret ul-Aziz (Harput/Kharpert), and the province of Trebizond on the Black Sea coast.[94] From the end of July, the measures were extended to the Armenians of central and western Anatolia, including the settlements around the Sea of Marmara. In September and October, the Armenians of Thrace met with the same fate. Meanwhile, Cilicia was continually revisited by deportation as the earlier measures against Zeitun and then Marash were repeated throughout the Adana district.[95]

Mass population movement was only half the story, however. With the Russian arrival at Van, Jevdet Bey withdrew westward over Lake Van to Bitlis. He was joined early in June by Enver's uncle, Halil, the

nt failed campaign in Persia had been handi-
sing. With reinforcements, they managed to
dvance into Anatolia. Thereafter, Jevdet and
th against the Armenian population of Bitlis,
task was not completed until late July be-
t Turkish actions evoked at Mush and Sasun.
djacent to both Bitlis and Van, had been on
way to being "cleansed" of Armenians since the end of May, a process culminating in July and August. The Armenian Genocide in each of these areas was characterized by on-the-spot massacres, though some deportations also took place.[96]

The Genocide in Perspective

The Armenian Genocide was a—perhaps *the*—archetypal example of a nationalist genocide. It was not a genocide of biological racism nor of religious fanaticism, though both of those motives certainly influenced various perpetrators. In its nationalist terms, the genocide was *a completely successful venture*, especially once the Russian revolutions of 1917 fortuitously let the Ittihadists off the hook in military terms. Though the deportations and massacres did not annihilate every last Armenian, they did remove the Armenian national presence from the lands that were later to form the Republic of Turkey. Control of the land and the homogeneity of the people on that land constituted the driving force behind the Ittihadist policy, and this would continue under Mustafa Kemal (Ataturk) with his organization for the defense of eastern Anatolia against the impositions of the Treaty of Sèvres, and with his subsequent intensified repression of the Kurds.

The Armenian Genocide represents a terrible but clear logic of ethnic nationalism when carried to its extreme in multinational societies. As regards the other forced population movements in Anatolia during World War I, particularly the deportation of the Kurds in 1916-17,[97] future research may show that the very introduction of the Armenian deportations and massacres was important in crystallizing broader Turkish aspirations for ethnic-national homogenization into action. The ramifications of the Armenian Genocide reverberate to this day.

Notes

1. Mehmet Sukru Hanioglu, *Preparation for a Revolution: The Young Turks, 1902-1908* (Oxford: Oxford University Press, 2001); Erik Jan Zürcher, "Young Turks, Ottoman Muslims and Turkish Nationalists," in Kemal Karpat, ed., *Ottoman Past and Today's Turkey* (Leiden: Brill, 2000), pp. 150-79, especially p. 151.
2. Hanioglu, *Preparation*, pp. 8, 84; David McDowall, *A Modern History of the Kurds* (London: I.B. Tauris, 1996), pp. 90-91.
3. Donald Quataert, *Social Disintegration and Popular Resistance in the Ottoman Empire, 1881-1908* (New York: New York University Press, 1983), pp. 1-2, 9-10; Hanioglu, *Preparation*, p. 35.
4. Roderic H. Davison, *Essays in Ottoman and Turkish History, 1774-1923* (Austin: University of Texas Press, 1990), p. 88.
5. Donald Quataert, "The Age of Reform, 1812-1914," in Suraiya Faroqhi et al., eds., *An Economic and Social History of the Ottoman Empire,* vol. 2: *1600-1914* (Cambridge: Cambridge University Press, 1997), p. 761. On British interest, see Akaby Nassibian, *Britain and the Armenian Question* (Kent: Croom Helm, 1984).
6. Hanioglu, *Preparation*, chapter 5.
7. Zürcher, "Young Turks," p. 151; Quataert, "The Age of Reforms," pp. 764-65.
8. Mark Levene, "Creating a Modern 'Zone of Genocide': The Impact of Nation- and State-Formation on Eastern Anatolia, 1878-1923," *Holocaust and Genocide Studies* 12:3 (1998): 403.
9. Hans-Lukas Kieser, *Der verpasste Friede: Mission, Ethnie und Staat in den Ostprovinzen der Türkei 1839-1938* (Zurich: Chronos, 2000), p. 339 and *passim*. For an individual case study, see Kieser, "Dr. Mehmed Reshid (1873-1919): A Political Doctor," paper presented at conference "Contextualising the Armenian Experience in the Ottoman Empire," University of Michigan-Ann Arbor, March 7-10, 2002.
10. On the origins of the Young Turks, see Wolfdieter Bihl, *Die Kaukasus-Politik der Mittelmächte*, vol. 1 (Vienna: Hermann Böhlau, 1975), pp. 143-44; Feroz Ahmad, *The Young Turks: The Committee of Union and Progress in Turkish Politics 1908-1914* (Oxford: Clarendon Press, 1969), pp. 166-81.
11. See especially Hanioglu, *Preparation*.
12. Zürcher, "Young Turks," pp. 154-55; Ahmed, *The Young Turks*, p. 154, compares Ittihadist ideology to a cake, the proportions of whose ingredients varied between adherents and over time. See also Roderic H. Davison, *Turkey: A Short History* (Huntingdon: Eothen Press, 1998), p. 128.
13. Kieser, *Der verpasste Friede*, pp. 244-47. See Jelle Verheij, "Die armenischen Massaker von 1894-1896," in Hans-Lukas Kieser, ed., *Die armenische Frage und die Schweiz* (Zurich: Chronos, 1999), pp. 69-129, for up-to-date accounts of these massacres that convincingly dispute the argument of Stephen Duguid, "The Politics of Unity: Hamidian Politics in Eastern Anatolia," *Middle Eastern Studies* 9 (1973): 139-55.
14. Reşat Kasaba, *The Ottoman Empire and the World Economy: The Nineteenth Century* (Albany, NY: State University of New York, 1988), chapters 3 and 4; Kieser, *Der verpasste Friede*, part 1.
15. For the best available analysis of the process, see Kieser, *Der verpasste Friede*, part 1.
16. Ibid., Stephan Astourian, "Genocidal Process: Reflections on the Armeno-Turkish Polarization," in Richard G. Hovannisian, ed., *The Armenian Genocide: History, Politics, Ethics* (Basingstoke: Macmillan and New York: St. Martin's Press, 1992), pp. 53-79. On the Kurdish persecutions, see Martin van Bruinessen, "Genocide in

Kurdistan?" in George J. Andreopoulos, ed., *Genocide: Conceptual and Historical Dimensions* (Philadelphia: University of Pennsylvania Press, 1994), pp. 141-70, especially pp. 149-54. See also United States, National Archives, Record Group 59, 867.00/465, Rockhill to Bryan, Jan. 21, 1913.

17. Harry Jewell Sarkis, "The Armenian Renaissance, 1500-1863," *Journal of Modern History* 9:4 (1937): 433-48.
18. Kieser, *Der verpasste Friede*, pp. 79-85 and *passim*.
19. Davison, *Turkey*, p. 115.
20. Astourian, "Genocidal Process," pp. 56-58; Levene, "'Zone of Genocide'," pp. 400-01. For the formation of Armenian elites outside Armenia at the beginning of the twentieth century, see Anahide Ter Minassian, "Élites Arméniennes en Suisse," in Kieser, ed., *Die armenische Frage und die Schweiz*, pp. 29-52.
21. Quataert, *The Ottoman Empire*, pp. 116-17. For statistics on the refugees, see Zürcher, "Young Turks," p. 171.
22. Astourian, "Genocidal Process," pp. 61-62, 66-67.
23. Ibid, pp. 58-60.
24. See, for example (in an article that does not seem to have overcome all of these stereotypes), Feroz Ahmad, "Vanguard of a Nascent Bourgeoisie," in Osman Okyar and Halil Inalcik, eds., *Social and Economic History of Turkey (1071-1920)* (Ankara: Meteksan, 1980), pp. 329-50, especially pp. 329-31; and, in the same volume, Moshe Ma'oz, "Intercommunal Relations in Ottoman Syria during the Tanzimat Era," pp. 205-10.
25. Astourian, "Genocidal Process," pp. 61, 64.
26. Ibid, p. 65; Ahmad, "Vanguard," p. 329; Ma'oz, "Intercommunal Relations," p. 207.
27. On the Turkish rhetoric on Anatolia, see David Kushner, *The Rise of Turkish Nationalism, 1876-1908* (London: Frank Cass, 1977), chapter 5.
28. On the pattern of massacre, see Raymond Kévorkian, ed., *La Cilicie (1909-1921)*, special issue of *Revue d'Histoire Arménienne Contemporaine* 3 (1999): 59-82; Astourian, "Genocidal Process," pp. 63-66.
29. Davison, *Turkey*, pp. 128-29; David McDowall, *A Modern History of the Kurds* (London: I.B. Tauris, 1996), pp. 90-91.
30. Taner Akçam, *Armenien und der Völkermord* (Hamburg: Hamburger Edition, 1996), p. 37; Vahakn N. Dadrian, *Warrant for Genocide* (New Brunswick, NJ: Transaction Publishers, 1999), chapter 9.
31. Ahmad, "Vanguard," pp. 332-33.
32. Quataert, *Social Disintegration*, pp. 144-45; Hanioglu, *Preparation*, p. 69.
33. Ahmad, "Vanguard," pp. 322-23; idem, "Unionist Relations with the Greek, Armenian and Jewish Communities of the Ottoman Empire, 1908-1914," in Benjamin Braude and Bernard Lewis, eds., *Christians and Jews in the Ottoman Empire*, vol. 1 (New York: Holmes and Meier, 1982), pp. 405-18, especially p. 409, on the pan-Hellenism of many Greek representatives in the National Assembly; Akçam, *Armenien*, pp. 41-42; Quataert, *Social Disintegration*, pp. 144-45.
34. Akçam, *Armenien*, p. 43; Marjorie Housepian Dobkin, *Smyrna 1922: The Destruction of a City* (Kent, OH: Kent State University Press, 1988), pp. 42, 46. For a breakdown of the figures, see Zürcher, "Young Turks," p. 171.
35. Johannes Lepsius, *Der Todesgang des armenischen Volkes* (Potsdam: Tempelverlag, 1919), pp. xiv-xv.
36. Levene, "'Zone of Genocide'," p. 403. On the developing role of the revolutionary parties, their composition, and operational bases, see Anahide Ter Minassian, *La Question Arménienne* (Roquevaire: Éditions Parenthèses, 1983), pp. 74, 108, 124-34. On the disappointments of 1878 and the background to the formation of the

revolutionary parties, see Christopher J. Walker, *Armenia: The Survival of a Nation* (London: Routledge and New York: St. Martin's Press, 1980), pp. 110-32.

37. Kieser, *Der verpasste Friede*, p. 123
38. Ibid., Jeremy Salt, *Imperialism, Evangelism and the Ottoman Armenians, 1878-1896* (London: Frank Cass, 1993), p. 84.
39. Kieser, *Der verpasste Friede*, p. 122.
40. Justin McCarthy, *Death and Exile: The Ethnic Cleansing of Ottoman Muslims, 1821-1922* (Princeton: Darwin, 1995).
41. See Gerayer Koutcharian, *Der Siedlungsraum der Armenier unter dem Einfluss der historisch-politischen Ereignisse seit dem Berliner Kongress 1878* (Berlin: Dietrich Reimer, 1989).
42. Fatma Müge Goçek, "Reading Genocide: Turkish Historiography on the Armenian Massacres and Deportations of 1915" (p. 5), paper presented at conference cited in note 9 above. Cf. James J. Reid, "Total War, the Annihilation Ethic, and the Armenian Genocide, 1870-1918," in Hovannisian, ed., *The Armenian Genocide*, pp. 21-52, especially pp. 40-41.
43. On these appointments, see Max Oppenheim, "Die revolutionierung des Islamischen Gebietes unserer Feindes," file 47, folio 36, Ernst Jäckh papers, Yale University Library.
44. Fikret Adanir, "Non-Muslims in the Ottoman Army and the Ottoman Defeat in the Balkan War of 1912/13," paper presented at the conference cited in note 9 above.
45. See Zürcher, "Young Turks," pp. 156-57.
46. This is also Adanir's implication in "Non-Muslims in the Ottoman Army."
47. Davison, *Turkey*, p. 132.
48. Akçam, *Armenien*, pp. 39-43; idem, "Rethinking the Ottoman Archival Material: Debunking Existing Myths/General Overview of the Ottoman Documents," paper presented at the conference cited in note 9 above.
49. Roderic H. Davison, "The Armenian Crisis (1912-1914)," *American Historical Review* 53 (April 1948): 481-505. More generally on Russian policy at the time, see Alan Bodger, "Russia and the End of the Ottoman Empire," in Marian Kent, ed., *The Great Powers and the End of the Ottoman Empire* (London: George Allen and Unwin, 1984), pp. 76-110.
50. Akçam, *Armenien*, p. 48; Davison, "The Armenian Crisis," p. 493.
51. Djemal Pasha, *Memories of a Turkish Statesman* (London: Hutchinson and Co., 1922), pp. 266-75.
52. Ibid., p. 276.
53. Haus- Hof- und Staatsarchiv, Vienna (HHSA), PA I, 942, Pallavicini to Berchtold, Dec. 23, 1914.
54. Mark Levene, "The Limits of Tolerance: Nation-State Building and What It Means for Minority Groups," *Patterns of Prejudice* 34:2 (2000): 21.
55. Gabriele Yonan, *Ein vergessener Holocaust: Die Vernichtung der christlichen Assyrer in der Türkei* (Göttingen: Gesellschaft für Bedrohte Völker, 1989).
56. Lepsius, *Todesgang*, p. xiv; Henry Morgenthau, *Ambassador Morgenthau's Story* (Garden City, NY: Doubleday, Page & Co., 1918), p. 347.
57. Davison, *Essays*, p. 88, and *Turkey*, pp. 129-30.
58. Donald Bloxham, "The Beginning of the Armenian Catastrophe: Comparative and Contextual Considerations," in Hans-Lukas Kieser and Dominik Schaller, eds., *Die armenische Völkermord und die Shoah* (Zurich: Chronos, 2002); idem, "Cumulative Radicalisation and the Armenian Genocide," paper delivered at the conference cited in note 9 above.

59. Raymond Kévorkian, ed., *Le sort des déportés Arméniens Ottomans dans les camps de concentration de Syrie-Mésopotamie (1915-1916)*, special issue of *Revue d'Histoire Arménienne Contemporaine* 2 (1998): 16, 60-61; Hilmar Kaiser, *At the Crossroads of Der Zor* (Princeton, NJ: Gomidas, 2001), pp. 10-12; Aram Arkun, "Cilicia and the Armenian Genocide," paper delivered at the conference cited in note 9 above.
60. Kévorkian, *Le sort des déportés Arméniens*, pp. 16, 60-61; Kaiser, *At the Crossroads*, pp. 67-69. See also Yves Ternon, *Les Arméniens: Histoire d'un génocide* (Paris: Seuil, 1977), chapter 17.
61. Akçam, "Rethinking," section 7, part c.
62. Ara Sarafian, "The Absorption of Armenian Women and Children into Muslim Households as a Structural Component of the Armenian Genocide," in Omer Bartov and Phyllis Mack, eds., *In God's Name: Genocide and Religion in the Twentieth Century* (New York: Berghahn, 2001), pp. 209-21.
63. See, for example, "Confiscation des biens des réfugiés arméniens par le Gouvernement turc" (Paris: Imprimerie Massis, 1929). More generally on the wartime theft and its function within the genocide, see Hilmar Kaiser, "The Ottoman Government and the End of the Ottoman Social Formation, 1915-1917," in Kieser, ed., *Die armenische Völkermord und die Shoah.*
64. Rhodes House Library, Oxford, MSS British Empire S22 G506, folder "Armenia," S.G.5489, 18.10.32, folio 2; SG.3119, 21.1.1930, folios 2-3; John H. Harris, *Salving the 'Outcasts of the War'* (London: Friends of Armenia, 1929), p. 2. On abducted Armenian women and children even at the end of the 1920s, see "The Rescue of Christian Slaves," *Slave Market News* (Jan. 1929). On the different "political" development of the Protestant *millet*, see Kieser, *Der verpasste Friede*, pp. 81-83. For correspondence concerning the treatment of non-Apostolic Armenians by Austria and Germany respectively, see HHSA, PA XII 209, Pallavicini to Burian, Sept. 3, 1915; *Deutschland und Armenien 1914-1918*, ed. Johannes Lepsius (Potsdam: Tempelverlag, 1919), doc. 148, p. 138.
65. Rhodes House Library, Oxford, MSS British Empire S22 G506, C.13 8.3.35, Feb. 7, 1935.
66. Artem Ohandjanian, *Der verschwiegene Völkermord* (Cologne: Böhlau, 1989), pp. 81-82.
67. G. Korganoff, *La participation des Arméniens à la Guerre Mondiale sur le front du Caucase* (Paris: Massis, 1927), pp. 20-21; Vahakn N. Dadrian, "The Role of the Special Organisation in the Armenian Genocide during the First World War," in Panikos Panayi, ed., *Minorities in Wartime* (Oxford: Berg, 1993), pp. 50-82, especially p. 53.
68. On this subject generally, see Bloxham, "The Beginning." For Russian overtures, see Bérard to Boghos Nubar, Feb. 5, 1915, in *Boghos Nubar's Papers and the Armenian Question 1915-1918: Documents*, ed. Vatche Ghazarian (Waltham, MA: Mayreni, 1996), doc. 2, pp. 5-6; Bihl, *Kaukasus-Politik*, vol. 1, p. 220. For specific contemporary Turkish fears, see *Documents* (vol. 1) and *Documents on Ottoman Armenians* (vol. 2) (Ankara: Directorate General of Press and Information, 1982-1986), vol. 1, nos. 4, 6, 8, pp. 9, 15, 21-22; vol. 2, nos. 1893, 1894, 1899, 1903, pp. 2, 4, 17, 44-54. For non-Turkish sources on desertion and defection, see Archives of the German Foreign Office, Abt. 1A, Türkei 183, vol. 36, Wangenheim to Bethmann, April 15, 1915; Raphael de Nogales, *Four Years beneath the Crescent* (New York: Charles Scribner's Sons, 1926), pp. 27-28; Maurice Larcher, *La guerre turque dans la guerre Mondiale* (Paris: Chiron, 1925), p. 395. On some of the circumstances of Armenian desertion, see Arkun, "Cilicia."

69. Dadrian, "Special Organisation," pp. 63-64; in greater detail, see Bloxham, "The Beginning."
70. Reid, "Total War," pp. 26-27.
71. Oppenheim, "Revolutionierung," folios 36, 39.
72. Stephen D. Shenfield, "The Circassians: A Forgotten Genocide?" in Mark Levene and Penny Roberts, eds., *The Massacre in History* (Oxford: Berghahn, 1999), pp. 149-62.
73. HHSA, PA I, 942, Trabzon, Dec. 12, 1914.
74. Sarafian, "Absorption," p. 214, citing evidence that in the case of Trebizond, murder of deportees was legitimated by authorizing the accompanying gendarmerie—among whom there was a high representation of former Muslim refugees—to kill in the name of "discipline," if not necessarily explicit policy.
75. HHSA, PA I, 943, Pera, Jan. 13, 1915, on the atrocities committed by irregulars and the lack of control of German officers over the political influence of Ittihadist activists.
76. Talaat's memoirs, cited in Goçek, "Reading Genocide." For another example of military pressure for deportation, see Turkey, *Documents*, vol. 1, no. 26, p. 71.
77. Jäckh papers, file 41, Enver's autobiography, folios 12-13, 18-21; Reid, "Total War," pp. 28, 38.
78. Bihl, *Kaukasus-Politik*, vol. 1, pp. 37-38.
79. Leo Kuper and Gary Remer, "The Religious Element in Genocide," *Journal of Armenian Studies* 4:1-2 (1992): 307-30.
80. Ternon, *Les Arméniens*, pp. 211-12; Arthur Beylerian, "L'échec d'une percée internationale: Le mouvement national arménienne (1914-1923)," *Relations internationales*, no. 31 (1982): 356.
81. *The Treatment of Armenians in the Ottoman Empire, 1915-16...with a Preface by Viscount Bryce*, ed., Arnold Toynbee (London: Sir Joseph Causton and Sons, 1916), doc. 57, pp. 236-40; Kieser, "Reshid."
82. Erik Jan Zürcher, "Ottoman Labour Battalions in World War I," in Kieser and Schaller, eds., *Die armenische Völkermord*; Jäckh papers, file 13, "Mitteilungen von Enver Pascha," Oct. 13, 1914.
83. Jäckh papers, file 23, "Sehr vertraulich! Besprechung mit Enver Pascha am 11. April," folios 4 and 5.
84. Akçam, *Armenien*, p. 59.
85. Bloxham, "The Beginning," section 2.
86. Akçam, *Armenien*, p. 59; Dadrian, "Special Organisation," pp. 66-67.
87. Kieser, "Reshid."
88. Bloxham, "Cumulative Radicalisation"; Arkun, "Cilicia"; Akçam, *Armenien*, p. 63.
89. On the rising in general, see Anahide Ter Minassian, "Van 1915," in Richard G. Hovannisian, ed., *Armenian Van/Vaspurakan* (Costa Mesa: CA: Mazda Publishers, 2000), pp. 209-44. For the specific explanation cited, see Donald Bloxham, "The Beginning."
90. Joseph Pomiankowski, *Der Zusammenbruch des ottomanischen Reiches* (Vienna: Amalthea, 1928), p. 147.
91. Arkun, "Cilicia." See also Kaiser, *At the Crossroads*, pp. 9-10.
92. See, for example, Kevork Yeghia Suakjian, "Genocide in Trebizond: A Case Study of Armeno-Turkish Relations during the First World War" (Ph.D. diss., University of Nebraska, 1981); Yves Ternon, *Mardin 1915: Anatomie pathologique d'une destruction* (Paris: Centre des l'Histoire Arménienne Contemporaine, 2000); Arkun, "Cilicia."
93. For a good summary of the routes, see Kévorkian, *Le sort des déportés Arméniens*. Lepsius, *Todesgang,* and Toynbee, ed., *Treatment of Armenians*, have yet to be

supplanted, albeit they do not provide explicit and overall links between deportations, rather examining them on a case-by-case and province-by-province basis.

94. Lepsius' chronological list of the major round-ups is given in G. S. Graber, *Caravans to Oblivion: The Armenian Genocide, 1915* (New York: John Wiley and Sons, 1996), p. 120.
95. Ternon, *Les Arméniens*, pp. 253-59.
96. Walker, *Armenia*, pp. 211-12, 222.
97. On the deportation of the Kurds, see Hans-Lukas Kieser, "Zwischen Ararat und Euphrat: Abendländische Missionen im spätosmanischen Kurdistan," in Kieser, ed., *Kurdistan und Europa* (Zurich: Chronos, 1997), pp. 113-51, especially pp. 135-36. For some of the differences between the Ittihadist treatment of Kurds and Armenians, see Hamit Bozarslan, "Der Kemalismus und das Kurdenproblem," in Kieser, ed., *Kurdistan und Europa*, pp. 217-36, especially p. 221.

4

The United States Response to the Armenian Genocide

Simon Payaslian

The United States had emerged as one of the principal contenders in global political economy when the Wilson Administration entered the White House in 1913. By then, the nation had developed deeply entrenched domestic and bilateral commercial and geopolitical configurations as shaped under the Open Door and Dollar Diplomacy policies of the preceding administrations. Although Woodrow Wilson and his first secretary of state, William Jennings Bryan, proposed to infuse humanitarian values into U.S. foreign policy, overarching commercial and geostrategic considerations in various parts of the world, including the Ottoman Empire, relegated the Armenian Question and the Armenian Genocide to a secondary concern. The Wilson Administration condemned the genocide, but its response initially stressed management of public opinion at home, followed by relief assistance to the survivors.

United States Foreign Policy toward the Ottoman Empire

The advent of the United States as a global power and the restructuring of the world political economy coincided with the internationalization of the Armenian Question in the nineteenth century.[1] The United States and the Ottoman Empire had developed commercial relations since the early decades of that century, and expanding interests underscored the strategic significance of naval stations across the Mediterranean basin.[2] Negotiations regarding naval arrangements led to the U.S.-Turkish treaty of 1830, followed by another treaty in 1862 for wider trade relations between the two nations.[3] The United

Navy facilitated the expansion and protection of American mercial and missionary interests, at times becoming involved in Ottoman political affairs, as during the Greek war of independence in the 1820s and in the British and French conflicts in Egypt in the 1880s.[4] In the aftermath of the Armenian massacres of 1894-96 during the reign of Sultan Abdul-Hamid II,[5] the second administration of Grover Cleveland dispatched the *USS San Francisco*, *Marblehead*, and *Minneapolis* to Ottoman waters to secure protection for American citizens and missionaries and to coerce the Turkish government to pay indemnity for the damages caused to missionary properties.[6] The administration of William McKinley (1897-1901) demanded compensation for the loss of American property, and in 1898 the two governments reached an agreement whereby the Sublime Porte would pay through purchase of an American-built ship.[7] Neither the Cleveland nor the McKinley Administration, however, considered raising with the Turkish authorities the issue of indemnification for the losses suffered by the Armenian victims during the massacres.

In the meantime, responding to the depression of the 1890s, the United States redoubled its efforts to expand economic relations with the outside world and relied on the Open Door policy and freedom of the seas for greater international competitiveness in Europe, East Asia, and the Ottoman Empire.[8] The total volume of U.S.-Turkish trade was $6.2 million in 1899,[9] and widening international operations by American companies such as Standard Oil, Singer Sewing Machine, and the American Tobacco Company contributed to the long-term strengthening of U.S.-Turkish bilateral relations. Further, expanding commercial activities by American companies across the Ottoman Empire coincided with the conversion from coal to oil as a principal source of energy in the industrialized economies, intensifying the geopolitical competition among Russia, Great Britain, France, and the United States over known and potential oil reserves in the Middle East and the Caucasus.[10]

Under the administrations of Theodore Roosevelt (1901-09), William Howard Taft (1909-13), and Woodrow Wilson (1913-21), the United States government functioned as the "promotional state," and its ambassadors to Turkey assumed the responsibility of promoting and protecting American interests in the Ottoman Empire while maintaining amicable relations with the Turkish authorities.[11] The much publicized railroad project proposed by Admiral Colby M. Chester and supported by the Department of State, though ultimately failing to materialize, exemplified the role of the United States government as the "promotional state."[12] In relations with Turkey, advancement of commercial interests implied avoidance of conflicts so long as the Turkish government respected the principles of Open Door as predicated upon the extraterritorial rights of foreign nations. The Turkish government, for its part, mired in European struggles for balance of power, looked to the United States as a potential alternative source for capital and technology to reverse the fortunes of its declining economy and military.[13] By the first decade of the twentieth century, the United States had become a major partner of Ottoman trade. The total value of U.S.-Turkish trade rose from $8.3 million in 1900[14] to $16.4 million in 1907,[15] and after the 1908 Young Turk revolution, from $14.9 million in 1909[16] to $25.5 million in 1913.[17]

Concurrently, American missionaries sought to spread American Protestant Christianity to the world.[18] The American Board of Commissioners for Foreign Missions (ABCFM) had led the missionary works in the Ottoman Empire since the early decades of the nineteenth century, and by the early twentieth century, five American missionary societies were active in the region.[19] In 1911 the American Board of Commissioners for Foreign Missions employed 1,181 native workers serving 15,398 communicants and 55,632 students.[20] Like their commercial compatriots, American missionaries insisted on the Open Door principle for the equal treatment of their institutions under Ottoman law.[21]

The influence of the missionaries extended beyond educational and religious activities, however, and caused intense friction between the American Protestants and the Armenian Apostolic Church. Although some Armenians welcomed the missionaries as a vehicle for Westernization and modernization, most resisted their growing cultural and political impact on their communities.[22] Nevertheless, in times of massacres and political and economic uncertainties, a growing number of Armenians, including students from missionary institutions, emigrated to the United States.[23] As they worked toward improving their life, the Armenian immigrants founded numerous societies in efforts to mobilize American public support for their compatriots in the Ottoman Empire. They organized mass meetings, circulated petitions and pamphlets, and published newspapers and journals, including, for example, the newspaper *Hairenik* [Fatherland], and the journals *Gotchnag* [Clarion] and *Armenia*. They published articles on the history of Armenia, its culture, religion, and traditions, and on the Turkish atrocities committed against the Armenians, all the while urging their compatriots back home to remain loyal to the Young Turk regime despite its failure to improve conditions.[24] They were unable to influence U.S. foreign policy, however. The Armenian community, too small in numbers and too inexperienced in American politics, could not compete with the incomparably greater powers of missionaries, corporations, and bureaucracies.

The Wilson Administration

When the Wilson Administration entered office in 1913, there had developed a network of U.S. interests in the Ottoman Empire, and not surprisingly the Administration, like its predecessors, assumed the responsibilities of the "promotional state" and continued to pursue the economic and geopolitical objectives of the nation.[25] Wilson was also heavily influenced by the Presbyterian religious tradition, although he viewed political support for missionary interests at home and abroad as a vehicle to realize his own ideals and political objectives.[26] While characterized as a utopian visionary by historians, Wilson "was also a calculating politician,"[27] whose opinions and actions revealed both optimism and pessimism as required by the immediate political circumstances. In matters of foreign policy, Wilson initially expressed opposition to European imperialism, the Rooseveltian "Big Stick," and Taft's Dollar Diplomacy. As president, however, he pursued policies not dissimilar to those of his predecessors and paid great attention to commercial and geopolitical considerations.[28]

The U.S. Navy continued its role as the "agent of enlightenment" and of commerce during the Wilson Administration.[29] The conversion of naval vessels from coal to oil, spearheaded by Secretary of the Navy Josephus Daniels, encouraged the Navy Fuel Board to coordinate policies with the oil and ship building industries, benefiting both the Navy and the industries in areas of technological developments in oil engines and oil refinement.[30] At the same time, the conversion to oil by the United States and European countries intensified international competition in the Middle East, and newly formed foreign combinations such as the Anglo-Persian and the Royal Dutch-Shell companies challenged Standard Oil in world markets.[31] The Wilson Administration, and the State Department in particular, extended diplomatic support to the U.S. oil industry in the Middle East, necessitating greater cooperation in U.S.-Turkish relations.

While promoting commercial and missionary interests abroad, the Wilson Administration also sought to maximize the president's chances for reelection in 1916. The effective management of domestic public opinion, therefore, became an integral component of its foreign policy.[32] In fact, Wilson's Cabinet appointments were aimed primarily at satisfying his constituency in the Democratic Party, with little regard for their experiences in international affairs. Most members of his Cabinet had little or no role in determining policy toward the Armenian Question; that policy remained confined to the secretaries of state and the U.S. ambassador to Constantinople.

Henry Morgenthau, as the Administration's first ambassador to Constantinople, was hardly prepared for his post at the Turkish capital when appointed in September 1913. Financially successful, he had contributed to New York and Democratic campaign politics, and his dedication to the Democratic Party in general and to Wilson's election in particular had earned him the confidence of the president and the ambassadorship.[33] He had no experience in foreign relations, however. Prior to his departure for Constantinople, Morgenthau spent a few days at the State Department for briefings,[34] and in October he attended an informative conference with several members of the American Board of Commissioners for Foreign Missions in New York regarding the political situation in the Ottoman Empire.[35] He arrived on November 27 in Constantinople, where he was greeted by more than twenty people, including the embassy staff and Oscar Gunkel, the regional manager of Standard Oil.[36]

During his first year in office as ambassador, Morgenthau was optimistic regarding the future of the Young Turk regime and sought to lend U.S. assistance to its efforts at modernization. He met frequently with Turkish officials on issues pertaining to the reorganization of their economy and finances, closer naval ties with the United States, and protection for missionaries and their institutions. A member of the Ottoman Parliament even expressed interest in reviving the Chester project.[37] On December 22, Morgenthau and Minister of the Interior Talaat Pasha discussed the possibility of extending a U.S. financial loan to Turkey.[38] The very next day, Morgenthau urged Standard Oil to transfer a loan to the Turkish government and cabled Secretary of State Bryan for approval to render such assistance by the company.[39] That evening, Morgenthau conferred with Minister of the Navy Mahmud Pasha and Minister of Justice Ibrahim Pasha.[40] Mahmud Pasha intimated that the Turkish fleet needed additional ships but was uncertain whether his government could obtain them any time soon. Ibrahim Pasha, who, Morgenthau noted, appeared sincerely interested in instituting "real justice," requested a copy of the U.S. civil, criminal, and federal codes.[41]

On December 27, Morgenthau met briefly with a group of leading Armenian representatives, including Archbishop Zaven Eghiayan, the Armenian Patriarch of Constantinople, and Professor Abraham Hagopian of Robert College.[42] In their conversation, Morgenthau learned that the Armenians in the Ottoman Empire, numbering about 2 million,[43] had become "like vassals to the Kurds," who descended from the mountains "whenever they need anything—and when one of the Kurd chiefs hears of or sees a nice and young Armenian bride or wife—and likes her, he unhesitatingly takes her away and puts her in his house." Being the U.S. Ambassador to Constantinople "is no easy job," Morgenthau confided in a letter, as Turkish "affairs are tremendously complicated."[44]

Meanwhile, the arrival of the German military mission of General Liman von Sanders at Constantinople in December 1913 and the elevation of Enver Pasha to the post of minister of war in January 1914 did not bode well for the Armenian reform measures sponsored by the Russian government and negotiated by the major European powers.[45] The reform plan was formally signed by the representatives of the Turkish and Russian governments on February 8, 1914, providing for the consolidation of the Armenian provinces into two inspectorates made up of the Trebizond, Sivas, and Erzerum *vilayets* and of the Van, Bitlis, Kharpert, and Diarbekir vilayets, and the appointment of a European inspector-general for each province.[46] The Wilson Administration was not a participant in these negotiations, perhaps because it had no ambassadorial representation in Constantinople until the arrival of Morgenthau, but also because, aware of Turkish resentment toward foreign intervention, it preferred to remain neutral so as not to antagonize the Young Turk government.

Prior to the outbreak of World War I, while Morgenthau began to express concern regarding the Young Turk leaders and the political situation in Turkey, he generally continued to remain optimistic.[47] In *All in a Life-Time* he explained: "The total failure of this party proved again the impossibility of true reform among the Turks. This was evident to careful observers long before my arrival at Constantinople, but I was so ardent in my desire to help that it took me nearly a year to become wholly disillusioned."[48]

As Europe became engulfed in the Great War and Turkey prepared to enter the conflict as an ally of Germany, the Wilson Administration adopted the policy of neutrality for international and domestic reasons. These included the isolationist tradition, Wilson's emphasis on moral diplomacy in contradistinction to European struggles for balance of power, and, more significantly, the Administration's hope to avoid loss of public support for Wilson prior to the presidential elections in 1916. Relations with Turkey continued on friendly terms even after September 1914, when the Turkish government announced the abrogation of the Capitulations. The United States and European governments protested the termination of this extraterritorial protection for their nationals and properties, but to no avail.[49]

Conditions deteriorated rapidly in Turkey during the second half of 1914, and public opinion in the United States expressed anxiety as reports from Smyrna (Izmir), for example, warned of impending massacres of all Christian communities in the city. The American Board of Commissioners for Foreign Missions and U.S. citizens in the Ottoman Empire urged Morgenthau and the State Department to dispatch one or two cruisers to Turkish waters for protection.[50] In early August, as the cruisers *USS Tennessee* and *North Carolina* sailed for Europe and Turkey, the governor of Smyrna, Rahmi Bey, threatened to raze the city to the ground if it was invaded or bombarded.[51] On August 27, 1914, the *Daily Telegraph* of London reported that Morgenthau had warned the State Department of the impending threat to the Christians and Jews in Turkey, both "seriously menaced by the Mohammedans, who are planning massacres while the great Powers are engaged in war." The report added that, according to Morgenthau, "no unbeliever will be permitted to escape if the Mohammedans have their way," and that the U.S. government was seriously considering sending the battleships *Tennessee* and *North Caro-*

lina to Turkish waters to assist Americans stranded in belligerent countries.[52] Talaat immediately requested that Morgenthau issue a statement to the press contradicting this assessment by the London newspaper, and Morgenthau complied by sending an unsigned statement to the Associated Press.[53]

On September 1, the State Department instructed Morgenthau to secure permission for the *North Carolina* to pass through the Dardanelles, as some Americans preferred to leave and needed safe passage.[54] Complaints were heard in political and missionary circles in the United States and Turkey that the Wilson Administration had failed to act quickly. Charles Arthur Reed, writing to Reverend Charles T. Riggs from Smyrna, noted that it was safe for American ships to enter Turkish waters and to reach Smyrna and that some Americans would "risk going up, or down, or whichever way Turkish mines would send a war ship, by meeting the vessel outside and coming in on board her. The Turkish government seems adept at bluffing, and the American authorities splendid victims."[55]

On the home front, Bryan sought to calm American public opinion and gave assurances that assistance had been sent to Americans in Turkey.[56] In December 1914, very much concerned about public opinion, Bryan dispatched a confidential telegram to Morgenthau stating that Americans were advised to leave Turkey if they deemed it necessary, but they were to avoid public attention in the United States. The matter was to be handled "very guardedly and confidentially," Bryan instructed Morgenthau. "If they send word to their friends at home they can simply state that they are intending to leave Turkey, without saying that they are advised to do so."[57]

In 1915, as the Turkish government launched its genocidal policy against the Armenian people, the Wilson Administration condemned the Turkish atrocities, but, opposing any military engagement against Turkey for humanitarian purposes or otherwise, it limited its response to official and unofficial representation to the Turkish authorities and subsequently to relief aid for the surviving refugees. The Administration placed a premium on neutrality and sought to maintain relations with Constantinople. Secretary of State Bryan and later Robert Lansing were particularly concerned with public opinion at home, as reports of potential Turkish violence against American interests kept the issue of a U.S. response on the national agenda. Thus, within the narrow confines set by the Administration's domestic and foreign policy priorities, Ambassador Morgenthau defined his role strictly with respect to implementation of policy as determined by the State Department, on the one hand, and as conveyor of reports received from the U.S. consulates and missionaries regarding the deteriorating situation and the atrocities committed against the Armenians, on the other hand.

Consular Dispatches

Policy recommendations submitted to Washington by the U.S. consuls ranged from appeals for accelerating relief work to maintaining good relations with the Turkish government, but there were also rare instances when a consul recommended military action. Numerous reports noted that the situation in Turkey was highly unpredictable and that those massacring Armenians today could easily massacre foreigners tomorrow. The copious reports submitted by Morgenthau were supplemented by equally copious dispatches from the consular offices.[58] Included here are a few examples of these reports with particular attention to their suggestions for a U.S. response.

As the war raged in Europe, Turks and Russians carried on their historic hostilities for land and sea, in particular for control of the Caucasus. Enver's disastrous winter campaign at Sarikamish had already cost more than 75,000 Ottoman casualties, and the Russian command now felt prepared to extend its campaign into Ottoman territory.[59] Russian destroyers attacked Trebizond on February 8, 1915[60] and Kerasond (Girasun) on April 20.[61]

While the military conflict continued, the Turkish government's genocidal scheme to annihilate the Armenian people unfolded province by province, as thousands of Armenians were killed and those surviving the bloodshed were marched to the desert in northern Syria. U.S. Consul Jesse Jackson at Aleppo frequently reported to Morgenthau and the State Department on the conditions in major towns, such as Marash, Zeitun, and Aintab, where Armenian lives were being destroyed and the land depopulated.[62] As early as April 1915, Jackson noted with concern that, despite official promises not to harm the population, the Turkish military was conducting house-to-house searches in these regions, "extorting money, carrying off property, and intimidating" the Christian population while disarming them.[63] Men, women, and children were separated and deported, with official instructions to escorting soldiers "to do what they pleased to the women and girls."[64] The flow of refugees increased rapidly, and Jackson reported in June that as more Armenians were resettled in northern Syria, "in the interior a perfect reign of terror exists." It was clear, Jackson concluded, that the Turkish government had carefully planned the thorough extinction of the Armenians, and all appeals by prominent individuals and authorities were ignored.[65] Jackson's communications continued to depict the horrors experienced by the refugees as they passed through Aleppo caravan after caravan, emaciated, half clad.[66] In a letter forwarded by Jackson on August 10, Reverend F. H. Leslie of Urfa described the situation in that city as "very dangerous":

> Fourteen "volunteers" from Stamboul (lately come from Diarbekir) have terrorized the governor, the gendarmery commander, the martial law examining commission and all the other chief officers of the local government so that they dare not move to protect the Christian population or to oppose the will of these murderers who now have everything under their control. They are nightly seizing the best and most prominent Christian citizens and after a period in prison here sending them on to the death-trap Diarbekir.[67]

In early June, the government arrested about 250 Armenian leaders in Trebizond and, on June 26, issued a proclamation ordering the Armenians of the city to deliver their properties to the government within five days and prepare for the trek to the interior on July 1. The proclamation assured Armenians of the right to reclaim their goods at the conclusion of the war.[68] On June 28, the U.S. Consul at Trebizond, Oscar Heizer, sent a copy of this proclamation to Morgenthau, and noted: "It is impossible to convey an idea of the consternation and despair the publication of this proclamation has produced upon the people. I have seen strong, proud, wealthy men weep like children while they told me that they had given their boys and girls to Persian and Turkish neighbors." As all vehicles were used for the war effort, the refugees would be forced to march on foot to Jazireh or Mosul, the intended destinations. "Even a strong man," Heizer added, "without the necessary outfit and food would be likely to perish on such a trip.... The People are helpless but are making preparations to start on the perilous journey."[69]

Also in June, Leslie A. Davis, the U.S. Consul in Harput (Kharpert), dispatched to Morgenthau eyewitness accounts of the atrocities in the city and the surrounding regions. Government persecutions of Armenians had intensified while thousands were and continued to be deported from Erzerum and Erzinjan to certain death "as part of the general plan to dispose of the Armenian race."[70] Davis advised Americans to leave Turkey as soon as possible, even if temporarily.[71] By the closing days of 1915, he was convinced, little could be done except to assist the refugees and "keep people alive for the present."[72]

U.S. Consul Stanley Hollis at Beirut was among the exceptions, stressing the necessity of military action and therefore challenging the Administration's policy of non-interference. As early as November 1914, even before the genocidal process had commenced, Hollis wrote of the rapidly deteriorating situation and advised that, if the U.S. government was interested in doing anything to protect Americans, foreigners, and local Christians, "naval forces in these waters should be strengthened by a number of small cruisers, or gunboats."[73] Rufus W. Lane, former U.S. Consul at Smyrna, shared this view and called for some form of military protection to halt the anti-Christian murders and deportations.[74] Adhering to the Administration's position, however, Morgenthau rejected such recommendations for military intervention. Although Morgenthau thought favorably with respect to deployment of cruisers so as to enhance U.S. prestige and to strengthen his position in Constantinople, he concurred that Americans would be safer if they trusted the Turkish government for protection. More direct intervention, Morgenthau maintained, might "render our position absolutely hazardous." He cautioned against the temperament of officials such as Hollis in order to avoid "any incidents" and insisted that deployment of cruisers should be reserved exclusively for refuge and moral influence.[75]

Thereafter, Hollis resigned himself to mere reporting but continued to advocate immediate action for relief. In July 1915, he relayed to the State Department a report titled "Persecution of Armenians," which noted that thousands of Armenians had been deported from Hajin, Sis, Hasan Beyli, and Dort Yol and that the survivors had become refugees scattered from Aleppo to Deir el-Zor and Baghdad. In many cases, men of military age were "bound tightly together with ropes or chains. Women with little children in their arms, or the last days of pregnancy were driven along under the whip like cattle." The report concluded: "If a means is not found to aid them through the next few months, until they get established in their new surroundings, two thirds or three fourths of them will die of starvation and disease."[76]

George Horton, the U.S. Consul General at Smyrna, reported in July that the Turkish authorities at Constantinople had accused seven Armenians in Smyrna of political offenses against the Turkish government and ordered them to be hanged. Horton appealed to Morgenthau to intercede to secure a delay for further investigation of the charges, for, Horton noted, neither the governor nor the military commander thought these men "guilty of any offence deserving death." The local authorities had petitioned their superiors in Constantinople for imperial clemency, but the central government, while granting the accused the right to petition for clemency under Ottoman law, nevertheless insisted that the court martial at Smyrna should "hang them immediately and send the petition afterwards." The true purpose for executing these men, Horton added, was "to intimidate the Armenian race."[77]

On August 7, 1915, the U.S. Consul at Mersina, Edward Nathan, informed Morgenthau of the Armenians being deported to Adana and of thousands being massacred in the interior.[78] The Turkish government had ordered a German orphanage at Haruniye closed, and the Americans feared that they would receive similar orders as well. Two months later, Nathan stressed the necessity of relief aid, as the unsanitary conditions and the lack of food threatened the lives of a stream of refugees arriving from other regions.[79]

By February 1916, more than 400,000 refugees had arrived in Syria, the great majority of them at Deir el-Zor.[80] Consul Jackson complained of restrictions imposed by Turkish authorities on the administration of relief to the destitute victims.[81] In September 1915, he estimated that more than a million Armenians had died and that the survivors, in need of assistance, amounted to "only 15 per cent of those originally deported."[82]

Morgenthau's Reports and Policy Recommendations

Ambassador Morgenthau sent hundreds of reports to the State Department regarding the deportations and massacres of the Armenians, and the Administration was fully apprised of the events transpiring in the Ottoman Empire. In his dispatches, Morgenthau recommended diplomatic efforts to alleviate the situation for the Armenians, and Secretary of State Bryan and then Lansing encouraged him to do so but with the clear understanding that no requests beyond such mitigating measures would be entertained.

Morgenthau expressed concern about the safety of American institutions and citizens after the Turkish government declared its abrogation of the Capitulations[83] and about the Armenian situation immediately after the sultan's declaration of *Jihad* (Holy War) against the Allied Powers in late 1914.[84] He submitted his first report regarding the persecutions on April 27, 1915, in the wake of the arrest of Armenian leaders in Constantinople. The confidential message stated: "Over hundred Armenians of better classes are arrested ostensibly to prevent revolutionary propaganda." Morgenthau added that their "lives are probably not in danger…but they are being deported to the interior," from where he had received "unfavorable reports about Armenians."[85] Three days later, on April 30, the ambassador informed the State Department: "Continued report of persecutions, plunder and massacres of Armenians in certain parts of empire had been received." Morgenthau wrote that, while Minister of War Enver Pasha justified these measures as a reaction to Armenian revolutionary activities in Van, Consul Jackson reported on the "incredible severity" of the government's treatment of the Armenians in Zeitun and Marash, as the authorities deported "a large number of the innocent population." Morgenthau concluded: "Apparently these measures are part of the campaign of repression against non-Turkish and non-Union-and-Progress elements and organizations," despite promises by the Grand Vizier Said Halim Pasha, Enver, and Talaat "that no general massacres or excesses will occur and that a number of Armenians who were not Dashnagists and were arrested by mistake will be released."[86]

As late as May, although aware of entire villages being destroyed and thousands of Armenians deported, Morgenthau did not believe that "as yet there have been any massacres on a large scale."[87] Later, in his *Story*, he explained:

> It was some time before the story of the Armenian atrocities reached the American Embassy in all its horrible details. In January and February fragmentary reports began to filter in, but the tendency was at first to regard them as mere manifestations of the disorders that had prevailed in the Armenian provinces for many years. When the reports came from Urumia, both Enver and Talaat dismissed them as wild exaggerations, and when, for the first time, we heard of the disturbances at Van, these Turkish officials declared that they were nothing more than a mob uprising which they would soon have under control. I now see, what was not apparent in those early months, that the Turkish Government was determined to keep the news, as long as possible, from the outside world. It was clearly the intention that Europe and America should hear of the annihilation of the Armenian race only after that annihilation had been accomplished. As

the country which the Turks particularly wished to keep in ignorance was the United States, they resorted to the most shameless prevarications when discussing the situation with myself and with my staff.[88]

In July, as the genocidal scheme became more obvious, Morgenthau observed that the Turkish authorities reacted to protests "with more drastic measures," adding: "I believe therefore, that nothing short of actual force, which obviously the United States are not in a position to exert, would adequately meet the situation and I suggest that belligerent nations and mission boards be informed of this."[89] A month later, Morgenthau presented three possible options for addressing the crisis in Turkey:

1) to urge the Turkish government to end immediately "the present campaign and to permit the survivors to return to their homes if not in the war zones, or else to receive proper treatment";

2) to extend an official appeal to the German government "to insist on Turkey" stopping "this annihilation of a Christian race";

3) to make "a vigorous official demand...without delay for the granting of every facility to Americans and others" to administer financial assistance to the victims of the deportations.[90]

Morgenthau recommended the third course. Although he did not discuss why the United States could not pursue the first two, the first option appeared most impracticable unless the Administration was prepared for an extensive military engagement in Turkey. It was clear that the Turkish government would resent such intervention, thereby undermining U.S.-Turkish relations and threatening commercial and missionary interests. As Morgenthau had mentioned in his earlier dispatch, the Administration was not ready for responsibilities of such magnitude as to involve not only the termination of the deportations and massacres but also to secure the return of refugees to their towns and homes. With the 1916 presidential elections fast approaching, the Wilson Administration would not take risks that could potentially jeopardize its credibility and prestige both at home and abroad, particularly at a time when Wilson hoped to serve as an impartial mediator and peacemaker among the warring powers. Policymakers in Washington would have rejected the first option, notwithstanding the moralistic pronouncements of principles of peace and democracy by the president. A staunch supporter of Wilson, Henry Morgenthau would not challenge the Administration's policy.

The second option was not more promising. Had Germany's Kaiser Wilhelm II been interested in intervening to prevent further massacres by his Turkish ally, no official appeals would have been needed from other governments. There was no reason to believe that Germany would show any interest in the welfare of the Armenians in Turkey. In his *Story*, Morgenthau noted that during the massacres of the 1890s the same kaiser had visited Abdul-Hamid II and decorated the "bloody tyrant's breast, and kissed him on both cheeks."[91] Further, German officials in Constantinople had repeatedly notified Morgenthau that their "*one aim was to win this war.*"[92]

Referring to the third option, Morgenthau argued that under the circumstances, assisting the Armenians would be the "most acceptable" course of action, as rendering such aid was a "matter of our right" and immediate action on behalf of the Armenians would also register the Administration's "protesting attitude."[93] Thus, at the urging of Morgenthau, in September 1915 a group of influential missionary, business, and government leaders, including James L. Barton, Cleveland H. Dodge, and Charles R. Crane, organized the Committee on Armenian Atrocities, followed, in November 1915, by the formation of the American Committee for Armenian and Syrian Relief (ACASR).[94] This third option, however, indicated a willingness on the part of the United States to accept the genocide as a fait accompli, and the primary focus of U.S. policy would be limited to extending assistance to the survivors. This remained the central feature of the U.S. response toward the Armenian Genocide as well as the short-lived Republic of Armenia (1918-20).[95] Moreover, as American policymakers were interested in maintaining normal relations with the Ottoman Empire, the Turkish view on national sovereignty conveniently coincided with the Wilson Administration's policy of neutrality and non-interference. Thus, when Ambassador Morgenthau left Constantinople in early February 1916, a key principle undergirding the policy of the Wilson Administration toward Turkey had been firmly established: the United States would serve as a mediator among the belligerent powers and would try to provide relief assistance to those in need, but it would not be willing to become the object of Turkish hostility.

Between February and October 1916, prior to the arrival of Morgenthau's successor, the U.S. Embassy was headed by the Chargé d'Affaires Hoffman Philip. During this period, Philip was preoccupied with issues pertaining to the protection of American rights in the absence of the Capitulations. The embassy continued its protests against the abrogation, noting that the United States would hold the Ottoman government "responsible for any injury which may be occasioned to the United States or to its citizens."[96] At the same time, communications exchanged between the two governments reaffirmed their determination to maintain good relations and to cooperate in matters of mutual interests. The Ottoman Ministry of Foreign Affairs sent instructions to "the provincial authorities to avoid frictions in all matters concerning American interests,"[97] and, for its part, the Wilson Administration agreed to protect Turkish interests in Mexico, as the Sublime Porte had no diplomatic representation in that country, which was mired in prolonged political upheavals.[98]

The new ambassador to Constantinople, Abram I. Elkus, presented his credentials on October 2, 1916.[99] Elkus had served as a judge in the state of New York and, like his predecessor, was among the influential circles in New York politics with close ties to the Wilson Administration. Ambassador Elkus continued to report on the conditions in Turkey and on several occasions interceded on behalf of relief workers for permission to carry on their work.[100] Soon, however, the rapid pace of events after Wilson's reelection moved the nation closer to war. Relations between the United States and Turkey were severed on April 21, 1917, and Elkus returned home.

Policymakers in Washington: Woodrow Wilson

President Wilson took great interest in the State Department and played a key role in the formulation of foreign policy.[101] His views on war and peace, autocracy and democracy, imperialism and self-determination, delineated the general contours of the Administration's international objectives. Despite the voluminous correspondence between Morgenthau and the State Department regarding the atrocities committed against the Armenians, however, Wilson seldom referred to these events in his public addresses, and in his communications to private inquiries he repeated the principle of non-interference as adopted by his Administration. For example, in December 1915, Reverend William Chambers, of the American Mission in

Adana, who had returned home on board the *USS Des Moines* to escape the horrors, wrote Wilson to inform him of the conditions in Armenia. He asked whether the president was interested in exerting greater influence to end the atrocities. Within days, Wilson replied that the United States, as a neutral country, was "doing everything that is diplomatically possible to check the terrible business."[102]

Before the presidential elections of 1916, Woodrow Wilson was mainly concerned with reminding the American public that he had kept the nation out of the European conflict. He also hoped to reaffirm his humanitarian convictions and in so doing to gain the political support of the progressives and Armenophile groups when he proclaimed October 21 and 22, 1916 as "Syrian and Armenian Relief Days."[103] Upon securing reelection to the White House, the Wilson Administration commenced mobilization of public support as the United States and Germany moved closer to war. In the process, Wilson directed American opinion against Germany, but without drawing attention to the Turkish massacres of Armenians when the United States declared war in April 1917. Wilson did not request a declaration of war against Turkey. Instead, he portrayed Turkey as the victim of "Prussian conquest and the Prussian menace." Turkey and Bulgaria, he argued, "are mere tools and do not yet stand in the direct path of our necessary action. We shall go wherever the necessities of this war carry us, but it seems to me that we should go only where immediate and practical considerations lead us and not heed any others."[104]

In February 1917, Talaat Pasha, now the grand vizier, related to Ambassador Elkus the sultan's desire to maintain friendly relations with the United States.[105] In case the United States went to war with Germany, he maintained, Turkey and the United States should continue their cordial relations. Although Turkey formally severed ties with the United States on April 21, both governments took care to avoid offensive actions.[106] The issue of war with Turkey resurfaced in December 1917 when Wilson requested from Congress a declaration of war against Austria-Hungary. Some members of Congress favored inclusion of Turkey in the declaration, but Cleveland Dodge and James L. Barton lobbied heavily against such action. Barton argued that conflict with Turkey would jeopardize not only American lives and institutions but also efforts to render assistance to the Armenian refugees.[107] Thus, by the time Wilson announced, in January 1918, his Fourteen Points for peace, including "an absolutely unmolested opportunity of autonomous development" for the nationalities under Turkish rule,[108] it was clear that his Administration would not deviate from the established patterns of policy toward Turkey.

William Jennings Bryan

A pacifist in ideological orientation, Bryan hoped to establish peace treaties for the promotion of international arbitration to replace war as an instrument of policy, and he was criticized by "realists" for his idealist aspirations. He was concerned primarily with strengthening the position of the United States as a neutral mediator on the international diplomatic stage and hoped Turkey would remain neutral "in the interest of humanity" and dissociate itself from German war plans.[109] With respect to the situation in Turkey, his principal task was the management of public opinion as the American public exhibited much anxiety regarding reports from Turkey of anti-Christian massacres and the threat posed to Americans lives and properties.[110]

Bryan's position vis-à-vis the Armenian massacres appeared to have changed briefly in the early months of 1915, when the European powers were preparing the declaration of May 24 condemning Turkish atrocities.[111] In a telegram dated February 18, he instructed Morgenthau to communicate to the Turkish authorities that they will be "held responsible for lives and property of Jews and Christians in case of massacre or looting."[112] Subsequently, Bryan requested that Morgenthau urge the Turkish government to use "effective means" to protect the Armenians from violence and that he investigate the truth of the Armenian massacres.[113] Yet, even while Bryan was in office, whether the Wilson Administration seriously entertained the idea of holding the perpetrators of the genocide "personally responsible for these crimes" seems debatable. Bryan resigned on June 9, 1915.[114] His successor, Robert Lansing, a legalist par excellence, no longer mentioned in his communications the issue of Turkish responsibility for the atrocities committed against the Armenians.

Robert Lansing

Secretary of State Lansing showed little interest in Armenian affairs. Whereas Bryan had begun to discuss such measures as holding responsible the perpetrators of the genocide, Lansing emphasized the importance of American public opinion and the negative impact "atrocity reports" exerted on United States-Turkish relations. Accordingly, Lansing instructed Morgenthau to continue to use his good offices to improve conditions and to inform the Turkish government that their persecutions were "destroying the feeling of good will which the people of the United States have held towards Turkey."[115] He added, however, that "the Department can offer no additional suggestions relative to this most difficult situation other than that you continue to act as in the past."[116]

Lansing's approach to the Armenian massacres was apparent before he became secretary of state, and his position did not change after taking office. His central concern as pertaining to a U.S. response to Turkish atrocities was the protection of American citizens and properties. This concern was not based on humanitarian considerations per se but rather on considerations of domestic public opinion. As prior to the 1916 presidential elections Wilson repeatedly promised to keep the United States out of the European war, Lansing feared that the possibility of Americans being killed in Turkey would compel the Administration to take military action, potentially creating a situation that would jeopardize the president's reelection. It was, therefore, necessary for Lansing to manage public opinion and public perceptions of U.S.-Turkish relations, especially as Turkish atrocities against Armenians had for years assumed such great saliency in the American press. Lansing justified the U.S. policy of non-interference on behalf of the Armenians on legal grounds. He considered national interests and national security as superseding humanitarian considerations. Atrocities committed in the name of national security and self-preservation, Lansing believed, might even be justified on grounds of national sovereignty. He maintained that it was difficult to render direct support for the Armenians in Turkey because of the assertion that "large bodies of Armenians are in armed rebellion against the Turkish Government, and that the Turkish Government claims that such measures as it has taken are only such as are necessary for its own protection against the members of its race."[117] The revisionist views so familiar today had already gained a certain acceptance at the official level in Washington even at the time of the genocide. In January 1919, when the victorious Allied Powers met in Paris, Lansing chaired the First Subcommission of the Commission on Responsibilities and Sanctions, but even in that capacity he showed little interest in matters pertaining to the perpetrators of the Armenian Genocide.[118]

The Return to Peace

By the end of World War I, nearly 300,000 Armenian survivors had become refugees in the Caucasus, and 400,000 others were scattered throughout Syria and in other countries. Thousands had set up camps on the outskirts of Aleppo, one of the principal destinations of the deportations, and across Syria.[119] Approximately half of the refugees in the Caucasus died of famine and poor health.[120] The Republic of Armenia, declared independent in May 1918 in a small part of Russian or Eastern Armenia, and whose very survival depended on external economic and military assistance, was ill-prepared to rectify the calamitous situation created by the genocide. Masses of refugees escaping death and in need of food, shelter, and medical relief crowded the streets of Erevan.[121]

With the support of the Wilson Administration, charitable organizations began to send assistance to the Armenian republic. By the end of 1919, about 30,000 metric tons of food and clothing had arrived through the American Committee for Relief in the Near East (ACRNE), incorporated in August 1919 by an act of Congress as the Near East Relief (NER), supplemented by tons of flour and grain delivered by the American Relief Administration (ARA).[122] The Near East Relief placed thousands of orphans in mission facilities, with the expectation that these orphans would soon "absorb American ideals of wholesome living and...grow into useful manhood and womanhood according to American standards and by American methods."[123] Philanthropic endeavors could not be sustained for long, however, as American attention quickly shifted to national priorities of economic growth and security.

With Germany now removed as a competitor in international markets, the United States reverted to the Open Door policy, and its commercial rivalry with the European economies, particularly those of France and Great Britain, intensified. Britain jealously watched its position in the world economy decline as the vortex of global finance gravitated away from London to New York.[124] An American mandate or protectorate over Armenia became inextricably intertwined with, and ultimately the victim of, Open Door aspirations and conflicts.[125] President Wilson commented in a letter to Undersecretary of State Frank L. Polk: "It is evident to me that we are on the eve of a commercial war of the severest sort, and I am afraid that Great Britain will prove capable of as great commercial savagery as Germany has displayed for so many years in her competitive methods."[126]

U.S. oil companies criticized British efforts to monopolize the oilfields in the Middle East and the American government for failing to exert sufficient influence to obtain concessions from the British. They urged the American peace delegation in Paris to take a more decisive stance on their behalf.[127] In response, stressing the necessity of access to adequate sources of oil for the industrial needs of the nation, the State Department sent instructions to its consular representatives to gather comprehensive data on oil reserves and foreign mining concessions and operations.[128] As the Middle East was one of the principal regions attracting U.S. oil policy for the exploration of reserves, it was not surprising that Rear Admiral Mark L. Bristol, the U.S. High Commissioner at Constantinople (August 12, 1919-June 25, 1927), representing the interests of the Navy and, by extension, of the oil industry, would oppose the assumption of the American mandate over Armenia.[129] As Bristol saw it, Great Britain and France arrogated to themselves the right to monopolize the oil fields in the Middle East at the expense of American economic and security interests. In a report dated July 12, 1919, he stated:

> The British believe they have discovered in Mesopotamia one of the greatest oil fields in the world. The examinations they have already made and the prophecies of geologists in the past bear out this idea. These oil fields are about 80 kilometers east of Bagdad. The British Government have already assumed control over these fields with the idea of keeping out any competitors.... I firmly believe they [the European Allies] are trying to force us into Armenia so that the European countries may be free to divide up the rest of Turkey.... Again, even at the risk of being tiresome by repetition, I must urge that we be not meddled with the mandatory over Armenia.[130]

The U.S. Senate rejected the mandate in June 1920, ending the tortuous debates on the issue.[131] In December of that year, Wilson requested a loan from Congress for the Armenian republic, but Congress rejected this as well.[132] Instead, the United States, having attained victory in war and returned to peace, resumed its commercial relations with Turkey. During the war the total annual value of U.S.-

Turkish trade had dropped to about $530,000, but that figure increased to $62.2 million in 1919 and to $82 million in 1920.[133]

Conclusion

From the perspectives of Washington and Constantinople, ephemeral episodes of aberrations and diversions, however horrific in their manifestations, would not be permitted to disturb a century-long history of U.S.-Turkish relations. Despite the challenges posed by the turn of events in Europe and the Ottoman Empire, the Wilson Administration continued the policy, as inherited from its predecessors, of maintaining amicable relations with the Turkish government. The Administration's immediate response to the Armenian Genocide was shaped by considerations for domestic public opinion and the security of U.S. economic and missionary interests in the Ottoman Empire. With rare exceptions, neither Morgenthau nor the consuls advocated policies deviating from that course. Although the United States extended public and private humanitarian assistance to the survivors of the genocide during and immediately after World War I, it was also determined, contrary to the expressed idealism and humanitarian principles, to continue the U.S. commercial and missionary presence in Turkey. The United States had become a major competitor in international economic relations, with growing economic and geopolitical interests in the Middle East.

Notes

1. Walter LaFeber, *The Cambridge History of American Foreign Relations*, vol. 2: *The American Search for Opportunity, 1865-1913* (Cambridge: Cambridge University Press, 1993); Richard G. Hovannisian, "The Armenian Question in the Ottoman Empire, 1876-1914," in Richard G. Hovannisian, ed., *The Armenian People from Ancient to Modern Times,* vol. 2: *Foreign Dominion to Statehood: The Fifteenth Century to the Twentieth Century* (New York: St. Martin's Press, 1997), pp. 203-38.
2. For the most compelling statement on the necessity of sea power for U.S. commerce and security, see Alfred Thayer Mahan, *The Influence of Sea Power upon History, 1660-1783* (Boston: Little, Brown, 1890; repr. Mineola, NY: Dover, 1987). For example, emphasizing the geopolitical significance of the newly constructed Suez Canal, George H. Boker, U.S. Minister to Constantinople, proposed in 1874 the annexation of Bab al-Mandeb Cape, strategically situated on the Red Sea between the canal and the Indian Ocean. See James A. Field, *America and the Mediterranean World, 1776-1882* (Princeton: Princeton University Press, 1969), p. 341; LaFeber, *American Search for Opportunity*, p. 84.
3. Leland James Gordon, *American Relations with Turkey, 1830-1930: An Economic Interpretation* (Philadelphia: University of Pennsylvania Press, 1932), pp. 42, 162-

63; Howard A. Reed, "Yankees at the Sultan's Port: The First Americans in Turkey and Early Trade with Smyrna and Mocha," in Jean-Louis Bacqué-Grammont and Paul Dumont, eds., *Contributions à l'histoire économique et sociale de l'Empire ottoman* (Louvain, Belgium: Éditions Peeters, 1983), pp. 353-83; Mira Wilkins, *The Emergence of Multinational Enterprises: American Business Abroad from the Colonial Era to 1914* (Cambridge, MA: Harvard University Press, 1970), p. 10; Field, *Mediterranean World,* pp. 150-51, 297.

4. Thomas A. Bryson, *Tars, Turks, and Tankers: The Role of the United States Navy in the Middle East, 1800-1979* (Metuchen: Scarecrow Press, 1980), pp. 23-24, 31-32; Field, *Mediterranean World,* pp. 121-40.

5. Johannes Lepsius, *Armenia and Europe: An Indictment*, trans. and ed. J. Rendel Harris (London: Hodder and Stoughton, 1897); Hovannisian, "Armenian Question in the Ottoman Empire," pp. 203-38; Richard G. Hovannisian, "The Historical Dimensions of the Armenian Question, 1878-1923," in Richard G. Hovannisian, ed., *The Armenian Genocide in Perspective* (New Brunswick, NJ: Transaction Publishers, 1986), pp. 19-26.

6. Barbara J. Merguerian, "The American Response to the 1895 Massacres," in *Genocide and Human Rights: Lessons from the Armenian Experience,* special issue, *Journal of Armenian Studies* 4:1-2 (1992): 53-83; Bryson, *Tars, Turks, and Tankers*, pp. 35-37.

7. Bryson, *Tars, Turks, and Tankers,* p. 37; Field, *Mediterranean World,* pp. 445-47; Lloyd C. Griscom, *Diplomatically Speaking* (Boston: Little, Brown, 1940), pp. 162, 169-74.

8. Thomas A. Bailey, *A Diplomatic History of the American People*, 2d ed. (New York: F.S. Crofts, 1944), pp. 458-60, 526-28; William H. Becker, "America Adjusts to World Power, 1899-1920," in William H. Becker and Samuels F. Wells, Jr., eds., *Economics and World Power: An Assessment of American Diplomacy since 1789* (New York: Columbia University, 1984), pp. 173-223; LaFeber, *American Search for Opportunity*, p. 112. See also Emily S. Rosenberg, *Spreading the American Dream: American Economic and Cultural Expansion, 1890-1945* (New York: Hill and Wang, 1982).

9. United States, Department of the Treasury, Bureau of Statistics, *The Foreign Commerce and Navigation of the United States for the Year Ending June 30, 1901*, 2 vols. (Washington, DC: Government Printing Office, 1902), vol. 1, pp. 32-35.

10. Gregory P. Nowell, *Mercantile States and the World Oil Cartel, 1900-1939* (Ithaca and London: Cornell University Press, 1994), p. 45; George Sweet Gibb and Evelyn K. Knowlton, *The History of the Standard Oil Company (New Jersey): The Resurgent Years, 1911-1927* (New York: Harper and Row, 1956), pp. 279-88; John A. DeNovo, "The Movement for an Aggressive American Oil Policy Abroad, 1918-1920," *American Historical Review* 61 (July 1956): 854-76; Henry Woodhouse, "American Oil Claims in Turkey," *Current History* 15 (March 1922): 953-59. On the international rivalry for railway concessions, see John A. DeNovo, "A Railroad for Turkey: The Chester Project, 1908-1913," *Business History Review* 33 (Autumn 1959): 300-29; M. S. Anderson, *The Eastern Question, 1774-1923: A Study in International Relations* (London: Macmillan, 1966), pp. 261-86.

11. On the role of the U.S. government as a "promotional state," see Rosenberg, *American Dream*, pp. 38-86 passim.

12. DeNovo, "Railroad for Turkey," 300-29; idem, "American Oil Policy Abroad," pp. 854-76; Woodhouse, "American Oil Claims in Turkey," pp. 953-59.

13. Field, *Mediterranean World,* pp. 165-75; Bryson, *Tars, Turks, and Tankers,* p. 24; Joseph L. Grabill, *Protestant Diplomacy and the Near East: Missionary Influence*

on American Policy, 1810-1927 (Minneapolis: University of Minnesota Press, 1971), pp. 36-37; Ernest R. May, *Imperial Democracy: The Emergence of America as a Great Power* (New York: Harcourt, Brace, 1961), pp. 9-15, 29.

14. U.S. Department of the Treasury, *Foreign Commerce and Navigation*, vol. 1, pp. 32-35.
15. United States, Department of Commerce and Labor, Bureau of Statistics, *The Foreign Commerce and Navigation of the United States for the Year Ending June 30, 1910* (Washington, DC: Government Printing Office, 1911), pp. 36-37.
16. Ibid.
17. United States, Department of Commerce, Bureau of Foreign and Domestic Commerce, *Foreign Commerce and Navigation of the United States for the Year Ending June 30, 1914* (Washington, DC: Government Printing Office, 1915), pp. xii-xiii.
18. Grabill, *Protestant Diplomacy*; Joseph K. Greene, *Leavening the Levant* (Boston: Pilgrim Press, 1916); Suzanne E. Moranian, "The American Missionaries and the Armenian Question, 1915-1927," Ph.D. Dissertation (University of Wisconsin-Madison, 1994).
19. Harlan Beach, *A Geography and Atlas of Protestant Missions*, vol. 1 (New York: Student Volunteer Movement for Foreign Missions, 1901), p. 417; Robert L. Daniel, *American Philanthropy in the Near East, 1820-1960* (Athens, OH: Ohio State University, 1970), pp. 6-16; Field, *Mediterranean World,* p. 68; A. L. Tibawi, *American Interests in Syria, 1800-1901* (Oxford: Clarendon Press, 1966), pp. 12-35; William Ellsworth Strong, *The Story of the American Board* (Boston: Pilgrim Press, 1910; repr. New York: Arno Press and the New York Times, 1969), pp. 80-82, 199.
20. James S. Dennis, Harlan P. Beach, Charles H. Fahs, eds., *World Atlas of Christian Missions* (New York: Student Volunteer Movement for Foreign Missions, 1911), pp. 92, 107. For the turn of the century, see Henry Otis Dwight, H. Allen Tupper, Edwin Munsell Bliss, eds., *The Encyclopedia of Missions*, 2d ed. (New York and London: Funk and Wagnalls, 1904), p. 31.
21. See, for example, United States, National Archives, Department of State, *Despatches from United States Ministers to Turkey, 1818-1906*, Leishman to Secretary of State, Feb. 27, 1906, encl., Howard T. Bliss to Leishman, Feb. 23, 1906 (microfilm, 77 reels, vol. 79, Jan. 1-Aug. 1906, roll 77).
22. *The Treatment of Armenians in the Ottoman Empire, 1915-1916: Documents Presented to Viscount Grey of Fallodon, Secretary of State for Foreign Affairs*, Miscellaneous no. 31, 1916, ed. and comp. Arnold Toynbee, (London: Sir Joseph Causton and Sons, 1916, repr. Beirut: G. Doniguian and Sons, 1988), p. 619. By the turn of the twentieth century, the Protestant community in the Ottoman Empire consisted mostly of Armenians. See Beach, *Geography and Atlas*, vol. 1, p. 413. For an example of Armenian criticism regarding American missionary activities, see Aramayis P. Vartooguian, *Armenia's Ordeal: A Sketch of the Main Features of the History of Armenia, and an Inside Account of the Work of American Missionaries among Armenians, and Its Ruinous Effect* (New York: n.p., 1896); Grabill, *Protestant Diplomacy,* p. 7.
23. In 1909, for example, about 3,100 Armenians moved to the United States, more than 5,500 in 1910, and 9,355 in 1913. See Robert Mirak, *Torn between Two Lands: Armenians in America, 1890 to World War I* (Cambridge, MA: Harvard University Press, 1983), pp. 46-47, 54-55, 57.
24. See, for example, Moushek Seropian, "The Truth about the Adana Massacres," *Armenia* 4 (April 1911): 10-11; E. Aknouni, "The Political Turmoil in Turkey," *Armenia* 5 (June 1911): 7-8. See also Mirak, *Torn between Two Lands*, pp. 66-67;

Manuk G. Chizmechian, *Patmutiun amerikahay kaghakakan kusaktsutiants, 1890-1925* [History of American-Armenian Political Parties, 1890-1925] (Fresno, CA: Nor Or, 1930).

25. William Appleman Williams, *The Tragedy of American Diplomacy*, 2d rev. ed. (New York: Dell Publishing, 1972), p. 71; Rosenberg, *American Dream*, pp. 63-86.
26. Thomas J. Knock, *To End All Wars: Woodrow Wilson and the Quest for a New World Order* (Princeton: Princeton University Press, 1992), pp. 4, 6. See, for example, Wilson's religious talk in *The Papers of Woodrow Wilson,* ed. Arthur Link, 69 vols. (Princeton: Princeton University Press, 1966-1994), vol. 12, pp. 273-74.
27. Lloyd E. Ambrosius, *Wilsonian Statecraft: Theory and Practice of Liberal Internationalism during World War I* (Wilmington, DE: Scholarly Resource Books, 1991), p. 1.
28. Ibid., pp. 3, 10-11, 13; Arthur S. Link, *Woodrow Wilson and the Progressive Era, 1910-1917* (New York: Harper and Row, 1954), p. 82. See also *Papers of Woodrow Wilson*, vol. 12, pp. 474-78.
29. See, for example, Josephus Daniels, *The Navy and the Nation: War-Time Addresses* (New York: George H. Doran, 1919), p. 24.
30. John A. DeNovo, "Petroleum and the United States Navy before World War I," *Mississippi Valley Historical Review* 41 (March 1955): 642, 648.
31. Ibid., p. 646.
32. See, for example, Robert C. Hilderbrand, *Power and the People: Executive Management of Public Opinion in Foreign Affairs, 1897-1921* (Chapel Hill: University of North Carolina Press, 1981).
33. Library of Congress, Division of Manuscripts, The Papers of Henry Morgenthau, Sr., General Correspondence, Container 6, Morgenthau to House, July 10, 1913.
34. Ibid., Bryan to Morgenthau, Sept. 9, 1913; Henry Morgenthau, *All in a Life-Time* (Garden City, NJ: Doubleday, 1922), p. 174.
35. Morgenthau Papers, General Correspondence, Container 6, Rev. E. W. McDowell, quoted in Robert E. Speer to Morgenthau, Oct. 23, 1913.
36. Morgenthau Papers, Diary, Nov. 27, 1913.
37. Ibid., Dec. 8, 1913.
38. Ibid., Dec. 22, 1913.
39. Ibid., Dec. 23, 1913. Morgenthau and the representatives of Standard Oil of New York in Constantinople maintained close relations during his tenure. See, for example, Morgenthau Papers, General Correspondence, Container 6, OG/D, Standard Oil of New York, to Morgenthau, June 24, 1914.
40. Morgenthau Papers, Diary, Dec. 23, 1913.
41. Morgenthau Papers, General Correspondence, Container 4, Morgenthau to Josie, Dec. 27, 1913, pp. 1-2.
42. Ibid., p. 9; Morgenthau Papers, Diary, Dec. 27, 1913.
43. Morgenthau Papers, General Correspondence, Container 4, Morgenthau to Josie, Dec. 27, 1913, pp. 9-10.
44. Ibid., pp. 1-2.
45. A.J.P. Taylor, *The Struggle for Mastery in Europe, 1848-1918* (Oxford: Oxford University Press, 1954), pp. 508-09; Liman von Sanders, *Five Years in Turkey* (Baltimore: Williams and Wilkins, 1928), p. 3; Roderic H. Davison, "The Armenian Crisis, 1912-1914," *American Historical Review* 53 (April 1948): 503.
46. Hovannisian, "Armenian Question," pp. 235-38. See the preliminary draft in Great Britain, Foreign Office Archives, FO 43989/19208/13/44, Marling to Sir Edward Grey, Sept. 26, 1913, in G.P. Gooch and Harold Temperely, eds., *British*

Documents on the Origins of the War, 1898-1914, vol. 10, pt. 1: *The Near and Middle East on the Eve of War* (London: His Majesty's Stationery Office, 1936), p. 517.

47. See, for example, Morgenthau Papers, Diary, Jan. 20 and 28, 1914, and Feb. 16, 1914.
48. Morgenthau, *All in a Life-Time*, p. 196.
49. Morgenthau Papers, General Correspondence, Container 7, Morgenthau to Said Halim Pasha, Grand Vizier and Minister of Foreign Affairs, Sept. 18, 1914. See also John A. DeNovo, *American Interests and Policies in the Middle East, 1900-1939* (Minneapolis: University of Minnesota Press, 1963), p. 91. On the legal requirements instituted after the annulment of the Capitulations as a measure reflecting the hardening nationalist sentiments of the Young Turk regime, see United States, National Archives, Record Group 59, 771.673/73, Chargé Hoffman Philip to Secretary of State, June 15, 1916, encl., Sublime Porte, Minister of Foreign Affairs, "Instruction to be Communicated to Officials as the Consequence of the Abrogation of the Capitulations." Record Groups in the National Archives will be cited hereafter as RG. See also in Department of State, *Papers Relating to the Foreign Relations of the United States, 1916* (Washington, DC: Government Printing Office, 1925), pp. 968-74.
50. Morgenthau Diary, Aug. 18, 1914; RG 59, 367.116/219, James Barton to Secretary of State, Oct. 24, 1914.
51. Morgenthau Diary, Aug. 25, 1914.
52. Morgenthau Papers, General Correspondence, Container 6, Morgenthau to Secretary of State, Sept. 15, 1914, encls., clipping from "Christians in Turkey, Danger of Massacres," *Daily Telegraph*, Aug. 27, 1914; Library of Congress, Division of Manuscripts, Papers of Robert Lansing, Lansing Diaries, Oct. 24, 1914. See also Paolo E. Coletta, *William Jennings Bryan*, vol. 2: *Progressive Politician and Moral Statesman, 1909-1915* (Lincoln: University of Nebraska Press, 1969), p. 260.
53. Morgenthau Papers, General Correspondence, Container 7, Talaat, Minister of the Interior, to Morgenthau, Sept. 13, 1914, and Container 6, Morgenthau to Secretary of State, Sept. 15, 1914.
54. Morgenthau Papers, Diary, Sept. 1, 1914.
55. Morgenthau Papers, General Correspondence, Container 6, Cass Arthur Reed to Rev. Chas. T. Riggs, Sept. 25, 1914.
56. RG 59, 367.116/222, John E. Osborne (Assistant Secretary) to Snyder, Sept. 24, 1914; and RG 59, 367.116/219/227, Lansing to Barton, Oct. 27, and Bryan to Barton, Nov. 9, 1914.
57. RG 59, 367.116/261a, Bryan to Morgenthau, Dec. 20, 1914.
58. For a useful summary of the consular and missionary reports, see Armen K. Hairapetian, "'Race Problems' and the Armenian Genocide: The State Department File," *Armenian Review* 37 (Spring 1984): 41-59. See also Suzanne Elizabeth Moranian, "Bearing Witness: The Missionary Archives as Evidence of the Armenian Genocide," in Richard G. Hovannisian, ed., *The Armenian Genocide: History, Politics, Ethics* (New York: St. Martin's Press, 1992), pp. 103-28.
59. *Current History* 2 (Sept. 1915): 1042; W.E.D. Allen, and Paul Muratoff, *Caucasian Battlefields: A History of the Wars on the Turco-Caucasian Border, 1828-1921* (Cambridge: Cambridge University Press, 1953), pp. 245-86, *passim*; Grabill, *Protestant Diplomacy*, pp. 50-60; Jon S. Kirakosyan, *Arajin hamashkharhayin paterazme ev arevmtahayutiune 1914-1916 tt.* [The First World War and the Western Armenians, 1914-1916], 2d ed. (Erevan: Hayastan, 1967), pp. 329-30; Christopher J. Walker, *Armenia: The Survival of a Nation* (London: Croom Helm, 1980), pp. 199-200; *Treatment of Armenians*, pp. 637-38.

60. *Current History* 2 (Aug. 1915): 870-72.
61. Morgenthau Papers, Diary, April 20, 1915.
62. RG 59, 867.00/761, Jackson to Secretary of State, April 21, 1915, encl. report of Rev. John E. Merrill, April 20, 1915, pp. 1-9.
63. Ibid., p. 2.
64. Ibid., pp. 4-5; RG 59, 867.4016/72, Jackson to Morgenthau, May 12, 1915.
65. RG 59, 867.4016/77/148, Jackson to Morgenthau, June 5, 1915 and Morgenthau to Secretary of State, Aug. 30, 1915, encl. Jackson to Morgenthau, Aug. 19, 1915.
66. RG 59, 867.4016/129/147/225, Jackson to Morgenthau, Aug. 3, Aug. 10, and Oct. 16, 1915.
67. Morgenthau Papers, General Correspondence, Container 7, Jackson to Morgenthau, Aug. 10, 1915, encl., F. H. Leslie to Jackson, Aug. 6, 1915. In his note accompanying Leslie's letter, Jackson warned that "there may be a very disastrous result to the Armenian question, as mentioned in Rev. Leslie's letter, and no time should be lost in having the belligerents removed before there is a conflagration in which they run great risk of being caught."
68. RG 59, 867.4016/114/85, Heizer to Secretary of State, July 12, 1915, and Heizer to Morgenthau, June 28, 1915. See also Haigazn G. Ghazarian, *Tseghaspan Turke* [The Genocidal Turk] (Beirut: Hamazkaine, 1968), pp. 74-77.
69. RG 59, 867.4016/85, Heizer to Morgenthau, June 28, 1915. This report also appeared in *Treatment of Armenians* as Document 72.
70. RG 59, 867.4016/122/269, Morgenthau to Secretary of State, Aug. 10, 1915, encl. Davis to Morgenthau, June 11, 1915, and Hoffman Philip to Secretary of State, Feb. 17, 1916, encl. Davis to Morgenthau, June 30, July 24, and Dec. 30, 1915.
71. RG 59, 867.4016/122, encl. Davis to Morgenthau, July 11, 1915.
72. RG 59, 867.4016/269, encl. Davis to Morgenthau, Dec. 30, 1915.
73. RG 59, 867.00/724, Hollis to Secretary of State, Nov. 16, 1914.
74. RG 59, 867.00/668/683, Charles R. Lane to Secretary of State, Sept. 29, and Oct. 10, 1914.
75. RG 59, 867.00/723, Morgenthau to Secretary of State, Dec. 12, 1914.
76. RG 59, 867.4016/97, Hollis to Secretary of State, July 6, 1915.
77. RG 59, 867.4016/150, Morgenthau to Secretary of State, Sept. 1, 1915, encl., letter by Horton, July 30, 1915.
78. RG 59, 867.4016/124, Morgenthau to Secretary of State, Aug. 15, 1915, encl. Nathan to Morgenthau to Secretary of State, Aug. 7, 1915, reporting also that a French warship visited the port "but left without taking any action."
79. RG 59, 867.4016/238, encl., Nathan to Morgenthau, Nov. 4, 1915.
80. RG 59, 867.48/271, Jackson to Morgenthau, Feb. 8, 1916; *Treatment of Armenians*, Document 139 (section d); Walker, *Armenia*, pp. 226-29.
81. RG 59, 867.4016/291, Jackson to Morgenthau, July 21, 1916.
82. RG 59, 867.4026/219, Morgenthau to Secretary of State, Nov. 1, 1915, encl. Jackson to Morgenthau, Sept. 29, 1915.
83. United States, Department of State, *Papers Relating to the Foreign Relations of the United States, 1914* (Washington, DC: Government Printing Office, 1922), pp. 1090-92.
84. Henry Morgenthau, *Ambassador Morgenthau's Story* (New York: Doubleday, 1918), pp. 169-70; Vahakn N. Dadrian, *German Responsibility in the Armenian Genocide: A Review of the Historical Evidence of German Complicity* (Watertown, MA: Blue Crane Books, 1996), p. 144.
85. RG 59, 867.4016/58, Morgenthau to Secretary of State, April 27, 1915.
86. RG 59, 867.4016/59, Morgenthau to Secretary of State, April 30, 1915. See also

867.4016/74, Morgenthau to Secretary of State, July 10, 1915.

87. RG 59, 867.4016/71, Morgenthau to Secretary of State, May 25, 1915.
88. Morgenthau, *Ambassador Morgenthau's Story*, p. 326.
89. Morgenthau Papers, General Correspondence, Container 7, Morgenthau to Secretary of State, July 16, 1915.
90. RG 59, 867.4016/90, Morgenthau to Secretary of State, Aug. 11, 1915; United States, Department of State, *Papers Relating to the Foreign Relations of the United States, 1915:* supplement, *The World War* (Washington, DC: Government Printing Office, 1928), p. 986, cited hereafter as *Foreign Relations, 1915*, supp.
91. Morgenthau, *Ambassador Morgenthau's Story*, p. 292.
92. Ibid., p. 383, emphasis in original.
93. RG 59, 867.4016/90, Morgenthau to Lansing, Aug. 11, 1915; *Foreign Relations of the United States, 1915*, supplement, p. 987.
94. Daniel, *American Philanthropy*, p. 153. The ACASR grew out of the merger of three organizations operating in the Middle East. These included the Persia War Relief Fund, established in March 1915 by the Presbyterian Board of Missions; the Syria-Palestine Committee, founded in April 1915 by Presbyterians and Jews; and the Committee on Armenian Atrocities, organized in September 1915 by the American Board of Commissioners for Foreign Missions. The latter requested $20,000 from the Rockefeller Foundation, which in turn required merger of the relief committees working in the Middle East. See Daniel, *American Philanthropy*, p. 150. Barton, as chairman of the ACASR, and Crane gained access to the files of the Department of State with permission to use all relevant documents for the purposes of the committee. See James L. Barton, *Story of Near East Relief, 1915-1930* (New York: Macmillan, 1930), pp. 4-10.
95. See Richard G. Hovannisian, *The Republic of Armenia*, 4 vols. (Berkeley, Los Angeles, London: University of California Press, 1971-1996), vol. 1: *The First Years, 1918-1919*, pp. 133-34, 300-01, 303, 312-17; vol. 2: *From Versailles to London, 1919-1920*, pp. 316-403; vol. 3: *From London to Sèvres, February-August 1920*, pp. 434-38; vol. 4: *Between Crescent and Sickle: Partition and Sovietization*, pp. 1-44.
96. RG 59, 711.673/69, Chargé Philip to Secretary of State, March 9, 1916, encls., American Embassy to Ministry of Foreign Affairs, Feb. 19, 1916, and Ministry of Foreign Affairs to American Embassy, March 7, 1916, in United States, Department of State, *Papers Relating to the Foreign Relations of the United States, 1916* (Washington, DC: Government Printing Office, 1925), pp. 963-64, cited hereafter as *Foreign Relations, 1916.*
97. RG 59, 711.673/72, Chargé Philip to Secretary of State, May 23, 1916, *Foreign Relations, 1916*, pp. 965-67.
98. RG 59, 312.67/65, Consul Alonzo B. Garrett to Secretary of State, March 24, 1916; Secretary of State to Special Representative Rodgers, April 5, 1916, *Foreign Relations, 1916,* pp. 797-99.
99. United States, Department of State, *United States Chiefs of Mission, 1778-1982* (Washington, DC: Government Printing Office, 1982), p. 238. Elkus was appointed in July but did not arrive in Constantinople until September.
100. RG 59, 867.4016/373, Jackson to Secretary of State, March 4, 1918, encl., report, "Armenian Atrocities."
101. Alexander L. George and Juliette L. George, *Woodrow Wilson and Colonel House: A Personality Study* (New York: John Day Company, 1956), pp. 115-16.
102. Library of Congress, Division of Manuscripts, Presidential Papers, Wilson Papers, Rev. William Chambers to Wilson, Dec. 10, 1915, and Wilson to Chamber, Dec. 15, 1915 (microfilm, reel 337, ser. 4, case files 2554). See also *Papers of Woodrow*

Wilson, vol. 35, pp. 337, 349.

103. United States, Department of State, *Papers Relating to the Foreign Relations of the United States, 1918:* supplement 1, *The World War* (Washington, DC: Government Printing Office, 1933), p. 892; James B. Gidney, *A Mandate for Armenia* (Kent, OH: Kent State University Press, 1967), p. 45; Richard G. Hovannisian, *Armenia on the Road to Independence, 1918* (Berkeley and Los Angeles: University of California Press, 1967), p. 251.
104. Address of the President, Dec. 4, 1917, United States, Department of State, *Papers Relating to the Foreign Relations of the United States, 1917* (Washington, DC: Government Printing Office, 1926), pp. xi, xiv.
105. RG 59, 867.00/793/804$^{1/2}$, Elkus to Secretary of State, Feb. 16, and March 2, 1917, United States, Department of State, *Papers Relating to the Foreign Relations of the United States: The Lansing Papers, 1914-1920,* 2 vols. (Washington, DC: Government Printing Office, 1939-1940), vol. 1, p. 787, cited hereafter as *Lansing Papers*.
106. See, for example, *Lansing Papers*, vol. 2, p. 121-22, 124-26, Lansing to Wilson, May 2 and May 18, 1918. See also Daniel, *American Philanthropy,* p. 154-55.
107. Morgenthau Papers, General Correspondence, Container 8, Barton to Morgenthau, Dec. 15, 1917, encl., Barton to Lodge, Dec. 10, 1917. See also Daniel, *American Philanthropy,* pp. 154-55.
108. Excerpt in Hovannisian, *Armenia on the Road to Independence*, p. 252.
109. RG 59, 763.72111/348, Morgenthau to Secretary of State, Aug. 25, 1914, and Secretary of State to Morgenthau, Aug. 26, 1914, in Department of State, *Papers Relating to the Foreign Relations of the United States, 1914:* supplement, *The World War* (Washington, DC: Government Printing Office, 1922), p. 77.
110. See, for example, RG 59, 367.116/233/234/241/247, B. Bowman to Secretary of State, Nov. 15, Arthur J. Brown to Secretary of State, Nov. 11 and Nov. 21, 1914, Brown to Secretary of State, Nov. 28, 1914, and J. C. Way to Secretary of State, Dec. 7, 1914.
111. RG 59, 867.4016/67, Sharp to Secretary of State, May 28, 1915.
112. RG 59, 367.116/309a, Secretary of State to Morgenthau, Feb. 18, 1915. Also in *Foreign Relations, 1915*, supp., p. 979.
113. Morgenthau Papers, Container 7, Secretary of State to Morgenthau, April 20, and May 1, 1915.
114. *Papers of Woodrow Wilson*, vol. 33, pp. 375-76, Bryan to Wilson, June 9, and Wilson to Bryan, June 9, 1915.
115. RG 59, 867.4016/218a, Lansing to Morgenthau, Oct. 4, 1915; *Foreign Relations, 1915*, supplement, p. 988.
116. RG 59, 867.4016/74, Lansing to Morgenthau, July 16, 1915; *Foreign Relations, 1915*, supplement, p. 984.
117. RG 59, 367.116/341, Lansing to Barton, July 19, 1915, *Foreign Relations, 1915*, supp., pp. 984-85. In August 1918, Elkus suggested that Lansing write on the role of Germany in Turkey, but Lansing rejected the idea. Lansing Diaries, Aug. 28, 1918.
118. James F. Willis, *Prologue to Nuremberg: The Politics and Diplomacy of Punishing War Criminals of the First World War* (Westport, CT: Greenwood Press, 1982), pp. 69-70. Lansing believed that punishment of war crimes would be best implemented if left to the military authorities of individual governments. President Wilson supported Lansing's position. See, for example, Commission on the Responsibility of the Authors of the War and on Enforcement of Penalties, "Report Presented to the Preliminary Peace Conference," March 29, 1919, reprinted in *American Journal of International Law* 14 (1920): 95-154.
119. Walker, *Armenia*, p. 230.

120. Hovannisian, *Armenia on the Road to Independence*, pp. 67-68.
121. Hovannisian, *Republic of Armenia*, vol. 1, pp. 44, 48, 130-33.
122. On the operations of ACRNE and the American Relief Administration in Armenia, see Hovannisian, *Republic of Armenia*, vol. 1, pp. 133-44. On relief work in Turkey and Syria, see Daniel, *American Philanthropy*, pp. 158-59.
123. *New Near East* 7 (June 1922): 6, quoted in Daniel, *American Philanthropy*, p. 158.
124. DeNovo, "Oil Policy," pp. 857-58.
125. On the mandate issue, see Gidney, *Mandate for Armenia*; Laurence Evans, *United States Policy and the Partition of Turkey* (Baltimore: Johns Hopkins Press, 1965); Benjamin Gerig, *The Open Door and the Mandate System* (London: Allen and Unwin, 1930).
126. Woodrow Wilson to Frank L. Polk, March 4, 1920, quoted in DeNovo, "Oil Policy," pp. 858-59.
127. Gerald D. Nash, *United States Oil Policy, 1890-1964* (Pittsburgh: University of Pittsburgh Press, 1968), pp. 40-41, 50.
128. Rosenberg, *American Dream*, p. 128; DeNovo, "Oil Policy," pp. 857-58.
129. Nash, *Oil Policy*, p. 44; Hovannisian, *Republic of Armenia*, vol. 1, p. 298n23, vol. 2, pp. 90-91.
130. RG 38, Chief of Naval Operations, Intelligence Division, Naval Attache Reports, 1880-1939, U-1-i, Box 1345, Mark L. Bristol, July 12, 1919, U.S.S. Scorpion Flagship, Constantinople. On Bristol's views regarding Armenia, see Hovannisian, *Republic of Armenia*, vol. 1, pp. 298-99, 325-26n114, vol. 2, pp. 47, 90-91; Evans, *Partition of Turkey*, pp. 292-322.
131. Gidney, *Mandate for Armenia*, pp. 233-37; Hovannisian, *Republic of Armenia*, vol. 4, pp. 3-24.
132. Hovannisian, *Republic of Armenia*, vol. 4, p. 303; Daniel, *American Philanthropy*, p. 165.
133. United States, Department of Commerce, *Foreign Commerce and Navigation of the United States* (Washington, DC: Government Printing Office, 1921), pp. x-xi.

5

The League of Nations and the Reclamation of Armenian Genocide Survivors

Vahram L. Shemmassian

Women and children constituted a special category of victims in the Armenian Genocide. Whereas the older boys and men were murdered summarily in the most gruesome manner, the women and children suffered immeasurably in terms of sustained physical, emotional, and psychological punishment. Along the deportation routes, those who did not succumb to starvation, disease, exposure, drowning, or outright massacre were abandoned, abducted, raped, or sold. As such, they involuntary became part of Muslim society in Turkey, Greater Syria, and Mesopotamia, serving as concubines, wives, servants, or slaves. While physical salvation might have been a desirable outcome in strictly human terms, the traumatic impact of separation, forced religious conversion, and all sorts of abuse defied description.[1] Be that as it may, although in time many victims became resigned to their fate, they were not forsaken altogether. Their efforts at search and rescue, or a fraction thereof, began as soon as conditions permitted.

At the end of World War I, Armenian individuals, organizations, and institutions operating in Allied zones of occupation in the Near East began to look for missing Armenians with assistance from British, French, American, and Arab military, political, and relief circles. Various compatriotic unions representing Armenians from particular districts, towns, and villages in the Ottoman Empire, Armenian church bodies in Constantinople, Aleppo, Baghdad, and Jerusalem, and charitable associations dispatched agents and teams to free enslaved Armenians.[2] Given the enormity and complexity of the problem, greater success hinged upon larger sums, manpower, support, and concerted effort. The League of Nation's involvement came as a major boost.

Genesis of the Commission of Inquiry

The League of Nations Covenant did not include a specific provision regarding the rescue and protection of deported women and children in the Near East or, for that matter, anywhere else. There was, however, enough room under Article 23—designed for the implementation of existing international regulations concerning the traffic in women and children—to initiate an inquiry into the matter. In 1920 the representative of Romania notified the League's Assembly of "the Eastern slave markets, where women and children were sold, which we know were flowishing [sic] in Armenia and Asia Minor.... Now with the return of Peace and relaxation of passport formalities it is to be feared that the traffic will take a new lease of life. International collaboration is the only means to fight against it."[3] This recommendation fell on receptive ears, as the following resolution was drafted for consideration:

> That the Assembly should nominate a temporary committee or entrust an existing body—*i.e.*, a Court of Justice in one of the countries represented—to receive applications from the families of deported women. This Authority would be empowered to institute enquiries, to deal direct with Governments, in short, to take all steps to enable these victims to return to their families. This Authority would be in constant and close touch with the Officer within the Secretariat charged with questions relative to the Traffic.[4]

An amendment to the draft resolution asked for the formation of a temporary judicial committee, composed of up to three persons including at least one woman, "with power to trace and liberate deported women and girls."[5] As this committee would conduct its investigation foremost in the Ottoman Empire, the representative of the Serb-Croat-Slovene State raised the issue of legality. According to international law, he contended, "a Commission could not be permitted to conduct inquiries, within the boundaries of a State, which affected the individuals of that State."[6] But his argument was dismissed as untenable, because the legal basis for initiating investigations in Turkey existed in Article 142 of the Treaty of Sèvres, signed on August 10, 1920. The article read in part:

> In order to repair as far as possible the wrongs inflicted on individuals in the course of the massacres perpetrated in Turkey during the war, the Turkish Government under-

takes to afford all the assistance in its power, or in that of the Turkish Authorities, in the search for and deliverance of all persons, of whatever race or religion, who have disappeared, been carried off, interned or placed in captivity since November 1st, 1914.

The Turkish Government undertakes to facilitate the operations of mixed commissions appointed by the Council of the League of Nations to receive the complaints of the victims themselves, their families or their relations, to make the necessary enquiries, and to order the liberation of the persons in question.

The Turkish Government undertakes to ensure the execution of the decisions of these commissions, and to assure the security and the liberty of the persons thus restored to the full enjoyment of their rights.[7]

The Assembly then drafted a resolution, calling upon the Council to appoint a committee of inquiry that would operate in Armenia and Asia Minor. Its membership would consist of three persons, including a woman, who were well informed of the issue at hand. The committee would convey its findings to the League Secretariat, which would also receive pertinent information from other states. The League would shoulder all costs.[8] Although the resolution was adopted unanimously, the geographical scope of investigation became the subject of a dispute. It started when the Danish delegate, Henni Forchhammer, suggested that the following clarification be made: "If it would be possible to introduce the word 'particularly' before the words 'in Armenia and Asia Minor,' it would not exclude the great spheres outside these regions which are mentioned."[9] Emboldened by this statement, the envoy extraordinary and minister plenipotentiary of Persia in Switzerland, Emir Zoka-ed-Dowleh, expressed desire to see his country included in that sphere. After arguing that Persia had suffered immensely at the hands of Imperial Russia during World War I, he concluded with a request: "I ask the League of Nations to take up the case of the women and children of Persia, who have been even more unfortunate than those of Asia Minor, Armenia, and Greece, who have lost their property and all that is dear to them. I ask the League to do all in its power for their repatriation."[10] But the Emir was reminded that the League had the right to intervene under the Treaty of Sèvres only in Armenia and Asia Minor. Even so, in order to end the haggling, "Turkey" and "territories adjoining these countries" were incorporated into the resolution alongside "Armenia and Asia Minor."[11] As the course of events would indicate, the expanded area remained largely untouched, the Commission of Inquiry concentrating its efforts only around Constantinople and Aleppo.

The official resolution, adopted on December 15, 1920, was submitted to the Council for approval. Meeting in Paris on February 22, 1921, the Council considered the formation of a commission of inquiry, but given the tenuous political and military situation in the Near East, deemed it unpropitious to dispatch an outside team.[12] The Italian representative, Marquis Guglielmo Imperiali dei Principi di Francavilla, expressed the prevalent apprehension:

> The question...arises whether this Commission could, at the present moment, arrive at any really useful results. It is perhaps permissible to doubt it. The fact is that there are at present in Turkey and the adjacent countries—if we except the territory occupied by the Allied troops—nothing but areas ruled over by Governments which are not recognised, and to whom no diplomatic representatives have been accredited. They are even in a state of war with certain Members of the League of Nations. It is still very uncertain whether it is possible to visit these regions. Such is the situation in the central part of Asia Minor and Armenia. In these circumstances, the appointment and despatch of a Commission of Enquiry into these regions could not offer any great advantages. The Commission would not be able to collect information fuller than that which the League could obtain, at present, by other means. Neither could it exercise any political influence in order to put an end to these deportations.[13]

The most expedient alternative, therefore, would be "to request a small number of persons (three) specially interested in this question, and who are already on the spot, to collect all the information which they can obtain on this subject, to make enquiries and to exchange views in order to draw up a programme of action which might be put into execution whenever it shall be possible to do so."[14] Having thus set the broader premises of the commission's functions, the Council called for nominations. The American Mission in Constantinople, Robert College, and Constantinople College recommended Emma D. Cushman; the British High Commissioner recommended Dr. W. A. Kennedy; and the French representative on the Council recommended Madame Georges Gaulis. Later, "various important Organisations" submitted the name of Karen Jeppe. Gaulis declined the offer after Jeppe accepted her "provisional appointment."[15]

Upon learning of the imminent formation of a commission that would deal with Armenian women and children "sequestered during the course of the war in Mesopotamia, in Asia Minor and recently at Kars and Alexandropol and whose number surpasses according to the most moderate evaluations, a hundred thousands," Vahan Papazian, speaking on behalf of the United Armenian Delegations in Paris, asked the League of Nations Secretary-General Sir Eric Drummond whether the Armenians could also assign one or two representatives on the commission.[16] Drummond replied: "To do valuable work, the Commission must be regarded as an entirely impartial Body, and I do not think therefore, that it would be advisable for any representative of the Countries directly concerned to be attached to it." He would, however, "transmit a copy of your letter to the Commission, when formed, asking it to get into touch with your Representatives."[17]

The nominees had impressive credentials. A Near East Relief worker, Emma Cushman had taken care of deported Armenian women and children at Konia during the war. When diplomatic relations between the United States and the Ottoman Empire were severed in the spring of 1917, she was offered safe passage to Constantinople. She refused to leave, however, because the Turkish authorities declined her request that her proteges be protected in her absence. She also had tended many Allied prisoners of war brought to Konia.[18] Dr. Kennedy was a British physician working among the refugees camped in and around Constantinople. As such, his nomination elicited a most favorable reaction in the Council.[19] Karen Jeppe, too, suited the job well. A native of Denmark, she had served in Dr. Johannes Lepsius' German Orient Mission at Urfa since 1903. In 1918 she returned to Denmark to recuperate from the shock she had sustained as a result of witnessing the wartime Armenian atrocities. Three years later she established herself in Aleppo in order to revive the vanishing art of medieval Armenia embroidery among female genocide survivors and thus create a source of livelihood for them.[20] Cushman and Kennedy oversaw the rescue operations from Constantinople, and Jeppe from Aleppo.

The Commission—officially known as the Commission of Inquiry for the Protection of Women and Children in the Near East—was to refrain from ascribing any "political significance" to its task, which aimed at the "reconstruction" of families torn apart and "reconciliation" among peoples. In other words, this was a purely humanitarian enterprise, and as such "complete impartiality" had to be maintained in dealing with the victims of different races and religions. War was perceived to be the culprit, and people in the Near East had been displaced, separated from their families, or enslaved due to the movements of enemy troops. Hence, no distinction was to be made between those on the one hand who were deported by government orders and forcibly converted to Islam and/or kept in Muslim harems, houses, and orphanages against their will and those on the other hand who were rendered homeless or parentless essentially as a result of the war. By officially adopting such a position, the League hoped to gain three things: credibility, cooperation of the Turkish government, and favorable world public opinion. The first two were deemed necessary for the commission to accomplish its mission, and the third for the success of any future League activity.[21]

The Work at Constantinople

After several months of preliminary investigation at Constantinople, the Commission informed the League of its findings. Kennedy and Cushman sent a report and a letter, respectively, accompanied by supplementary documents. Since it had been "impossible to classify the details" pertaining to the Armenian deportees, recourse to previously compiled information about them had become imperative. The sources consulted included the Armenian-Greek section of the British High Commission, the Armenian Patriarchate, the Near East Relief, the Armenian Refugees' Fund of the Lord Mayor of London, as well as American missionaries, officers, and private citizens, and reclaimed persons.[22]

The information provided by the British High Commissioner, Sir Horace Rumbold, pertained to some 2,300 women and children who had been interrogated and subsequently retrieved from bondage. Utmost caution was exercised "to avoid injustice to any of the parties concerned."[23] The Armenian Patriarchate records included "official birth certificates, undoubtedly false, of Christian children, who make allegations that they are Moslem; official letters from Turkish officials in which untrue statements are made in regard to Christian children; and the nominal rolls of Turkish orphanages which have been seized by the Allied police, in which the names of Christian children have been struck out and Moslem names super-imposed." Furthermore, the Armenian authorities believed that the Armenians constituted about half of the wards in Turkish orphanages, a claim that Kennedy considered as "roughly true, although it is probably somewhat exaggerated."[24] The rosters of orphans kept in Turkish institutions revealed that the overwhelming majority of names were Kurdish, something that aroused suspicion. During the war, thousands of Armenians were deported through Kurdish-inhabited territory, making it highly probable that many of the children abducted en route were given Kurdish names. Moreover, it was questionable whether the Turkish government had any keen interest in the well-being of Kurdish children. And finally, there was no indication that a great many Kurdish youngsters were separated from their families during the war. Unfortunately, it would be impossible to check all Turkish orphanages across the empire, unless "systematic means of examination" were devised.[25]

The Armenians similarly maintained that there existed in and around Constantinople an additional 6,000 Armenian children in Muslim homes. A Turkish organization, "affiliated with the [Turkish] Red Crescent Society under the patronage of such leading Moslems as [Genocide masterminds] Talaat Pasha, Enver Pasha, [the Turkish nationalist intellectual-feminist] Halideh Edib Hanum and other prominent ladies and gentlemen," had collected Armenian youngsters—estimated at more than 2,000—in northeast Syria for distribution among Muslim families. According to the chief of the Turkish Refugee Commission during the war, Hamdi Bey, "no effort was made in this work to distinguish between a Moslem and a Christian child." Interestingly, no children were placed in Christian families.[26] After conducting its own cross-examinations of recovered children, the Commission concluded that they had been brainwashed as Muslims through various intimidation and deception tactics.[27]

Kennedy asked the League to empower the Commission with the actual emancipation and protection of as many captives as possible before it was too late. He also hinted at the immediate necessity for a mixed inter-Allied body to oversee the rescue operations in a concerted manner, thereby alleviating the British from a most onerous burden.[28] Finally, he wished to see the Neutral House of Constantinople change hands, as explained:

> This was an institution established by the Near East Relief to observe reclaimed children. At first there were Moslem representatives, and its aim was to determine the nationality of doubtful cases. It soon became evident that claims made on behalf of alleged Christian children were usually substantiated, with the result that the Moslem representatives withdrew and it became a sort of transition institution where Armenian children were kept pending their assignment to another institution or to their relatives. This plan appears to be very desirable from some points of view, and if the Neutral Home could be made an inter-Allied Headquarters to deal with the whole subject, considerable progress might be made.[29]

Cushman's letter dwelled primarily on the Turkish methods of brainwashing Armenian children. After speaking "of the unique and very clever manner in which the Turks contrive to conceal the identity of these [Armenian] children," Cushman wrote:

> They [Turks] try to bring about not so much a change of name and locality, but rather a complete change of mind in the child.... The reasons given by the children for their denial of nationality are varied. With the girls, experience has taught me that this attitude of mind is usually brought about by gifts of clothing, personal adornments, such as beads, cheap jewellery, etc.; with the boys, it seems to be largely produced by fear, threats, blows, etc., until the child really believes that he is being protected by the Turks from a much worse fate.[30]

Cushman also stated that many of the freed children tried to return to their captors who lured the waifs back with food and gifts. After acknowledging the very difficult and delicate nature of the Commission's task, Cushman concluded her report with statistics. The total number of Armenian orphans reclaimed since the Mudros Armistice of October 30, 1918 was 90,819. Of these, 12,480 were rescued in areas in Asia Minor that were not occupied by the Allies, 11,339 in areas occupied by the Allies, and 67,000 in Armenia, Georgia, Egypt, and Cyprus. Still, 73,350 Armenian orphans were believed to remain in Turkish institutions and homes, with 60,750 in the unoccupied areas and 12,600 in the occupied areas.[31]

The Kennedy-Cushman reports were discussed in the League's Council on August 30, 1921, and in the Assembly the following month.[32] On September 23 the Assembly translated its favorable reactions and unequivocal support to both the reports and recommendations into five resolutions, which stated:

> I. That there shall be appointed in Constantinople a Commissioner of the League of Nations, whose appointment shall be officially notified to the Allied and Associated High Commissioners, to the representatives of the other interested countries and Members of the League, to the Turkish Government and to the ecclesiastical authorities of the deported populations, namely, the Greek and Armenian Patriarchs;
>
> II. That the League request France, Great Britain and Italy to instruct their High Commissioners to constitute themselves as a Committee, whose duty it will be to concert action with a view to giving all possible assistance and powers to the League of Nations Commissioner for the carrying out of his duties;
>
> III. That there shall be established, under the Commissioner of the League, a mixed Board to deal with the reclamation of women and children. This Board would be composed of the present Members of the League of Nations Commission of Enquiry, with power to co-opt in particular cases members of each interested nationality. This Board would look to the Allied Commissioners and to the co-operation of the Greek and Armenian Patriarchs for the necessary support in the carrying out of its decisions. The Assembly emphasises the desirability of encouraging the work of charity already being carried on in the different centres by various establishments;

IV. That the Neutral House for the temporary reception and examination of women and children reclaimed from Turkish houses should be reorganised and placed under the direct management and supervision of the Commission of Enquiry;

V. That further Neutral Houses may be opened in other centres as circumstances permit.[33]

On October 2, 1921, the Council invited Dr. William W. Peet of the American Bible Mission in Constantinople as chief commissioner. Following an extensive correspondence that lasted until June 10, 1922, Peet declined.[34] One of his colleagues associated with the American Board of Commissioners for Foreign Missions doubted as early as January 28 whether Peet would ever assume that role: "There seems to be little likelihood that he will accept because of the small opportunity of service which it will actually afford him and the large degree of uncertainty surrounding the attitude which would be maintained by the other commissioners and the Turkish government towards his position if he were so to be appointed."[35] Five days later, on February 2, his superior, Dr. James L. Barton, confirmed: "The matter is in correspondence and he has declined to accept the position on the ground that his influence would be less under the conditions of the appointment than he now has as missionary and as free adviser of the different Embassies."[36] Kennedy, as the logical alternative, therefore replaced Peet.

In May the Council authorized the Commission to proceed with the reclamation of deportees. Pending the employment of a chief commissioner, the funds allocated for his usage in the 1922 budget would be spent on the rescue operations.[37] Towards the end of June, the Commission officially accepted the executive authority vested in it. It also informed the concerned organizations in Constantinople of the League's five resolutions, opened its headquarters at 53-55 Union Han, Galata, rented another building at 19 Rue Telegraphe, Pera, to receive the rescued, and hired a staff of three, namely, R. W. Graves (office manager), Felix Friand (secretary-archivist), and Caris Mills (directress of the House), to run the day-to-day operations in Constantinople. The Armenian orphanage, which until then had served as the Neutral House, was consequently closed and the "doubtful cases" transferred to the new League House. For the maintenance of the Armenian children there, the Patriarchate pledged an annual sum of 1,800 Turkish liras. Also in line with the new arrangements, the request forms utilized by the British High Commission for the doubtful cases were replaced by ones that did not make mention of religion or race. This change would give equal opportunity to Muslim women "who may happen to be illegally detained in Christian houses or institutions."[38]

So long as the Commission's activities were confined to the capital and its vicinity, no personnel or budgetary augmentations would be necessary. More manpower and money would be needed, however, once Nationalist-controlled Anatolia was pacified and opened. Not only was this projection based on the knowledge that there still existed large numbers of victims awaiting deliverance but also that many more would be enslaved by the time the war in Anatolia was over.[39] But without awaiting its outcome, Kennedy, in the introduction to his report for 1922, criticized the Turkish government for its continued policy of persecution. He wrote:

> The Turkish Government should eventually see that deportation of women and children is an evil that prevents its co-operation with European nations and furnishes the gravest reasons for lack of confidence in its willingness to adopt methods of government and treatment approved by the League of Nations and by the world at large. Any subsequent relations of Turkey with the League should be regulated by her readiness to guarantee effectively to assist in the reclamation of these women and children, and to remove the causes that expose children, and to remove the causes that expose thousands of them to utter desolation and despair.[40]

These scathing remarks elicited a spirited debate in the Assembly. The Swiss representative deemed the criticism "too severe" toward the Turkish government "and somewhat political in nature, although the Chairman [of the Fifth Committee of the Third Assembly] had expressedly requested the Commission not to introduce politics into the discussion." It is true that the Swiss representative had no intention of condoning Turkish policy as such; in all fairness the accused should be given a chance to defend itself before a verdict could be reached. The Romanian representative responded, by saying: "The Turkish representative at Berne had officially declared that the question [of deportation and reclamation] had been dealt with somewhat summarily, and that the Turkish Government was entirely innocent. This declaration constituted the Turkish Government's defence, and therefore that Government had had its say." The Danish and French representatives, on the other hand, proposed that Kennedy's remarks be omitted from the report so as to eliminate any misconceptions about the Commission's work. According to the French representative, "politics should be entirely banned. This was essential in view of the possible co-operation of the Turkish Government.... The Committee should limit its actions to verifying the facts and should not give birth to the idea of responsibility weighing upon any Government." The representative of New Zealand downplayed the controversy by reminding all that the report itself was not debatable. That actually being the case, the final resolution approved "the conclusions of the report."[41]

Ominous political clouds looming over Constantinople jeopardized the rescue work temporarily. The advance of the Turkish Nationalist army forced the closure of orphanages run by the Lord Mayor of London's Armenian Relief Committee, and the British High Commissioner advised the British staff of the Commission of Inquiry (that is, Kennedy and Graves) to leave the city at once. Before his departure for Corfu, Greece on November 20, 1922, Kennedy asked Dr. Fridtjof Nansen's Refugee Commission in Constantinople to look after the Commission of Inquiry's affairs. Despite the expressed fears, it was later learned that temporary shelter was actually provided to liberated women and children who had no male relatives.[42]

The Commission's report for 1923 passed silently over the turmoil. The work evidently continued, as children were gathered, returned to relatives, placed in schools, encouraged to emigrate, given up for adoption, and/or sent to hospitals for special medical treatment. Dr. Esther Pohl Lovejoy, the president of the American Women's Hospitals, extended considerable financial aid. Similarly, the Christian Science Relief Committee of America distributed significant amounts of food among women and children in the large refugee camps. To be sure, "no distinction of any kind has been made in regard to race or religion, although the majority of applications for aid come from the non-Turkish population." As for the emancipated Armenian women, they were reunited with their kin or sent to the United States.[43] Also in 1923, "a hopeful sign for the future" came from an unexpected source—Turkish women in Constantinople who took "interest in the work of the Home." The Commission's "humanitarian work" set to benefit people of all nationalities "appeals to the imagination of the man in the street" and "helps...to rally behind the League that support of public opinion without which the League cannot live."[44]

This optimistic outlook notwithstanding, the Supervisory Commission of the Fourth Committee of the Fourth League Assembly now maintained that "the special relief work involved was not primarily the work of the League of Nations, but was a matter rather for Governments or for the various Red Cross organisations," and therefore "the contribution of the League of Nations to the relief work in question should be brought to an end as soon as possible." But the Supervisory Commission also "recognised the disadvantages of immediately breaking off this work." Accordingly, a sum of 75,000 gold francs of "supplementary credits" was voted upon for the first nine months of 1924, the balance to be raised through other channels.[45]

The period from July 1923 to July 1924 proved fruitful. As many as 1,327 children and 960 women benefited from the Commission's services, primarily without visiting the House. Most rejoined their relatives or emigrated to the United States. But an increasing number, suffering from "nerve strain, unemployment, and under nourishment," entered the Greek Hospital. During the same period, the international character of the Commission's tasks became more apparent. For example, half of the 200 pounds sterling, as well as the 500 pounds of cocoa and 117 bundles of old clothes donated by the British Save the Children Fund, were distributed among Turkish orphans with the assistance of a distinguished Turkish woman, Madame Hussein Bey, and the Turkish Red Crescent. Moreover, the Commission raised 1,300 Turkish liras for the *Ecole des Mineures*, the city's "only school for the rescuing of children from white slave traffic." Other youngsters were enrolled in the British School for Russian Children, American schools, and "national" schools.[46]

At the end of this successful period, the Council once again considered the question of subsidizing the Commission. British representative and rapporteur to the Council, Lord Parmoor, based on private and official reports under his disposal, was convinced that the Commission should carry on its mission. This was imperative because of the termination of certain charitable societies of their business in Constantinople, the elimination of most of the impediments hampering the work thus far, and the League's inevitable gaining of prestige by its according of "magnanimous protection" to liberated women and children. Consequently, the Council budgeted 75,000 francs for 1925, again to be shared equally by the Constantinople and Aleppo branches of the Commission.[47]

The Commission's annual report covering the second half of 1924 and the first half of 1925 mirrored the increasing acuteness of war ravages. The Commission protected, hospitalized, counseled, delivered to relatives, sent abroad, or placed in houses and schools a record 1,414 children and 1,456 adults.[48] But Austen Chamberlain, the British representative on the Council, was "not wholly convinced that all the work undertaken comes within the limit of the responsibilities laid down for the Commission," a criticism approved by the Council and leveled particularly at the excessive emphasis on placement services.[49] Given the closure of the International Emigration Bureau and the curtailing of relief measures undertaken by other organizations such as the American Red Cross and Near East Relief, the Commission had no choice but to loan small amounts to create jobs and place in apartments females relinquished to its care. "This in itself is a necessary form of protection under present conditions and a measure of prevention," the Commission maintained in its report, while simultaneously giving aid to the *Ecole de Bonheur* that collected and educated children abandoned in the streets.[50]

The report also revealed that the American Women's Hospitals had increased its monthly subsidy from $500 to $700, enabling 620 women and 315 children to receive medical treatment. Ailing Russians in the city, bereft of proper care, also benefited from that service. Similarly, the British Save the Children Fund sent 575 pounds sterling to feed undernourished children in the House and to assist youngsters of all nationalities, especially Turks. And the Christian Science Relief of America gave another $1,000 for the travel expenses of emigrants and the needs of Armenian orphans in refugee camps. These and other private contributions amounted to $14,418.[51]

At this time Kennedy informed the League that he would be unable to continue his work on the Commission. Although published League documents do not mention the reasons for his resignation, both the Assembly and the Council asked him to stay to preserve "continuity in leadership." Should he decline to reconsider his decision, however, the Council ought "to take all necessary measures for the continuation of this work." Even so, the Council budgeted only 30,000 francs for Constantinople and 45,000 francs for Aleppo, thereby hinting that the work in the former place was winding down.[52]

The Commission lasted one more year, during which 1,319 children and 1,550 adults received help.[53] Despite the plea of the House directress, Caris Mills, for another year of support, the League declined. As a last gesture of goodwill, however, it lent her the furniture and equipment of the House so that she could run it as a social service center with the help of the American Women's Hospitals and friends.[54] Thus came to an end the Constantinople branch of the Commission of Inquiry in 1926, after having touched the lives of 4,000 children and 4,000 adults during the four years of its existence. While the percentage of Armenians and other Christians rescued and/or receiving care cannot be readily determined, in all likelihood they constituted a majority.

Outreach from Aleppo

Unlike the expanded scope of the Commission's work carried out in Constantinople, that which was conducted by the Aleppo branch dealt exclusively with the recovery and rehabilitation of Armenians in bondage. To be sure, serious complications dictated the adoption of a cautious approach to salvaging Armenian remnants in the Syrian hinterland. Muslim nomadic society, which had absorbed Armenian women and children, was reluctant to give up its coveted wartime spoil unless forced to do so. Then, with the passage of time, strong human bonds had been established between captors and captives, and between Armenian mothers and their children born of Muslim fathers. Thus, the yearning for a return to the Armenian fold had been diminished if not altogether extinguished in many a woman, who at any rate would be punished if caught running away. Others had given up all hope of freedom after being told that no Armenians were left to receive them. And children in particular had been raised as staunch Muslims akin to the fanatical "Janissaries of old."[55]

Difficulties of a political nature hampered the rescue work as well. When Karen Jeppe approached High Commissioner General Henri Gouraud for letters of recommendation to canvass the Syrian countryside in search of survivors, she was told that, "in spite of the Franco-Turkish convention, the Beduin [sic] tribes of Jezireh are sometimes brought under outside influences which excited their religious fanaticism, and that the proposed [rescue] mission would be of a nature to create a fresh ferment of anti-foreign hostility and might produce results quite contrary to those intended."[56] Therefore, the Commission "had to be very careful not to provoke an 'Armenian Question'." Indeed, "the less said about them [Armenians] the better."[57] Meanwhile, at least 30,000 Armenian women and children scattered across the French zone of occupation (minus the regions of Diarbekir, Kharpert, and Cilicia) awaited deliverance.[58]

The lack of adequate relay stations and shelters constituted another deterrent to escape from captivity. Since such facilities did not exist at the end of war, thousands of Armenians converging on Aleppo after the Mudros Armistice were compelled to return to the Muslims.[59] But things began to change because of the establishment of two outposts, one at Rakka and one at Jarablus,[60] so that by August 1922, Jeppe was able to shelter 100 persons in the League of Nations Home, dubbed "a center of refuge and moral cleansing."[61] Also known as the Reception House, the Home was situated in the vineyards of Sheikh Taha on the northern outskirts of Aleppo along the Kweik River. In 1928, that is, one year after the League dissolved the Commission, Jeppe transferred the Home to a 10,000 square meter lot in the Meidan (Nor Giugh) neighborhood of Aleppo to continue the rescue work in a private capacity.[62]

From the outset Jeppe faced financial difficulties. The 500 pounds sterling allocated to her for the first year constituted but a fraction of the total cost. Although the subsidy for 1923 trebled to 1,500 pounds, it still would not have sufficed had it not been for the contributions of such charitable organizations as the Danish Friends of Armenia Committee, the Swedish Friends of Armenia Committee, and the Armenian Red Cross of London.[63] Jeppe traveled to Geneva in the summer of 1923 on learning of "a rumor that the League of Nations was going to stop the work done there [in Aleppo] because it did not seem of sufficient importance for the League to deal with it." After stressing the indispensability of such a humanitarian endeavor, she responded to the question of whether it was worthwhile to salvage only a few while the majority would not be reached at all: "It is a very little candle, but the night is dark."[64]

Financial problems did not sidetrack the actual progress made in the field. Between August 1922 and July 1923, some 300 women and children were received at the Home, of whom 200 were returned to relatives or taught trades to become self-sufficient. The rest stayed at the Home for up to six months until they, too, could readjust to normal life. Stress was laid on the acquisition of skills to manufacture goods that would also benefit the Syrian economy. Jeppe tried hard to render the refugees economically productive as soon as possible, so that the generally poor Arab population would not consider them as an additional financial burden to the country. As a further incentive to the training program, the Danish and Swedish Friends of Armenia established an industrial department that consisted of a carpentry, a shoe making shop, a tannery, and an embroidery atelier. It was also suggested for the first time that an agricultural colony be established to help increase the produce of the country and bring "international reconciliation."[65]

Not all went well in 1923. In the spring, a fire demolished the Home. Fortunately, the mild climate allowed for the erection of tents in the adjacent lot, and a barrack was constructed in the garden across from the Home. Subsidized by the Armenian Red Cross of London, the barrack could accommodate at least 200 persons. It had two other merits. Being situated in a garden, it presented a village-like ambiance to which the inmates had been acclimatized during their captivity; an urban setting would have made the transition from rural to city life much more cumbersome. Moreover, the Commission saved money by not paying rent, which ran very high in Aleppo.[66]

The projected increase of new arrivals in the Home would cause heavy congestion, in which eventuality it would be necessary to relocate some of them elsewhere. The United States seemed to be the most logical destination, because many Armenians had relatives there. Hence, at the request of the League, the U.S. Senate considered the issue and adopted a special bill that would allow Armenian women and children from Aleppo to enter the country. The bill was then sent to the House of Representatives for similar action. The deliberations in the House, however, dragged on inconclusively. Given the isolationist impulse in the country in the 1920s, the House failed to adopt the bill in 1923.[67]

In the spring of 1924, the rescue work took a turn toward the better, primarily for two reasons. First, political stability in Syria ushered in a period of relative peace, during which both France, as the mandatory power in Syria, and the Arab government lent support to Jeppe more readily. Second, the groundwork done during the previous two years bore fruit. Statistics show that from March 1 to December 31, 1922, some 200 Armenians were rescued; from January 1 to December 31, 1923, 213 Armenians; and from January 1 to June 30, 1924, 187 Armenians, for a total of 600 persons. Of these, 359 were boys and 241 were women and girls.[68] The relatively low number of females could be explained by the difficulty encountered in leaving their Muslim harems or homes, especially if they had borne children in captivity.

The rescued originated from numerous places in Anatolia. Statistics covering the period from 1922 through May 1924 provide the following picture concerning 546 cases: 116 came from Diarbekir; 103 from Kharpert; 33 from Brusa; 33 from Mush and Bitlis; 32 from Kghi; 30 from Sivas; 28 from Palu; 27 from Erzerum; 27 from Urfa; 19 from Adiaman; 17 from Marash and Zeitun; 16 from Adana; 10 from Kayseri; 10 from Malatia; 9 from Aintab; 7 from Arabkir; 6 from Izmid; 4 from Divrig; 4 from Tekirdagh; 4 from Girasun, Ordu, and Bafra; 3 from Erzinjan; 3 from Van; 2 from Gurun; 1 from Khozat; 1 from Amasia; and 1 from Konia.[69] The fact that these localities dotted the entire span of Anatolia, from north to south and from east to west, attested to the comprehensiveness of the Armenian Genocide.

Three more stations were inaugurated in March 1924—at Deir el-Zor, Hasake (Hasiche), and Mardin. The captives arriving at those outposts did so voluntarily, without being forced by the Commission. To be sure, in some instances persuasion was applied in order to provide the slaves with additional guarantees of protection and good treatment once freed. This fear of abandonment and abuse stemmed from the tragic experiences endured during the deportations, fear that Jeppe and her associates could not alleviate instantly. Only when news got out about the well-being of liberated Armenians did many more captives become convinced of the Commission's sincere intentions. This, in turn, emboldened rescued Armenians themselves to participate in the reclamation efforts, which yielded better results.[70]

The French and Arab governments supported the stations at Deir el-Zor and Hasake by issuing permits for the inmates to reach Aleppo safely. The two governments likewise formed a committee whose task it was to examine special cases. The committee consisted of two Muslim clerics, two Christian clerics, and Krikor Haygian, the Commission's agent at Deir el-Zor. Such overt blessing notwithstanding, Jeppe and associates continued to maintain a low key to avoid antagonizing the Bedouins. By proceeding in this manner, Jeppe succeeded in gaining the cooperation of some Muslim notables.[71]

As indicated, the liberated Armenians could not stay at the Home for more than six months. Exceptions to the rule existed, especially pertaining to the sick who required extended treatment and those who for various reasons could not be released by the stated deadline. The latter could stay another three months, provided that they paid more than half of their expenses by working in a trade. The boys would then leave to start life anew, whereas the females would be turned over to their relatives, placed in respectable families as maids, or allowed to work in the Home or its embroidery department, fully paying for their expenses. These rules were explained to the inmates from the outset to avoid aimless lingering.[72]

Forty-eight percent of the recovered cases up to June 1924 eventually rejoined their kin. And since many others had somehow established contact with their relatives, Jeppe estimated that 80 percent of those rescued "*are restored to the natural family life.*" Two venues made such an accomplishment possible. First, numerous Armenians contacted the Commission in Syria inquiring about lost relatives. Second, the Commission itself continuously advertised about found persons. "And what scenes do we not witness," wrote Jeppe, "when brothers and sisters unexpectedly meet or when fathers and mothers clasp a child in their arms—a child they never thought they would see again."[73] The Commission placed fifty-eight children with no relatives in the orphanage of Near East Relief. Eventually they were transferred back to the League Home and taken care of by the Danish Friends of Armenia.[74]

Thanks to a school run by the Danes adjacent to the barrack, the inmates underwent a program of reorientation. In order "to change the inside along with the outside" of the rescued, teaching the Armenian language was imperative. Language and mathematics were taught during the day for a month after admission into the Home. Those engaged in the trades, especially the boys, continued taking evening classes, so that at the time of their release from the Home they were able to write a simple letter and do the four arithmetical operations.[75] The very young ones from both genders, who had forgotten the Armenian language and "everything else with it," attended the day school to learn additionally Armenian history and geography. At nights, they took singing lessons.[76]

In the same vein, Jeppe cooperated closely with the Armenian Prelacy of Aleppo to reestablish the national-legal identity of the liberated people. She provided the Prelacy with detailed lists that included names, surnames, parents' names, gender, age, places of origin, and so forth. The Prelacy, in turn, registered such information in the baptismal ledgers of the various churches under its jurisdiction and obtained identification papers for each rescued person from the local government. Jeppe likewise sought the services of the Apostolic Church in a bid to re-expose people under her care to their Christian faith. Given the distance of Sheikh Taha from existing places of worship in the city, priests visited the Home on Sundays to preach and console the sick; on holidays all attended church in town, sometimes led by Jeppe herself.[77] All the efforts at re-Armenianization notwithstanding, the acculturation of some children in Muslim society had been so thorough that they eventually returned to their wartime families. Such cases, however, amounted to less than 6 percent of the total reclaimed.[78]

The cost of search, rescue, and rehabilitation naturally increased with the growth of the work itself. Money spent on the recovery operations alone increased from 275 pounds sterling in 1922 to 425 pounds in 1923 and to 525 pounds up to June 1, 1924. The combined total of all activities, excluding school expenses, amounted to 5,100 pounds for the period March 1922 to July 1924. Of this sum 300 pounds were appropriated for bedding and other utilities, and the balance of 4,800 pounds was spent for the upkeep of 600 persons. Therefore, an average of 8 pounds was spent on each case, as follows: rescue work, travel, stations, and others, 2 pounds; medical care, 0.5 pound; clothing, 1.5 pounds; and board (average of four months per person), 4 pounds. The relative high cost of clothing and medical care was not surprising, given the neglected state in which the Armenians were retrieved. Clad in rags often covered with vermin, they needed new outfits without which they could not enter the Home. Similarly, having been exposed to harsh, unsanitary living conditions for many years and, in the case of females, having been subjected to rape and other unsafe sexual activities, they carried a host of eye, skin, venereal, and other diseases that required immediate attention. But the tattoos imprinted on females according to Bedouin tradition could not be eradicated with any corrosives, thereby symbolizing the permanence of the deep emotional and psychological scars left behind by the genocide. Fortunately, none of the patients in the Home died. On the contrary, all but one who suffered from incurable lunacy experienced remarkable recovery, notwithstanding the fact that some cases required extensive treatment.[79]

Despite these successes, time was running out on thousands of other captives who awaited emancipation. According to Jeppe, 5,000 to 10,000 Armenians could be saved in four or five years if 40,000 to 50,000 pounds were raised. But realizing that the League could not or would not provide such large sums for this purpose, she offered a more practical alternative—the establishment of an agricultural colony. It would be very cost-effective and the savings would be used to salvage more Armenians; it would help improve Syria's economy; and it would "build up a strong and thriving peasantry fit to understand and be understood by the native population." Despite these advantages, discussions about the colony's realization were postponed for a year.[80]

During the second half of 1924 and first half of 1925, the rescue work experienced some setbacks. Jeppe's agent at Deir el-Zor, Krikor Haygian, died of a heart disease. Since he was solely responsible for the operations in that region, his loss dealt a heavy blow. Although his widow carried on his duties for a while, the Deir el-Zor station had to be shut down once the survivors could be entrained from Hasake to Aleppo via Ras el-Ain, circumventing Deir el-Zor. But financial hardships forced the station at Hasake to close temporarily; its proximity to Mardin in Turkey—where an Armenian Catholic priest by the name of Krikor had been acting as an important rescue link—greatly facilitated the infiltration of numerous fugitives, who were now left in the cold. Vasil Sabagh, the manager at Hasake, continued to recover a few more Armenians on his own. However, he met a tragic death at the hands of Arabs, who felt that he had taken away too many Armenians from them. Sabagh's successor at the Hasake station, which reopened in late 1925, was not as productive. The Turkish-Kurdish clashes that same year further curtailed his operations by making it impossible for Armenian refugees to enter Syria via Mardin because of the closure of the border. Even so, the Commission somehow succeeded in receiving 250 survivors.[81]

The virtual standstill at the frontier now compelled Jeppe to shift focus to Syria proper, especially to "the region of Ras-el-Ain, where, in 1916, the remnants of the deportations, over 80,000 of Armenians, were slaughtered, and consequently thousands of young girls and boys were sold. Although the greatest number have been carried away to other parts of the country, it is supposed that about 2,000 are still found in the regions around or behind Ras-el-Ain."[82]

The rescue work would be facilitated by the existing regular train service between that town and Aleppo, travel safety being assured by the French military presence along the railroad. By this time, experience had taught the Commission how to find relatives in a shorter interval and/or come up with more efficient ways of training the new arrivals in a trade. For these reasons no more than 100 inmates stayed at the Home at a time. Concurrently, the Danish Friends of Armenia sent a helper by the name of Jenny Jensen to boost education in the school, oversee the industrial work, and nurse the infirm at the Home and among the Armenian refugees in general.[83]

The realization of the oft-mentioned colonization scheme was delayed by bad weather. Even so, some boys at the Home were relocated to an existing rural settlement near Rakka, called Tal Saman (Simen), where they engaged in agriculture, built cottages, and eventually got married.[84] The role of Tal Saman in the rescue work came about in the following way. The two chieftains of the influential Aneze tribe in north Syria, Hashim Pasha and Mejhim Pasha, wanted Armenian refugees to populate parts of their uncultivated domains fearful of possible French expropriations and/or other tribal encroachments. The inhabitants of Garmuj village near Urfa, who had been expelled from Turkey in 1924, would be ideal settlers. The two chieftains successfully negotiated with Jeppe and her adopted son, Misak Melkonian, to establish the desired village. Besides his duties as its headman, Melkonian led a team of armed Armenian and Arab horsemen that embarked on search and rescue expeditions in the contiguous areas, sometimes penetrating Turkish territory. The municipality at Tal Saman thus functioned as a relay station as well, and the village itself hosted a number of inmates from the Aleppo Home. The municipality also served as a school, where children studied Armenian and mathematics during the day, and adults studied at night. Saturday evenings were reserved for singing and Armenian history, and Sunday mornings for Bible study under the guidance of visiting priests.[85]

But agricultural expansion could not come about by a single settlement. Many more would be needed because "it is very important that there should be an *Armenian population to which our young people can adhere.*" As 10,000 pounds would suffice to start a colony, Jeppe once again implored the League for its approval of the scheme:

> Nothing could possibly be more encouraging and helpful to the people of Syria than the League of Nations manifesting its confidence in the future of Syria by inaugurating a conspicuous colonisation scheme. Everybody knows that the future of Syria depends upon an intense cultivation of her fertile soil, but for this a stronger feeling of confidence must be created. The capital hangs on in the cities, where it cannot even be fully utilised, and the people are crowding together there seeking employment in vain, while the land is waiting for capital and the workers to come. It is a very distressing situation, but, if the means were available, much might be done.[86]

On September 5, 1925, the Eighth Meeting (public) of the Council considered the issue. French representative and President Paul Painlevé let it be known that such a project required his country's supervision. France, he said, would always extend its patronage and aid to Jeppe's work. "It should be clearly understood, however, that in a mandated territory only the mandatory Power could assume the supervision over all the social work being carried out throughout that territory; in particular, that Power must be careful to ensure that persons pursuing work of this kind, however well-intentioned, should not exceed their mission and encroach upon the administrative or economic domain." Clearly, "this was in the interests of good administration, so that there should be no contradiction between the work of private individuals and that carried on by the Government of the mandatory Power."[87] That understanding ultimately resulted in the establishment of two colonies for rescued Armenians by 1926, one called Tal Arman (Armenian Hill) at Kherbet el-Rez, not far from Tal Saman along the Balikh River, and one called Charb (Sharb) Bedros, north of Tal Saman.[88] It was hoped that, "when these little colonies are more developed and consolidated, they will to a certain degree be able to replace the stations and the Reception House when the latter cease to exist."[89]

During the year following July 1925, as many as 300 Armenians were rescued. They emerged from among three groups. The first was a gypsy gang that included two "dancing girls"; they were freed by force. The second consisted of certain marauding Bedouin tribes, which appeared at particular intervals; the Commission would send agents in search of Armenians as the tribes surfaced. Kurdish *ashiret*s (tribes) fleeing persecution in Turkey constituted the third group. During the winter of 1925-26, as many such tribes took refuge in Syria, albeit temporarily, a "unique opportunity" arose for Armenians forcibly cohabiting with the Kurds to be liberated. Since a significant number of the captors were killed during the Turkish-

Kurdish fights, the task of reclamation became easier. A station at Arab Punar investigated the incoming Kurdish refugees mainly.[90]

Two new stations, those of Bab and Munbij, had a different mission: to search for and free Armenian remnants in the area west of the Euphrates River, which hitherto had not been explored duly. Even though the majority of captive Armenians in the Near East had been assimilated in Muslim society, Jeppe wanted "to leave no stone unturned and *to make sure that at least within Syrian territory no Christians are detained among Moslems without their own free consent, and that the opportunity of returning to their people has been offered to every one of them.*"[91] Another station could be opened in Nisibin in 1926, but "our experience in our old areas have shown us that a station which can only be kept open one year does more harm than good. It not only incurs great expense, but, in addition, it creates interest and awakens expectations in the minds of many people whom in such a limited time it is not able to rescue, and who would be left unhappier than they were before."[92]

Jeppe was reluctant to inaugurate a new station, because in 1926 the Assembly resolved "that the mission for the rescue of women and children...shall be prolonged for [only] one year more" and that Jeppe herself was "of [the] opinion that her task will be discharged during the coming year." And indeed, the League dissolved the Aleppo branch of the Commission of Inquiry after December 1927. But since Jeppe was determined to continue her mission in a private capacity, the League, as in Constantinople, allowed her to use its property for another year.[93] The League's decision to close down the Aleppo branch came under criticism. The representative of Norway expressed skepticism as to whether "utterances" of appreciation made to Jeppe without substance "would suffice to preserve, for so much as one single day, the existence...of the Armenians."[94] In turn, the representative of Great Britain elected to "pass over the anomalous position that the League of Nations will get the palm without the dust."[95] And the representative of Australia commented: "Huge sums were voted for organisation and for propaganda, but nothing for those things which touched the very heart and conscience of the masses of the people. It was the smaller matters—particularly the work of the women—that constituted the most fruitful propaganda the League could devise."[96]

In her final report to Geneva, dated May 31, 1927, Karen Jeppe summed up the Commission's five-year accomplishments as follows: A total of 1,600 Armenians had been recovered, of whom 1,400 had entered the Home. An additional 200 persons had been reclaimed in collaboration with relatives.[97] "We do not doubt that," Jeppe remarked, "*as far as Syrian territory* [excluding the region around Nisibin] *is concerned*, practically all the deported women and children, detained since the war against their will among the Moslems, will have been offered an opportunity to return to their own people, before, *in December* 1927, *we finally close the stations,*" adding: "*Those who remain have chosen to stay.* They mostly consist of women who have given birth to children, whom naturally they cannot leave."[98] Thirteen percent of the rescued were girls or young women over eleven at the time of their enslavement in 1915. Nearly all were violated upon abduction. Most who expressed willingness to return to the Armenian fold had children from prewar marriages. Seventeen percent were six- to eleven-year-old girls in 1915. They were treated by their captors relatively well as "children of the house" and eventually "sold in marriage." Therefore the harm had already been done. Thirty-seven percent were six- to twelve-year-old boys in 1915; boys over twelve were killed with the men. Having been utilized as slaves, they expressed readiness to be freed. Fifteen percent were four- to six-year-old boys in 1915. As such, they needed much help in learning about their national origins. And the remaining 18 percent were boys under four in 1915. Since their link with the past had completely vanished, and because they were manipulated "for immoral purposes," they had to be rescued with the assistance of relatives or acquaintances, sometimes by force.[99]

"From the very beginning," Jeppe went on to say, "our sole strength was *the righteousness of the cause* and *the atmosphere of confidence* we created around us." With the passage of time, "*the leading men among those who detained these people began to realise that they* [Armenians] *had a right to return to their families, and that it was our duty to protect them and to help them on.*" As a result, "we have…tried not to break up friendly relations or to disturb family life…. *We have rescued only those who could not adapt themselves to this life and so were profoundly unhappy.*" This accounted "for the comparatively small number rescued." Had the Commission been "unscrupulous, we could have had very different figures to show."

But "as it is, we know that, *although the scope of our work has been limited, within those limits it has done nothing but good.*"[100]

Conclusion

The full extent of the quantitative and qualitative damages caused by the Armenian Genocide is still under investigation. Indeed, no attempt at understanding or comprehending this human tragedy can ever do justice to what befell the Armenian people during and after World War I. Notwithstanding, a comprehensive assessment of the causes, processes, and consequences of mass murder is necessary for historical, political, retributive, restitutive, and preventive purposes, not to mention countless other reasons. Exposing the fate of Armenian women and children absorbed by Muslim society in Anatolia and the Arab Near East constitutes an important component within the overall framework of genocide study.

This chapter has examined the League of Nation's involvement in the reclamation of survivors held captive among Turks, Kurds, Arabs, and other Muslims. The League formed a Commission of Inquiry for the Protection of Women and Children in the Near East to deal with the reclamation of enslaved Armenians and others, emphasizing strict impartiality and the avoidance of politics. The Commission consisted of two branches, those of Constantinople and Aleppo. As per League instructions, the Constantinople branch used a wider compass to accommodate any ethnic group, including Turks, although the bulk of beneficiaries seemed to be Armenians and other Christians. The Aleppo branch, on the other hand, focused its attention exclusively on Armenians.

These somewhat divergent approaches between the two branches beg an explanation. Differences in the personalities of commissioners Kennedy, Cushman, and Jeppe could not have played a role, because all three were dedicated humanitarians intimately familiar with the plight of the Armenian people. The answer may lie in location and politics. Constantinople was the cosmopolitan capital of the Ottoman Empire, a center of a kaleidoscope of people, and a hub of international political-economic rivalry. Therefore, any activity there, especially by no less a body than the League of Nations, would be carefully watched through the magnifying glass. This was also a time of transition from the Ottoman Empire to the Turkish republic, whereby the European powers, some of the very constituent members of the League, positioned themselves to curry favor with the emergent regime. Aleppo, on the other hand, while a regional center of inland trade, certainly did not match up with Constantinople in importance. Equally significant, as part of Syria, Aleppo and the outlying districts were under French mandate as sanctioned by the League of Nations. With such a defined sphere of influence, there seemed to be no outside force (perhaps with the exception of Turkey) desirous to control or coveting Aleppo and north Syria in general. And while cognizant of political realities in Syria as related to indigenous aspirations and agitation, the French for the most part supported the Commission's exclusive embrace of the Armenian cause.

The League clearly stated that it would fully fund the Commission. But as the work progressed, the League began to distance itself from its financial obligations, instead asking individual states and philanthropic organizations to carry the burden. Despite the criticism leveled by certain members at this about-face, the League terminated its association with the reclamation effort, after supporting it for four years in Constantinople and five years in Aleppo.

All said, the League made two important contributions. First, it liberated and returned several thousand Armenians to their people, who were badly decimated as a result of the genocide and thus needed regeneration. Indeed, the rescue work in Syria continued without the League through the rest of the 1920s and the first half of the 1930s by Karen Jeppe and associates, the British Friends of Armenia, and the Syrian Armenian Relief Society. An additional number of slaves was thus emancipated, although the overwhelming majority remained permanently in Muslim hands in Turkey, Greater Syria, and Mesopotamia. Second, being the international body of nations between the two world wars, and as the precursor to the modern United Nations, the League's findings add weight to at least the slavery aspect of the Armenian Genocide, although the term "genocide" had not yet been coined at the time.

Notes

1. For the fate of women and children during the Armenian Genocide, see Donald E. Miller and Lorna Touryan Miller, *Survivors: An Oral History of the Armenian Genocide* (Berkeley, Los Angeles, London: University of California Press, 1993), pp. 94-117; Richard G. Hovannisian, "Intervention and Shades of Altruism during the Armenian Genocide," in Richard G. Hovannisian, ed., *The Armenian Genocide:*

History, Politics, Ethics (New York: St. Martin's Press, 1992), pp. 173-207; Yair Auron, *The Banality of Indifference: Zionism & the Armenian Genocide* (New Brunswick, NJ and London: Transaction Publishers, 2000), pp. 68-69. For descriptions of life in captivity among Muslims by Armenian survivors themselves, see Agheten Veraproghner [Survivors of the Catastrophe], *1915: Aghet ev veradznund* [1915: Catastrophe and Rebirth] (Paris: Araks Press, 1952); idem, *Ter-Zor* [Deir el-Zor] (Paris: P. Elekian Press, 1955).

2. The rescue attempts at the end of World War I are treated in Ruben Herian, "Hay aghchikner arabneru tunerun mech" [Armenian Girls in the Homes of Arabs], *Hayastani Kochnak* [Clarion of Armenia] 19:35 (Aug. 30, 1919): 1122-23; Maritsa Chopurian, "Miatini jambordutiuns (1919 hunis 17-i oragires endorinakvats)" [My Trip to Miyadin (Copied from My Diary of June 17, 1919)], *Hayastani Kochnak* 19:36 (Sept. 6, 1919): 1148-50; Madteos M. Eplighatian, *Azgayin khnamatarutiun: Endhanur teghekagir arachin vetsamsia 1 mayis 1919 -31 hoktember 1919* [National Caretaking Agency: General Report for the First Six Months, May 1, 1919-October 31, 1919], 2d ed., preface by Catholicos Garegin II (Antelias, Lebanon: Catholicosate of Cilicia, 1985), pp. 82-87; Archbishop Zaven [Ter-Eghiayan], *Patriarkakan hushers: Vaveragirner ev vkayutiunner* [My Patriarchal Memoirs: Documents and Testimonies] (Cairo: Nor Astgh, 1947), pp. 287-98; Stanley E. Kerr, *The Lions of Marash: Personal Experiences with American Near East Relief, 1919-1922* (Albany, NY: State University of New York Press, 1973), pp. 43-48; Lawrence Diran Cretan, "The Armenian Remnants in Turkey, 1918-1923," seminar paper, University of California, Los Angeles, March 1976, pp. 13-18; Levon Marashlian, "Finishing the Genocide: Cleansing Turkey of Armenian Survivors, 1920-1923," in Richard G. Hovannisian, ed., *Remembrance and Denial: The Case of the Armenian Genocide* (Detroit: Wayne State University Press, 1998), pp. 120-22.
3. League of Nations, *The Records of the First Assembly: Meetings of the Committees* (Geneva: [League of Nations], 1920), Annex 25, pp. 261-62.
4. Ibid., p. 262.
5. Ibid., p. 263.
6. Ibid., p. 163.
7. Ibid., p. 263.
8. League of Nations, *The Records of the First Assembly: Plenary Meetings (Meetings Held from the 15th of November to the 18th of December 1920)* (Geneva: [League of Nations], 1920), p. 546; League of Nations, *Resolutions Adopted by the Assembly during Its First Session (November 15th to December 18th 1920)* (Lausanne: Imp. Réunies, S.A., [1920]), p. 21.
9. *Records of the First Assembly: Plenary Meetings*, pp. 546-47.
10. Ibid., pp. 548-49.
11. Ibid., pp. 548-51.
12. League of Nations, *The Records of the Second Assembly: Plenary Meetings (Meetings Held from the 5th of September to the 5th of October 1921)* (Geneva: [League of Nations], 1921), p. 121.
13. League of Nations, *Official Journal*, 2d year, no. 2 (March-April 1921), pp. 118-19.
14. Ibid., p. 119.
15. Ibid., no. 3 (May 1921), p. 294, and no. 5-6 (July-Aug 1921), p. 606.
16. Armenian Revolutionary Federation Archives, Boston (now Watertown), Massachusetts, File 158/57 *H.H. Patvirakutiun, 1921 t.* [R(epublic) of A(rmenia) Delegation, 1921], Vahan Papazian to Sir Eric Drummond, Feb. 28, 1921.

17. Ibid., Drummond to Papazian, March 10, 1921.
18. James Levy Barton, *The Story of Near East Relief (1915-1930): An Interpretation* (New York: Macmillan, 1930), p. 68.
19. League of Nations, *The Records of the Second Assembly: Meetings of the Committees,* II, Annex 16 (Geneva: [League of Nations], 1921), pp. 481-82.
20. Hakob Cholakian, *Karen Eppe hay goghgotayin ev veratsnundin het* [Karen Jeppe with the Armenian Calvary and Rebirth] (Aleppo: Arevelk Press, 2001), pp. 5-48; Hebe Spaull, *Women Peace-Makers* (London: George G. Harrap & Co., 1924), pp. 51-59; Ida Alamuddin, *Papa Kuenzler and the Armenians* (London: Heinmann, 1970), pp. 43, 65, 74-80; Sv. Cedegreen Bech, "Karen Jeppe," *Dansk Biografisk Leksikon* 7 (Copenhagen: Gyldendal, 1981): 340-41; Armenian Red Cross and Refugee Fund (ARCRF), *Seventh Annual Report* ([London]: n.p., 1921), p. 10; *Piunik* [Phoenix] (Beirut), July 19, 1924.
21. League of Nations, *Official Journal,* Special Supplement No. 23: *Records of the Fifth Assembly: Text of the Debates* (Geneva: [League of Nations], 1924), p. 164; League of Nations, *Work of the Commission for the Protection of Women and Children in the Near East*, A.69.1923.IV (Geneva: Imp. Jent, S.A., 1923), p. 1; League of Nations, Assembly, Fifth Committee, *Protection of Women and Children in the Near East: Report Submitted to the Assembly by the Fifth Committee,* A.103.1923.IV (Geneva: Imp. Albert Kundig, 1923), pp. 1-2; League of Nations, *The Records of the Third Assembly: Meetings of the Committees: Minutes of the Fifth Committee (Social and General Questions)*, Annex 16 (Geneva: [League of Nations], 1922), pp. 136-37; *First Assembly: Plenary Meetings*, p. 547.
22. *Official Journal*, 2d year, no. 10-12 (Dec. 1921), p. 1088.
23. Ibid.
24. Ibid., p. 1089.
25. Ibid.
26. Ibid.
27. Ibid., pp. 1089-90.
28. Ibid., p. 1090.
29. Ibid.
30. Ibid., p. 1091.
31. Ibid., pp. 1091-92.
32. *Second Assembly: Meetings of the Committees*, II, Annex 16, pp. 474-75.
33. League of Nations, *Official Journal*, Special Supplement No. 6*: Resolutions and Recommendations Adopted by the Assembly during Its Second Session (September 5th to October 5th, 1921)* (Lausanne: Imp. Réunies, 1921), p. 33.
34. *Third Assembly: Meetings of the Committees*, Annex 7, p. 113; League of Nations, *The Records of the Third Assembly: Plenary Meetings*, II, Annexes: *Reports on the Work of the Council and Reports Adopted by the Assembly* (Geneva: [League of Nations], 1922), p. 80; *Official Journal*, 3d year, no. 6 (June 1922), p. 525; Annex 341, p. 608; no. 8, part 2 (Aug. 1922), Annex 371, p. 832. For the duties of the chief commissioner, see *Official Journal*, 2d year, no. 10-12 (Dec. 1921), p. 69.
35. Archives of the American Board of Commissioners for Foreign Missions, Houghton Library, Harvard University, Cambridge, Massachusetts, ABC: 3.2, vol. 359, Ernest W. Riggs to District Secretary, Jan. 28, 1922.
36. Ibid., James L. Barton to Dr. Sproule, Feb. 2, 1922.
37. Parliament of the Commonwealth of Australia, *League of Nations: Third Assembly (September 4th-September 30th, 1922): Report of the Australian Delegates* (State of Victoria: Albert J. Mullett, 1923), p. 19; League of Nations, *Third Assembly: Meetings of the Committees*, Annex 7, pp. 113-14.

38. *Third Assembly: Meetings of the Committees*, Annex 7, pp. 113-14.
39. Ibid.
40. Ibid., Annex 8, p. 33.
41. Ibid., pp. 32-33 in regular text (not annex); League of Nations *Official Journal,* Special Supplement No. 9*: Resolutions and Recommendations Adopted by the Assembly during Its Third Session (September 4th to 30th, 1922)* (Lausanne: Imp. Réunies S.A., 1922), p. 32. It should be noted that Cecil Harmsworth, the representative of the British Empire on the League Council, in his January 13, 1922 report to the Council on the "Proposed Enquiry by the Chief Commissioner of the League in Constantinople into the Atrocities Committed by Turks and Greeks in the Near East," had made the following proposal: "That Dr. Peet's services should be utilised if the case unfortunately arises and it becomes necessary to investigate future accusations with regard to atrocities which may be committed either by the Turkish or non-Turkish authorities in Asia Minor and adjacent countries." See *Official Journal*, 3d year, no. 2 (Feb. 1922), Annex 308, pp. 171-73. Concurring with Harmsworth, the Council had adopted the following draft resolution: "The Council of the League of Nations, having heard with great concern the various reports of excesses alleged to have been committed both by Turkish and non-Turkish inhabitants in Turkish and Greek territories, instructs the Commissioner of the League at Constantinople to investigate any report of atrocities committed in those territories in the future, and to report to the Council thereon." See p. 106 in regular text (not annex). That responsibility must have fallen on the shoulders of Dr. Kennedy, who, upon Dr. Peet's refusal to accept the position of Chief Commissioner, assumed that role.
42. *Official Journal*, 4th year, no. 3 (March 1923), Annex 451, p. 278; League of Nations, *The Records of the Fourth Assembly: Text of the Debates* (Geneva: [League of Nations], 1923), p. 266.
43. *Work of the Commission*, A.69.1923.IV, pp. 1-2; *Official Journal*, 4th year, no. 11 (Nov. 1923), Annex 547, pp. 1374-75.
44. *Fourth Assembly: Text of the Debates*, p. 111. See also League of Nations, *The Records of the Fourth Assembly: Meetings of the Committees: Minutes of the Fifth Committee* (Geneva: [League of Nations], 1923), p. 19.
45. League of Nations, *The Records of the Fourth Assembly: Meetings of the Committees: Minutes of the Fourth Committee (Budget and Financial Questions)* (Geneva: [League of Nations], 1923), p. 296.
46. *Official Journal*, 5th year, no. 10 (Oct. 1924), Annex 664, pp. 1442-43.
47. Ibid., p. 1288; Annex 659a, p. 1391; League of Nations, *Official Journal,* Special Supplement No. 28: *The Records of the Fifth Assembly: Meetings of the Committees: Minutes of the Fifth Committee (General and Humanitarian Questions)* (Geneva: [League of Nations], 1924), Annex 10, pp. 46-47, 105.
48. *Official Journal*, 6th year, no. 10 (Oct. 1925), Annex 791a, p. 1451.
49. Ibid., Annex 791, p. 1448.
50. Ibid., Annex 791a, p. 1451.
51. Ibid., pp. 1451-52.
52. Ibid., pp. 1339, 1403, and Annex 812, p. 1538; League of Nations, Special Supplement No. 33: *Records of the Sixth Assembly: Text of the Debates* (Geneva: [League of Nations], 1925), pp. 134-35; League of Nations, *Verbatim Record of the Sixth Assembly of the League of Nations: Seventh Plenary Meeting, Friday, September 25th, 1925, at 3:30 p.m.* (Geneva: "Tribune de Genève," 1925), p. 9; League of Nations, *Official Journal,* Special Supplement No. 32: *Resolutions and Recommendations Adopted by the Assembly during Its Sixth Session (September 7th to 26th, 1925)* (Geneva: Imp. Albert Kundig, 1925), p. 26; League of Nations, Sixth Assem-

bly, *Protection of Women and Children in the Near East: Resolutions Proposed by the Fifth Committee and Adopted by the Assembly on September 25th, 1925 (Afternoon)*, A.141.1925.IV (Geneva: Imp. Jent, S.A., 1925), p. 1.

53. League of Nations, *Report of the Commission for the Protection of Women and Children in the Near East: Report from July 1st, 1925 to June 30th, 1926*, A.25.1926.IV (Geneva: Imp. d'Ambilly, 1926), p. 3.
54. Ibid.; League of Nations, Assembly, Fifth Committee, *Protection of Women and Children in the Near East: Report of the Fifth Committee to the Assembly*, A.106.1926 (Geneva: Imp. Jent, S.A., 1926), p. 2; *Official Journal*, Special Supplement No. 58: *Records of the Eighth Ordinary Session of the Assembly: Meetings of the Committees: Minutes of the Fourth Committee (Budget and Financial Questions)* (Geneva: [League of Nations], 1927), pp. 38-40.
55. Karen Jeppe, "Prisoners of War Not Yet Rescued: The League of Nations at Work in Syria," *Friend of Armenia*, n.s., Third Quarter, no. 96 (1925): 9-10. See also First Quarter, no. 90 (1924): 11.
56. *Third Assembly: Meetings of the Committees*, p. 115.
57. Great Britain, Public Record Office, Foreign Office Archives (FO) 371/9098, file pp. 182-83, League of Nations, "The Work of the League of Nations among the Deported Women and Children in Syria and Mesopotamia," n.d.
58. Ibid.; *Third Assembly: Meetings of the Committees*, pp. 114-15; ARCRF, *Seventh Annual Report*, p. 11.
59. *Third Assembly: Meetings of the Committees*, p. 114.
60. *Piunik*, July 19, 1924.
61. *Third Assembly: Meetings of the Committees*, p. 115.
62. Cholakian, *Karen Eppe*, p. 55. For details about the Home, see *Friend of Armenia*, Fourth Quarter, no. 97 (1925): 12.
63. *Third Assembly: Meetings of the Committees*, p. 115.
64. Rachel E. Crowdy, "'Am I My Brother's Keeper?' League of Nations Strives to Answer Questions," *League of Nations News* 3:55 (July 1926): 3-4.
65. *Work of the Commission*, A.69.1923.IV, p. 2. See also *Piunik*, July 19, 1924.
66. *Work of the Commission*, A.69.1923.IV, pp. 2-3; *Fourth Assembly: Text of the Debates*, p. 320; *Official Journal*, 4th year, no. 11 (Nov. 1923), Annex 547a, p. 1376; ARCRF, *Ninth Annual Report* ([London]: n.p., 1923), pp. 9-10.
67. *Fourth Assembly: Meetings of the Committees*, pp. 19-21; *Protection of Women and Children*, A.103.1923.IV, p. 1.
68. *Work of the Commission*, A.69.1923.IV, p. 2.
69. *Piunik*, July 23, 1924.
70. *Official Journal*, 5th year, no. 10, Annex 664, pp. 1443-44. See also *Friend of Armenia*, First Quarter, no. 90 (1924): 11.
71. Ibid.; *Piunik*, July 19, 1924. For the improving relations between the Armenians and Arabs, see also League of Nations, *Verbatim Record of the Fifth Assembly of the League of Nations: Twentieth Plenary Meeting, Thursday, September 25th, 1924, at 4 p.m.* (Geneva: "Tribune de Genève," [1924]), p. 9.
72. *Official Journal*, 5th year, no. 10, p. 1444.
73. Ibid. See also Cholakian, *Karen Eppe*, pp. 55, 58.
74. *Official Journal*, 5th year, no. 10, Annex 664, p. 1445.
75. *Piunik*, July 23, 1924.
76. Ibid.; *Official Journal*, 5th year, no. 10, Annex 664, p. 1445; Spaull, *Women Peace-Makers*, pp. 59-60.
77. Cholakian, *Karen Eppe*, pp. 64-91.
78. *Official Journal*, 5th year, no. 10, Annex 664, p. 1445.

79. Ibid.; Spaull, *Women Peace-Makers*, p. 60; ARCRF, *Ninth Annual Report*, p. 8; *Slave Market News* 1:11 (July 1926): 4-5, and *Supplement to the Slave Market News* (Jan. 1926), copies in Foreign Office Archives, 371/11545, E4504/663/44; *Slave Market News* 1:14 (April 1927): 3-4, copy in FO 371/12331, E2157/2157/44; Emily Robinson to Ronald McNeill, M.P., Under Secretary of State, FO, April 8, 1925, in FO 371/10864, E3315/228/44. An official at the Foreign Office, G. W. Rendel, was skeptical about information concerning tattoos published in an unspecified issue (1925?) of the *Slave Market News*. Considering the pamphlet "of no importance" and the evidence therein "of no value," he wrote: "It contained photographs of Armenian refugee girls with marks on their foreheads & faces (which appeared to have been drawn in on the negatives)." See FO 371/10864, E1490/228/44, Rendel minutes, March 10, 1925, also signed by L. Oliphant. For the health conditions of Armenian refugees (including liberated captives) in Aleppo at the end of World War I, see George Lyman Richards, ed., *The Medical Work of the Near East Relief: A Review of Its Accomplishments in Asia Minor and the Caucasus during 1919-20* (New York: Near East Relief, 1923), pp. 19-23.
80. *Official Journal*, 5th year, no. 10, Annex 664, p. 1446. The estimate of 5,000 to 10,000 Armenians was later scaled down to 2,000 for them to have a realistic chance of rescue within two to three years. See *Verbatim Record of the Sixth Assembly*, p. 10.
81. *Official Journal*, 6th year, no. 10, pp. 1448-49. For the Mardin station, see *Piunik*, July 19, 1924. For the deaths of Haygian and Sabagh, see also *Friend of Armenia*, Fourth Quarter, no. 101 (1926): 12.
82. *Official Journal*, 6th year, no. 10, p. 1449.
83. Ibid., p. 1450.
84. Ibid. See also S. S. Manukian, "Tel Samende Ermeniler" [The Armenians at Tal Saman], *Rahniuma* 7:34 (Sept. 12, 1925): 534-35.
85. Cholakian, *Karen Eppe*, pp. 51, 53-54, 58, 121, 126. See also FO 371/10864, E4833/228/44, Hough to FO, Aug. 16, 1925. For the expulsion of the inhabitants of Garmuj village from Turkey, see also United States, National Archives, Record Group 59, 867.4016/973, Aleppo Consul Parker W. Buhrman to Secretary of State, March 11, 1924. The incursions of Melkonian's team into Turkey were the exception, as deduced from the following statement: "These [Commission of Inquiry] agents seldom or never cross the Turkish frontier. Their work is carried on within [French] mandated territory [in Syria]." See *Verbatim Record of the Sixth Assembly*, p. 9.
86. *Official Journal*, 6th year, no. 10, p. 1450.
87. Ibid., p. 1339. See also League of Nations, Assembly, Fifth Committee, *Protection of Women and Children in the Near East: Report of the Fifth Committee to the Sixth Assembly*, A.111.1925.IV (Geneva: Imp. Jent, S.A., 1925), pp. 1-2; Parliament of the Commonwealth of Australia, *League of Nations: Seventh Assembly (6th September to 25th September, 1926): Report of the Australian Delegation* (State of Victoria: H.J. Green, 1927), pp. 60-61.
88. Cholakian, *Karen Eppe*, pp. 110-22. For life at Charb Bedros and other sites, see League of Nations, *Report of the Commission for the Protection of Women and Children in the Near East from July 1st, 1925, to June 30th, 1926*, A.25.1926.IV (Geneva: Imp. d'Ambilly, 1926), pp. 2-3. For the understanding between the Commission and the French, see League of Nations, *Official Journal*, Special Supplement No. 44: *Records of the Seventh Ordinary Session of the Assembly: Text of the Debates* (Geneva: [League of Nations], 1926), p. 139.
89. *Official Journal*, Special Supplement No. 49: *Records of the Seventh Ordinary Session of the Assembly: Meetings of the Committees: Minutes of the Fifth Commit-*

tee (General and Humanitarian Questions), A.V/14.1926, Annex 4b (Geneva: [League of Nations], 1926), p. 101; Parliament of the Commonwealth of Australia, *League of Nations: Seventh Assembly*, p. 61.

90. *Report of the Commission*, A.25.1926.IV, pp. 1-2; *Protection of Women and Children*, A.106.1926, p. 1; Parliament of the Commonwealth of Australia, *League of Nations: Seventh Assembly*, p. 61.
91. *Report of the Commission*, A.25.1926.IV, p. 2.
92. Ibid., p. 3.
93. League of Nations, Seventh Ordinary Session of the Assembly, *Protection of Women and Children in the Near East: Resolutions Adopted by the Assembly at Its Meeting Held on September 25th, 1926 (Afternoon)*, A.127.1926.IV (Geneva: Imp. Jent, S.A., 1926), p. 1; *Official Journal*, Special Supplement No. 44, p. 139, No. 49, p. 40; *Official Journal*, Special Supplement No. 59: *Records of the Eighth Ordinary Session of the Assembly: Meetings of the Committees of the Fifth Committee (General and Humanitarian Questions)* (Geneva: [League of Nations], 1927), p. 11, and Annex 1, p. 50; League of Nations, *Verbatim Record of the Eighth Ordinary Session of the Assembly of the League of Nations: Fifteenth Plenary Meeting, Tuesday, September 12th* [should be 20th], *1927, at 10 a.m.* ([Geneva: "Tribune de Genève," 1927]), p. 8.
94. League of Nations, *Official Journal*, Special Supplement No. 48: *Records of the Seventh Ordinary Session of the Assembly: Meetings of the Committees: Minutes of the Fourth Committee (Budget and Financial Questions)* (Geneva: [League of Nations], 1926), p. 57.
95. *Official Journal*, Special Supplement No. 44, p. 139.
96. *Official Journal*, Special Supplement No. 48, p. 63.
97. League of Nations, *Report of the Commission for the Protection of Women and Children in the Near East: Aleppo, July 1st, 1926-June 30th, 1927*, A.29.1927.IV (Geneva: Imp. Kundig, 1927), p. 2. It was estimated that about 75 percent of the total reclaimed rejoined their relatives.
98. Ibid., p. 1.
99. Ibid., pp. 3-4.
100. Ibid., p. 3.

6

Bitter-Sweet Memories: The Last Generation of Ottoman Armenians

Richard G. Hovannisian

The last generation of Armenians born in the Ottoman Empire was virtually eliminated in the period between the empire's entry into World War I in 1914 and the proclamation of the Republic of Turkey in 1923. By the latter date, less than 5 percent of that generation remained within the borders of Turkey. All the rest either had perished through outright massacre and death marches or else had been driven into permanent exile.

The affected generation was never able to comprehend fully what had occurred or the reasons for their victimization. The absolute disruption of a way of life caused unending bewilderment and bitterness. Moreover, the trauma was compounded by the lack of acts of contrition and redemption by the perpetrator side. At a time when the treatment of traumatic and post-traumatic stress was only just evolving, the survivors tried to cope in various ways ranging from tight repression of memory to obsessive recounting of their tribulations. Donald and Lorna Miller have categorized survivor responses into the five overlapping categories of reconciliation, resignation, repression, revenge, and rage.[1] These categories are fluid, for even those who find solace in religious conviction and who profess forgiveness and reconciliation bristle with resentment and outrage when speaking about lost loved ones and the horrendous scenes of which they had been a part. The UCLA Armenian Oral History collection was initiated in the 1970s when the reality was brought home that the last generation of Ottoman (Western) Armenians was rapidly disappearing. With it were being lost firsthand memories of life before the genocide—town and country, family and community, church and school, games and holidays, marketplace and workshop, intra- and inter-racial and religious relations—as well as the details of the sudden disruption, prolonged agony, occasional life-saving intervention, and ultimate rescue and revival.

The UCLA collection has now grown to more than 800 taped audio interviews, averaging two hours, with some as long as five to eight hours in duration. The interviews are of mixed quality, as they were conducted by students, some of whom were excellent questioners whereas others could do little more than allow the interviewees to tell their individual stories without much additional inquiry. As a whole, the collection contains invaluable information and detail. This is all the more the case in view of the fact that few of the interviewees are now alive.

The pool of interviewees includes individuals born throughout the Ottoman Empire, from the European shores at Rodosto (Tekirdagh) and Constantinople (Istanbul) to the nearer Asiatic districts such as (names given here in the form used by survivors or in common usage at the time) Brusa, Banderma, Izmid, Bardizag, Adabazar, Bilejik, and Sogut; the whole of Anatolia, where Armenians constituted a relatively small percentage of the population and lived intermixed as an ethno-religious minority in places such as Eskishehir, Kutahia, Afion-Karahisar, Konia, Karabunar, Nigde, Ayash, Chankiri, Yozgat, Boghazliyan, Kirshehir, Kastamuni, and Kayseri (Kesaria; Caesarea); all along the seacoasts from Selefke and Adalia to Smyrna (Izmir), the Dardanelles, Zonguldak, Samsun, Unieh, Ordu, Kerasond, Trebizond, and Rize; and the greater Cilician region that included the then-large *vilayet* or province of Adana (with districts such as Hajin, Sis, Mersina, Osmaniye, and Dort Yol) and the contiguous counties (*sanjak*s) of Marash, Aintab, and Alexandretta. To the east of these regions lay the six vilayets of "Turkish Armenia," that is, Sivas (Sebastia), Kharput (Kharpert) or Mamuret ul-Aziz, Erzerum (Karin), Bitlis (Baghesh), Diarbekir (Tigranakert), and Van. These six large provinces encompassed rather disparate districts. For example, Sivas took in the areas of Chorum, Marsovan, Amasia, Tokat, Shabin-Karahisar, Divrig, Zara, Gemerek, and Gurun. Kharput/Kharpert also incorporated Malatia, Adiaman, Charsanjak, Chemeshgedzak, Agn (Egin), and Arabkir, while the Erzerum vilayet extended from Kemakh and Erzinjan to Mamakhatun, Baiburt

(Baberd), Kghi, Khnus, Tortum, Alashkert, and Bayazid. The UCLA collection also includes a sizable number of natives of the northern Iranian districts of Tabriz, Khoi, Salmast, and Urmia, an area that was subjected to invasion and massacre in 1914-15 and again in 1918. Besides this main collection of 800 interviews, there are some fifty interviews with children of survivors, which might serve as a basis to assess trans-generational memory and trauma as well as the degree of distancing from and depersonalization of the calamity.

The fact that the survival rate of Armenians from the Cilicia region was much higher than that of persons born in the eastern provinces of Turkish Armenia is reflected in the geographic breakdown of the collection. There are, for example, fewer than fifteen interviews with natives of the Bitlis vilayet (Bitlis, Mush, Sasun, and Sghert or Siirt) as compared with some seventy for the city of Aintab alone and more than 200 for greater Cilicia as a whole. It is well documented that most of the Armenian population of the Bitlis region was massacred outright without regard to age and sex, so that there were few deportation caravans from the area and the death rate was higher here than in any other province. One might argue that relocation patterns in California might have affected this ratio, in that many people who moved to Southern California from the Middle East during the closing decades of the twentieth century were natives of Cilicia and lived much of their lives in Syria, Lebanon, or Egypt. Still, there has been such massive immigration to California from diasporan communities around the world and from Armenia itself that a relatively reliable, though unscientific, correlation between survival ratios and geographic origins might be deduced from the UCLA collection.

This point having been made, other factors, too, must be considered. Unlike the pattern of decimation in Bitlis province, the process of destruction was by and large consistent in most other regions of the Ottoman Empire—segregation and mass killing of community leaders and the adult male population, followed by the deportation in caravans (*barkhana*) of the women, children, and elderly toward the Syrian and Mesopotamian wastelands. Hence, the UCLA collection contains more than 100 interviews with natives of the Kharpert vilayet, primarily the woman and child survivors who escaped death through religious conversion, being assisted by Muslim notables or else kidnapped by tribesmen, or somehow numbering among those fortunate enough to survive in the vast open-air zone of concentration lying within the great irregular triangle of Urfa-Mosul-Deir el-Zor. The figure is undoubtedly also affected by the fact that there was significant emigration from Kharpert to the United States prior to 1914 by adult males trying to save up enough money to return home and purchase a plot of land or gain greater economic security for their family. It was natural that these men would do everything possible after World War I to rescue and reunite with any surviving relatives, so that the percentage of natives of Kharpert who arrived in the United States in the postwar years was probably higher than of those born in most other regions of the Ottoman Empire.

There appears to be some correlation between the time that the individual interviewee was in the United States and his/her coping with the trauma sustained in childhood. Many persons who spent most of their lives in America and achieved financial success and stability, witnessed the achievements of children and grandchildren, and resigned themselves to the intermarriage and acculturation of subsequent generations were more likely to have repressed the past or found means to reconcile with it. Where Armenian identity was preserved more intensely, such as in the Arab world, the immediacy of the events and the resentment of survivors are often, though not always, more abiding and verbalized.

Before the Deluge

A few comments should be made about the pre-genocidal life of the last generation. Nearly all survivors, regardless of social and economic status or place of residence, remember their childhood with idyllic nostalgia. They recall fondly and cherish the simple pleasures of playing games such as jacks (with bone joints) or marbles, jump rope, and hide-and-seek; a protective, extended family of grandparents, parents, siblings, and often uncles, aunts, and cousins, as well as mutually supportive friends and neighbors; the excitement and celebration of holidays such as the New Year, Christmas, Easter, the frolic with water on *Vardavar* (Feast of the Transfiguration of Christ), and the blessing of grapes on *Astvatsatsin (*Assumption of Holy Mother of God), and especially the wedding festivities that lasted "for seven days and seven nights." Although often rushing ahead to speak of their harrowing experiences during the deportations and massacres, when questioned properly the survivors give in detail the layout of their homes, the central room with its oven-fireplace or *tonir-ojakh*, the lofts or mats for sleep, the distribution of labor within and outside the household, the animals and corrals, the fields and threshing floors, and all the daily routines. They describe with expressive terms the rippling streams, gurgling brooks, and cold, pristine water gushing from natural springs, and the gardens and wonderful aromatic fruits and vegetables, the likes of which they have never seen or tasted since their expulsion. They seek with tears and sorrow that lost time, trying to reconnect, but in that process also realize and mourn that all of this is gone and non-recoverable. They grieve over murdered parents and siblings who were integral to those joyous scenes.

As far as social and ethnic relations are concerned, the survivors by and large speak of segregated lives, remaining in their own villages and city quarters, interacting with their own kind, going to their own schools and churches, and, if they were women or children, having few non-Armenian friends or acquaintances. Community and religious leaders and the men-folk, few of whom survived, were the ones who interacted with members of other ethnic and religious groups, as it was they who represented the collective ethnoreligious group or were involved in the trades, crafts, and professions. But even those who dealt on a daily basis with Turks and other Muslims usually restricted that relationship to the marketplace and to business hours. A few survivors do remember living in mixed quarters and having cordial relations with their Muslim neighbors, some of whom would come to serenade the Armenians on Christian holidays and receive sweets and money in appreciation.

A number of survivors speak of having gotten along with Turks and other Muslims while at the same time having been cautious because of an awareness of potential danger. They had as children either witnessed personally or heard stories of the terrible massacres of the 1890s and, if in Cilicia, also of 1909, but they are quick to add that they believed that those tragic days had passed, especially as the Armenians were swift to rebuild and reestablish themselves throughout the Ottoman Empire. The survivors knew of the existence of Armenian political parties, although from what they could tell the young men who participated in the meetings of these semisecretive groups were trying to find ways to protect their people from the rampant lawlessness and oppression that afflicted the interior eastern provinces of the empire. Members of Protestant denominations tend to have a less favorable attitude toward the political parties and view them as having been very naïve or even harmful to the welfare of the Armenian people.

Looking ahead to what was to happen to them, the survivors point out the progressiveness of the Armenian community, the spread of an educational network throughout the empire, as demonstrated in the fact that nearly every town and sizable village operated schools for the predominant Apostolic (Orthodox) community, as well as for the smaller Protestant element and in some places for the even smaller Catholic community. Most school-age girls of this last generation were enrolled in elementary-level schools, and some had already advanced to become college graduates and teachers. Armenians constituted the majority of students and faculty in the American-sponsored schools and institutions operating from Constantinople to Cilicia, Marsovan, Sivas, Kharpert, Bitlis, and Van.

The Genocidal Process

The 800 interviews in the UCLA collection corroborate the documentary and other evidence that the deportations and massacres beginning in 1915 were intended to eliminate the Armenian population from the width and breadth of Anatolia and the eastern provinces, generally referred to as Turkish Armenia. The process was so thorough that even the small isolated and completely defenseless communities in western Anatolia were not spared from the same fate that befell the Armenians from Sivas and Kharpert eastward to and beyond the frontiers of the Russian Empire and Persia. In interview after interview the genocidal process is described as a consistent pattern:

- Conscription of the adult male population prior to and during the first months of the war and their subsequent segregation into labor battalions and ultimate execution.
- Disarmament of the Armenians by demanding that each household turn in weapons and when these did not exist driving the terrified population to purchase and deliver guns to avoid the threatened severe punitive action.
- Arrest and imprisonment of community leaders, including teachers, priests, and intellectuals, and the closure of schools.
- Proclamation through town criers of the decree for deportation, which was to follow within a week.

- Pandemonium of trying to prepare for the journey, selling household goods for a pittance, hiding valuables or entrusting them to Turkish acquaintances, and, in the case of "connected" Armenians, desperately seeking the intercession of American missionaries or Turkish officials for exemption or at least a delay in enforcement of the decree.

- Separation of the remaining adult male population and killing of most of these men a short distance from their native towns and villages, especially at prearranged sites such as river crossings, isolated vales, or mountain passes. ("All of those who were gathered were tied together and thrown into the Euphrates River. Those who were older were taken aside and shot.... Everything was fully planned by the Turks, everything was organized to the last detail in that massacre."[Ohannes Akaragian].[2] "We came and what did we see? Bodies lying at the river, one groaning, 'my head,' one, 'my leg,' one, 'my back.' The rest were dead, and those still barely alive would moan something to themselves every once in a while." [Hagop Garabedian]).[3]

- The death marches of the women, children, and elderly toward the deserts, a process lasting weeks and months during which the majority perished from thirst, hunger, fatigue, disease, and repeated physical abuse. ("Thousands of people with no protector or helper, people forced to strip and shot. Where have such things been seen?" [Ohannes Akaragian].[4] "They lined us up one by one like soldiers and they searched everyone, taking everything—money, rings, goods. They then led us down into Sheitan valley and suddenly we were surrounded by *ashirets* [tribesmen], who started to massacre. We all ran, I in one direction, my mother in another, my sister in another." ... "The next morning, *Vay, vay, vay,* they had brought people from Aintab, from Marash, from Kilis and piled them on top of each other. There was no count. They had come from everywhere." ... "On the road to Rakka, the fields were filled with carcasses—human corpses." [Hagop Garabedian]).[5]

The methodical process of the genocide is made clear, for example, in that survivors from Arabkir, Kharpert, and Malatia describe the caravans of deportees passing through their towns "like a tribe of walking dead people" (Hachadour Kalustian) weeks before they themselves were notified of their own impending departure.[6] During that intervening period they tried to help the pitiful Armenian masses originating from regions farther east and north, all the while continuing to tend their fields and harvest their crops, wanting to believe the explanation that those unfortunate deportees had been forced to leave their homes because they were situated in a war zone. Yet, after the last caravan from the northeast had passed, the same process started in the Kharpert vilayet, and with rare exception neither the intercession of American missionaries or consular officials nor anyone else was able to attenuate the full force of the cleansing process. In some instances, Protestants and Catholics felt relieved that they were not among the first to be deported, only to find that in a matter of weeks, they, too, were put on the road to exile. Even the Turkish-speaking Armenian Catholic villages deep within Anatolia in the districts of Yozgat and Angora (Ankara) found no reprieve and were subject to some of the most horrific massacres of 1915.

The descriptions of the dehumanization and gratuitous cruelty on the routes of deportation are heartrending. Repeated stories of disembowelment of pregnant women and persons suspected of trying to conceal a piece of gold by swallowing it, of being stripped naked and forced to walk blistered and bloodied under a scorching sun in a state of utter degradation, and of kidnappings, separation, and suicides are all a part of the collective testimony of survivors from as far west as Banderma to as far east as Erzerum. A number of interviewees insist that they are not speaking figuratively when they say that there were so many massacred Armenians in the Euphrates River that the water ran red and was clogged with bodies at many points (e.g., Haigaz Bonaparte).[7] At Ordu, Dikranouhi Baghdassarian's nine-month old babe was snatched away, her father's throat was slit, and her mother was decapitated. She cries that many children in her town were impaled or thrown into the Black Sea.[8] Only in a few places was resistance offered, and the survivors state almost in disbelief that they were "herded like sheep" by a few gendarmes. Survivors from Van, Urfa, Musa Dagh, and the several other localities where the Armenians took arms to defend themselves display a strong sense of pride, almost superiority, at the fact that while most of them may have died they were not "slaughtered like sheep."

Within these descriptions of the genocidal process are also stories of the "miraculous" survival of "one in a thousand" through intervention, whether for selfish or altruistic motives, of Turks, Kurds, Arabs, and Greeks.[9] Krikor Ananikian, for example, cannot forget how when he was an abandoned waif his eyes met those of a Turkish peasant woman, "who pulled me close to her breast and told me in the most motherly voice that she would take care of me."[10] Some Armenians survived by assuming a new identity through religious conversion and absorption into the dominant group. There is often a sense of shame among such survivors, who feel the need to rationalize this phase in their life and to insist that even while saying prayers in a different language and in a different religion they kept the true faith in their hearts. These same individuals often speak with fondness of their new parents, who were tender and loving and raised them with compassion. The repeated trauma of separation, this time from their new families following the war, remains strongly etched in the memory of many survivors. But there were also the untold thousands of young girls who had been forced into concubinage and had borne children to their captors. For them the choiceless choice was one of abandoning their children or else forsaking their own families and people to whom they could not return with the living evidence and constant reminder of their violation and shame.

A compelling development in this time of extreme crisis was the role of leadership into which women were thrust. It was women who became the heads of the family, who had to make critical decisions, such as whether the family would stay together at the price of dying together or whether it was necessary to save a part of the family by sacrificing some of its members by giving them away or even abandoning them. They became the primary negotiators with Turks, Kurds, and Arabs for their own survival and that of their loved ones. It was women taken into Muslim households who did everything possible to assist others even more unfortunate and miserable than themselves. If the Armenian family was preserved during this period of unprecedented horrors, much of the credit belongs to the last generation of Ottoman Armenian women, who assumed unconventional roles in the desperate struggle for survival.

Explaining the Inexplicable

The survivors who have recounted their experiences in the UCLA Armenian Oral History Program are almost without exception at a loss to explain what happened to them and why. They insist that even a simple understanding of what took place is unattainable for anyone who did not experience firsthand the incessant torment of those years. Ohannes Akaragian says: "Such things happened that it is impossible to describe, the human mind is incapable of imagining that such things could occur on earth. Yesterday's Turk who had eaten your bread, who was your friend, suddenly became your enemy."[11] The survivors feel deeply wronged and especially aggrieved by the absence of recognition of their suffering. They repeatedly stress the peaceful, law-abiding nature of their families and find that their only guilt was being Armenian Christians. They believe that their people represented a sedentary, progressive element within a mixed society plagued by the lawlessness of nomadic and tribal elements, but they are also insistent that what happened to them was a demonic scheme enacted by the very government that was supposed to protect them. For this, they are bitter and unforgiving.

Many of the survivors try to find some explanation or rationalization, the most common being the dominant element's fear and envy of the economic, educational, and cultural advances of the Armenian people. Franklin Hadian says: "The Turks were jealous towards Armenians. They saw the Armenians so successful, so they robbed and killed them.... All the beautiful homes, all the good businesses, were run by the Armenians, while the Turks were not educated to run any."[12] Armenians are portrayed as being industrious and ambitious for their children and advancing from a strictly traditional society to one receptive to external, especially Western, influences, again in contrast with the dominant element, a fact that was exploited by Enver, Talaat, and other Young Turk organizers of the genocide. There is also a religious component, as the pejorative label *gavur* (infidel) given to Armenians and the associated negative religious connotations of the term are often mentioned. There is also occasional self-blame, as several survivors note that the Armenian political parties, while perhaps not the source of the problem, only aggravated it and gave the Turkish leaders a desired excuse to destroy the entire Armenian population.

While some survivors find solace in their religious faith and thank God for rescuing them and allowing them to create a new home in a new country with a loving, successful family, others have been so traumatized as to question the existence of a supreme being. Vehanush Bagdasarian says: "I don't believe in God. I have seen so many things. At that time, I used to pray. I was a Protestant. I had a good heart. After the massacres I would ask myself, 'God, where were you? Did you not see so many things happening?' So many unreal things happened. If God exists, why was there so much injustice?"[13]

A number of survivors who have long lived in the United States and prospered profess a readiness to get on with their lives. David Dingilian, who attained a higher education, does a self-analysis: "The only way you can keep your sanity is by repression.... I know from my clinical experience that a young child who is traumatized is flooded by stimuli so overwhelming that he cannot cope...all he can do is build repressive machinery as far as possible to stay alive himself. That must have happened to me." He adds, as if in compensation, "Peril can be a great stimulator—you never can let adversity trip you up" and "any pain can be a stepping stone" to improving life.[14] Rose Andrews, who was taken in by Arabs ("Arabs are wonderful people") before being rescued and arriving in the U.S. in the 1920s, says: "Nobody should be vengeful; the new generation had nothing to do with it,"[15] and Euphrates Kazanjian, who is a contemporary of the survivors but happened to be born in the United States, tells her grandson: "There are good Turks and bad Armenians and the other way around—nobody is all good or all bad—it was the government's fault."[16]

But the above statements of resignation and reconciliation reflect the view of a small minority. Many more share the sentiments of Beatrice Hagopian, who, while explaining that her family never spoke of the horrors that had been experienced during the genocide (her earliest memories are of countless bodies floating down the Euphrates River), admitted that she froze and then walked away the first time she met a Turk in the United States during the 1950s.[17] Another survivor voices a festering resentment and rage that is not limited to the survivor generation: "It is my opinion that a Turk, at whatever generation, is always a Turk. After all these years, they are the same people. They act the same way towards Armenians."

Most survivors express deep concern about maintaining a national existence and cohesion in the Diaspora. They fear the loss of identity through a "white massacre," that is, through intermarriage and assimilation, and they often preach in their interviews about the need to speak Armenian, maintain Armenian traditions, and advance the Armenian cause. Even as they profess hope and pride in the "new generation," they betray an anxiety that the impact of the genocide has not yet run its full course.

The survivor generation of the Armenian Genocide is all but gone at the start of a new century and new millennium, yet a few hundred recorded voices may serve as a reminder of the inhumanity of exclusivist nationalism and racism in the twentieth century. There is an impressive resilience among survivors, whose chief yearning is that not only they but also the perpetrators and bystanders confront the face of evil and know the truth of their suffering.

Notes

1. Donald E. Miller and Lorna T. Miller, "An Oral History Perspective on Responses to the Armenian Genocide," in Richard G. Hovannisian, ed. *The Armenian Genocide in Perspective* (New Brunswick and London: Transaction Publishers, 1986), pp. 187-203. See also Donald E. Miller and Lorna T. Miller, *Survivors: An Oral History of the Armenian Genocide* (Berkeley, Los Angeles, London: University of California Press, 1993).
2. Ohannes Akaragian, born in Agn (Egin),1900, interviewed by Knar Kouleyan, Los Angeles, California, May 6, 1977, and Rubina Peroomian, Los Angeles, California, May 31, 1980.
3. Hagop Garabedian, born in Agn, 1904, interviewed by Nareg Keshishian, Los Angeles, California, February 22, 1990.
4. Ohannes Akaragian interview, May 6, 1977, and May 31, 1980.
5. Hagop Garabedian interview, February 22, 1990.
6. Hachadour Kalustian, born in Arabkir, 1901, interviewed by Anahid Nazarian, Sherman Oaks, California, May 13, 1977.
7. Haigaz Boneparte, born in Malatia, 1898, interviewed by Kathy Albarian, Los Angeles, California, February 25, 1979.
8. Dikranouhi Baghdasarian, born in Ordu, 1901, interviewed by Mary Astadourian, Los Angeles, California, May 10, 1980.
9. On the subject of intervention and altruism during the deportations and massacres, see Richard G. Hovannisian, "The Question of Altruism during the Armenian Genocide of 1915," in Pearl M. Oliner, Samuel P. Oliner, Lawrence Baron et al., eds., *Embracing the Other: Philosophical, Psychological, and Historical Perspectives on Altruism* (New York and London: New York University Press, 1992), pp. 282-305.
10. Krikor Ananikian, born in Trebizond, 1906, interviewed by Ani Shahbazian, Beverly Hills, California, May 28, 1996.
11. Ohannes Akaragian interview, May 31, 1980.
12. Franklin Hadian, born in Agn, 1896, interviewed by Craig Williams, Glendale, California, May 29, 1980.
13. Vehanush Bagdasarian, born in Marsovan, 1909, interviewed by Ani Shahbazian, Glendale, California, May 4, 1996.
14. David Dingilian, born in Kharpert, 1908, interviewed by Craig Williams, Rancho Palos Verdes, California, June 5, 1980.
15. Rose Kalajian Andrews, born in Kharpert, 1905, interviewed by Craig Williams, Los Angeles, June 11, 1980.
16. Euphrates Kazanjian, born in Pasadena, California, 1904, interviewed by Douglas Kazanjian, Pasadena, California, November 21, 1999.
17. Beatrice Hagopian, born in Kharpert, 1913, interviewed by Robert Malkasian, Orinda, California, February 2, 1992.

7

Raphael Lemkin and the Armenian Genocide

Steven L. Jacobs

Introduction

That the genocide of the Armenian people during World War I at the hands of the Young Turk regime provided foundational support for Turkey's German collaborators and supporters in the Nazi slaughter of Jews during World War II is fact. That the genocide also impacted the life of a unique individual, himself a Polish Jewish refugee to the United States, is far less well known. That the Armenian Genocide, along with other genocides, both energized and motivated him during his formative and his productive years is equally little known except to a handful of concerned scholars and historians. Gradually, however, a half century after the death of Raphael Lemkin, his story is being told and retold in a variety of venues, and his pioneering work and vision are becoming increasingly appreciated as knowledge of him and his voluminous writings on the subject of genocide makes its way into the public arena.[1]

Who Was Raphael Lemkin and Why Genocide?

Raphael Lemkin was born in 1900, the son of a Jewish farmer, in the Polish town of Bezewodene. In his still unpublished autobiography, *Unofficial Man: The Autobiography of Raphael Lemkin*, he describes his fellow Poles as "tolerant" of their Jewish neighbors, removed as they all were from the centers of both Jewish and non-Jewish life and Polish officialdom. With an accuracy born of hindsight, he regarded his growing-up as neither unusual nor significantly different from other Jews in similar environments in the early decades of the twentieth century—with one notable exception.

Sometime during his teenage years—he does not tell us precisely when—he read and was profoundly affected by 1905 Polish Nobel Laureate Henryk Sienkiewicz's novel *Quo Vadis*, which tells of Nero's almost successful attempt to exterminate the Christians of his realm. He writes:

> I asked my Mother, "Why did the Christians permit themselves to be thrown to the lions without calling the police?" Her answer was, "Do you think the police could help them?"
>
> I started to read about other attempts to destroy national, religious and racial groups. Soon I understood that something more is required than the assistance of local police to stop this evil for which I have later coined the name "Genocide." The cases of Genocide in history caught my imagination. My thinking was so intense that I have been almost seeing the events with my own eyes. I saw the French King, Charles XII, who enjoyed from the balcony of the royal castle the execution of the Huguenots and ordered more light to be thrown on their faces so he can better see their tortures. I saw the Catholics of 17th Century Japan being compelled to drink water, after which all openings of their bodies were cemented and heavy loads put on their bodies until they exploded. I saw the Moslems of Spain crowded half-naked on the decks of boats under the murderous African sun buying from the sailors the right to sit in the shade so that their miserable existence can be prolonged before their bodies are thrown into the sea. And I heard the screamings of Jews in pogroms, when their stomachs have been opened, filled with feathers, and tied with ropes.
>
> I identified myself more and more with the sufferings of the victims, whose numbers grew, and I continued my study of history. I understood that the function of memory is not only to register past events, but to stimulate human conscience. *Soon contemporary examples of Genocide followed, such as the slaughter of the Armenians* [emphasis mine]. It became clear to me that the diversity of nations, religious groups and races is essential to civilization because every one of these groups has a mission to fulfill and a contribution to make in terms of culture. To destroy these groups is to oppose the will of the Creator and to disturb the spiritual harmony of mankind. I had decided to become a lawyer and work for the outlawing of Genocide and for its prevention through the cooperation of nations. These nations must be made to understand that an attack on one of them is an attack on all of them. My mature years I have devoted to this work.[2]

Lemkin went on to study law at the University of Lwow (also known as Lemberg, Lvov, Lviv) in Poland and the University of Heidelberg in Germany, becoming Secretary of the Warsaw Court of Appeals in 1927. From 1929 until 1935, he served as Secretary on the Committee on Codification of the Laws of the Polish Republic and then privately practiced law until the start of World War II. In 1933, he had hoped to attend the League of Nations meeting in Madrid, there to propose a ban on mass slaughter and the destruction of cultures (his terms were "barbarism" and "vandalism") but was prevented at the last moment from attending by his superiors. Though he had sent his written materials in advance, the reticence of the League to act doomed his proposal to failure.

While still a student in Lwow, Lemkin followed with great interest the trial of another student, Soghomon Tehlirian, who in 1921 assassinated Talaat Pasha, a prime architect of the Armenian Genocide, on a Berlin thoroughfare. In his autobiography, Lemkin expresses disappointment and concern that the perpetrators of the Armenian Genocide had not been punished by the Allied Powers:

> In Turkey, more than 1,200,000 Armenians were put to death for no other reason than they were Christians. They were driven from their homes, along the Euphrates River. Then, suddenly, the escorting gendarmes were starting shooting at both ends of the line and they would accuse the Armenians of shooting, finally, they mow them down.
>
> After the end of the war, some 150 Turkish war criminals were arrested and interned by the British government on the island of Malta. The Armenians sent a delegation to the peace conference at Versailles. They were demanding justice. Then, one day, the delegation read in the newspapers that all Turkish war criminals were released. I was shocked. A nation was killed and the guilty persons were set free. Why is a man punished when he kills another man? Why is the killing of a million a lesser crime than the killing of a single individual? The Turkish criminals released from Malta dispersed all over the world. The most frightful among them was Taalat Pasha, the Minister of the Interior of Turkey, whose name was identified with the destruction of the Armenian people. Taalat Pasha took refuge in Berlin. One day, he was stopped in the streets by a young Armenian with the name of Tehliran [Tehlirian]. After identifying Taalat Pasha, Tehliran shot his interlocutor with the words, "This is for my mother." Tehliran was one of the survivors of a massacre. He was saved because the body of his dead mother had fallen over all around him. Tehliran was tried. Factually the trial was transformed in[to] a trial of the Turkish perpetrators. The sinister panorama of the destruction of the Armenians was painted by many witnesses, which the Armenians brought to court. Through this trial, the world finally obtained a real picture of the tragic events in Turkey. The same world which was conveniently silent at the time when 1,200,000 were murdered intended to hide the fact by releasing 150 Turkish war criminals after the war. But the world was compelled to listen to the truth after the fatal shooting in Berlin.
>
> The court in Berlin acquitted Tehliran. It decided that he has acted under psychological compulsion. The man who upheld with his shooting the moral order of mankind was classified as a so-called insane defendant who was incapable to discern the moral nature of his act. Tehliran acted as the self-appointed legal officer for the conscience of mankind. But can a man appoint himself to mete out justice? Will not passion sway such a type of justice and rather make a travesty of it? At that moment, my worries about the murder of the innocent became more meaningful to me. I didn't know all the answers but I felt that a law against this type of murder must be accepted by the world.
>
> In Lwow University where I enrolled for the study of law, I discussed this matter with professors. They invoked the argument about the sovereignty of states. "But sovereignty of states," I answered, "implies conducting an independent foreign and internal policy, building of schools, construction of roads, in brief, all types of activity directed towards the welfare of people. Sovereignty," I argued, "cannot be conceived as the right to kill millions of innocent people."

With the outbreak of World War II marked by Germany's invasion of Poland on September 1, 1939, and the blitzkrieg victory in a few short weeks, Lemkin joined the Polish underground. In a little more than one year, however, he was to leave his native Poland, via Sweden and Switzerland, arriving in 1941 in the United States, where he taught law at Duke and at Yale. At war's end, he served as an advisor to Justice Robert H. Jackson at the International Military Tribunal in Nuremberg, Germany.[3] Prior to this appointment, in 1944, he published his major work, *Axis Rule in Occupied Europe: Laws of Occupation, Analysis of Government, Proposals for Redress*.[4]

Significantly, Part I, Chapter IX, pages 79-95, of that work is titled "Genocide," with three subheadings:

1. Genocide—A New Term and New Conception for Destruction of Nations;

2. Techniques of Genocide in Various Fields—Political, Social, Cultural, Economic, Biological, Physical, Religious, and Moral;

3. Recommendations for the Future—Prohibition of Genocide in War and Peace—International Control of Occupation Practices.

While Lemkin used the term "genocide" throughout the work and his commitment since his early years to alleviate the causes and consequences of this horrific crime remained unwavering, he was prepared linguistically to accept another word possibility to describe his concept, namely *ethnocide*:

> Another term could be used for the same idea, namely, *ethnocide*, consisting of the Greek word "ethnos"—nation—and the Latin word "cide."[5]

Returning to the United States at the conclusion of the Nuremberg trials, Lemkin would spend the next three years intensively and aggressively pursuing with single-minded purpose his desire to have the United Nations, now the successor to the League of Nations, endorse a resolution condemning and outlawing genocide. His efforts would meet with success in December of 1948, under the leadership of then President of the General Assembly Herbert V. Evatt of Australia, when the United Nations adopted the "Convention on the Prevention and Punishment of the Crime of Genocide."

For the remaining ten years of his life, until his death in 1959, Lemkin would invest the bulk of his prodigious energies in two areas:

1. Doing everything within his own power and urging others to join forces to get the United States, his adopted and beloved country, to ratify the Genocide Convention.[6]

2. Writing a number of important books on genocide, all of which would be rejected for publication on the grounds of lack of interest and/or an adequate market.[7]

Manuscript No. 1: Book-Length Manuscript on the Armenian Massacres

Found among Lemkin's more than 20,000 pages of letters and correspondence, articles, interviews, editorials, newspaper clippings, and manuscripts are two relevant to this essay: a 139-page manuscript, untitled by its author, but given the name by the cataloguer of his papers, "Book-Length Manuscript on the Armenian Massacres," and a six-page manuscript, also untitled, but given the name "Short Manuscript on the Armenian Massacres," neither of which is dated.[8] The former cites twenty-two bibliographic sources[9] and is divided into the following seven sub-sections: 1. Armenians: Background; 2.Taxation [an area in which Lemkin was particularly interested given the legal focus of much of the material in his volume *Axis Rule in Occupied Europe*]; 3. Massacres of the 1890s; 4. Massacres of 1909—Adana; 5. Massacres and Deportations of 1915-1916; 6. Intent to Kill—Who Is Guilty?; 7. Reactions Abroad. These subtitles are Lemkin's own. The "short manuscript," on the other hand, includes no bibliography but does cite five sources in its footnotes.

Quoting liberally from all of his sources and integrating and interweaving these into a single coherent manuscript, Lemkin was not afraid to quote even the most horrific of graphic descriptions for his future readers, as witnessed by the following, taken from Frederick Davis Greene's book of 1895, *The Armenian Crisis in Turkey*:

> The following letter's authenticity is vouched for by twenty outstanding Americans, but at the time of its publication neither the name of the author not the place from which it was written could be revealed for fear of Turkish reprisals:
>
> Nov. 16, 1894
>
> A number of able-bodied young Armenians were captured, bound, covered with brushwood and burned alive. A number of Armenians, variously estimated, but less

than a hundred, surrendered themselves and pled for mercy. Many of them were shot down on the spot and the remainder were dispatched with sword and bayonet.

A lot of women, variously estimated from 60 to 160 in number, were shut up in a church, and the soldiers were "let loose" among them. Many of them were outraged to death and the remainder dispatched with sword and bayonet. Two stories are told. 1. That they were carried off to harems of their Moslem captors. 2. That they were offered Islam and the harems of their Moslem captors; refusing, they were slaughtered. Children were placed in a row, one behind another, and a bullet fired down the line, apparently to see how many could be dispatched with one bullet. Infants and small children were piled one on the other and their heads struck off. Houses were surrounded by soldiers, set on fire, and the inmates forced back into the flames at the point of the bayonet as they tried to escape.[10]

Most likely, this manuscript was written after adoption by the United Nations of the Convention on the Prevention and Punishment of the Crime of Genocide (1948), because his energies between the years 1945 and 1948 were all-consuming and focused as the horrors of the Nazi slaughter of the Jews came to light. Whether it was written prior to or during the Korean War (1950-53) or during its euphoric aftermath, when the United States experienced unprecedented economic growth and when the "Cold War" with the Soviet Union dominated political thought and reality cannot be determined. Given the rejection by publishers of his other attempts to place genocidal concerns before the American public in the mid-1950s, however, one might assume that the writing of this manuscript was undertaken at approximately the same period of time.

Without minimizing the horrors of the Armenian Genocide with which Lemkin himself so closely identified, and knowing of the loss of forty-nine members of his own family at the hands of the Nazis, what is most surprising, even shocking perhaps, is his bitter and angry condemnation of the Turks and the Germans in the next to the last section of the manuscript, titled "Intent to Kill—Who is Guilty?" He also excoriated the Koran itself, all this from someone who was politically savvy and astute enough to enlist the support not only of the West but of the Communist-controlled East and the Islamic countries as well. One can only speculate that, given the collective horrors of the genocides of history with which his research led him to become increasingly familiar, his legal training and scholarly objectivity mandated for him the responsibility to marshal the best evidence available and present it, together with his own commentary, to those who shared his ongoing concerns. Perhaps, too, in the aftermath of his success at the United Nations, he saw yet another opportunity to harness primarily American support for the deterrence and prevention of genocide: educating through his writing and teaching about genocides past and present. Alas, however, these are only speculations: Lemkin himself has left us no record of the rationale behind this particular manuscript nor the condemnations it contains.

He, Polish Jewish refugee from the Holocaust, begins this section with the following statement:

> The persecution of the Armenians, a strong Christian element existing in the heart of the Mohammedan religion, was inevitable as the fundamental principles of the Koran were in direct opposition to the teachings of Christ.[11]

Two pages later, he continues:

> No Mohammedan ruler, or follower of Mohammed's religion, dared do otherwise than what was taught him in the Koran and therefore none of the grants, permits, promises of reform, liberty of religion, protection of persons, honor and property of the Christian subjects of the empire, made by the sultans under pressure from foreign countries were intended to be kept. The rulers could not have put such laws into effect and remained conscientious and faithful Mohammedans.
>
> The history of Mohammedanism has been one of constant warfare against Christianity, and the Armenians have been slaughtered and persecuted ever since their conversion to Christianity. The massacres of the 1890s were religious in character although the Sultan was too clever openly to wage war on his Christian subjects without concocting the excuse of a threatened revolution to excuse his tactics to the outside world. It was convenient for the European and British governments to accept the Sultan's accusations against the Armenians and pretend to believe in their rebellion rather than admit that they were being persecuted for religious reasons alone.[12]

While we today, and others—and here I single out, for example, the important work done by Vahakn Dadrian and Richard Hovannisian—may have views differing somewhat from Lemkin's understanding of the Koran's teachings about other religious traditions, as well as the root and extended causes of the Armenian Genocide, for him, it was "undeniable that the Ottoman Government is a politico-religious system" and, therefore, there was "no place in the Ottoman Empire for persons of Christian faith."[13]

Additionally, Lemkin's reading of the evidence strongly pointed to collaborative support of Germany, Turkey's ally, for the near annihilation of the Armenians:

> The Government felt that with Germany as its ally it need have no fear of future retaliations for its plan of complete extermination, as it was convinced that Germany would win the war and would shield Turkey from the vengeance of the Western Powers and of Russia.

> The crime was worked out systematically and there is evidence of identical procedure from over fifty places, including every important town in Armenia proper and Eastern Anatolia, as well as Ismid and Broussa in the west and a number of places in Thrace.[14]

Having condemned Turkey for its genocide of the Armenians based on the evidence presented, Lemkin then goes on to draw a connection to the Jews in the Holocaust prior to his condemnation of the Germans:

> A strong parallel may be drawn between the extermination of the Armenians by the Turks and the extermination of the Jews by the Germans. The position of the Armenians in the Ottoman Empire closely approximated that of the Jews in Germany. The Armenians were the industrious citizens of the Empire, with a talent for handicrafts and intellectual pursuits. They had the same gift for commerce as the Jews, and in Asiatic Turkey it was the Armenian who was the skilled workman and the man of business. Every town in Anatolia had its prosperous Armenian quarter, the centre of local skill, intellectual life and trade, as well as of the town's commercial relations with Constantinople and Europe.[15]

Establishing this linkage, Lemkin proceeds to castigate Germany for its complicity in the genocide of the Armenians:

> There is every evidence that the persecution of the Armenians met with full favor in Germany.... Had Germany wished she could have stopped the atrocities merely by withdrawing her support.... It is unlikely that the German authorities initiated the crime, but it is clear that the Germans made no move to stop it.... From the above evidence there can be little doubt that the plan of extermination was well conceived and put into execution by the Turkish Government with the full recognition and support of Germany.[16]

Manuscript No. 2: Short Manuscript on the Armenian Massacres

There is nothing particularly distinguishable about this abbreviated account of the Armenian Genocide. It details some further examples of atrocity, cites several sources,[17] has neither introduction nor conclusion, and equally provides no rationale whatsoever for its writing, but it nonetheless ends with the statement: "There are innumerable accounts of heroic actions on the part of the Armenians, and their fortitude in the face of overwhelming disaster was admirable."[18]

Conclusion

For Raphael Lemkin, Polish Jewish refugee to the United States, author of the word *genocide*, and motivating presence behind the successful passage in 1948 of the United Nations Convention on the Prevention and Punishment of the Crime of Genocide, the Armenian Genocide *did* occupy a central place in his thinking, along with the Holocaust against his own Jewish people and the genocidal barbarity practiced against so many others. That it led him to write not one but two manuscripts specifically about these tragic events is confirming evidence enough of the primacy it occupied in his own desire to rid the world of such horrors. For one who saw a direct causal linkage between what was done to the Armenians by the Turks, with the full knowledge of their German allies, and what was done to the Jews by the Nazis and their allies, Adolf Hitler's rhetorical question in August 1939, on the eve of World War II, "Who now remembers the extermination of the Armenians?"[19]—was answered affirmatively by one whose own moral courage and integrity led him to translate words into challenges and the devastation of others into preventative actions.

Notes

1. See, for example, Steven L. Jacobs, *Raphael Lemkin's Thoughts on Nazi Genocide: Not Guilty?* (Lewiston, NY: Edwin Mellen Press, 1992); "The Papers of Raphael Lemkin: A First Look," *Journal of Genocide Research* 1:1 (1999): 105-14; "Genesis of the Concept of Genocide According to Its Author from the Original Sources," *Human Rights Review,* forthcoming.
2. Here, I disagree somewhat with Vahakn N. Dadrian's assessment: "In fact, evidence indicates that his interest in the codification of the crime of genocide under international law was first triggered by his emotive, as well as intellectual, reaction to the horrors of the Armenian genocide." See Vahakn N. Dadrian, *The Key Elements in the Turkish Denial of the Armenian Genocide: A Case Study of Distortion and Falsification* (Toronto: Zoryan Institute, 1999), p. 35. To be sure, the Armenian Genocide was a decisive factor in Lemkin's relentless drive to internationalize criminal punishment for acts of genocide, but it was not his first nor primary motivation.
3. Eight references to Lemkin are found in the seventy volumes associated with those trials: four in the 42-volume *International Military Tribunal*; two in the 11-volume *Nazi Conspiracy and Aggression*; and two in the 16-volume *Nuremberg Military Tribunal.* See James Joseph Sanchez, James Joseph, Kelly Reed, Brian Peck, Valerie Caquias, and Vickey Bishop, co-compilers, *Nuremberg War Crimes Trials* (Seattle: Aristarchus International Law Database Series, 1995), CD-Rom.
4. Raphael Lemkin, *Axis Rule in Occupied Europe: Laws of Occupation, Analysis of Government, Proposals for Redress* (Washington, DC: Carnegie Endowment for International Peace, 1944), 674 pages.
5. Ibid., p. 79n1.
6. Almost three decades after Lemkin's death, the United States would in 1988 finally adhere to the Genocide Convention, in no small measure because of the support of conservative President Ronald Reagan and a tireless advocate, Senator William Proxmire of Wisconsin. For the fullest discussion of the political maneuvers asso-

ciated with ratification of the Convention, see Lawrence J. LeBlanc, *The United States and the Genocide Convention* (Durham, NC: Duke University Press, 1991).

7. The manuscripts include the following: *Totally Unofficial: The Autobiography of Raphael Lemkin*; *Introduction to the Study of Genocide*; *The Hitler Case*; and *A History of Genocide in Three Volumes.* It is my intent, as editor of his more than 20,000 pages of letters and correspondence, articles, interviews, editorials, newspaper clippings, and manuscripts first to catalogue and inventory all these materials and then to seek publication of these important works under one imprint, as well as a collection of his shorter writings and a critical evaluation of both the man and his work. For a detailed discussion of his papers, see my "The Papers of Raphael Lemkin: A First Look."
8. A chapter on the Armenian Genocide was also to be included in his three-volume *A History of Genocide*, specifically in volume 3, *Modern Times*, in addition to this particular manuscript. It has, however, not appeared, leading to the conclusion that Lemkin died before he was able to write it.
9. As Lemkin himself listed the sources, they are as follows:

BIBLIOGRAPHY ON ARMENIAN MASSACRES

The Tragedy of Armenia, Henry Morgenthau, London, 1918
Great Britain, Miscellaneous No. 31 (1916), *The Treatment of Armenians [in the Ottoman Empire]*, Preface by Viscount Bryce
Armenia, a Martyr Nation, M. C. Gabrielian, London, 1918
Turkey and the Armenian Atrocities, Rev. Edwin Munsell Bliss, 1896
The Armenian Crisis in Turkey, Frederick Davis Greene, 1895
Turkish Cruelties upon the Armenian Christians, Rev. Edwin Munsell Bliss, 1896
Les Turcs ont passé là, George Brèzol, Paris, 1911
Horrors of Armenia, William Hillard Howard, New York, 1896
Shall This Nation Die? Rev. Joseph Naayem, New York, 1921
The Blackest Page of Modern History, Herbert Adams Gibbons, New York, 1916
Massacres d'Arménie, Pierre Loti, 1919
Beginning Again at Ararat, Mabel Evelyn Elliott, 1924
Hadjin and the Armenian Massacres, Rose Lambert, 1911
Germany, Turkey and Armenia, London, 1917—A selection of documentary evidence relating to the Armenian atrocities from German and other sources
Letters on Turkey, [Abdolonyme] Ubicini, Vol. II
Nineveh, [Austen Henry] Layard, Vol. I
Armenia and the Campaign of 1877, [Charles Boswell] Norman
Annual Cyclopedia, Appelton [publisher], 1880
The Armenian Crisis in Turkey, [Frances D.] Greene
Armenia and Europe, [Johannes] Lepsius, Berlin, 1896
Transcaucasia and Ararat, [James] Bryce, 4th edition
Fifty Years in Constantinople, [George] Washburn

10. As cited in Raphael Lemkin, "Book-Length Manuscript on the Armenian Massacres," pp. 32-33. Original in Frederick Davis Greene, *The Armenian Crisis in Turkey* (New York: G. P. Putnam's Sons, 1895), pp. 13-15.
11. "Book-Length Manuscript," p. 85.
12. Ibid., p. 87.
13. Ibid., pp. 89-90.
14. Ibid., p. 92.
15. Ibid., p. 93.

16. Ibid., pp. 95ff.
17. As noted in Lemkin's footnotes, the sources are the following: 1. *Sonnenaufgang,* October, 1915; 2. *Germany, Turkey and Armenia*; 3. New York Journal, *Gotchnag*, August 28, 1915; 4. *Treatment of Armenians*; 5. *Beginning Again at Ararat.*
18. "Short Manuscript," p. 6.
19. For an exploration and analysis of the context in which Hitler put this self-serving and self-justifying question, see Kevork B. Bardakjian, *Hitler and the Armenian Genocide* (Cambridge, MA: Zoryan Institute, 1985).

8

The Armenian Genocide and International Law

Joe Verhoeven

The word "genocide" was coined by Raphael Lemkin during the closing years of World War II, mostly to characterize the atrocities committed by the Nazi regime against the Jews. His paternity of the term is, in this sense, indisputable. That does not mean, however, that "genocide" should relate only to the suffering of the Jewish people under the Nazis or that such monstrous action was beyond the scope of international law before the word was created to condemn the crime. There is no doubt, for instance, that the Armenian massacres of 1915 were contrary to international law at the time they were perpetrated by the Turks; that is, they were illegal or unlawful even if no specific procedures then existed to prosecute the perpetrators. The culpable parties could be held accountable, even if only in accordance with the rules generally applicable to illegal acts or conduct such as murder, kidnapping, and so forth. This was evidenced, at least partially, by the Turkish war-crimes trials that were held after World War I.

Consequently, the object of the 1948 United Nations Genocide Convention was not to render illegal what had previously been considered lawful. It was simply to make genocide a specific crime and to impose on the contracting states a duty to prevent and punish that crime. Such a duty certainly now possesses a customary nature, which implies that it binds not only the states that have explicitly adhered to or ratified the Convention, but also those that have not. This point is presently undisputed. Together with war crimes, crimes against humanity, and crimes against peace, the crime of genocide now constitutes the central core of a developing international criminal law aimed at offenses that are linked by their exceptional gravity and involve some of the most basic individual values—life and human dignity. The crimes are almost always "state-implicated" in one way or another.

It is true that these developments do not encompass the Armenian Genocide, for the obvious reason that the crime against the Armenian people was committed before the adoption of the United Nations Convention in 1948 and of the international treaties and resolutions intended to criminalize specifically such odious conduct. As the immediate perpetrators are now dead, criminal proceedings against them have lost their *raison d'être*. For the time being at least, implicated states as such escape "punishment." Obviously, this does not mean that the story of the Armenian Genocide has come to an end. Quite the contrary, the very fact that there was no punishment and even no official recognition of the genocide by the perpetrator side keeps the wounds open and prevents healing. It should be for law, including international law, to determine what mechanisms or procedures should be used to have the Armenian Genocide recognized officially by the relevant authorities and what are the remedies available to the victims. This raises certain "technical" issues, but before addressing them, it would be useful to analyze the evolution of international practice since the time when the United Nations General Assembly adopted the Genocide Convention. Although this evolution does not concern the Armenian people specifically or singly, it is nonetheless decisive for the future of mankind and cannot but be of importance to a people who were among the first victims of this colossal crime.

Genocide—The Evolving Practice

The purpose of the 1948 United Nations Genocide Convention was twofold (Article 1):

1) to define genocide, so as to distinguish it from other related offenses;

2) to take measures for the prevention and the punishment of what is confirmed to be a crime under international law.

The term "confirm" refers to Resolution 96-I, adopted on December 11, 1946, by which the General Assembly of the United Nations, during its very first session, officially condemned genocide as a crime under international law. It is probable that such a confirmation was also intended to remind the "peoples of the United Nations," as mentioned in the Preamble of the Charter, that genocide had a criminal character—even if unspecified—before the Convention's entry into force in 1948. The 96-I Resolution had no binding effect as such, but it explicitly contemplated the negotiation of a binding compact on the crime of genocide. Despite fierce criticisms within the General Assembly's committee charged with drafting the agreement, the Convention was completed in less than two years, remarkable by usual diplomatic standards.[1]

As far as characterization is concerned, three elements are required in any genocide (Article 2):

1) the existence of "a national, ethnical, racial, or religious group";

2) the "intent to destroy" such a group "in whole or in part";

3) the intent enacted in one or more of the ways enumerated by the Convention (killings, inflicting conditions of life calculated to bring about physical destruction, preventing procreation, forcibly transferring children of one group to another, and so forth).

As far as prevention and punishment are concerned, the provisions of the Convention actually remain general and somewhat ambiguous. The central provision is probably the one stipulating that persons charged with genocide are to be tried by a court of the state where the act was committed or—what is totally new—"by such international penal tribunal as may have jurisdiction with respect to those Contracting Parties which shall have accepted its jurisdiction."

Apart from this point, the most important specification is that persons committing genocide shall be punished "whether they are constitutionally responsible rulers, public officials, or private individuals," it being understood that for purposes of extradition acts constituting genocide would not be considered as political crimes. Clearly, the originality of the Convention is not that persons committing genocide can be punished. It would be sheer nonsense to maintain that they were not previously accountable. Still, it could be difficult to bring officials and public authorities before a public court, not only because of their possible control of the judicial machinery but also because they might legally possess some immunity in jurisdiction. The specifications given in Article 4 of the Convention confirm in this respect that the intent of the contracting states is both to have genocide effectively punished and possibly to exclude any defense based on jurisdictional immunity. As genocide is to a large extent "state-implicated," such a specification is quite important. There is no doubt that the claim of immunity must be disregarded when it is made before a national court of the state of which individuals accused of genocide are public officials or authorities. It is another matter to determine whether those persons enjoy immunity when they are prosecuted in the courts of a foreign state. Some scholars consider that such an "international" immunity is also to be disregarded. In its judgment of February 14, 2002, in the case concerning the arrest warrant of April 2000 (Democratic Republic of Congo versus Belgium), the International Court of Justice decided, however, that there is no exception to immunity from criminal jurisdiction and inviolability even when an incumbent minister of foreign affairs is suspected of war crimes or crimes against humanity. There is nothing to suggest that the rule should be different where genocide—which is another international crime—is concerned or that is should not be applicable to other persons (heads of state, diplomatic agents, and so forth) normally enjoying "international" jurisdictional immunity. The Court of Justice did not explicitly decide on these points, but its implicit ruling is unambiguous.

From the very beginning, certain provisions of the Genocide Convention have been met with varied and sometimes fierce criticism, yet no one has called into question the principle of an international treaty prohibiting the crime. The main criticism of the definition of genocide is simply that it is too narrow, because the legal specifications adopted resulted in the exclusion of many abuses that are genocidal in nature. True, the specificity of law, especially in criminal matters, requires that the constitutive elements of an offense be clearly determined, so as to leave no doubt as to what does and does not qualify. The critics do not disagree on this point, but they still dispute the narrowness of a definition that could have been made much broader without endangering the basic principles of criminal law. Furthermore, each of the three elements mentioned in Article 2 above give rise to specific criticisms.

It is argued that there is no reason to define restrictively the groups whose destruction constitutes genocide. Originally, a major concern related to political groups, a category explicitly included in the draft prepared by a special committee of the U.N. Economic and Social Council prior to submission to the General Assembly for adoption. The reason for the ultimate omission of political groups was simply the desire of the Western governments to have the Soviet Union and its allies ratify the Convention, something that would have been highly problematic were the Stalinist purges and suppression of non-Communist parties to fall within the ambit of the document. That said, political elements are not the only "other" vulnerable group that could have been included in Article 2.

The requirement of "intent" in genocide has also been widely criticized, as it renders the Convention almost inapplicable, since hard evidence of intent to destroy a group, in most—if not all—cases, appears impossible to produce according to normal judicial standards of proof. It allows states to evade criminal prosecution simply by maintaining that there was no guilt intent, without minding the disastrous consequences of their policies, as, for instance, in the cases of native Indian peoples in Paraguay and Brazil.

According to Article 2 of the United Nations Convention, the intent must be to destroy a group "in whole or in part." The exact meaning of these terms is uncertain. The intent to destroy a group in whole, even if actually eliminating only a part of it, is quite understandable, but how can there be the intent to destroy a group only in part, except when such a part is by itself constitutive of a specific subgroup?[2] This will explain why, at the time that ratification of the Convention was being considered by the United States Senate, Undersecretary of State Dean Rusk declared that genocide requires the intent to destroy the entire group.[3] This conclusion clearly is difficult to reconcile with the wording of Article 2, but it still seems to be the best explanation of what was intended in the article. The logical implication of such a definition seems to be that the number of victims is irrelevant as such if it can be established that the intent is to reach beyond the individual to the group to which the individual belongs. Such a view clearly contradicts the ordinary—let us say journalistic—meaning of the term "genocide," which usually supposes mass killings or deportations. Without officially endorsing this interpretation, some states are not far from accepting it in practice. This was made clear, for example, in the declaration of the United States in 1973 that it intended to add to its ratification of the Convention the wording: "The U.S. government understands and construes the words 'intent to destroy'...appearing in Article 2 to mean the intent to destroy a national, ethnical, racial or religious group...in such a manner as to affect a *substantial part* of the group concerned," it being understood that "substantial part means a part of a group of such numerical significance that the destruction or loss of that part would cause the destruction of the group as a viable entity."[4] No such declaration was actually made when the United States finally ratified the convention in 1988, the emphasis being only that there must be *express* intent. This does not mean, of course, that the precise meaning of Article 2 is now unambiguous.

Another criticism is that the enumeration of acts constituting genocide is too restrictive. One of the main regrets is that the destruction of the cultural or historic heritage of a group was not criminalized under the 1948 Convention. In this respect, it clearly stands back from the draft transmitted to the General Assembly by the Economic and Social Council. The second paragraph of Article 3 of that draft included the destruction of libraries, schools, museums, historic monuments, churches, and other cultural institutions or property of a group. That aspect is directly relevant for the Armenian people, taking into account the actions of Turkish authorities since the 1915 genocide. The provision was deleted in the final draft, however, the main consideration once more being to avoid rejection of the Covenant by states concerned about the uncertain implications of the paragraph.

The "repressive" part of the 1948 Convention is obviously rather poor, even though making genocide "a crime under international law" may be considered noteworthy progress. The symbolic value of such an explicit condemnation cannot be disregarded. Nevertheless, the fact is that the operative part of the Convention as far as the prevention and punishment of genocide are concerned is virtually non-existent. There really is no prevention at all, apart from the deterrent that might result from criminalizing genocide in international law. The provisions for punishment, moreover, are far from being explicit. The central provision makes punishment the responsibility of the involved territorial state or by an international criminal court of justice. It is not surprising that the territorial authorities may not be motivated to punish the perpetrators of a genocide, which to a large extent is "state-implicated," and it is well known that states traditionally oppose the compulsory jurisdiction of a permanent international court, even if they recently decided to establish an International Criminal Court.

Up to the present, the definition of genocide has remained substantially unchanged, even if the reading of its terms is somewhat less restrictive than originally understood. To meet the criticisms to which the definition of genocide has given rise, the Convention must be modified. Despite many such proposals, no agreement has been reached to amend the compact. Moreover, the statutes of the international tribunals that were created in the 1990s to punish genocide in Rwanda and the former Yugoslavia define the crime in terms identical to those in the United Nations Convention. This means that the definition of genocide has remained within its narrow parameters. Still, even without formal revision of the 1948 text, some changes have occurred in national or international judicial practice.

The main trend in contemporary practice seems to be stretching the definition of genocide. Many proposals have been made in this respect. According to Helen Fein, for instance, "genocide is the calculated murder of a segment or all of a group defined outside the universe of obligation of the perpetrator by a government, elite staff or crowd representing the perpetrator in response to a crisis or opportunity perceived to be caused or impeded by the victims."[5] For Israel Charny, "genocide in the generic sense is the mass killing of substantial numbers of human beings, when not in the course of military actions against the military forces of an avowed enemy, under conditions of the essential defenselessness and helplessness of the victims."[6] These definitions have never been admitted as such in legal practice, but the conduct of states is clearly demonstrating a willingness to go beyond the restrictive terms of the United Nations Convention. Some national statutes, notably in France, now consider the destruction of "any" group as such as constituting the crime of genocide.

The International Criminal Tribunal for Rwanda (ICTR) affirmed in its judgment in the Ayakesu case (which sentenced a mayor of a Rwandan community in which 2,000 Tutsi were massacred) that the drafters of the 1948 Genocide Convention intended to protect any group having a stable and permanent character. The exact significance of its decision has given rise to divergent interpretations.[7] It remains unclear whether, by making this comment while discussing the ethnic character of the Tutsi group, the Tribunal's purpose was actually to extend or, on the contrary, to reduce the interpretation to be given to the groups identified in Article 2 of the Convention. The extent to which practice is prone to accept that any group will be taken into account in defining genocide therefore still remains to be seen. It could in fact be dangerous to disconnect totally the rules prohibiting genocide from the ones protecting groups whose destruction is regarded as genocidal, the result of which would be to allow perpetrators to invent a group ("any" group) devoid of the objective bases permitting "positive" protection, as in the case, for example, of minorities or indigenous peoples.

No progress has been made regarding the issue of intent. Actually, the requirement is basically sound. How could such a monstrous crime be committed if there is no intent to destroy a group as such? It is not surprising therefore that the need of a specific intent was reaffirmed by the ICTR Chamber in its Ayakesu judgment, even if the crime need not be premeditated. Premeditation is a superfluous factor. Clearly, it is still criminal to expose a group to the risk of destruction, by adopting a particular conduct or policy, even if at first sight it might seem "objectively" justified. No doubt, punishment is legitimate in such a context. That said, it is still a totally different matter to adopt a conduct or policy with a view to destroying a group, in whole or in part. A possible evolution might alleviate the burden of proof without impairing the basic principles of criminal law. For instance, the presumption that a large number of victims proves genocidal intent is problematical and in any case should not be deemed irrefutable. The interested party must always be allowed to establish that it never had such intent. This might differentiate ethnic cleansing, as used in the former Yugoslavia, from genocide, no matter how reprehensible the forced displacement of persons to create ethnically homogeneous political or territorial units.

What appears to be the least detrimental to the effective protection of groups is the restrictive list of acts constituting genocide according to the Convention. After all, the terms are already broad enough to cover most genocidal practices without breaching the rules of legal interpretation. The main reservation relates to what is called "cultural genocide," the deliberate attempt to destroy a culture without necessarily physically eliminating all members of the group. The term "ethnocide" is sometimes used to distinguish this crime from physical genocide or genocide *sensu stricto* (in a strict sense). Proposals have been made to modify the 1948 Convention or to draft a special protocol to criminalize and lay down punishment for policies of cultural genocide.[8] Up until now, these suggestions have not gone forward. Political factors explain the difficulty of changing the terms of the Genocide Convention. Moreover, there is significant resistance to equating "cultural" with "physical" genocide. It is difficult to put on the same level the elimination of groups with the disappearance—however regrettable—of their specific culture. Often, the goal of cultural genocide is the opposite of physical genocide, as it is intended to assimilate another group, not to destroy it as such.[9]

Apart from ethnocide, it has been proposed to incriminate specifically a crime of "ecocide," the harmful and often irreversible alterations of the environment as the result of human activities (nuclear testing, massive industrial pollution, and so forth). No doubt, safeguarding the environment is critical in many respects for present and future generations, which easily explains the wish to criminalize conduct jeopardizing this objective. But this does not mean that "ecocide" should be equated with genocide, even though wanton cultural or environmental misconduct may certainly be taken into consideration in determining whether genocide is being or has been perpetrated. These acts simply need to be viewed within the broad categories used in Article 2 of the 1948 Convention to be criminalized as such, provided that the intent to destroy the group is established.

The fact that odious conduct may fall beyond the scope of the 1948 Convention does not mean that it is to be tolerated and cannot be criminally prosecuted. No! It simply means that it is not punishable as genocide, which does not exclude punishment under either a national (murder, kidnapping, etc.) or an international (war crime, crime against humanity) legal code. What is of specific interest in the case of an international crime is that it is not subject to a statute of limitation and may fall within the jurisdiction of an international court.

The punishment of genocide has remained theoretical for forty years. Since the end of the Cold War, things are changing, as evidenced by the first conviction for the crime of genocide in the Akayesu decision by the International Criminal Tribunal for Rwanda. Clearly, there is no intrinsic link between the Cold War and the Rwandan

Genocide. The fact remains that the changing atmosphere in international relations has made possible the punishment of perpetrators. It surely is too early to formulate any firm conclusion in this respect, but there is a good chance that the time of complete impunity is over and that those who perpetrate genocide, no matter at what level, will be held accountable.

In contemporary practice, genocide is prosecuted both at the national and international levels. At a purely interstate level, not implying criminal proceedings against individuals, it is noteworthy that Bosnia-Herzegovina and Croatia referred to the International Court of Justice (ICJ) the case of alleged genocidal practices committed by Serbia during the Yugoslav crisis. Serbia counter-charged Croatia for genocide against the Serbs. The case is still pending, but it is significant that this is the first time that genocide is the object of an interstate dispute, brought before the judicial organ of the United Nations, the International Court of Justice.

At an international level, the punishment of genocide is one of the responsibilities entrusted to the International Criminal Tribunal for Rwanda (ICTR) and the International Criminal Tribunal for Yugoslavia (ICTY), established pursuant to the decisions of the Security Council based on Chapter VII of the United Nations Charter. The punishment of the serious crimes committed during the Yugoslavian and Rwandan crises was considered to be part of the "measures" that the Security Council is entitled to adopt under this chapter in order to restore international peace and security. Genocide clearly is at the center of the jurisdiction of the Rwandan tribunal, whereas the tribunal for the former Yugoslavia has been somewhat more cautious, since in principle ethnic cleansing is not equated with genocide. Although the functioning of the tribunals, especially the ICTR, has been criticized, this does not change the fact that the creation of these international judicial bodies is an extraordinary development.

It is even more amazing, by ordinary international practice, that the Statute of the International Criminal Court (ICC) was adopted in July 1998. The ICC has jurisdiction over genocide when national courts are unable or unwilling to act, which means that its role is to be "complementary," and not subsidiary, as some commentators suggest. The specific conditions under which the ICC is to exercise its responsibility are stipulated in the Statute, with the respective roles of the court and the prosecutor being clearly defined. This, too, is a remarkable development. Despite certain criticism and the voiced opposition of some countries such as the United States, the statute entered into force in April 2002, more than sixty states having ratified its provisions.

At a national level, the United Nations is negotiating with Cambodian authorities on the modalities of trials of the Khmer Rouge by a Cambodian court, with international assistance so as to constitute a "credible" panel. This confirms that the territorial courts constitute the "natural" judges of genocidal acts, but it also implicitly attests to the difficulties faced by those courts in rendering justice in such extreme circumstances.

At a purely national level, there are also courts claiming so-called universal jurisdiction to punish perpetrators of genocides committed abroad and not having any territorial or personal link with the state in which such courts function. This explains, for example, how in Belgium, where a specific statute was adopted in 1999, complaints were lodged against individuals implicated in genocides in Rwanda and in Cambodia or how in Spain, apart from Pinochet (probably erroneously in that case), former military leaders of Guatemala have been charged with genocidal practices against Indian natives.

Such a variety of approaches clearly shows that the time when persons committing genocide were left unpunished has passed. Each of these techniques has its own merits, largely dependent on the specifics of the particular case. That said, at an international level, a permanent court, having a role complementary to national tribunals, is clearly to be preferred to ad hoc institutions created for specific needs, as legitimate as they might be. Ad hoc bodies are likely to be seen as expressing more the will of some unilateral power than of common justice. For the same reasons, there is no illusion about universal jurisdiction, especially when it is exercised by Western powers imposing their own views about democracy and justice on the rest of the world. That might satisfy some immediate need of the victims but would not meet the requirements of justice in the long run.

To the extent discussed above, progress in international law regarding genocide is noticeable. Nevertheless, two major defects remain. The first one is concerned with the prevention of genocide, which is as important, or even more important, than punishment. Only a few limited things have been achieved in this respect. The difficulty is that prevention has to do with the causes of genocide, which usually are far from being clear. Even if those causes were fully understood, it still would be necessary to determine how to handle the situation. It would be helpful in this respect to develop education programs and information campaigns, as suggested for instance in the report submitted by committee rapporteur Benjamin Whitaker.[10] The work in this direction has been insufficient. Certainly, some non-governmental organizations play a role in hindering genocide. At least, they are the watchful bodies whose alarm signals are the most effective. But this is not enough as evidenced in recent developments. It is incumbent on the United Nations and the world community to determine appropriate measures and define common policies regarding prevention.

The second basic defect pertains to the persistence of denial or negationism. Genocide is such a horrendous crime that it will almost always be denied by those who are its authors. And this point brings us directly back to Armenian history. It is a matter of law when an alleged crime is committed to establish what are the relevant facts and their legal bearing, so as to ascertain whether they fit its constitutive elements. What is a matter of law becomes a matter of history when there no longer is room for criminal proceedings because of the death of the perpetrators. And normally it is not for a court or for any other judicial or political body to rule on history. That said, it still is unacceptable that a state denies and persists in denying, contrary to reliable evidence, a genocide perpetrated by former authorities. Negationism perpetuates suffering and denies a people the right to have its memory restored. It should be the elementary right of the victims to have access to an independent (international) body simply for the truth to be established officially. And it should be the obligation of the state concerned to cooperate with such a body. No such right or obligation presently exists or is clearly admitted. It should be the task of any honest man to fight for its recognition, saving the international community from becoming merely a sham or a mockery, for that would be disastrous for individuals, groups, peoples, and nations alike.

“Technical” Legal Issues

Obviously, genocide raises “fundamental” questions that go far beyond the technicalities of law. Still, some legal issues are necessarily involved and must be addressed. These are different in character and importance. The principal ones relate to:

1) punishment of the perpetrators of a genocide;

2) official recognition of the existence of a genocide;

3) compensation of the victims of a genocide.

It is not possible to discuss thoroughly in the present brief contribution the various legal aspects of the three points, but several general comments can be made in this regard.

Punishment

It is an accepted principle of law that criminal proceedings may be brought against only living persons. Consequently, the punishment of those responsible for the Armenian Genocide is no longer possible. In contemporary international law, on the other hand, the idea of criminal liability of states is affirmed, and genocide was listed among the international crimes in Article 19 of the initial draft articles on state responsibility, adopted by the International Law Commission (ILC). Such an assertion opens the way to international "punishment" of the state to which the genocidal acts are attributable, as would be the case of Turkey should it be held responsible for the 1915 massacres. Such a perspective is quite interesting. Serious doubt exists, however, regarding the customary character of the distinction made between internationally wrongful acts that constitute a "crime" and a "delict" respectively. There is nothing in the ILC draft to suggest that the state to which the crime is attributable may be "punished," and the specific consequences of its criminal conduct remain rather vague. This explains why any reference to a "crime" was finally deleted in the draft of the ILC, even if it still makes mention of a "serious breach of an obligation arising under a pre-emptory norm of general international law," which is far from being much clearer.

Recognition

It is not for a judge or any other political authority to establish the truth in case facts or situations are disputed between contesting parties. As far as the judge is concerned, his task is to decide whether to take a given fact or situation as having been established and, if so, to determine what are its consequences according to the law. His judgment has all the binding effects given by law (*res judicata*). The same goes *mutatis mutandis* for the judgment of a political authority. To this extent, there exists some judicial or political truth that cannot, however, be confused with historical truth, even if it is hoped that both are in agreement.

The point is relevant for genocide as well as for the determination of any other legal situation. It implies that a tribunal can never be asked directly to recognize the existence of a genocide, as in most cases such recognition is purely incidental to the punishment of the perpetrators or the compensation of the victims, that is, to the legal case that is referred to it. At the international or interstate level, it is conceivable that a claim could be brought before an international tribunal by Armenia against Turkey concerning certain legal consequences of the Armenian Genocide, but this implies that the genocide has been accepted as fact. This remains only a theoretical possibility. The difficulty is not—although it cannot be dismissed—that Armenia was non-existent as a state at the time the genocide was committed, but rather that no interstate court has jurisdiction unless it is accorded that prerogative by the interested parties. Its jurisdiction exists only when and to the extent that those parties have so agreed. The form of such an arrangement is irrelevant, but mutual consent must be given. To date, no such an agreement exists in the relations between Armenia and Turkey, either by treaty, the exchange of optional clauses of compulsory jurisdiction in accordance with Article 36 of the Statute of the International Court of Justice, or any other arrangement. And I would be most surprised if Turkey ever agreed to submit to the ICJ or any other international tribunal a dispute that could call into question its denial of the Armenian Genocide.

The only court of compulsory jurisdiction to which Turkey has adhered is the European Court of Human Rights (ECHR), whose seat is at Strasbourg, France. This is an international but not interstate court, in the sense that it is established by international treaty to decide claims of individuals against contracting states for breach of the European convention on human rights, signed at Rome in 1950 and since then supplemented by several protocols. Once a state has ratified or adhered to the convention and its relevant protocols, which is the case for Turkey, no further consent is needed from it to hear a case.

To my knowledge, the ECHR is the only international court before which Turkey, being a party to the European system of protecting human rights and fundamental freedoms, could presently be brought without its consent. The difficulty lies in finding a claimant and a claim, that is, a breach of the European convention on human rights and a person entitled to sue the Turkish authorities for such a breach. This is rather problematic. Any person within the jurisdiction of Turkey may bring action before the ECHR if he claims to be the victim of a violation of the provisions of the Rome convention. Clearly, a genocide as such would violate those provisions, but it could be judged only if it occurred after the convention entered into force. Hence, the Armenian Genocide would not fall within the purview of the ECHR. The only possibility therefore would be to assert that the persistent denial of the genocide by the Turkish authorities violates one of the basic human rights guaranteed by the European convention. What right? Possibly the right of any person not to be subjected to inhuman or degrading treatment, which could be said to occur by the negation of crimes that profoundly affect the very identity of the Armenian people. The argument obviously is not ill founded. Still, the construction is somewhat strained and probably goes beyond the scope of the original intent of the Rome convention. This does not imply that it is without merit, but it is unlikely that the ECHR would accept such a method of recognizing the reality of the Armenian Genocide. In any case, local remedies, that is, Turkish remedies, have to be exhausted before any complaint can be lodged before the European Court of Human Rights.

It is also possible for national courts to decide "indirectly" on the existence of a genocide. This is necessarily the case when a person is brought before a tribunal for the crime of genocide. As far as the Armenian Genocide is concerned, that hypothesis has lost any relevance, since, as previously noted, all the perpetrators are now dead. The only possibility, therefore, is to argue the legal consequences of the genocide as regards mainly compensation due to the victims. The mere fact that those responsible for the genocide are no longer alive does not exclude the right of compensation. The important point is to establish the fact of the massacres and other violence and to determine what are their legal consequences. In this context, it is relatively immaterial that those massacres were of a genocidal nature.

Compensation

Compensation under international law cannot be confused with compensation under national law. It is theoretically conceivable that Armenia could make a claim against Turkey for the continuing consequences of the 1915 genocide. The difficulty is that the state of Armenia was non-existent at the time of the massacres, which would give grounds to dispute its claim for compensation. The objection is serious, and in any case claims cannot be brought before a judge, arbitrator, or tribunal without the consent of the parties concerned. There is little chance that Turkey would agree to refer such a case to an international body.

At first sight, another possibility is that Armenia exercise its right to diplomatic protection of its nationals. It is not disputed that a state may claim compensation for the injury caused to its nationals by a foreign state that violates its international obligations. In this respect also, the difficulty is that the victims of the genocide were not Armenian nationals at the time the genocidal massacres took place but rather subjects of the Ottoman Empire. This circumstance is clearly inconsistent with the rule requiring that the persons for which a state is exercising the so-called diplomatic protection be its nationals "continuously" from the time the injury occurred until the time the claim for compensation is made. The only possibility—and that, too, is problematic—would therefore be to assert that denial of the genocide by Turkey is a violation of its international obligations and is harming Armenian nationals. In any case, local Turkish remedies must be exhausted by the interested private parties before any claim could be made by the Armenian authorities with the consent of Turkey. The slim chance of such an eventuality requires no further comment here.

When the issue of compensation is raised under national law, the tribunal having jurisdiction must first be determined as does the law that is to be applied, which raises problems when the case is connected with two or more legal systems. Each state has its own rules, and this makes solutions more complicated. It is generally agreed that when immovable goods and properties are involved, the tribunal having jurisdiction is the one in the district or country where the goods are located; that in contractual matters such as insurance the parties are free to choose the tribunal before which the claims are brought; and that when no special rule exists, the judge is one in the domicile of the respondent. It is probable that in many if not most cases those rules will result in giving jurisdiction to Turkish tribunals, because the property or assets whose restitution is claimed are located in Turkey or because the public and private entities that are accused of causing the damage are domiciled in that country. Even so, it cannot be excluded that claims for compensation might be brought before foreign tribunals, as there is a recent trend of such courts asserting jurisdiction on "extraordinary grounds" in order to provide compensation to the victims of an international crime. Where Turkish tribunals are concerned, it is for the Turkish law to decide to what extent Turkish authorities might be brought before the courts. Moreover, before a non-Turkish tribunal, those authorities are normally entitled to claim the benefit of the immunity of jurisdiction, at least when they have been acting in their sovereign capacity (*jure imperii*). There is nonetheless a tendency in contemporary practice to disregard the claim for immunity when it comes to acts constituting an international crime, which genocide undisputedly is.

It is another matter to determine what law is to be applied to the substance of the claim. It may be necessary to resort to the rules pertaining to conflict of law. The law in force at the place where the immovable goods and properties are located (*lex situs*) normally governs the claims concerning their legal status, as for instance the claim for restitution for illegal acquisition. Actually, the same criterion is used *mutatis mutandis* to determine the law applied to movable goods, which usually makes applicable the *lex situs.* As far as tort liability is concerned, the applicable law generally is the law in force at a place where the tort was committed (*lex loci delicti*) or at the tribunal before which the action is brought (*lex fori*). In most cases, the applicable rules would probably be the law of Turkey. And there is a good chance that contractual claims will also be governed by that law if the parties did not explicitly agree in the contract on the applicability of some other law.

No doubt, such claims for compensation will not be easily granted. Apart from any political consideration, factual and legal reasons are involved. Factually, one of the major difficulties will be to produce the evidence to support a claim for restitution or damages more than eighty years after the occurrence of the massacres. And this passage of time raises legal difficulties because statutes of limitations could bar action. Doubts exist as to the law governing time limitations, the dominant view being that it is for the law applicable to the substance of the case to decide the question. Each national law has its own rules in this respect. Whatever the applicable law, it would be most unusual that the admissibility of a claim could surmount the passage of more than eighty years. On the other hand, recent cases suggest that judges do not always adhere to strict limitations when it comes to such "basic" issues.

Conclusion

From the above discussion, one may conclude that the prospect of having the Armenian Genocide officially recognized or of receiving compensation remains legally weak, especially in the present political context. That does not mean, however, that it is simply sheer nonsense. Above all, that does not mean that recognition and compensation can be achieved only by application of and in accordance with the rules of law. Recent practice has shown that more than fifty years after the Nazi genocide, compensation has been afforded and assets or properties returned to its victims without strict adherence to the technicalities of any system of law and without the formal intervention of public institutions. The important point seems to be that the victims, invoking some natural law of a new kind independent of the political interests of any state, organize so as to negotiate a settlement effectively and that public opinion—and some influential public authorities—be influenced so as to sustain and reinforce the legitimacy of their claim. No doubt, the Armenian people, who would probably be more efficient than the Armenian state, still have much progress to make in this respect. While the global context may not be favorable to them, there is no doubt that the concept of justice supports their cause.

Notes

1. On the story of the Convention, see Pieter N. Drost, *The Crime of State*, vol. 2 (Leiden: A.W. Sythoff, 1959); William A. Schabas, *Genocide in International Law* (Cambridge and New York: Cambridge University Press, 2000).
2. See Nathan Robinson, *The Genocide Convention: A Commentary* (New York: Institute of Jewish Affairs, 1960), p. 63.

3. See Lawrence J. LeBlanc, *The United States and the Genocide Convention* (Durham, NC and London: Duke University Press, 1991), pp. 37ff.
4. Lawrence J. LeBlanc, "The Intent to Destroy Groups in the Genocide Convention: The Proposed U.S. Understanding," *American Journal of International Law* 78 (1984): 370, 380.
5. As quoted in Israel W. Charny, ed., *Genocide: A Critical Bibliography Review* (London: Mansell, 1988), p. 3.
6. "Towards a Generic Definition of Genocide, " in George J. Andreopoulous, ed., *Genocide: Conceptual and Historical Dimensions* (Philadelphia: University of Pennsylvania Press, 1994), p. 75.
7. William Schabas, "L'affaire Ayakesu et ses enseignements sur le droit du génocide," in Katia Boustany and Daniel Dormoy, eds., *Génocide(s)* (Brussels: Bruyland, 1999), pp. 111ff.
8. See, for instance, the revised and updated draft of the report presented by Benjamin Whitaker on the prevention and repression of genocide before the subcommittee of the U.N. Human Rights Commission, Doc. E/CN.4/Sub2/1985/6, July 2, 1985, §§ 32-33.
9. See Jean-Michel Chaumont, "Génocide et ethnocide," in Boustany and Dormoy, *Génocide(s)*, pp. 253-55.
10. U.N. Human Rights Commission, Doc. E/CN.4/Sub2/1985/6, July 2, 1985, §§ 78-82.

9

New Directions in Literary Responses to the Armenian Genocide

Rubina Peroomian

To Conceptualize the Catastrophe

The history of the Armenian people is replete with persecutions and massacres, traumatic collective experiences that have triggered the last cries of the victims and the urge in the survivors to comprehend and give meaning to the cataclysm so that life may continue. Armenian literature is a repository of echoes of these responses to catastrophe. These are not reactions in a vacuum but are shaped and reshaped through time by multiple layers of influences such as Judeo-Christian teachings, cultural determinants, historical archetypes, as well as evolving national ideals and political aspirations.[1] Within this context, literary responses to genocide are the amalgamation and the echo of all these factors, and, at the same time, they surmount all responses in scope, depth, and intensity, as the Armenian Genocide culminates all catastrophes in the history of the Armenian people in terms of its eschatological nature and impact. Hence arises the grouping of the literature of genocide as a topical genre of Armenian literature, paradoxically, whether the genocide is a literary theme or only a hidden motif.

The Armenian diasporan post-genocide literature, therefore, to a large extent embodies the attempts to conceptualize the Catastrophe (*Aghet*) or Great Crime (*Eghern*), to come to terms with its impact, to reconcile with its undying memory, or to vent rage and frustration against the denial by the perpetrator and the indifference of the world. Nearly all Armenian diasporan literature relates in one way or another to the Armenian Genocide. Diaspora is regarded as the offspring of the Genocide:

Children of massacre,
children of destruction,
children of dispersion,
oh, my Diaspora...
someone was calling
in my dream.[2]

These lines are a poetic rendering by Diana Der Hovanessian of the make-up of the interrelationship between the Diaspora and the Genocide. But the Genocide is more than a physical source of being. It is an end and a beginning. In a study of North American Armenian literature, Lorne Shirinian writes: "1915 functions as a symbol through which Armenians have knowledge of themselves and see themselves. Having survived genocide, not only do they have to believe in themselves, but they have to convince others of their existence. Armenian diasporan literature is an expression of this necessity."[3]

Now, at the beginning of a new millennium, as the Catastrophe slips into the past century, as factual memories are fading, and as generations of Armenians are growing more and more aloof from the wounds of the past and weary of the image of a victim people, is there a reason for the continuation of genocide literature? And if there still exists a milieu open to its development, what direction will these literary responses take? Will they follow the same paradigm? Or is there a change in the making that can result in new directions? Certainly, historical documents will still be discovered, and new historical texts will continue to shed light on the Catastrophe, affirming the truth and the reality of the crime. And political and civic organizations will undoubtedly keep on striving for world recognition of the Armenian Genocide. At the same time, new conceptualizations in the literary representations of the Genocide will enrich the topical genre and, together with the responses of the past generations of survivors, will play an important role in the process of nation building.

On the Scope of the New Literary Responses

The Armenian Genocide has generated a plethora of literature, both prose and poetry, but writers have aspired in vain to write, and critics are still awaiting, the novel of novels—one that encompasses the Genocide in its entirety. It has not materialized. The fact is that the most successful novel of this kind, *The Forty Days of Musa Dagh* (1933), was written by a non-Armenian, Franz Werfel. And now there is a promising more recent novel, one that won the 1989 Alfred Döblin Award, given by the Günter Grass Foundation, one with a different scope and a different approach, *The Story of the Last Thought*, by another non-Armenian, Edgar Hilsenrath.[4] Despite the success and importance of these novels, they are not the awaited masterpieces of literature on the Armenian Genocide. Yet, I cannot point to any work by an Armenian author in any genre that is nearly as thorough a representation and as popular as these, except perhaps Paruyr Sevak's *Anlreli zangakatun* [Immutably Tolling Bell Tower]. Leonardo Alishan writes: "There is no proper genre for giving an artistic expression to the genocide. The novel comes closest but that too does not suffice. The particular bears witness to the general. But though this witness tells the truth and nothing but the truth, it fails to tell the whole truth."[5] My contention is that one has to live the hell in order to be able to create its representation in art; yet even such representation will be a mimesis, according to Platonic logic, one step removed from the Truth of the unthinkable reality of genocide.

Elie Wiesel has said that only one who has been there has the right to speak, and Alvin Rosenfeld asserts that "the best portrayals of 'life' in Nazi concentration camps are produced by those who themselves experienced the meaninglessness of the two categories of life and death."[6] The generation with firsthand experience of the Armenian Catastrophe did not succeed in creating that masterpiece. The most talented writers and poets were massacred at the outset. The attempts of the surviving few, such as Hagop Oshagan and Aram Andonian, did not bear fruit.[7] It is thus unreasonable to hope that succeeding generations of Armenian writers would be able to reach that pinnacle.

Materialization of the Novel of the Armenian Genocide is unlikely. Still, I believe that the next generations of Armenian literati—some obsessed with the Genocide, others only now discovering the traumatic past, the cause of the unspoken pain in the family, and still others finding the freedom to entertain the topic as they choose—have strong potentials. With the distance of time and space in their favor, with a deeper knowledge of history, and with a talent for grasping the poetics of violence, they have favorable possibilities to be able to confront the Genocide. They may accomplish the imperative, the preponderant component of the totality of literary responses to the Genocide. Their work is likely to encompass the echoes of the nation's collective psyche shaped by the violence, the pain of dispersion, the wounds of self-accusation, the search for identity or the struggle to cope with a dual identity, the effects of the past, and present role of the perpetrators and world bystanders.

The Functionality of Genocide Literature

Let us briefly consider the functionality of literary responses to catastrophe. This is based on an assumption accepted by many sociologists and literary critics that fiction is socially conscious. In this connection Melvin J. Vincent writes: "Fiction and drama make possible an imaginative penetration into human character and social events. When presented with consummate literary skill, this offers a more precise and deeper insight into both human character and events and their significance."[8]

The fictionalized Armenian Genocide provides that deep insight into the Catastrophe with a potential impact that works in two distinct dimensions. The internal dimension is built upon the responses of the victims and survivors, coming across from within the text. It accounts for the cathartic quality and therapeutic effect that such artistic expressions exert upon the author and the reader as well. It also works as an essential fuel to keep the fire burning in the soul, to keep alive the Armenian consciousness of a colossal injustice awaiting redress, to keep the collective memory of the Armenian Genocide alive and functional. The external dimension deals with the potential impact of such literature on world public awareness, which consequently can help the realization of world recognition of the Armenian Genocide and eventual reparation.

But this is a difficult task to assign to genocide literature. If it is produced with such a goal in mind, it may easily cross the boundary of pure art. It may become tendentious art, identified with a political cause, or, at best, a desperate protest against denial. The Turkish government's stance and its tacit acceptance by the world are detrimental influences. Alishan spells out the end result: "The artist is caught between serving his art and convincing people of his own people's collective catastrophe. He plays both the role of the detached artist and the passionate propagandist. Consequently, there is a chaotic confusion of genres and roles, resulting in a frustrated failure."[9]

Anne Frank did not need to convince the world that the Holocaust happened. Yet her work in the simple form of a diary has had a powerful impact. For some, it is the only source of information on the genocide of the Jews. Published in English translation in 1952, *The Diary of a Young Girl*, as Alvin Rosenfeld attests, was the first to penetrate the American consciousness and shape the American, or rather the universal, reception of the Holocaust. Then came the Broadway production (1955) and the full-length film (1959) of the *Diary*. Part of the success of the book, the play, and the film was the subtlety of the subject: not too harsh, not too Jewish, not too disturbing.[10] Then came Steven Spielberg's *Schindler's List*, with an impact surpassing Anne Frank's *Diary*. This was a completely new approach to the Jewish tragedy, one that portrayed not the victimization of the Jews, but the confrontation of good and evil, the good German and the evil German, the savior and the executioner, and the conclusion was not a depressing one but a happy reunion of survivors, now mostly affluent people. This is a new direction in Jewish responses, or rather a new representation of the Holocaust that incidentally has drawn much criticism but one that the public can readily grasp.

What does the public know about the Armenian Genocide?

The Paradigm of Responses

The survivors of the Armenian Genocide, scattered around the world, and in particular those who reached America, did not in most cases speak of their horrible experience, especially to their children. For many, there was this inexplicable shame, the shame of having survived while other members of the family had suffered gruesome death. Then, there was this inner compulsion to leave everything behind and live in the New World integrated in the society like everyone else, fearing that, if they told their stories, it would set them apart. There was also the burden of daily struggle for survival in a new, unfamiliar environment. The prejudice of mainstream society against newcomers contributed to that conduct, and, on top of it all, there was the desire to spare their children, to protect them against the paralyzing memory with which they had to live. Whatever the reasons, their response to the genocide was silence. It needed an Edgar Hilsenrath to write in his novel, *The Story of the Last Thought*:

> I told the silence the story of the genocide. I made the silence aware of how important it is that it should be spoken of in public. I said: "Everyone ought to know!" For how will genocide be prevented in future if everyone declares they knew nothing about it, and they did nothing to prevent it because they couldn't even imagine such a thing.[11]

For some, this period of silence was never broken. It was only after their death that their children discovered, through fragmented memorabilia, the tremendous burden of memory that weighed so heavily upon their parents and caused their special, unfathomable, sometimes peculiar behavior. Virginia Haroutounian's *Orphan in the Sands* (1995) is the story of the author's mother, who only in the final days of her life shared with her daughter her terrible ordeal during and after the Genocide. It is the story of the daughter, who resented her mother's strange behavior and strove all her life to adjust to it only to learn in the end that it was the Genocide and its aftereffects that had ruined her mother's and her own life.

David Kherdian speaks of the same experience:

> Why have I waited until your death
> to know the earth you were turning
> was Armenia, the color of the fence
> your homage to Adana, and your other
> complaints over my own complaints
> were addressed to your homesickness
> brought on by my English.[12]

In another poem, Kherdian describes his father, who "always carried a different/look and smell into the house when he/returned from the coffee houses in Racine":

> Years later, reading the solemn and bittersweet
> stories of our Armenian writer in California,
> who visited as a paperboy coffeehouses in
> Fresno, I came to understand that in these
> cafes were contained the suffering and
> shattered hopes of my orphaned people.[13]

The burden of tragic memories had been transmitted indirectly yet effectively, for it fit perfectly into the family atmosphere and father-and-son relationship experienced by the generation born to the survivors of the Genocide.

Other survivors were able to overcome all the inhibitions and communicate their ordeal, pass on the memory, even put it in writing and publish it for everyone to know. With the politicization of the Diaspora in the late 1960s, these survivors gradually acquired a certain status: they became primary sources of information and their memoirs were welcome additions to genocide literature. It is significant that even today, when this generation is almost gone, the memoirs keep appearing. They are being written by the second, even the third, generation. In some cases, the author is simply reproducing what was left in writing by the survivor. Hovhannes Mugrditchian's diary is an example. The diary, whose English version is published by his son as *To Armenians with Love: The Memoirs of a Patriot*, begins with stories of Turkish rape and persecution of Armenians even before Hovhannes was born. It then continues with the author's childhood memories in Cilicia and the tragic events leading up to and including the deportations and massacres of 1915, the resettlement of the survivors in their Cilician towns and villages after World War I, and finally their irreversible exodus in 1921. This is followed by life in the United States, repatriation to Soviet Armenia, and eventual return to America.[14]

In other cases, the raw material, survivor testimonies, is elaborated and embellished to become the response of the new generation to the memory of their parents, to the genocide of their people. Peter Balakian's *Black Dog of Fate* (1997) is an example of a well-written melange of memoir-documentation. It is an attractive source of reference for non-Armenians and new-generation Armenians. It is, as the author himself puts it, a "polyphonic, multilayered memoir" in which "personal discovery and history merge."[15] *Efronia, An Armenian Love Story* (1994) is another example. Here, Efronia Katchadourian's memoirs of some 500 pages were translated into English by her son and turned into a nicely-wrought piece of imaginative literature by her non-Armenian daughter-in-law, Stina Katchadourian.[16] In *Rise the Euphrates* (1994), Carol Edgarian skillfully blends the facts of the Armenian Genocide and the traumatic experience of the survivor generation with the attractions and multiple opportunities and fun that American culture can offer a third-generation Armenian teenager.[17] It is clearly manifest in Edgarian's work that no matter how deeply assimilated with the culture and lifestyle of the mainstream, no matter how aloof from the Armenian past, this American-born generation still carries traces of the wounds of the Genocide.

The success of these memoirs or other sub-genres of genocide literature in prose and poetry can be attributed to the fact that they are being produced within the conventions of American culture. They are palatable to the American taste and acceptance of horror stories. The second and third generation poet or writer has mastered the criteria. As Arpiné Konyalian Grenier puts it, the new writer "faces the tragedy, accepts it, mourns it and transcends it." Later she adds, however: "It is tricky and slippery to face emotion and express it in unadulterated fashion."[18] It is indeed a challenging task, for it is sometimes impossible not to succumb to the waves of irrepressible emotion.

Leonardo Alishan has never been able to transcend, or rather he has never tried to transcend, the tragedy that was his grandmother's, the tragedy that became his fate at the age of nine. His strongest literary creations are about his "Granny" and "bearing witness to her agony." He shares her agony; he is a part of it: "I try to be a spectator of that tragedy which culminated in a London hospital room in 1978 where Granny saw Turkish horsemen around her bed before she died. But, alas, I am not the spectator. I am a character caught in that play which never, never, never reaches its equilibrium."[19] Alishan is still gripped by the nightmare of genocide. His Granny, "Gayané, the living martyr," as he defines her, still governs his life and his emotions. She is a constant presence in his dreams, in his waking thoughts. It is through his grandmother, as it is the case of most second- or third-generation writers, that Alishan sees the Armenian suffering, the Genocide:

In the center of my dream
there is a church of stone in Van
sealed from outside
exhaling screams and smoke from the inside,
its congregation of Armenian folk
replacing the candles with their flesh.
There is a church in my dream
made with the bones of dead gods,
babies and parrots' prayers;
always, all night, in flames

but never burning to the ground.
And in the church burns a statue of Mary
With my Granny's face, wax dripping down her eyes
drop by drop, on the skin of my dreams.[20]

The memory of the Armenian Genocide, even though not at peak intensity and not as devastating as it was for the first-generation survivors, has been transmitted to subsequent generations and is still now inspiring literary creations. The topoi associated with the Genocide appear as fragmented images imposing themselves upon everyday life in the New World. Many of Peter Balakian's poems in *Sad Days of Light* (1983) illustrate this duality. Through a commingling of images past and present, Balakian registers the replay of the tragedy of 1915 in his grandmother's mind.[21]

These responses are definitely different from the immediate reactions of those who experienced the Genocide. Indeed, the Armenian poets and writers of the 1920s and the 1930s attempted to recapture in art the hell through which they themselves had lived, the horrifying experience of an entire people half-murdered, half-eradicated from their homeland and cast into foreign lands. They tried to find the source of the evil in the character of the Turk, the victimizer. They tried to explain the Catastrophe, laud the spirit of self-defense, chastise the cowards and their lowly, despicable means of survival. They tried to interpret the calamity as a twist in the relationship between man and God; they even defied God, casting doubt on His existence or His oneness. Hagop Oshagan, Aram Andonian, Vahan Tekeyan, and Shahan Natali, among others, produced the best examples of these themes.

The next generation, the orphans of the desert who began their adult life in the Diaspora, strove to cope with the new situation in alien lands. They expressed the pain of orphanhood, took refuge in the world of dreams. For their misfortune, they blamed the past generation Armenian literati and the values and traditions they had transmitted to them. The artistic expressions of Vazken Shushanian, Shahan Shahnur, Shavarsh Narduni, and Nigoghayos Sarafian embody this predicament. Others, like Aram Haigaz and Hamasdegh, buried their powerful nostalgia in the fictionalized and mythified Old World they recreated.

Quest for Self-Identity with the Genocide at Its Core

The *Aghet* is now sliding into the past, leaving increasingly foggy memory, but the questions still persist: Why did it happen? Why did the world let it happen? Why this terrible injustice? These are questions that have no answers and cause frustration and anxiety. Justice has not been rendered, and the Armenians cannot put their dead to rest. One and a half million souls seem to haunt them, demanding action. There are two other underlying reasons that Armenians are still so obsessed with the Genocide and that the subject keeps surfacing in their literature, reflecting the way they think and perceive the world. One is the denial of the crime by the perpetrators and their use of intrigue to secure allies and distort history. And perpetrators always find excuses. "Where do they find them?" asks the storyteller's shadow in *The Story of the Last Thought*. "In their fears," replies the storyteller.[22] "In their fears!" No explanation could be as expressive as this one word—"fears." Then, there is also the vague image of a lost homeland that kindles a sense of deprivation even in the most integrated or acculturated Armenian in the Diaspora, a homeland never seen but still somewhere in the unconscious. This phenomenon has grown deeper under the influence of the general trend in the United States in the 1960s and the 1970s to search for one's roots, a sense of belonging, and an identity connected to the past, to history, and to the other members of the group. American culture of the time facilitated group affiliation and identification. The Armenian past was obviously associated with the massacres and deportations, a captive homeland swept clean of its indigenous people, and a decimated family. The modern responses to genocide were thus shaped by looking back to that historical source of self-understanding, self-consciousness, and self-identity. It does not matter whether the individual Armenian has lost family members in the death marches. All are survivors of genocide. "We are children of DerZor," writes Diana Der Hovanessian:

Even though your mother was a baby
in Worcester, and safe
and your father a young soldier
in Mourad's mountains
and you a generation from being born,
. . . .
even without a single

relative who lived to march,
lived past the march.
We are children of DerZor.[23]

Coinciding with the trend of searching for one's roots in America, the widespread commemoration of the fiftieth anniversary of the Armenian Genocide in 1965 and the heightened political activism of the Diaspora played a pivotal role in sensitizing the new generation, in directing attention to the unhealed wound. This was a beginning for the new diasporan reality, which called for a stronger commitment to the cause, to national ideology. It kindled self-consciousness and self-recognition among a stratum of youth who were now thoroughly immersed in the mainstream culture yet still searching for the source of their own particularity.

The echoes of this search reverberate both in the works of immigrant writers and of those born in America. Among the second-generation survivor-writers in the United States, Peter Najarian stands out with his *Voyages* (1971), in which the painful reconciliation between the past and the present and the constant references to the Genocide speak of the struggle to find one's identity and adjust to the adopted country. The quest for self-identity takes imaginative literature along different paths; yet the Genocide and the reconstruction of the memory of it remain at the core, the leitmotif. Najarian's *Daughters of Memory* (1986) and Peter Balakian's *Black Dog of Fate* are examples in which the Armenian component is gradually pulled out of a nebulous memory hole to become an important dimension in the self-identity of diasporan Armenians.

Vahé Oshagan, an emigrant from the Middle East, portrays the assimilated, alienated generation in America against a backdrop of national traditions, a past, and roots beckoning the generation, demanding action, be it in the most unconventional way, for example, by staging shockingly scandalous scenes and even generally unacceptable political violence.[24]

The pain and frustration resulting from the struggle to adjust to one's dual identity as well as the search for an ideal image of a diasporan Armenian echo in almost the entire literary output of Hakob Karapents. His characters are ordinary Armenians in the New World. In one of his stories, "Voreve teghits minchev aystegh" [From Any Place to Here, 1970], Karapents describes his protagonist: "An Armenian like any other Armenian. He was young and old like any other Armenian, because he had suffered.... He lived his life passively, without will or effort, like the survivor of a catastrophe."[25] Nubar Agishian and Beniamin Noorigian are other immigrant writers who develop an array of characters caught in the turmoil of dual identity and intermarriages leading to assimilation.[26]

Then come the newer poets and writers, all emigrants from Middle Eastern countries—Vrej Armen, Boghos Kupelian, Vahé Berberian, Vehanush Tekian, and Ishkhan Jinbashian—who write in Armenian and whose artistic creations portray the painful transition, the makeup of the new diasporan Armenian. The hardship of dislocation, the memory of the dead family, have become a part of the Armenian legacy and are transmitted from generation to generation. How they have responded to their Armenian heritage depends on that linkage, whether they love and cherish it and live stranded within it, or hate it, run away and try to free themselves from it. In all cases, the response is an act of desperation.

The intensity of this struggle for an Armenian identity does not necessarily exist to the same degree in other diasporan communities. In some cases, this struggle is only that of the intellectual elite, and the wound of the Genocide bleeds through the literary works they produce. Sevda Sevan's novel, *Rodosto, Rodosto* (written in Bulgarian, 1981), permeates the Bulgarian Armenian poetess-writer's motivation to capture the impact of genocide on the mental state of its survivors and the perpetrators' perception of the event, as well as their unchanged attitude toward the few remaining Armenians.[27]

In a recent poem, "Voghjoyn kez nor dar" [Greetings to You, New Century, 1999], Iranian-Armenian poet, Varand, hails the New Century with hope and expectations for the deliverance of the nation. And, significantly, the source of his chagrin and the tears he sheds is the continued captivity of his homeland, symbolized by Mount Ararat. "For the star-reaching captive did not return home yet," he reasons, and the crime against the nation remains unresolved: "For the righteous blood boiling in my veins is the blood I shed on the roads to Deir el-Zor."[28] Azat Matian, another Iranian-Armenian poet, uplifted by a young woman singing the famous song "Krunk" [Crane] during a vigil at the Genocide monument, writes the poem "April 24, 1996 (to Gariné for singing Krunk)." He expresses his bewilderment with unanswered questions and fading memories. He struggles to come out of this hopelessness:

> Where are we
> and bound for where?
> . . . .
> Who are we
> and heading for what?
> Hating, hating this endless pain
> and one another
> . . . .
> and believe again
> in the eternal life of my stricken race.[29]

Hilda Kalfayan-Panossian, a native of Constantinople residing in France, laments the loss of the Armenian language in the Diaspora (*Spiurk*). She sees the Diaspora as a bleeding wound: "Spiurk is my pain/like an agony that never ends/unable to speak/and yet full of hope." Spiurk for her is the site of "demolition and disintegration," the outcome of the Genocide that obliterated all rules and regulations, effaced order and value in the life of Armenians thrust in the Diaspora, caught in a prolonged agony.[30]

For all intents and purposes, the new response has stemmed from the attempt to confront the Genocide in order to grasp its historical and psychological impact, to enhance the fading memory or to construct one to which to relate and identify. And the constructed reality can be an imagined one. Hilsenrath's *The Story of the Last Thought* sets a perfect example. It constructs brick by brick the reality of Thovma Khatisian's family history, "from the little idyllic mountain village to the torture chambers of the Turkish rulers."[31] Khatisian's family was wiped out completely during the Genocide. As a young boy, he was raised in a Turkish family. Dagmar Lorenz notes in his review of this novel, Khatisian had a choice of self-identities: Turkish, Swiss, or Armenian. "The last was for him the hardest to attain, since he had to reconstruct or even construct an entire biography and national history. Yet he chooses to become a survivor of the massacres and a witness."[32] Thovma's inquiries led him to patch together his own story, albeit an imagined reality. And, one day, he says, "I had a genuine family history. I knew my roots. I had a father and a mother again, and I had many relatives. I also had a name with a tradition, one that I could pass on to my children and grandchildren."[33]

Indeed, nowhere in Armenian or non-Armenian-language creative writing, particularly in the genre of the novel, has the theme of the search of survivors' self-identity been so masterfully laid out and so naturally developed as in Hilsenrath's *The Story of the Last Thought*. And this is so, despite the fact that, contrary to others, it is constructed around a purely fictitious and imaginative setting. I am not aware of any survivor story of the Armenian Genocide that covers so much ground and treats such a vast array of issues pertaining to the atrocities, the victimization, the survival, the pain of losing one's home, family, and identity, of being thrown into an unknown world helpless and alone, and then, above all, of being denied truth and justice. And all this is crafted in a breathtaking narrative against a rich background of Armenian and Turkish affairs, customs, traditions, morés, beliefs, superstitions, and folklore. Hilsenrath is compelling as he interweaves imagination, dream, and reality in the thoughts of Thovma Khatisian at the end of the long and torturous road that is called "life." His last thoughts, as those of all Armenian survivors, fly back to Mount Ararat, to *Hayastan*. Perhaps, their thoughts never left these places. Perhaps, Armenians never left these places.

The dead Armenians whisper, Hilsenrath suggests, and "when Armenians whisper at night, the Turks have nightmares,"[34] because in every Armenian's dream "Anahit, the mother of Armenia," will find Hayk, "her lost son." It is significant that toward the end of the novel the storyteller calls Thovma by the name of Hayk to invoke "the first of the Armenians," and Thovma's mother is named Anahit. Hayk "will be fruitful and have many descendents. And the children of Hayk and their children's children, will people this land, which was always meant for them." Finally, as with the last thought of Thovma Khatisian, the last thoughts of all Armenian survivors, before they draw their last breath, "will fly back into the gaps in the Turkish history books."[35]

A Mutual Ground for New Directions

New directions in the responses to the Armenian Genocide were generated in the Diaspora, particularly in America. In fact, in recent years the increasing fragmentation and particularization of American culture, the prevailing theory of multiculturalism, and the political atmosphere have played as the catalyst and booster of the new Armenian-American response to the past, to history, to genocide.

These new directions will certainly influence the literary output in the Republic of Armenia. That is one of the goods, the commodities if you will, that we shall see crossing the Diaspora-Armenia bridge to reach the thinkers and the ordinary citizens of Armenia. Literature will become one of the major footings of mutual awareness and eventual unification. This will come about, as Vahé Oshagan puts it, from "the strong attachment of all poets to the national ethos." One important reason, Oshagan continues, "is that throughout the past centuries, the Armenian literary elite has always been involved with national ideology, i.e. survival of the nation and the preservation of the culture. This in itself is a political ideal, and all poets, diasporan or Armenia-based, have been and are committed to it."[36] Sooner or later, the "Armenia-based" literati will rid themselves of the constraints of the Soviet era and its lingering ideologies; the forced detachment from the Armenian past and the Genocide in particular will be lifted off the intellectual atmosphere as it is lifted off the political atmosphere; interest in addressing these issues will increase; and Armenia will join the Diaspora in responding to the past, to history, to the Genocide.

There was a time when government policy dictated the need to forget, to cease writing about the harrowing experience of the past, and to move ahead. It was even planted in people's minds that writing about the Genocide was masochism. This dictum hovered over Soviet Armenia for decades and penetrated certain segments in the Diaspora. Such mentality is gradually losing ground, although there are still persons among the leadership of Armenia who believe that the Armenian Question should be the concern and cause solely of the diasporan Armenians. In any event, judging by the present state of Armenian-Turkish political affairs and the Armenia-Diaspora relationship, there is plausible cause to predict that literary responses to the Genocide will continue as an important intellectual endeavor both in Armenia and the Diaspora. These responses will serve to build and enhance the monument of the Armenian collective memory, but more important they will become a vehicle through which to find a way to overcome the Catastrophe and make national survival possible.

Throughout this literary analysis in pursuit of new directions in literary responses to Genocide, two thoughts are underscored: First, a just resolution of the Armenian Question is viewed as a condition for national survival, and genocide literature is treated as an important avenue to reach that resolution. Second, literary representations of the Genocide are suggested as important factors in the nation-building process. These thoughts may seem irrelevant to the main thrust of the subject and may even impart political overtones to this discourse. But they result, I contend, from delving into the characteristics and attributes of genocide literature. In fact, these thoughts are the underlying *raison d'être* of this literary analysis. In order for these thoughts to materialize, however, there should be a commonality or at least a parallelism between the genocide literature produced in Armenia and in the Diaspora. The diasporan literature relates to the Genocide by nature and by circumstance. What about the Soviet and post-Soviet Armenian literature?

Despite Soviet restrictions and censorship, the Genocide did not cease to occupy the minds of Soviet Armenians, be it as a painful memory secretly transmitted from generation to generation, be it as a covert leitmotif in literature, or be it as innocent reminiscences of native village or hometown. Eghishe Charents, Gurgen Mahari, Khachik Dashtents set the example. The fiftieth anniversary of the Armenian Genocide was a turning point in the evolution of political thought in Soviet Armenia, as it was in the Diaspora. On the morning of April 24, 1965, for the first time in Soviet Armenian history, an enormous crowd took to the streets in Erevan and marched in commemoration of the victims of the Genocide, demanding the return of their ancestral lands and calling for a just solution of the Armenian Question. Silva Kaputikyan, a poetess-writer and participant in these demonstrations, reminisces about the event:

> They were going
> To claim their orphaned dead and orphaned tombs,
> To kneel and kiss the orphaned sacraments
> Of Maruta Monastery,
> To bring back the land
> And pull out of it the Lightening Sword,
> To bring back the rock and bring out Kurkik Djalali
> To say that we are able to saddle our father's dragon-slaying horse,
> To say that we are the owners, the lords of the House of Sasun
> And the cause of Sasun.
> The month was April,
> And the day was right.[37]

After that day, nothing was the same. The Khrushchev thaw was succeeded by the Brezhnev restrictions and renewed censorship; yet masterpieces like Paruyr Sevak's *Anlreli zangakatun*, Mushegh Galshoyan's "Tsirani poghe" [The Purple Horn], and Hrand Matevosyan's "Metsamor" (the name of a district in Armenia), as well as Gevorg Emin's poems of rage and tears for the victims, were produced. The Soviet Armenian dissident literature prepared the ground for the Karabagh movement in 1988, a nationalistic uprising calling for the unification of Karabagh (an adjacent Armenian enclave in the Soviet Republic of Azerbaijan) with Armenia. Parenthetically, it should be noted here that dissidence in Soviet Armenia did not have the same meaning as in Moscow or other parts of the Soviet Union. Whereas Soviet dissidents fought against the Communist regime, the Armenian dissident movement was patriotic, sensitive to the past, to history, to the Genocide, and to the lands lost to Turkey.

Rediscovering the past, writing about the Genocide, and dealing with previously forbidden historical subjects in literature, however, have not gained momentum in today's relatively free atmosphere, while historical research in these areas has come a long way. Rare are the voices like that of the young poet Ludvik Turyan, who expresses disillusion and at the same time the aspiration for justice for all of mankind. In his poem "Justice," Turyan begins by treating Justice like a toy, when he knew little about the fate of his people and about Justice that was denied to them:

> Justice, if you had been given to me
> as a toy when I was a child,
> I am sure I would have broken you
> to bits to find what made you tick.

Shattered at the thought that there is no Justice in the world, he continues with a pessimistic note. He sees no light at the end of the tunnel:

> What healer
> you could have been, had you arrived
> centuries ago
> . . . .
> But Justice, our globe is aging, aging,
> You are, too, and I am afraid you may die
> of old age before you really arrive.[38]

The independence of Armenia since 1991 has provided unprecedented freedom for the literati but paradoxically has brought about, especially in the first years, a socioeconomic atmosphere quite unfavorable for artistic endeavors. "There are no literary impulses and directions. In this freedom, we have grown tired of freedom," asserts Abgar Apinyan in an editorial in *Nor Dar* [New Century].[39] He suggests a collective and conscious effort to revive literary activities and above all to learn about the conventions that govern the diasporan literature. I would say that the stimulus is there; however, most Armenian writers and poets have chosen other avenues to express their suppressed feelings. Other previously forbidden topics are at center stage in literary creations.

Sporadically, we hear voices that sing the song of the orphaned lands of Armenia and the calamity that befell the nation. These creations are mostly in the genre of lamentation. Gurgen Gabrielyan, a poet of Artsakh (Karabagh), compares the value and significance of land, of homeland, to those of the mother, and writes:

I remember so well the Catastrophe
And the Golgotha of our people,
The blood-soaked plough
I remember so well.
And in all my life
My heart is full
With the grief
And the gloom of Armenians.

Robert Esayan, a younger poet of Artsakh, searches in history, in the destruction of his people in Western Armenia, for the source of the present plight in Karabagh and the carnage that went on for years at the hands of the Turkic Azeris. He laments the pain of the nation:

At the tombs and dreams plundered
our pain has been made a theatre
for the world to stage a play,
a play pregnant with the final destruction.

Esayan then looks to God for an answer to his supplications:

My arms that are the closed windows of heaven,
will they open again oh God, to my soul's dawn,

or...is that life of dream
yet another illusion, all decked in splendour?[40]

In a poem dedicated to the sixteen hundredth anniversary of the creation of the Armenian alphabet, Ruben Vardanyan paints with sullen darkness and morbid metaphors the landscape of Armenian history and the Armenian Genocide. In the voice of Mesrop Mashtots, the inventor of the Armenian alphabet, he laments the calamity and appeals to God for mercy and guidance. The poem ends with a portrayal of current bleak situation, the exodus of Armenians, the white massacre (*spitak jard*), and the homeland becoming increasingly bereft of her beloved sons and daughters.

Silva Kaputikyan, whose mother and grandmother were refugees from Van, remembers their ordeal and that of her people in "Hin karote" [The Old Yearning, 1992].[41] The poem captures Kaputikyan's preoccupation with the fate and the unresolved cause of the Armenian people. In her imagination, three generations—her grandmother, her mother, and herself—walk together through life as girls of the same age harboring the same yearnings, the same unfulfilled dreams, the same shattered hope for return to the ancestral home. Kaputikyan implies that national pain and aspirations do not diminish with the succession of generations.

Hovik Hoveyan's collection of poems, *Aregakn ardar* [The Righteous Sun] opens with a piece called "Anapat" [Desert], a reference to the Syrian deserts where the Armenian survivors of massacres and deportations met their death. The poet imagines himself as a piece of bone, one of the millions scattered on the desert sand, blown about by the wind. His life is empty and meaningless since he is unable to shake the indifference of the world: "The empty caravan is passing/The golden bell is not ringing,/My cry is still asleep in silence/In the dragging camel's lazy ear."[42]

The theme of genocide, if entertained at all in the poetry of Armenia, is within the framework of old responses. Only in a few cases, when the atrocities against the Armenians of Azerbaijan and Karabagh are lamented, is a new accent added: a thread is passed through history to link these pogroms to the Genocide, and the new Azeri perpetrator is identified with the Turk of yesteryear. New voices are rare, and they are heard in the most unexpected contexts and conceptualizations. An expressive example in prose is Aghasi Ayvazyan's "Antun turke" [The Homeless Turk]. In this imaginative interaction with the Turk, the nation's resentment and rage pour out. Fate brings the Armenian and the Turkish wanderers together under a freeway overpass in Pasadena, where the homeless hang out. The Armenian blames the Turk for their plight: "You Turks, if you had not invaded Armenia from Central Asia, or wherever you came from...if you had not driven my grandfather out of his home in Bitlis or Kars or wherever...if you had not slaughtered the children and the old...I could welcome you in my house in Bitlis or wherever. We could drink wine together." Surprisingly, the Turk accepts the blame and does not object, but the outcome is an impasse. The rapprochement, despite the similar conditions and fate that drew the Armenian and the Turk together, is fruitless.[43]

Another example, this one in poetry, of such an innovative voice in literary responses to genocide in Armenia is Henrik Edoyan's "Hey, Turkish Poets." The author addresses the Turk, and, at the same time, he intimates the importance of the role of literati, in this case the Turkish intellectuals at the time of the Genocide. Edoyan believes that they could make a difference and prevent the atrocities. The first stanza sets the pattern:

> If one of you, just one, had spoken up
> "Why kill this trembling kid,
> his slaughtered parents were enough,"
> We might have raised a glass together
> if not a monument.

The poem continues in the same mood, reproaching Turkish poets for not speaking out when "innocent girls," children, women, old men, "the old gods who walked and worked this land" were being killed, when "manuscripts [were] soaked in blood again." And if they had taken sides and said, "'Let's not kill the genuine poets/at least not them.'/You too could have been the real thing." Turkish poets have remained silent, and their silence is deemed as complicity, unbefitting a real artist, as Edoyan sees it.[44] The Armenian poet's attempted dialogue can be considered not only as a call to account but also as an invitation to today's Turkish men of letters to assume their indispensable role in society, to take a stand and to act. I wonder if Edoyan has read Nazim Hikmet's poetry of rage and admonishment, but, on the other hand, he was but a voice in the wilderness.[45]

In the literary works of a larger dimension, Berj Zeytuntsyan's *Verjin arevagale* [The Last Dawn] stands alone. This historical novel, with Grigor Zohrap (Krikor Zohrab) as its protagonist, embodies the author's perception of the Genocide. The general title of the book is *Vark metsats* [Life of the Great Ones], but the narrative is a selective, arbitrary, and often not very convincing portrayal of Zohrap's character, views, and activities. It is neither a novel, as identified in the title page, nor a true-to-life biography. Nonetheless, it is an effort to add a voice to the literature of the Armenian Genocide.[46]

Literary works on the themes of Armenian suffering, and especially the inflicted injustice, may be few in Armenia because of the lingering effects of the past restrictions. However, taking into consideration the current efforts to enhance national themes in education and to broaden involvement in the struggle for a just solution of the Armenian cause, one can presume that the inclination to address these issues will increase and that genocide literature will soon form an independent corpus and find new directions.

It is my belief that, although historians will continue their research and new documents will shed more light on the issue, it is primarily the literary representations that will shape the understanding of the Armenian Genocide of future generations, that will pass the memory on to them and will shape their commitment to the cause. Indeed, it is the artist's creative power that can capture the unthinkable horrors of the Genocide and bring them down into the frame of the reader's comprehension. Notwithstanding Yehuda Bauer's warning against the Holocaust being understood through the works of imaginative writers and his labeling that kind of understanding a "metaphysical comprehension," the power and intensity of the impact that a literary representation of genocide can make is profound and the role it can play is important.[47]

Paraphrasing Emil Fackenheim's words, I conclude with this thought: to renew the past for present life has always been an essential obligation of the historians, the philosophers, and, I may add, the literati as well, and never before has this task been so essential and so difficult.[48] Therefore, I submit that future responses to the Armenian Genocide, be they fragmented and incoherent, as an imposition of the theme itself, will stand as a monument to the Armenian aspiration to revived nationhood. They will provide the needed dialogue between history and literature to place the Armenian Genocide within the ongoing saga of a living people, to find a way to resolve the tragedy, and to ensure national survival and evolution.

Notes

1. For an analysis of paradigms of responses to collective sufferings in national catastrophes through time, see Rubina Peroomian, *Literary Responses to Catastrophe: A Comparison of the Armenian and the Jewish Experiences* (Atlanta: Scholars Press, 1993).
2. Diana Der Hovanessian, *About Time* (New York: Ashot Press, 1987), from a poem titled "Diaspora," p. 22 (quotation marks by the author).
3. Lorne Shirinian, *Armenian-North American Literature, A Critical Introduction: Genocide, Diaspora, and Symbols* (Lewiston, Canada: Edwin Mellen Press, 1990), p. 60.
4. Edgar Hilsenrath is a survivor of the Holocaust and a well-known novelist in Germany. *The Story of the Last Thought* was first published in German in 1989 as *Das Märchen vom letzten Gedanken*. The English translation is by Hugh Young (London: Scribners, 1990, and Sphere Books, 1991). Citations in this chapter are to the 1991 edition. A short paragraph on the back cover of that edition explains the scope of the work:

   > The story is that of the best-forgotten crime of the century; the holocaust of the Armenian people by the Turks in 1915. Yet here it is both history and fable, told in a sequence of beautifully written conversations and stories, polished by exotic myth and vivid imagery. It takes the Armenian Thovma Khatisian back to the past to see the atrocities as his forebears saw them, tracing his father's life from an idyllic mountain village to the torture chambers of the Turkish rulers, delving far back into Armenian history, vividly recreating the folklore, legends and traditions of an early Christian people.

5. Leonardo Alishan, "An Exercise on a Genre for Genocide and Exorcism," in Richard G. Hovannisian, ed., *The Armenian Genocide: History, Politics, Ethics* (London: Macmillan, and New York: St. Martin's Press, 1992), p. 352.
6. See David Roskies, "The Holocaust According to Literary Critics," *Prooftext* 1 (May 1981): 209-16.
7. In this article, the transliteration of the names of Armenian authors depends on the dialect and preference of the writer; hence, Hagop Oshagan (Western Armenian) but Hakob Karapents (Eastern Armenian). The names of contemporary writers in Armenia are transliterated according to the system adopted in Soviet Armenia; hence, Kaputikyan, rather than Kaputikian.
8. See Bernard Cohen, *Sociocultural Changes in American Jewish Life as Reflected in Selected Jewish Literature* (Ruthford, Madison, Teaneck, NJ: Fairleigh Dickinson University Press, 1972), p. 32.
9. Alishan, "An Exercise," pp. 352-53.
10. See Alvin H. Rosenfeld, "The Americanization of the Holocaust," in Alvin H. Rosenfeld, ed., *Thinking about the Holocaust after Half a Century* (Bloomington and Indianapolis: Indiana University Press, 1997), pp. 141-44.
11. Hilsenrath, *The Story of the Last Thought*, p. 14.
12. David Kherdian, "For My Father," in a collection of poems titled *Homage to Adana* (Fresno, CA: The Giligia Press, 1970), pages are not numbered. This and the poem quoted next are examples of many that resonate the ineffaceable, tormenting memory of the Genocide indirectly transmitted to the author through his father.
13. David Kherdian, "My Father." The reference to "our Armenian writer in California" is to William Saroyan.

14. Hovhannes Mugrditchian, *To Armenians with Love: The Memoirs of a Patriot* (Hobe Sound, FL: Paul Mart, 1996).
15. Quotation from *The Chronicle of Higher Education*, June 12, 1998, p. B7.
16. Stina Katchadourian, *Efronia, An Armenian Love Story* (Boston: Northeastern University Press, 1994). For a brief analysis of this work, see the review by Rubina Peroomian, *Journal of the Society for Armenian Studies* 7 (1994): 205-08.
17. Carol Edgarian, *Rise the Euphrates* (New York: Random Books, 1994).
18. Arpiné Konyalian Grenier, "The Apprentice in Exile: Toward an Armenian-American Poetics," *Aspora* 1:1 (Fall 1993): 17-32 (quotations, 26-27).
19. Alishan, "An Exercise," p. 352.
20. From an unpublished poem, "*ECCE HOMO*."
21. For an analysis of these images in "The History of Armenia," see Shirinian, *Armenian-North American Literature*, pp. 110-15.
22. Hilsenrath, *The Story of the Last Thought*, p. 345.
23. Part 2 of the three-part poem, "Tryptich." The quoted part is titled "Why Sand Scorches Armenians." See Der Hovanessian, *About Time*, p. 14.
24. "Odzum" (Consecration, 1988) and "Telefone" (The Telephone, 1988) are two examples in which Oshagan illustrates how a shocking event in the life of the Armenian community (in "Odzum,"an act of sacrilege deliberately staged in an Armenian church by three youths belonging to an extremist terrorist group, and in "Telefone," the news of the suicide mission of an Armenian youth group against the Turkish Embassy in Lisbon) may stir generally indifferent, largely assimilated American Armenians.
25. Hakob Karapents, "Voreve teghits minchev aystegh" [From Any Place to Here] in the collection of stories titled *Antsanot hoginer* [Unfamiliar Souls](Beirut: Atlas Press, 1970), pp. 152-53.
26. For a brief thematic analysis of works by these authors, see Rubina Peroomian, "The Transformation of Armenianness in the Formation of Armenian-American Identity," *Journal of the Society for Armenian Studies* 6 (1992-93): 119-45.
27. A chapter of this novel, translated by M. Terzian into Armenian, is published in *Otaralezu hay groghner* [Armenian Writers Writing in Foreign Languages] (Erevan: Erevan State University, 1989), pp. 404-56.
28. Varand, "Voghjoyn kez, Nor Dar" [Greetings to You, New Century], *Nor Dar* 2 (1999): 232.
29. Azat Matian, "April 24, 1996 (to Gariné for singing Krunk)," trans. Vahé Oshagan, *RAFT* 10 (1996): 55-57.
30. Hilda Kalfayan-Panossian, "The Wake," trans. Vahé Oshagan, *RAFT* 9 (1995): 15-16.
31. From the back cover of the book.
32. For Dagmar C.G. Lorenz's book review, "Hilsenrath's Other Genocide," see the *Simon Wiesenthal Center Annual* 7 (n.d.), quotation, p. 3.
33. Hilsenrath, *The Story of the Last Thought*, p. 16.
34. Ibid., p. 462.
35. Ibid., pp. 464-65.
36. I concur with Oshagan that the Armenian literati have always been committed to a national ideology. That commitment has echoed down through time and has given Armenian literature its defining character. It has assumed the mission of national survival and perpetuation and will undoubtedly continue in this manner regardless of new trends or approaches in literary criticism. There is little need, therefore, for Oshagan to offer the apology that "this may seem slightly outdated at a time when Western poetry has abandoned the notion of a mission and has become an expres-

sion of total independence and purely personal vision." See *RAFT* 8 (1994): 3-4.

37. Silva Kaputikyan, *Ejer pak gzrotsnerits* [Pages from Locked Drawers] (Erevan: Apolon Press, 1997), p. 678. There are a few references here to the Armenian national epic "David of Sasun." David used the ancestral Lightening Sword to fight and slay the enemy. Kurkik Jalali is the legendary horse belonging to this family of Armenian epic heroes. According to an Armenian legend, after fighting against injustice and all the evil in the world, David's son, Pokr Mher, was imprisoned in a cave, and one day this last figure of the epic will ride his horse back to the world to set the Armenians free. "The House of Sasun" here has a more general sense than the region of Sasun. It is a reference to Armenia.
38. Ludvik Turyan, "Justice," trans. Diana Der-Hovanessian, *RAFT* 11 (1997): 45-46.
39. Abgar Apinyan, "Mer nor grakan kyanki herankari masin" [About the Future of Our New Literary Life], *Nor Dar*, no. 3-4 (1996): 3-4.
40. Robert Esayan, "Hesitation," trans. Vahé Oshagan, *RAFT* 10 (1996): 42-43.
41. Kaputikyan, *Ejer pak gzrotsnerits*, p. 658.
42. Hovik Hoveyan, *Aregakn ardar* [The Righteous Sun] (Erevan: Nairi Press, 1997), pp. 3-4. This is the fourth volume of Hoveyan's poetry. The theme of genocide is not entertained in the fifth and final volume, *Taparakan areve* [The Wandering Sun] (Erevan: Nairi Press, 1999).
43. Aghasi Ayvazyan, "Antun turke" [The Homeless Turk], *Nor Dar*, no. 2 (1999): 58-60.
44. Henrik Edoyan, "Hey, Turkish Poets," trans. Diana Der Hovanessian, *RAFT* 6 (1992): 11.
45. Nazim Hikmet (1902-1963), a Turkish Marxist writer-poet, a rebellious soul against oppression, also speaks about the Armenian massacres. In the poem "Evening Walk," written in 1950 (or "Evening Stroll" in a 1954 publication of Hikmet's poems by another translator), he has this to say:

    The grocer Karabet's lights are on.
    This Armenian citizen has not forgiven
    the slaughter of his father in Kurdish mountains.
    But he loves you,
    because you also won't forgive
    those who blackened the name of the Turkish
    people.

    As with most of Hikmet's writings, this poem is also autobiographical, and he himself is his addressee (the "you" throughout the poem). See *Selected Poems of Nazim Hikmet*, trans. Randy Blasing and Mutlu Konuk (New York: Persea Books, 1975), p. 60.
46. Berj Zeytuntsyan, *Verjin arevagale* [The Last Dawn] (Erevan: "Arevik" Press, 1989). Grigor Zohrap (Krikor Zohrab) was a writer, political activist, and Armenian deputy in the Ottoman Parliament who was arrested in 1915 and murdered on the way to exile.
47. James E. Young, *Writing and Rewriting the Holocaust* (Bloomington and Indianapolis: Indiana University Press, 1988), p. 7.
48. See Michael L. Morgan, "To Seize Memory, History and Identity in Post-Holocaust Jewish Thought," in Rosenfeld, *Thinking about the Holocaust,* p. 172.

10

Looking Backward and Forward: Genocide Studies and Teaching about the Armenian Genocide

Joyce Apsel

This chapter emphasizes the challenges of introducing genocide studies into the curriculum and focuses on trends and curriculum developments in genocide studies throughout the United States during the past several decades.[1] It also explores challenges to effective human rights education and proposes ways the subject of genocide, in particular the genocide against the Armenians, may be introduced to a wider audience through genocide studies, world survey courses, and teacher-training programs. The following questions reflect the pedagogical dilemmas of attempting to raise awareness and teach about the possibilities of human construction while teaching about the recurrent patterns of human destructiveness:

- Is taking part in genocide learned behavior?
- If it is learned behavior, can people be taught to "unlearn" it?
- Can becoming aware of the danger signs have any effect on preventing or halting genocide?
- Through educating about the history of atrocity, of intentional mass destruction of men, women, and children—genocide—are we teaching about remembrance and justice and are we constructing a background for individuals to develop an inclusive, caring community, or are we reinforcing views of a hierarchy of victims and of the destructiveness of humankind?

Historical Approach: The Armenian Genocide in the Century of Genocide

The twentieth century was characterized by a series of genocides in which various perpetrator states, individual killers, and their accomplices were able to escape punishment for mass murder in the vast majority of cases.[2] Under this culture of impunity, most individuals who planned or participated in mass killings were never brought to justice. In many nation states during the last century, it was more likely that an individual could get away with murder as part of a genocidal plan than for a single, isolated homicide.

The Armenian Genocide of 1915 represents the earliest example of genocide in Europe and Asia Minor during the twentieth century. By 1918 the Turkish perpetrators and their accomplices had carried out the destruction of more than one million Armenians. As Robert Melson points out, "hundreds of thousands of other victims had become homeless and stateless refugees.... By 1923 virtually the entire Armenian population of Anatolian Turkey had disappeared."[3] But this event was written out of history and became "the forgotten genocide."[4] As Gary Bass explains: "When the Ottoman Empire was defeated, it faced war crimes trials; when Ataturk drove Britain and Greece back, the new peace treaty dropped those demands."[5]

During World War I and the "restructuring" from Ottoman Empire to Turkish statehood, domestic genocide proved an effective mechanism to promote nationalism, modernization, and elimination of a civilian minority. Turkish state denial of the genocide has gone through different stages and intensified over time, providing a case study of the tragic repercussions of international failure to enforce accountability and prosecute perpetrators.[6] The ongoing denial campaign underscores the likelihood that state refusal to admit responsibility will result in the persistent and broadening pattern of fabrication and violation of human rights norms in the perpetrator state.[7]

In recent times, geopolitical changes after the breakup of the Soviet Union and the establishment of new independent states, including Armenia and Azerbaijan, and the ongoing conflicts in Nagorno-Karabagh and elsewhere undermine stability in the region. The conflict between the Turkish policy of denial and Armenian efforts to gain recognition of the genocide have complex repercussions for the new Armenian state, other small and large states in the region, and the Armenian Diaspora.[8]

Armenian Studies and Modern Armenian History

A brief survey of Armenian Studies will link in with the subject of genocide awareness. Armenian Studies began in the United States in the 1950s,[9] and endowed chairs in history and in language and literature were eventually established at Harvard University,[10] the University of California, Los Angeles (UCLA), and Columbia University. The positions were initially filled by scholars who concentrated on pre-modern history and culture.[11] Modern and contemporary studies became anchored with additional funded chairs at UCLA, the University of Michigan-Ann Arbor, California State University, Fresno, Tufts University, and most recently the University of California, Berkeley, and Clark University in Worcester, Massachusetts. Visiting and part-time faculty taught Armenian studies courses as well, a pattern that continues up to the present.[12] Among other institutions offering courses in Armenian studies are the University of Chicago, Wayne State University, Glendale Community College, Pasadena City College, University of Southern California, and California State University, Northridge. A series of educational and cultural institutions was developed, among them the Armenian Resource Center at the University of Michigan-Dearborn by Dennis Papazian. In 1974, the Society for Armenian Studies (SAS) was formed to promote scholarship, teaching, and research in Armenian Studies, including publication of a newsletter and journal and sponsorship of panels and conferences.[13] Modern Armenian history has emerged as an academic field, and a small group of scholars has now produced works on Armenian nationalism, the Armenian Genocide, the first Armenian republic, Soviet Armenia, as well as literary and cultural expressions of the modern Armenian experience.[14]

Around the fiftieth anniversary of the Armenian Genocide in 1965, survivors of the "forgotten genocide" began to speak more about their experiences:

> The survivors were able to penetrate the wall of silence around them just a little and to voice their pleas for international recognition and rectification of an outstanding crime against humanity. Many younger Armenians, affected by the transgenerational trauma of genocide, became involved in political and demonstrative activities.[15]

Beside the emergence of political violence that sought to reverse years of denial, projects multiplied to record eyewitness accounts before the remaining survivors died and to commemorate the event publicly.[16] Armenian-American writer Marjorie Housepian Dobkin's 1966 article in *Commentary Magazine* brought "The Unremembered Genocide" to the attention of a wider audience.[17] Members of the Armenian community, in response to the expansion of denial and falsification into the academic realm, raised funds for research, oral history projects, and other genocide-related programs.[18]

From the late 1960s on, a group of American academics and activists began the process of writing back into history various groups and events that had been distorted, ignored, excised, or forgotten. New social history enlarged areas of research and teaching to include groups previously neglected—workers (labor studies), African-Americans, Native Americans, women, and immigrants—and made popular tracing one's "roots."[19] Rediscovery of the past entailed "unsilencing" patterns of discrimination and historic atrocity such as destruction of indigenous peoples, slavery, and genocide. A variety of ethnic and area studies, including the Middle East and Russia/Soviet Union, gained popularity. These left their imprint on the development of Armenian Studies.

The influence of the Vietnam War and questioning and/or protest of U.S. actions in Southeast Asia was a further impetus to reanalysis of the individual and national past. For example, in an essay published in 1979, second generation Armenian American Leon Chorbajian traced his radicalization and commitment to civil rights as a reaction to the Vietnam War and death of more than one million Southeast Asians as well as his background as the child of Armenian genocide survivors:

> Born to parents who had survived a genocide, it was a particularly jarring experience for me to understand that my government was practicing a genocidal foreign policy. I came to spend a part of my life working in the civil rights and anti-war movements. These were choices which enormously broadened and enriched my life, and I am convinced that it was through these struggles that I was able to fully become Armenian. I saw that my parents and their generation had experienced a horror and violence which was shared by other people in the modern world. It was from this realization that my own political activity during the 60s was inspired, and this is why I have advocated that the Armenian experience be understood in the larger context from which it stems. This is the foundation of pride, dignity and action which is faithful to the history of our people.[20]

The Armenian Studies Program at California State University, Fresno, began with historian Louise Nalbandian's courses in Armenian history and culture.[21] As Dickran Kouymjian, Haig and Isabel Berberian Professor and director of the program, writes: "Due to the surge in interest in ethnic studies, and perhaps in part to the university's agreement to offer an Ethnic Studies Program after widespread unrest on campus, including the bombing of the computer center, Louise Nalbandian was able to push for more Armenian content courses."[22]

Specialized courses in modern Armenian history, which included the Armenian Genocide, developed primarily in areas where there was an Armenian student population that organized in clubs and/or where the Armenian community was willing to support a chair or program. Initially, Armenian Studies had focused on pre-modern subjects and the particularity of Armenian history and culture. But now, influenced by larger political and academic developments in the United States and worldwide and by demands of Armenian students for a relevant curriculum (part of the larger student advocacy of moving away from the ivory tower notion of learning to teaching about issues immediately relevant to their lives and current events), a few Armenian Studies programs began to address more modern, controversial themes and to establish links with ethnic studies programs or centers of Russian/Soviet and Middle Eastern studies.

Armenian Studies at UCLA

One of the earliest Armenian Studies programs in the United States began at UCLA in 1960:

> [The program] focuses on the 3,000-year history and culture of the Armenian people, both in their native homeland between the Mediterranean, Black, and Caspian seas, and in the dispersion. Unique in the context of Near Eastern Civilizations, the Armenians maintained their Indo-European language and developed a distinct culture that drew inspiration from and served as a link between the Orient and the Occident.[23]

In addition to the graduate program, an undergraduate Armenian Studies minor and a major through individual petition are available "to provide a systematic study of Armenian culture."[24] The program is now anchored with endowed chairs in the Department of History and the Department of Near Eastern Languages and Cultures.[25]

Richard G. Hovannisian, holder of the Armenian Education Foundation Chair in Modern Armenian History, joined the UCLA faculty in 1962 and served as associate director of the G. E. von Grunebaum Center for Near Eastern Studies from 1978 to 1995. Hovannisian has been a pioneer in developing curriculum and scholarship in modern Armenian history in the United States.[26] Aside from a variety of undergraduate courses that he offers, the graduate program in history has prepared a select group of scholars and community leaders.[27]

Seminars on comparative genocide, integration of new techniques such as oral history, the organization of conferences, including commemoration of the Armenian Genocide and international symposiums on historic Armenian cities and provinces, and community outreach characterize the UCLA program. At the same time that historian Hovannisian taught an undergraduate honors course on the comparative study of genocide, which included the Armenian Genocide, other faculty offered courses on genocide from different perspectives and a cross-over and cooperation among scholars and course offerings came to exist.[28] Anthropologist Hilda Kuper (1911-1992) taught a course on "Destruction and Survival of Indigenous Societies." Sociologist Leo Kuper (1908-1994) was a pioneer in genocide scholarship who incorporated the Armenian Genocide in his writings and courses.[29]

In 1965, Avedis K. Sanjian joined the Department of Near Eastern Languages and Cultures and in 1969 became the first occupant of the Grigor Narekatsi Chair in Armenian. For thirty years he offered undergraduate and graduate courses in language and literature. The Narekatsi Chair is now held by S. Peter Cowe, who has introduced new courses such as Armenian Film and Art, as well as Politics and Nationalism in Modern Armenian Literature.[30] Other Armenian language courses are available and taught by part-time faculty.[31] The University Research Library, where Gia Aivazian is the Armenian bibliographer, holds the largest collection of Armenian materials housed by a university in the United States.[32] The Armenian Studies program sponsors symposiums on aspects of Armenian culture and has organized exhibitions of Armenian art and architecture in cooperation with the UCLA Museum of Cultural History, now relocated and renamed the Fowler Museum.[33]

Challenges Ahead for Armenian Studies in the United States

Major strides have been made in Armenian Studies in the United States since its beginnings in the 1950s. In particular, both scholarly works and accessible general studies on modern Armenian history and the Armenian Genocide are now available in English. Several endowed university chairs and programs in Armenian Studies are well established. There are nonetheless significant challenges facing the field. First, retirement of prominent faculty and the complex politics of replacement will figure in how Armenian Studies programs develop. Second, generating student interest in the field from both the general student population and students of Armenian background will remain a concern, including how to promote language study and scholarship. Third, the complex geopolitics of Armenian statehood and developments in the Caucasus and throughout the region present new challenges of interpretation and add to the complexity of the modern Armenian experience. Fourth, the Turkish policy of denial distracts scholars of modern Armenian history and takes up much of their time in the need to refute the ongoing misrepresentation and falsification of history.

Comparative studies in literature, history, politics, and the phenomenon of genocide provide an important way to introduce aspects of Armenian Studies to a larger audience. International scholarship and academic trends in fields such as social history, gender studies, and ethnic and nationality studies, together with the increasing interest in the Caucasus region, may prompt new syntheses and interpretations. For example, Khachig Tololyan, founding editor of *Diaspora: A Journal of Transnational Studies*, discusses in "Memoirs of a Diasporan Nationalist" how "since 1975, I have been trying to balance my life as a professional, academic, and scholar with my life as an Armenian intellectual."[34] The *Armenian Forum*, a journal established in 1998, has included exchanges on the state of Armenian Studies in the United States, Turkish-Armenian dialogue, and differing analyses of factors leading to the Armenian Genocide.[35] Courses on History and Memory and on the Armenian-American Experience, as well as summer language programs in Armenia such as the one sponsored by the University of Michigan offer new directions and possibilities.[36] To what extent scholarship and teaching of the modern Armenian experience, including the Armenian Genocide, will be taken up by a new generation of scholars and students and made accessible to non-specialists is one of the challenges in looking forward.

Some Suggestions for Teaching about Genocide in the Twenty-First Century

It is against the background of Armenian Studies and current developments that the following questions are posed: What are the most effective ways to include genocide in the curriculum and teach about the Armenian Genocide in the twenty-first century? Who is the audience? The two teaching methods that I want to emphasize are the promoting of courses and curriculum that offer genocide studies and human rights as a framework rather than those dominated by one particular genocide, and the integration of material on genocide and human rights into general studies, education courses, and other offerings.[37]

The preponderance of courses taught about genocide in the twentieth century focuses on one genocide, the Holocaust. Holocaust studies are an important, demanding field of study and have generated interest and impetus to study other genocides and related subjects. They introduce students to the processes of intentional destruction of the majority of European Jewry and sometimes include other Nazi targeted groups such as the Roma Gypsies. The quantity of documentation, scholarship, films, and memoirs has provided valuable resources for a range of courses such as the History of Anti-Semitism, Memory and Representation, and Holocaust and Film. Generally, such courses reinforce the Holocaust as unique and the hegemonic model.[38] There also have developed institutional structures (university and/or community affiliated Holocaust centers, funding designated for Holocaust courses and public education, the U.S. Holocaust Memorial Museum, and state education mandates) focused on the Holocaust.[39]

At the same time, Holocaust studies have generated interest and impetus to study other genocides. In part because of scholarship linking the Armenian Genocide as a precursor to the Holocaust,[40] speakers, conferences, commemorative events, and exhibits, and on occasion courses on the Armenian Genocide are supported by some Holocaust centers.[41] It seems likely that Holocaust/Genocide centers (a few also include Human Rights in their name or description) will continue to expand their programs in teacher education and sponsor programs in genocide studies, as well as civil and human rights issues, and provide an important vehicle for public education.

The Genocide Studies Model

The genocide studies curriculum model provides a comparative approach to teach about mass destruction. Study of the Holocaust is an integral part of this model. Debates among genocide studies scholars on such issues as definition, typology, partial/total annihilation, and inclusion/exclusion provide challenging subject matter for classroom discussion and debate:

> The comparative study of genocide entails diligent and respectful scholarship of individual cases of genocide in human history, analysis of the known causes, sequences and outcomes of these events, and then comparison of each event with other events. In the traditions of scholarship and science, the purpose is to build up a body of knowledge of common patterns as well as differences between events, thus laying a groundwork for systematic thinking about the root causes of genocide, thinking about how to intervene when genocide looms as a threatening possibility, and also thinking about how to intervene as early as possible once an event of genocide has begun to form in order to save as many human lives as possible.[42]

It is important to note that comparative genocide emphatically does not mean a comparison of degrees of suffering or degrees of evil of perpetrators. Rather, it is based on the rationale that looking at genocidal events over time can lead to deeper understanding and analyses of mass violence and strategies of genocide prevention. Comparative genocide studies attempt to raise awareness both of human destructiveness and of human resistance and to face the limited success to date in efforts to protect life integrity and human rights. On the one hand, it is natural that people will have greater feeling when a group of which they are members or to which they have some personal connection is being studied.[43] However, study of different genocides may reduce tension and resentment among victim groups and provide educational/therapeutic value by allowing individuals to see the effects of genocide on other targeted groups, thereby reducing somewhat the sense of profound isolation and particularity of victimization.[44]

Genocide studies combine the specific history of mass destruction of a targeted people with examination of processes and repeated patterns, techniques, and reactions. There is acknowledgment that genocide does not end when the killing stops, as seen in the issues of denial, ongoing politics of refugees, justice and recovery, and ways in which state policy, including that of the United States, results in complicity in failure to bring perpetrators to justice. Finally, this pedagogy encourages a discussion of present-day human rights norms, including issues of state terror, torture, and political prisoners, as well as early warning systems, intervention, humanitarian aid, and international tribunals. Rather than focus on numbers killed, uniqueness, or competitive victimization, this model analyzes the enormity of human destructiveness and demystifies genocide by study of how often "ordinary people" take part in mass murder. It also challenges current mal-education and banalization, which all too often result in popular notions of any bad person being another Hitler and all violence being tantamount to genocide. Students grapple with the complexity of evil and political efficacy of genocide in different states and times under different political regimes.

The establishment of an organization for scholars and teachers as well as new publications have provided networks and resources for teaching more effectively about genocide. The Association of Genocide Scholars was founded in Berlin in 1994 by Israel Charny, Helen Fein, Robert Melson, and Roger Smith.[45] In *Teaching about Genocide: A Guidebook for College and University Teachers: Critical Essays, Syllabi and Assignments*,[46] all of the course syllabi listed under History, Sociology, Political Science, and Psychology include sections on the Armenian Genocide. The number of courses that use a comparative model is relatively small but growing. Students analyze several or a range of genocidal events perpetrated by diverse peoples and states. One approach is to cover the entire span from ancient to modern times in two semesters (the pattern developed by Frank Chalk and Kurt Jonassohn at Concordia University in Montreal and out of which their book *History and Sociology of Genocide* evolved).[47] Another approach is reflected in the collection *Century of Genocide: Eyewitness Accounts and Critical Views* that includes analyses of specific events in the twentieth century along with eyewitness testimony.[48]

One approach to teaching a course in genocide studies is to begin the course with a discussion of the definition of terms such as genocide, crimes against humanity, ethnic cleansing, democide,[49] omnicide,[50] and justice, reconciliation, and human rights. Also, using the classroom as an opportunity to talk about what events are included and excluded in the syllabus reflects the larger debates of scholars on what are the parameters and content of genocide studies. Students may debate whether or not the destruction of Native American peoples, the institution of slavery, the atomic bombing of Hiroshima and Nagasaki, the sanctions against Iraq, or terrorism constitute genocide. These discussions provide critical background for thinking about the implications of definitions and categorization and link to the U.N. Convention on the Prevention and Punishment of the Crime of Genocide, international tribunals, and most recently the International Criminal Court. Teaching within a multidisciplinary and comparative studies framework creates a pedagogical model that raises awareness of the relevance of genocide here and now and of foreign policy patterns from the past to the present. For example, post-World War II genocide in Cambodia, Guatemala, and Rwanda and the accomplice roles of the United States and other nation-states from providing training to supporting denial are not widely studied. Since so far in the twenty-first century there is no indication that intentional mass killing will stop, this methodology provides an ongoing approach to evaluate current events as well as those in the past.

In *Literary Responses to Catastrophe,* under the heading "The Monotony of Genocide Literature," Rubina Peroomian writes: "Genocide literature can be monotonous.... Stories of horror, no matter how startling, or mournful lamentations, no matter how catching they may sound, in repetition after repetition make for tiresome reading."[51] Monotony may be the reaction of some students to reading about atrocity after atrocity. One of the challenges of teaching about genocide is to vary the materials from film to memoir to anthropological and historical texts. It is important to point out to students that some of the numbing they may feel and the emotional roller coaster from monotony to despair reflect the gravity of the material and an awareness of the need to resist the feelings of paralysis. Assignments such as asking students to perform unusual acts of kindness or engage in discussions of altruism, rescuers, or other ways to devise alternatives to destructive patterns and to create caring communities provide models of construction and a psychological relief in a course focusing on mass violence. Courses may also include sections on prevention strategies. The fact remains, however, that courses in genocide studies fundamentally challenge students to confront issues of radical evil and reflect upon the implications for their own lives and choices.

Comparative genocide courses cannot include all genocidal events; hence, some rely on chronological while others follow a thematic approach. Robert Melson's *Revolution and Genocide: On the Origins of the Armenian Genocide and the Holocaust* is a pioneer work in comparative genocide and excellent for graduate and undergraduate courses.[52] Alex Alvarez's study, *Governments, Citizens and Geno-*

cide: A Comparative and Interdisciplinary Approach, is an important new work in the field, emphasizing the degree of "participation and complicity of ordinary citizens" and the necessity to study genocide as a crime in the context of murder.[53]

In my own courses, War, Revolution and Genocide and Twentieth Century Genocide, themes of mass violence and societies in transformation are emphasized. Students often want to discuss Native American history, slavery, the Irish famine, and most recently, terrorism. Such topics are further explored through research papers and discussions of definitions of genocide and the question of intent or premeditation. I also spend the end of the course addressing types of humanitarian intervention, denial, donor fatigue, reconciliation, and the ongoing state politics of justice and injustice. Both courses include the Armenian Genocide. Roger Smith has pointed out:

> The Armenian Genocide, in fact, illuminates with special clarity the dangers inherent in the political manipulation of truth through distortion, denial, and intimidation. In no other instance has a government gone to such extreme lengths to deny that a massive genocide took place. That democratic governments have supported Turkey in that effort raises significant questions about governmental accountability and the role of citizenship in a world in which truth increasingly comes in two forms—"official" and "alleged."[54]

While the focus is on the genocide and its denial, students also learn about the past and present of the Armenians or other peoples being studied. Hence, the goal of the perpetrators to destroy the history and culture of the victim group is in part resisted by including aspects of that history and culture as well as life after the genocide.

Introducing the Armenian Genocide into General Studies and Education Courses

An important way to educate about genocide is to incorporate the subject in general studies, honors programs, and survey courses. In the fall of 2000, the first book students read in my course, Individual and Society III General Studies, at New York University was *Devastation of the Indies* by Bartolome de las Casas, an eyewitness account of the Spanish atrocities against the Amerindians.[55] The previous spring in the Individual and Society IV class, I focused on World War I in several sessions, with one class devoted to the Armenian Genocide. Students read Paul Fussell's *War and Modern Memory* and looked at his analysis through literature written at the time of how the first total war dichotomized thinking and how truth and relativity were lost in the "Great War."[56] Then students were assigned essays from Richard Hovannisian's *The Armenian Genocide: History, Politics, Ethics*. The day before the reading was due, I asked students to think about the implications of James Reid's assertion that the "ethics of total war permitted the total destruction of the enemy."[57]

Only two students, one educated in Poland, and the other educated in Europe and Jewish, had heard of the Armenian Genocide. Students were genuinely shocked to read about the genocide and its continued denial. They wondered to what extent their ignorance of the events had to do with the effectiveness of the politics of denial. The class discussion was lively on the following issues: What is human nature? What is civilization and progress? What is nationalism and how are nation-states built? Several students whose parents are from India or Pakistan discussed the Armenian Genocide in terms of religious and cultural prejudice. One student talked about the warfare in Chechnya, what should be considered an internal domestic matter, and when should there be intervention and by whom.[58] This prompted my raising the issue of what is the distinction between a genocide, as in the Armenian case, and instances of ethnic conflict, and do these differences in definition matter. After reading Reid's chapter, one student chose to do his research paper on genocide and famine. Finally, on the midterm, I included a question on how the Armenians were defined—a hostage people—within a larger question about World War I, mass destruction, and historic memory. Most students were able to answer the question, and some cited the Armenians as being "defined outside the universe of moral obligation" (Helen Fein's terminology in *Accounting for Genocide,* which I had used in my introductory remarks.)

Teaching about genocide, including the Armenian Genocide, and issues of human rights and wrongs needs to be introduced more widely in courses in departments of education across the country. At a time when schools of education and in-service courses are directed toward inclusive (multicultural) curricula, the preparation of future teachers cannot ignore the study of prejudice, genocide, and denial, as well as law, civic responsibility, and human rights.

My own experience conducting workshops for student teachers around the country is that all too often guidelines for "inclusive curriculum" and Holocaust or Holocaust/Genocide mandates fail to encompass a range of genocides or human rights issues. Plays, stories, and other methods rely on "not a tear was dry" pedagogy, that is, moving students to tears rather than curriculum with content and depth. Another common technique is the "monster" theory of history, promoting one leader as responsible for the Holocaust or other genocides. This removes focus on how often ordinary people take part in mass murder and the personal implications of studying prejudice and mass violence. Current pedagogy that relies on the opposing viewpoint perspectives, that is, there are two sides or more to every story, needs to be countered with critical thinking techniques. These will lead to the judgment, for example, that writers who deny the Armenian Genocide or the Holocaust are not telling the truth and are thereby falsifying history.[59] Even when there are Holocaust/Genocide mandates, teachers usually do not have materials available which integrate these complex events in one text with accessible teaching materials and lesson plans that can be utilized within the assessment-driven (that is, state testing standards) classroom. Finally, the reality is that middle and high school teachers in classrooms across the country have limited time to introduce new materials, and this is often matched by limited interest in the subjects of genocide and human rights. Hence, educating student teachers before they enter the classroom full-time is imperative.

Lessons in Curriculum: Facing History and Ourselves

Since the 1970s, the Facing History and Ourselves National Foundation has been a prominent, national educational foundation training teachers and conducting workshops on issues of tolerance, the Holocaust, and the Armenian, Cambodian, and other genocides.[60] It has organized conferences on multiculturalism, slavery, war crimes trials, the South African Truth and Reconciliation Commission, and related subjects.[61] I consider it to be unfortunate, therefore, that the innovative comparative genocide curriculum introduced in the first resource book published in 1982, *Facing History and Ourselves: Holocaust and Human Behavior,*[62] was subsumed under the Holocaust model in the revised and expanded version released in 1994.[63]

The original text begins with an "Overview: Confronting 20th-Century Genocide," in which two twentieth-century genocides were introduced: the Holocaust and the Armenian Genocide. Co-authors Margot Stern Strom and William S. Parsons discuss the value of their comparative approach:

> By acknowledging the tension between the universal and the particular characteristics of these two events, teachers can answer those who fear that a study of the Holocaust and the genocide of the Armenian people together will denigrate or cheapen the significance of each event. Consequently, they will fully honor and recognize the potential of their students to make meaning of history. They can be faithful to the uniqueness of each historical event, and make universal connections where appropriate.[64]

Teaching about these events, they continue, requires confronting "the power that revisionism, universalism and denial have for educators and their students."[65]

> In the case of the Ottoman Armenians, one can begin to recognize how easily certain history is forgotten. It is obvious from the label "the forgotten genocide" that the impulse to cope with the history of the genocide of the Armenian people by ignoring, denying, or revising has almost been successful.[66]

Designed specifically for adolescents, the 1982 *Resource Book* promotes "awareness of the history of the Holocaust and the genocide of the Armenian people, an appreciation for justice, a concern for interpersonal understanding and a memory for the victims of those events."[67] Study of these genocides deepens the sensitivity of students to issues such as "the use and abuse of power, obedience, loyalty, decision making, and survival as they further develop their notions of justice. They identify the role and responsibilities of the individual within a given society in times of choice."[68] Chapters 3 through 10 use multidisciplinary materials to analyze the history of anti-Semitism and the Holocaust.

Chapter 11 (pages 317-82) on the Armenian Genocide introduces Adolf Hitler's chilling remark in a speech prior to the invasion of Poland in 1939: "Who still talks nowadays of the extermination of the Armenians?"[69] Strom and Parsons emphasize that if the world had responded more vigorously to the mass killings of the Armenians, "the Holocaust might not have occurred."[70] The chapter on the Armenian Genocide includes survivor, eyewitness, newspaper, and scholarly accounts, as well as materials on resistance, Allied response, tracing the history of the Armenians in the Ottoman Empire, maps of the region, Turkish denial, and the effects of the genocide on the Armenian community. The final chapter of the resource book links study of the past with confronting current controversy, including debating issues of the "moral majority," the use of nuclear technology, and what an individual might do to affect decision making.

Facing History's 1994 revised resource book (expanded from 400 to 576 pages) deletes the chapter on the Armenians and the earlier comparative overview. There is some acknowledgment of the connection between the Holocaust and other cases:

> Important connections can be made with the events that led to the genocide of the Armenian people during World War I; the enslavement of Africans; the destruction of Native American nations in the years that followed European colonization of the Americas; and mass murders during World War II in Nanking, China, and the Soviet Union and more recently in Cambodia, Laos, Tibet, and Rwanda.[71]

Nonetheless, the preface clearly states that "the series of events that led to the Holocaust is the focus of this book,"[72] with material on the Holocaust increased and a new chapter, "Bystanders and Rescuers," which integrates recent scholarship and films.[73]

Additional materials on violence, racism, and multiculturalism are interconnected to materials on the Holocaust and World War II. Crucial issues of definitions of genocide, the United Nations and the Convention on the Prevention and Punishment of Genocide, listing of some post-1945 genocides and international tribunals, and additional resources are presented in four pages (459-62).[74] The final chapter, "Choosing to Participate," raises issues about citizenship and stresses community involvement and volunteerism.[75]

The 1994 *Resource Book* has limited material on the Armenian Genocide interspersed throughout the text.[76] At present, under the auspices of Facing History and Ourselves and with funding from Armenian sponsors, Facing History is producing a separate resource guide on the Armenian Genocide. However, the question is whether teachers will have sufficient time or interest to utilize this separate source and, if so, when and under what circumstances?

Comparing the two editions of the Facing History *Resource Book* makes it clear that the focus on one dominant model of destruction, in this case the Holocaust, lessens the likelihood of students and teachers having access to materials and hence learning about genocidal events in different places and affecting different peoples. The "forgotten genocide" of the Armenians that is studied in the first resource book is much less accessible to the reader in the second edition. The repercussions of U.S. foreign policy in the genocides in Cambodia, Guatemala, and Rwanda are not highlighted. Hopefully, there will be a third edition of the Facing History *Resource Book* that will return to and develop the earlier comparative genocide analysis, with a more global perspective and the addition of post-1945 human rights issues (the term human rights does not appear in the index at all). David Moshman has pointed out in "Conceptual Constraints on Thinking about Genocide":

> Although Holocaust curricula serve important purposes, they may instill or reinforce Holocaust-based conceptions of genocide. American students, for example, may fail to recognize the annihilation of indigenous cultures of the Americas as genocidal if their central image of genocide is Auschwitz or Treblinka. Curricula that addresses multiple genocides and that encourages students to articulate and apply formal definitions of genocide are critical if we want students to understand history more objectively. Only through such curricula, moreover, can we have students develop the sort of conceptual structures that will enable them to perceive and analyze the human rights catastrophes of the future.[77]

Destruction and Construction

Finally, genocide studies need a further pedagogical shift to include issues of prevention, justice, human rights norms, and recognition. Other important subjects to examine in resource books, syllabi, and research papers are early warning systems, intervention, international tribunals, truth commissions, and the roles and choices of individual citizens, states, and non-governmental organizations. The range of perpetrator responses after genocide—from some form of state recognition and acceptance of responsibility as in the case of Germany (along with the rise of neo-Nazi groups) to more than eighty years of state education and foreign policy of denial as in the case of Turkey (along with recent recognition of the Armenian Genocide by a small circle of Turkish students and academics)—needs to be explored. Recent ethnic cleansing and other atrocities in the former Yugoslavia provide a telling example of how the legacy of victimization may provide part of the rationale for aggrieved groups to commit atrocities generations later. Genocide is the crime of mass murder and raises profound issues of individual and state responsibility not only in the past but now as well.

Is there a way to promote dialogue between communities of victims and victimizers? What is the toll that denial and the holding on to memories of victimization may take? How can remembrance and memory provide impetus for a person and community to begin healing and move forward? What may be the advantages to the perpetrator state of acknowledging past crimes? Looking at issues of justice, healing, and reconciliation is crucial not only for their intellectual and political content but also because they provide an educational/therapeutic value for those students and communities whose lives have been affected by genocide or other types of mass violence.

The study of destruction also needs to consider ways to construct and reconstruct. This is said with a deep awareness of the extreme difficulty for communities that have been devastated by genocide and continue to fight its denial. As courses in genocide studies, human rights, and societies in transformation increase, teaching about the Armenian Genocide becomes integral to understanding the failure of international norms and the politics of state building through genocide. It also serves as an object lesson in the continuing search of a community for healing, remembrance, and renewal in the face of continued denial. The ongoing human suffering caused by a century of genocide reminds us of the immediate demanding challenge of genocide prevention.

In the twenty-first century, those of us committed to teaching about genocide and human rights recognize the enormous challenges in the classroom and in the world to instructing about human destructiveness while seeking ways to affirm human dignity and rights in the face of injustice and denial. Teaching about the Armenian Genocide represents an integral part of this ongoing narrative of humankind.

Notes

1. The term genocide (*genus*: people and *cide:* killing) was coined by Raphael Lemkin and first appeared in print in his study, *Axis Rule in Occupied Europe* (Washington, DC: Carnegie Endowment for International Peace, 1944), p. 79. In this paper, genocide studies refer to the multidisciplinary comparative analyses of events of intentional mass destruction of civilian populations targeted because of their real or alleged belonging to an ethnic, racial, political, economic, or other grouping. For examples of the debate on definition, typology, and its implication, see essays by Leo Kuper, Frank Chalk, Israel W. Charny, and Helen Fein in "The Conceptual Dimensions of Genocide," in George J. Andreopoulos, ed., *Genocide: Conceptual and Historical Dimensions* (Philadelphia: University of Pennsylvania Press, 1994), pp. 29-108. My appreciation to Roger Smith for his helpful comments on an earlier draft of this paper and to Aram Arkun of the Krikor and Clara Zohrab Information Center in New York for assistance in locating relevant sources.
2. See Naomi Roht-Arriza, ed., *Impunity and Human Rights in International Law and Practice* (New York and Oxford: Oxford University Press, 1995), which lists violations of human rights from torture and disappearances to genocide. Most perpetrators were never prosecuted.
3. Robert Melson, "The Armenian Genocide," in *Encyclopedia of Genocide*, Israel W. Charny, ed., vol. 1 (Santa Barbara, CA: ABC-Clio, 1999), p. 61.

4. See Richard G. Hovannisian, "Foreword," in Richard G. Hovannisian, ed., *The Armenian Genocide in Perspective* (New Brunswick, NJ and Oxford: Transaction Publishers, 1986), p. 11. See also Vahakn N. Dadrian, *German Responsibility in the Armenian Genocide: A Review of the Historical Evidence of German Complicity* (Cambridge, MA: Blue Crane Books, 1996).
5. Gary J. Bass, *Stay the Hand of Vengeance: The Politics of War Crimes Tribunals* (Princeton: Princeton University Press, 2000), p.144.
6. For sources on the growing literature of denial, see Levon Chorbajian, "Introduction," in Levon Chorbajian and George Shirinian, eds., *Studies in Comparative Genocide* (New York: St. Martin's Press, 1999), pp. xxxii-xxxiii. On deniers of different genocides, see "Denials of Genocide," in *Encyclopedia of Genocide*, vol. 1, pp. 159-87.
7. Mark Levene, "Creating a Modern 'Zone of Genocide': The Impact of Nation- and State-Formation on Eastern Anatolia, 1878-1923," *Holocaust and Genocide Studies* 12:3 (1998): 393-433.
8. See Raffi K. Hovannisian, "State and Nation: Their Roles after Independence" in this volume. For a contrasting interpretation, see Gerard J. Libaridian, *The Challenge of Statehood: Armenian Political Thinking since Independence* (Watertown, MA: Blue Crane Books, 1999), pp. 109-18.
9. For a brief history of Armenology as a discipline and Armenian Studies in the United States and Europe, see Dickran Kouymjian, "The Purpose and Direction of Armenian Studies in the Diaspora," *Society for Armenian Studies Newsletter* 6:3 (1981): 3, 6, 8. See also Hagop J. Nersoyan, "Armenian Studies in the Next Decade: Observations and Reflections," in *Journal of Armenian Studies* 11:1 (1985): 1-5; Ronald G. Suny, "Report on the Status of Armenian Studies in the United States," *SAS Newsletter* 4:3 (1979): 1, 8.

   Armenian Studies programs remain small and are located primarily in California, Massachusetts, New York, and Michigan, where Armenian-American communities are concentrated. Many of the enrolled students are of Armenian background. For a recent academic roundtable on the history of the chairs, issues of purpose and content, employment and research difficulties, and other challenges facing Armenian studies in the United States, see the *Armenian Forum* 1:1 (1998): 95-101; Levon Avdoyan, *Armenian Studies and the Armenian American Community: An Old Curmudgeon's Viewpoint* (New York: Zohrab Information Center, 1995).

   For a discussion of what constitutes Armenian modernity, see Boghos Levon Zekiyan, "Modern Armenian Culture: Some Basic Trends between Continuity and Change, Specificity and Universality," in *Armenian Perspective: 10th Anniversary Conference of the Association Internationale des Études Arméniennes,* ed. Nicholas Awde (Richmond Surrey, UK: Curzon Press, 1997), pp. 323-54, and in the same volume, Dickran Kouymjian, "Response to 'Modern Armenian Culture'," pp. 355-61. The history and tensions within Armenian Studies are complex and affected by developments in Armenia and the worldwide Armenian communities, as well as larger political and cultural forces.
10. The first chair was established at Harvard University more than forty years ago and was occupied by Robert W. Thomson, a scholar of patristic literature who held the chair for three decades. The challenges of setting up these chairs in terms of raising funds and political obstacles were substantial. Richard N. Frye, at the time Agha Khan Professor of Iranian at Harvard and a founding member of the National Association for Armenian Studies and Research, mentions earlier failed attempts to establish a chair. "I emphasize the importance of the Armenian Chair at Harvard as a matter of major significance not only to Armenians of the world but beyond that,

and very importantly, to all the peoples of the world who are interested in preserving their identity and culture," *Journal of Armenian Studies* 1:1 (1975): 2.

11. Avedis K. Sanjian became chair holder in Armenian language and literature at UCLA in 1969. He served as chairman of the SAS Administrative Council, the first editor of the *Journal of the Society for Armenian Studies,* and chairman of Department of Near Eastern Languages and Culture (1970-74). Nina G. Garsoian was instrumental in establishing Armenian Studies at Columbia University and in 1979 became the first holder of the Centennial (now Avedissian) Chair in Armenian History and Civilization. She also served as chairperson of the Department of Middle Eastern Languages and Culture at Columbia University and as the chair of the Administrative Council of the SAS in 1975 (source http://www.umd.umich.edu/deot/armenian/sas). Louise Nalbandian taught courses in Armenian history for a year at UCLA and then in 1967 pioneered the Armenian Studies program at Fresno State until her untimely death in 1975. See Dickran Kouymjian, "Louise Nalbandian: Pioneer of Armenian Studies at Fresno State," in *Hye Sharzhoom* (May 2000): 3. Despite the pioneering work of Garsoian and Nalbandian, faculty and graduate students in Armenian Studies have been preponderantly male. A new trend may be emerging with the increase in recent years in the number of female faculty and Ph.D. candidates in the field.
12. "In all, over twenty-five institutions of higher education in the United States now offer accredited courses and programs in Armenian language, civilization, and history on the undergraduate, graduate, or adult-education levels." See *Journal of Armenian Studies* 11:1 (1985): 82.
13. Gia Aivazian, "SAS and Its Role in Promoting Armenian Scholarship in the U.S.," *SAS Newsletter*, 22:1 (1998): 13. The Society for Armenian Studies was founded at the initiative of Richard Hovannisian, in cooperation with Nina Garsoian, Dickran Kouymjian, Avedis Sanjian, and Robert Thomson. The SAS has some 220 members and affiliated early on with the Middle East Studies Association (which has more than 2,000 members) and later with the American Historical Association and Slavic Studies Association. See www.umd.umich.edu/dept/armenian/sas.
14. Richard G. Hovannisian has emphasized modern Armenian history as a national entity and placed the Armenian Genocide as central to the Armenian experience. Hovannisian has written and edited numerous books and articles, among them: *Armenia on the Road to Independence* (Berkeley and Los Angeles: University of California Press, 1967); *The Armenian Holocaust: A Bibliography Relating to the Deportations, Massacres, and Dispersion of the Armenian People, 1915-1923* (Cambridge, MA: Armenian Heritage Press, 1978); *The Armenian Image in History and Literature* (Malibu, CA: Undena Press, 1983). *The Republic of Armenia*, published by the University of California Press (1971-1996), is in four volumes: *The First Year, 1918-1919*; *From Versailles to London, 1919-1920*; *From London to Sèvres, February-August, 1920*; and *Between Crescent and Sickle: Partition and Sovietization*. Edited collections by Richard Hovannisian include *The Armenian Genocide in Perspective* (New Brunswick, NJ: Transaction Publishers, 1986); *The Armenian Genocide: History, Politics, Ethics* (London: Macmillan and New York: St Martin's Press, 1992); and *Remembrance and Denial: The Case of the Armenian Genocide* (Detroit: Wayne State University Press, 1999).

    Sociologist Vahakn N. Dadrian focuses on the Armenian Genocide. Besides his numerous articles, books by Dadrian include: *The History of the Armenian Genocide: Ethnic Conflict from the Balkans to Anatolia to the Caucasus* (Providence, RI and Oxford: Berghahn Books, 1995); *German Responsibility in the Armenian Genocide* (see note 4 above); *Warrant for Genocide: Key Elements of Turko-Arme-*

nian Conflict (New Brunswick, NJ and London: Transaction Publishers, 1999); *The Key Elements in the Turkish Denial of the Armenian Genocide: A Case Study of Destruction and Falsification* (Cambridge, MA: Zoryan Institute, 1999).

Ronald Grigor Suny, first Alex Manoogian Professor of Modern Armenian History and director of Armenian Studies at the University of Michigan-Ann Arbor, now teaches political science at the University of Chicago. He is a specialist in the history of the non-Russian peoples of the Caucasus and author and co-editor of works on a range of topics including *The Baku Commune, 1917-18: Class and Nationality in the Russian Revolution* (Princeton: Princeton University Press, 1972). Suny's books in modern Armenian history are *Armenia in the Twentieth Century* (Chico, CA: Scholars Press, 1983); and *Looking toward Ararat: Armenia in Modern History* (Bloomington and Indianapolis: Indiana University Press, 1993). His work, *The Revenge of the Past: Nationalism, Revolution, and the Collapse of the Soviet Union* (Stanford: Stanford University Press, 1993), is used in courses on nationalism and revolution and integrates the Armenian Genocide and modern Armenian history into regional studies.

Besides the publications in literature, poetry, religion, art history, and other cultural aspects, two memoirs have been most influential in introducing the Armenian Genocide and issues of Armenian identity to a larger reading public. These are Michael Arlen, *Passage to Ararat* (New York: Farrar Strauss Giroux, 1975), and Peter Balakian, *Black Dog of Fate: A Memoir* (New York: Basic Books, 1997).

15. Hovannisian, "Preface" in *Armenian Genocide in Perspective*, p. 2.
16. Donald E. Miller and Lorna Touryan Miller, *Survivors: An Oral History of the Armenian Genocide* (Berkeley, Los Angeles, London: University of California Press, 1993), p. 212. The authors discuss the growth of oral history programs and list film, photography, and musicology projects using oral history research methods.
17. Marjorie Housepian Dobkin, "The Unremembered Genocide," *Commentary* 42:3 (1966): 55ff.
18. For a brief discussion and references, see articles by Peter Balakian, "Combating Denials of the Armenian Genocide in Academia" and Rouben Paul Adalian, "Deniers of the Armenian Genocide," in *Encyclopedia of Genocide*, vol. 1, pp. 163-65 and 177-78. For a typology on the continuum from innocent to malevolent denial, see Israel W. Charny, "'Innocent Denials' of Known Genocides: A Further Contribution to a Psychology of Denial of Genocide (Revisionism)," *Human Rights Review* 1:3 (2000): 15-39. See also Israel Charny, "The Psychological Satisfaction of Denials of the Holocaust or Other Genocides by Non-Extremists or Bigots, and Even by Known Scholars," on-line journal *Idea* at http://www.ideajournal.com/charny-denials.html.
19. See Joyce Freedman-Apsel, "Teaching about Genocide," in Joyce Freedman-Apsel and Helen Fein, eds., *Teaching about Genocide: A Guidebook for College and University Teachers* (Human Rights Internet, 1992; rev. ed., Washington, DC: American Sociological Association, 1998), pp. 17-21.
20. Leon A. Chorbajian, "Massacre or Genocide: An Essay in Personal Biography and Objective Experience," *Armenian Review* 32:2 (1979): 170-71. Chorbajian is professor of sociology at the University of Massachusetts, Lowell. His recent work coedited with George Shirinian, *Studies in Comparative Genocide*, is based on a conference on comparative genocide held in Erevan, Republic of Armenia in April 1995. The book's dedication is "To all victims and survivors of genocide."
21. Dickran Koumjian, "Louise Nalbandian: Pioneer of Armenian Studies at Fresno State," (May 200):3. Koumjian points out that Nalbandian was the first female to

enter the all male bastion of the history department. Louise Nalbandian received her Ph.D. from Stanford University, and her thesis was published as *The Armenian Revolutionary Movement: The Development of Armenian Political Parties through the Nineteenth Century* (Berkeley and Los Angeles: University of California Press, 1963).

22. Kouymjian, "Louise Nalbandian," p. 3. By 1972, a minor in Armenian language was offered, and five university courses were listed in the 1974 catalog. With the untimely death of Dr. Nalbandian, the program lapsed. After the appointment of Dickran Kouymjian in 1977, the Armenian Studies program was reestablished and over time developed a multidisciplinary minor and sponsored guest lectures and publication of *Hye Sharzhoom* [Armenian Action], in cooperation with the Armenian Students Organization. It was reported that in the fall semester of 2000: "Some 170 students are registered in eight sections of Armenian Studies courses" and "nearly 100 students or 60% are non-Armenian, an extraordinary statistic which makes it clear that our Armenian Studies course offerings have become incorporated into the general university curriculum." See Dickran Kouymjian, "Banner Semester for Armenian Studies Program: A Report," *Hye Sharzhoom* 21:4 (May 2000): 2.
23. http://www.sscnet.ucla.edu/history/centers/armenian/history.
24. Ibid.
25. Ibid.
26. "University-level instruction in modern Armenian history began with a single course at UCLA…it was taught by Richard Hovannisian." See George Bournoutian, "Comments," in *Armenian Forum*, 1:1 (1998), p. 99. History seminars offered include the following: Armenian History, Armenian Oral History, The Caucasus under Russian and Soviet Rule, The Armenian Diaspora and the Armenian Genocide. Hovannisian edited *The Armenian Genocide in Perspective,* essays ranging from the impact of denial to the psychological consequences of the trauma of genocide. This collection was the first of its kind to provide much needed multidisciplinary material for general college classroom use.
27. In addition to their scholarship, for example, Rouben Adalian is executive director of the Armenian National Institute. "The primary goal of the Armenian National Institute (ANI) is reaffirmation of the worldwide recognition of the Armenian Genocide, and it is dedicated to the study, research, and affirmation of the Armenian Genocide" (*ANI Annual Report*, 1998). George Bournoutian, who was the recipient of the second Ph.D. degree awarded from the UCLA Armenian Studies Program, is professor of history at Iona College, has taught Armenian, Russian, and Middle Eastern history as a visiting professor at various universities, and has published, among other works, a two-volume survey of Armenian history for classroom use, *A History of the Armenian People*. Gerard J. Libaridian, an early graduate of the UCLA program, served from 1991 to 1997 as adviser to the former president of Armenia, Levon Ter-Petrosian, and then became a Senior Research Fellow at the East-West Institute in New York.
28. For syllabi of the three courses offered, see Freedman-Apsel and Fein, *Teaching about Genocide*.
29. Leo Kuper is the author of path-breaking works in the field of genocide studies: *Genocide: Its Political Use in the Twentieth Century* (New Haven: Yale University Press, 1982), and *The Prevention of Genocide* (New Haven: Yale University Press, 1985).
30. Professor Cowe has published primarily in ancient and medieval Armenian studies. According to a recent biographical sketch, "When S. Peter Cowe wasn't laboring this summer over medieval translations of 5th century Armenian manuscripts, he

was proofreading translations of late-20th century Armenian plays and laying the foundations for an 18th century Armenian cultural history." See www.today.ucla.edu.

31. Courses listed under Armenian Language and Literature include the following: Survey of Armenian Literature; Arts, Politics and Nationalism in Modern Armenian Literature; Issues in Armenian-American Literature and Culture; Armenian Literature of 19th and 20th Century. Language courses include Modern West Armenian, Modern East Armenian, and Elementary Classical Armenian and are offered when there is sufficient enrollment, often by part-time faculty. See http://www.sscnet.ucla.edu/history/centers/armenian/courses.html.
32. http://www.scnet.ucla.edu/history/centers/armenian/program.htm. For a history of the acquisition of the valuable Minasian collection, see Avedis K. Sanjian, "The Historical Setting," in Thomas Mathews and Avedis K. Sanjian, *Armenian Gospel Iconography: The Tradition of the Glajor Gospel* (Washington, DC: Dumbarton Oaks, 1991). "The Glajor Gospel, by reason of its extraordinary wealth of iconography and its excellent state of preservation, must be ranked as the most important manuscript from Greater Armenia to have reached the New World." p. 5.
33. http://www.scnet.ucla.edu/history/centers/armenian/program.html.
34. See Khachig Tololyan, "Memoirs of a Diasporan Nationalist," in Ronald G. Suny and Michael D. Kennedy, eds., *Intellectuals and the Articulation of the Nation* (Ann Arbor: University of Michigan Press, 1999), p. 106.
35. Vincent Lima and Ara Sarafian edit this new journal and promote debate on issues of scholarly interpretation as well as political and community interest and seek to "bridge the gap between Armenian scholars on both sides of the Atlantic as well as the Middle East." See http://www.gomidas.org/forum/editors.htm. For a report in the *Armenian Forum* on a workshop on the Armenian Genocide, held at the University of Chicago between Turkish, Armenian, and other scholars, see http://www.gomidas,org/forum/Chicago.htm. See also Ronald Grigor Suny, "Empire and Nation: Armenians, Turks, and the End of the Ottoman Empire," *Armenian Forum* 1:2 (1998): 217-52, and in the same volume, pp. 53-136, an exchange of views by Turkish historians Engin Deniz Akarli and Selim Deringil and Armenian Genocide specialist Vahakn Dadrian.
36. For courses at the University of Michigan-Ann Arbor, see www.umich.edu/~iinet/asp, which includes a range of subjects such as The Post-Genocide Literature of the Armenian Dispersion, The Writings of William Saroyan, and History, Memory and Identity. Kevork Bardakjian, Marie Manoogian Professor of Armenian, currently heads the program.
37. Given the large number of offerings on aspects of the Holocaust, popularity of courses on cultures of violence, primarily studying Latin America and other regions outside the United States, and the recent field of violence studies concerned with past and present U.S. behavior, from destruction of the Native Americans to contemporary hate groups, genocide studies in fact overlap with each of these fields. Interestingly, all these studies reflect U.S. societal preoccupation with violence and evil. In contrast, courses on utopias and communes and peace studies are much less popular than they were in the late 1960s and 1970s.
38. The amount and different types of materials available, commitment to the "uniquely unique" perspective on the Holocaust, and personal emotional involvement all can be factors in the resistance to including discussion of other genocides in courses on the Holocaust. In informal discussions with clergy or other Christians who are committed to teaching about the Holocaust for deeply religious/personal reasons (including profound disturbance at the history of anti-Semitism in Christianity), there is great reluctance, sometimes a reaction akin to the suggestion of apostasy, to

the idea of including information or giving students the option of doing research on other genocides. Teachers focused on teaching the Armenian Genocide or Cambodian Genocide also may want to keep their course directed on one genocidal event, but it is more likely that they have to take into consideration the Holocaust. However, the fact that people of different backgrounds teach and do research about the Holocaust has enriched the field greatly.

Most courses spend little time on the Nuremberg trials and later developments such as the U.N. Declaration of Human Rights and the U.N. Convention on the Prevention and Punishment of the Crime of Genocide. Successful lobbying and the politics of education have also contributed to funding and support for teaching about the Holocaust in the United States and establishment of the U.S. Holocaust Memorial Museum. See Peter Novick, *The Holocaust in American Life* (Boston: Houghton Mifflin, 1999).

39. For a listing of some of the major Holocaust organizations and centers, published yearly, see William L. Shulman, ed., *Association of Holocaust Organizations Directory* (New York: Holocaust Resource Center and Archives, Queensborough Community College, 2000).

40. See Robert Melson, "Revolution and Genocide: On the Causes of the Armenian Genocide and the Holocaust," in Richard G. Hovannisian, ed., *The Armenian Genocide: History, Politics, Ethics* (London: Macmillan and New York: St. Martin's Press, 1992); Robert Melson, *Revolution and Genocide: On the Origins of the Armenian Genocide and the Holocaust* (Chicago: University of Chicago Press, 1992); Helen Fein, "A Formula for Genocide: A Comparison of the Turkish Genocide (1915) and the German Holocaust (1939-1945)," *Comparative Studies in Sociology* 1 (1978): 271-93, and her *Accounting for Genocide: National Responses and Jewish Victimization during the Holocaust* (New York: Free Press, 1979); Vahakn N. Dadrian, "The Convergent Aspects of the Armenian and Jewish Cases of Genocide: A Reinterpretation of the Concept of Holocaust," *Holocaust and Genocide Studies* 2 (1988): 151-70.

Several books widely used in Holocaust courses include references to the Armenians. See, for example, Yehuda Bauer with Nili Keren, *A History of the Holocaust* (Danbury, CT: Franklin Watts, 1982). "The massacre of the Armenian people in Turkish Anatolia parallels the Holocaust." (p. 57.)

41. For example, according to Director William L. Shulman, the Holocaust Resource Center and Archives at Queensborough Community College commissioned, sponsored, and displayed the exhibit, "The Armenians, Shadows of a Forgotten Genocide," from August 1999 to June 2000. The University of Minnesota's Center for Holocaust and Genocide Studies under the direction of Stephen Feinstein has sponsored lectures and teacher workshops on the Armenian Genocide and is a pioneer in innovative programs and exhibits on a wide range of topics in genocide studies. See *Center for Holocaust and Genocide Studies Newsletter*, 1998-2000. In the fall of 2000, the Casperson Graduate School at Drew University in Madison, New Jersey, in conjunction with the Holocaust/Genocide Center offered a course on the Armenian Genocide and the Politics of Denial.

42. Charny ,"Comparative Study of Genocide" in *Encyclopedia of Genocide*, vol. 1, p. 9.

43. Israel W. Charny, "Introduction," in *Century of Genocide: Eyewitness Accounts and Critical View*, Samuel Totten, William S. Parsons, and Israel W. Charny, eds. (New York: Garland Publishing Co., 1997).

44. Unfortunately, different victim groups often express resentment toward other groups who they feel have too much political power or get too much attention. There is

particular anti-Jewish sentiment, including resentment over use of the term "Holocaust" exclusively for the Nazi genocide against the Jews, frequent newspaper and motion picture coverage, and the U.S. Holocaust Memorial Museum. Frustration and anger manifest themselves in criticisms of other victim groups. This type of competition and hostility makes the work of educators who teach about genocide particularly challenging.

45. Roger Smith, "Introduction," in Roger W. Smith, ed., *Genocide: Essays toward Understanding Early-Warning and Prevention* (Williamsburg, VA: Association of Genocide Scholars, 1999). All four of the organizing scholars have written and lectured about the Armenian Genocide in a comparative framework. For information on the Association of Genocide Scholars and other such organizations and for periodicals and articles on genocide studies, see the two-volume *Encyclopedia of Genocide*, edited by Israel W. Charny, an important recent reference source.
46. Freedman-Apsel and Fein, *Teaching about Genocide*.
47. Frank Chalk and Kurt Jonassohn, *The History and Sociology of Genocide: Analysis and Case Studies* (New Haven: Yale University Press, 1990).
48. Totten, Parsons, and Charny, *Century of Genocide*. The section on the Armenian Genocide, written by Rouben Adalian and followed by Armenian Genocide survivor testimonies, is a valuable introduction for students. Other chapters in this volume cover the following cases: Hereros; Soviet man-made famine in the Ukraine; Soviet deportation of whole nations; the Holocaust: Jews, Gypsies, and Disabled Peoples; Indonesia; East Timor; Bangladesh; Burundi; Cambodia; Indigenous Peoples; Rwanda; Bosnia-Herzegovina.
49. Rudolph Rummel introduced the term democide as "the murder of any person or people by a government, including genocide, politicide and mass murder." See R.J. Rummel, "The New Concept of Democide," in *Encyclopedia of Genocide*, vol. 1, p. 18. See also Rummel's study, *Power Kills: Democracy as a Method of Nonviolence* (New Brunswick, NJ: Transaction Publishers, 1997), which includes a bibliography of his extensive statistical and analytic work on democide and his essay, "When and Why to Use the Term Democide for 'Genocide,'" from *IDEA: A Journal of Social Issues*, at www.ideajournal.com/rummel-democide.html.
50. The term omnicide was coined by philosopher John Sommerville "to convey the new dimension of mass killing inherent in nuclear weapons." See the entry on "Omnicide" by Eric Markusen, *Encyclopedia of Genocide*, vol. 2, p. 451.
51. Rubina Peroomian, *Literary Responses to Catastrophe: A Comparison of the Armenian and the Jewish Experience* (Atlanta: Scholars Press, 1993).
52. Robert Melson's *Revolution and Genocide* (see note 40 above) is a unique contribution to the field of comparative genocide studies and sets a high standard for rigor and clarity.
53. See Alex Alvarez, "Introduction," in his *Governments, Citizens, and Genocide: A Comparative and Interdisciplinary Approach* (Indianapolis: Indiana University Press, 2001).
54. Roger W. Smith , "The Armenian Genocide: Memory, Politics and the Future," in Hovannisian, *The Armenian Genocide: History, Politics, Ethics*, p. 2.
55. Bartolome de las Casas, *The Devastation of the Indies* (Baltimore and London: Johns Hopkins University Press, 1992).
56. Paul Fussell, *The Great War and Modern Memory* (London and New York: Oxford University Press, 1975).
57. James J. Reid, "Total War, the Annihilation Ethic, and the Armenian Genocide, 1870-1918," in Hovannisian, *The Armenian Genocide: History, Politics, Ethics*, p. 32.

58. Students had no knowledge of either the forced famine in the Ukraine or the Soviet deportation of several ethnic groups and were surprised to learn that past Soviet excesses contributed to the recent warfare in Chechnya.
59. Greenhaven Press, for example, puts out the "Opposing Viewpoints" series on issues from human rights to social justice and the Third World. The goal is to develop critical thinking and evaluate different opinions.
60. Margot Stern Strom and William S. Parsons co-founded Facing History. Strom is its executive director. Parsons is the former director of education and now chief of staff for the U.S. Holocaust Memorial Museum in Washington, DC. He wrote the study guide, *Everyone's Not Here: Families of the Armenian Genocide*, produced for the Armenian Assembly of America in 1989.
61. For a description of goals, pedagogy, and publications, see Margot Stern Strom, "Facing History and Ourselves," in *Encyclopedia of Genocide*, vol. 1, pp. 223-26. The foundation sponsors a wide-ranging series of teacher training workshops. For example, in 1992, it cosponsored with the Institute for the Study of Genocide a conference at the Runkle School that became the basis for *Teaching about Genocide: A Guidebook for College and University Teachers* by Freedman-Apsel and Fein. See also Martha Minow, *Between Vengeance and Forgiveness: Facing History after Genocide and Mass Violence* (Boston: Beacon Press, 1998), which is an outgrowth of a Facing History conference cosponsored with the Harvard Law School Graduate Program in 1997 on "Collective Violence and Memory: Judgment, Reconciliation, Education, Facing History and Ourselves." In October 1999, Facing History, in cooperation with the Armenian National Committee of San Francisco, sponsored a workshop for teachers, "Exploring Responses to Genocide and Mass Violence." Jack Weinstein, Bay Area program director for Facing History, "led teachers through an examination of the responses to the Holocaust and the Armenian Genocide, comparing the governmental and societal reactions to each event." http://wwwancsf.org/press_releases.htm.
62. Margot Stern Strom and William S. Parsons, *Facing History and Ourselves: Holocaust and Human Behavior* (Watertown, MA: Intentional Educations, 1982).
63. *Facing History and Ourselves: Holocaust and Human Behavior Resource Book* (Brookline, MA: Facing History and Ourselves National Foundation, 1994).
64. Ibid., p. 6.
65. Ibid.
66. Ibid.
67. Ibid., p. 13.
68. Ibid.
69. Ibid., p. 319.
70. Ibid. The Armenian Genocide material is placed out of chronological order and after the chapters on the Holocaust.
71. *Facing History and Ourselves Resource Book* (1994), p. xvii.
72. Ibid. The preface adds (p. xviii):

    > Perhaps the most important is that it helps students better understand the modern world and ultimately themselves. In no other history are the steps that resulted in totalitarianism and ultimately genocide so carefully documented not only by the victims but also by perpetrators and bystanders. It is a history that clearly shows the deadly consequences of unexamined prejudices, unfaced fears, and unchallenged lies. It shows too the dangers of charismatic leaders who manipulate the young by appealing to prejudice, fear, and ignorance. We do not want yet another generation of young people influenced by propaganda to march blindly in someone else's parade.

73. The preface (p. xxvi) explains:

    The new edition also contains more social history and reflects the insights of current scholarship, particularly scholarship on issues related to violence and racism. Two important chapters in the earlier edition have been deleted and their content added to other chapters. As a result, anti-Judaism and antisemitism are discussed within the context of particular eras rather than in an isolated chapter. The same is true of the Armenian Genocide. It too has been placed within a chronological framework.

    New materials relevant for U.S. students include problems of violence and gangs as well as African American, Latino, and Asian American issues. Post-1945 U.S. foreign policy and genocide are not addressed. In the 1994 edition, chapter 8, "Bystanders and Rescuers" (pages 363-417), includes some material from the earlier resource book, such as "What Did People Know?" Most of the chapter, however, integrates more recent materials, such as discussion of the film *Schindler's List* (for which Facing History has prepared a study guide); Samuel and Pearl Oliner's, *The Altruistic Personality*: *Rescuers of Jews in Nazi Europe* (New York: Free Press, 1988); Gay Block and Malka Drucker, *Rescuers: Portraits of Moral Courage in the Holocaust* (New York:Holmes and Meier, 1992), among others.
74. Chapter 9, "Judgment," (pp. 418-69) is introduced with a quotation by Maya Angelou and focuses on Nuremberg, the Nazis, and Germany after 1945, including the topic of restitution.
75. The chapter is a selection from a larger volume on civic education published by Facing History and Ourselves, *Choosing to Participate*. The other cross-referenced Facing History publication is *Elements of Time*, "a companion manual" to a collaborative project with the Fortunoff video collection of Holocaust survivor testimonies housed at Yale University.
76. In chapter 2, "The Eve of World War I," for example, there is a section, "Creating Enemies of the State: The Armenians," with related "Connections" (pp. 102-06). Except for a mention as precedent for Nuremberg (p. 423), material on the Armenian Genocide appears again only in chapter 11 with a personal account, "Truth the Last Victim of Genocide" and "The Politics of Denial," and in both sections there are connections to further resources available about the Armenian Genocide (pp. 497-505). Everything in the chapter relates back to the dominant model of the Holocaust.
77. David Moshman, "Conceptual Constraints on Thinking about Genocide," *Encyclopedia of Genocide*, vol. 1, p. 13.

11

Reconstructing the Turkish Historiography on the Armenian Massacres and Deaths of 1915

Fatma Müge Göçek

"A Muezzin's Summons to Prayer"

On a July night replete with peace and repose, a darkness descends to the ground;
And to the sky at once raises a sound:
It is the muezzin's voice, summoning to prayer the Muslims all around,
Atop a white minaret he calls, divine love within abound.

Blending into the shore's breeze, they journey on together,
And that penetrating voice, slowly ascends layer upon layer,
Then into the world of eternity, it wanes and disappears
All along with the sweetly caressing morning breeze.

Oh, that muezzins voice! Lost in far away lands...
That prayer wanes by the moment, but the feeling left inside intense,
Yes, such a prayer, loaded with mystery and despondence,
Raises at times and then, replete with sadness, fades into the distance.

Confessions of a sad and pale heart this prayer beholds,
To me it appears sometimes as my weeping inner voice,
Yes, such a voice, longing to leave all sadness in the winds' embrace!...

And what's done is done; right then all slowly unfolds,
Yes, in my heart arrive and settle peace and repose,
Happiness and relief fill me inside, peace my whole existence envelops,
Because he wept for me tonight, for my sadness and sorrows...

This poem was written by Hraçya (Hrachia) Surenyan, also known as the poet Armen Dorian. Born in Sinope in 1892, Dorian first attended the Pangaltı Mekhitarist School and then the Sorbonne University in Paris.[1] At the age of twenty-one, he composed exclusively in French to become one of the founders of the pantheist school of poetry. After his return to Istanbul in 1914, he died at the age of twenty-three in Anatolia, where he had been sent in accordance with the Ottoman Decree of Relocation in 1915.

Dorian's poem clearly demonstrates how, for centuries, the Armenians and Turks lived and shared a world together and made that world theirs by imbuing it with particular meanings. The poetry of the summons to prayer demonstrates how the young poet had found in the muezzin's call an emotion he could make his own. He must have felt all the more betrayed to be first accused of sedition and then killed by the same Muslims about whom he wrote. And the same Muslims destroyed so much of a rich world of meaning Dorian had helped create. I chose to start my chapter with this poem not only to mark the tragic and timeless death of a gifted poet but also to emphasize the rich world that Turkish society so senselessly lost as a consequence of the Armenian massacres of 1915.

Contemporary Turks are only now being introduced to the literary world of the Turkish Armenians through recent translations into Turkish of works by authors such as Hagop Mintzuri,[2] Antan Özer,[3] Yervant Sırmakeşliyan,[4] and Krikor Zohrab.[5] Reading for the first time the novels, short stories, and poetry that these Turkish Armenians produced inevitably reveals to a Turkish audience how a world replete with meaning was lost with the massacres of the Armenians, leaving behind a culturally impoverished society. Yet, the Turkish people unfortunately are unable fully to acknowledge, understand, and mourn the tragic demise of the Armenians because of the policy of the Turkish nation-state that denies the Armenian massacres of 1915. I maintain that the mourning so necessary also for the Turks can only commence if the Turkish historiography on the events of 1915 is freed from the hegemony of the Turkish nation-state and contextualized within a larger historical framework.

I argue here that Turkish historiography on the Armenians can be viewed within three historical periods that contain distinct narratives. These are as follows:

1) *The Ottoman Investigative Narrative* based on accounts of the time pertaining to the Ottoman Armenians, including the Armenian deaths of 1915, published either by the Turkish state or by opposing political groups;

2) *The Republican Defensive Narrative* based on the works, often published or kept in circulation by the Turkish state, that have been written with the intent to justify and prove the nationalist master

narrative of the Turkish state, which explicitly denies the allegation that an Armenian genocide occurred;

3) *The Post-Nationalist Critical Narrative* found in works that are directly or indirectly critical of the nationalist master narrative but with a few exceptions do not focus specifically on the Armenian massacres. Their concern is much more with the silence in contemporary Turkish society pertaining to its history and resultant ethnoreligious composition.

Reading the events of 1915 within this framework can create a new space for a different Turkish interpretation, one that would ultimately recognize the depth of the Armenian tragedy.

The Ottoman Investigative Narrative on the Events of 1915

Works in this category are composed of the memoirs of Ottoman officials such as Said, Kamil, and Talat pashas, Mehmed Asaf, and Dr. Reşid Bey,[6] the investigative records of the postwar military tribunals that tried persons accused of perpetrating the massacres,[7] the official reports prepared by the Ottoman state such as the one by Hüseyin Nazım Pasha,[8] the petitions of groups associated with the postwar Ottoman government,[9] the accounts of the Turkish negotiations of the Treaty of Lausanne,[10] and the collections of documents published by the Turkish nation-state ostensibly from the Ottoman state and military archives to deny the genocide allegations.[11] Each work is reviewed in detail in a larger book project, but here I shall merely outline the general patterns of meaning I discern in these publications that make up the Ottoman investigative narrative.

My reading of the works issued during the Ottoman period on the Armenian relocations and deaths reveals that two characteristics distinguish the Ottoman investigative narrative from others. First, since all of these works were originally written around the time of the events of 1915, they do not question the occurrence of the Armenian "massacres" (genocide was not a term then employed) but focus instead on the question of what happened and why. Later, however, as the temporal distance between the events and the scholarship increases, the events become distant memories and the narratives of both the Republican and post-nationalist periods concentrate more on the meanings that the events acquired rather than the events themselves.

Second, the Ottoman investigative narrative reveals a very strong tension between two world views. Some of the authors maintain a more traditional Ottoman imperial view and regard the existing structure of empire as just and the problems of the Armenian subjects within it as resolvable. They also blame the events of 1915 on both the errant Armenian subjects and corrupt Muslim officials. Other authors, however, display a more "proto-national" state view and perceive the existing structure of the empire as inadequate and the position of the Armenian subjects within it as problematic. While they are not quite clear about how to deal with the situation, they give priority to the preservation of the state and its Muslim element over all other concerns and justify their actions accordingly.

The central tension of the Ottoman investigative narrative emerges over the attribution of responsibility for the crimes. When reviewed chronologically, the memoirs of Ottoman officials reveal a transformation in the assumption of responsibility as the later ones, more and more imbued with proto-nationalist sentiments, shirk from the charge of perpetration of crimes against the Armenians. The tension over responsibility mounts especially after the Ottoman defeat in World War I, when the Treaty of Sèvres between the Allied Powers and the Ottoman Empire makes the Armenian tragedy a reason not only to detach Ottoman lands having significant minority populations but also to establish an independent Armenian homeland extending into eastern Anatolia. During this period, the Ottoman state acknowledges what happened and publishes as supplements to the semi-official newspaper *Takvim-i Vekayi* the proceedings of the Ottoman military tribunals that tried some of the perpetrators. Yet the advent and eventual victory of what became known as Turkish War of Independence nullified efforts of the Allied Powers to bring the perpetrators to justice. With the triumph of nationalism, the newspaper issues that contain the records and verdicts of the military tribunals begin to disappear, to such a degree that at present no complete set exists in any Turkish public library.

Soon after the suspension of the military tribunals, especially during the transition from the Ottoman Empire to the Turkish nation-state, the responsibility for the crimes gradually shifts from the perpetrators to the victims. The first Ottoman official report addressing the events of 1915 cites the seditious activities of the Armenian revolutionary committees and the atrocities against the Turks (even though these occurred much later in the eastern provinces) as a way to justify the Armenian massacres and deaths. Significant in this shift is the strong connection between the Committee of Union and Progress (CUP; Young Turks), which rationalizes the Armenian tragedy as an unfortunate consequence of the need to protect the Ottoman state, and the Turkish nationalist movement, which gradually adopts this Unionist position as its own. The Ottoman state documents published by the Turkish nation-state repeat this same argument. And this argument in turn continues to subsist in an even more essentialized and radicalized form during the subsequent Republican defensive narrative that begins to be articulated in the 1950s.

The intervening thirty years before the emergence of the Republican defensive narrative are crucial in understanding the current stand of the Turkish nation-state in view of the fact that the connection between Ottoman and Turkish rule has never been extensively documented and studied. The Republican rhetoric dismissed, and still dismisses, any connection with the Committee of the Union and Progress, which lost the Ottoman Empire. Yet the works in this category, especially the military tribunal records, clearly demonstrate the strength of the connection between these two political entities in terms of the transfer of wealth, ideology, and personnel. Many of the organizers and perpetrators of the Armenian massacres escaped to Anatolia in order to evade Allied attempts to bring them to justice. Those perpetrators who evaded apprehension by the Allies as well as the silent participants in the massacres simply stayed in their locations and threw in their lot with the burgeoning nationalist movement. Once the oppositional struggle in Anatolia commenced and assumed the form of an independence movement that eventually triumphed in establishing the Turkish nation-state, the former perpetrators, some of whom now occupied significant positions in the nationalist camp and had become the patriotic citizens of a new country, could no longer be accused because there was no political entity left to indict them. The Allied Powers had retreated, the reigning sultan had been deposed, and the empire was now defunct.

The new nation-state and its leader, Mustafa Kemal, could not take a stand against the perpetrators who had become comrades in the struggle and who initially were needed in sustaining the new state. But Mustafa Kemal understood that it was essential to have his country recognized by the Western powers, which still took issue with what occurred during the Unionist leadership, and was anxious to win credit for the establishment of a nation-state (actually built through the resources provided by the Committee of Union and Progress). He therefore eventually took a public stand against the Unionists, denied his CUP credentials, liquidated those Unionists who challenged his authority, and exalted his passage to Anatolia on May 19, 1919 as the starting point of the War of Independence leading to the Turkish nation-state and its international recognition in the Treaty of Lausanne in 1923.

The treaties of Sèvres and Lausanne also become important historical landmarks in the discussion of the Armenian deaths and massacres of 1915 because the former confirms and the latter ignores them. Even though it initially could have been possible to have equity and also preserve the basic aspirations on both sides through reforms, this unfortunately did not happen due to a number of factors, including the conflicting viewpoints among the Ottoman officials about the necessity, applicability, or sustainability of such reforms, frequent diplomatic intervention by the Western powers about the execution of the reforms, as well as the impatience of the Armenians. While the reforms strove for the security of life, family, and property, the eventual polarization of the two groups strengthened, on both sides, the positions of those initially fringe groups that advocated the creation of separate independent nation-states. In the Treaty of Sèvres, the Armenian massacres helped establish the conditions for an Armenian homeland reaching into Anatolia. Even though for the Armenians the Sèvres treaty was a certificate of "rebirth" that accorded them a political entity that they could call their own, one that would establish their own country, the Muslim Turks interpreted the same treaty as a death sentence that guaranteed their disappearance as a political entity. As a result of these different interpretations, the two communities took different courses of action. The Armenians relied on and cooperated with the Allied Powers to attain their promised homeland and to bring to justice the perpetrators of the massacres. For their part, the Muslims of Anatolia, who now began to define themselves with a new, once radical, identity, that of "Turk," which had not been embraced by the Ottomans because of its exclusivity and limited scope, started to fight against the same Allied Powers and the Armenians.

The Turkish War of Independence culminated in victory largely because of Allied withdrawal of support for the Armenian cause. This success was predicated, however, on the injustice that the Unionists committed against the Armenian people in the name of a proto-nationalist ideal. First, they physically removed the Armenians from their homeland and eventually settled in their stead Muslim refugees (*muhajirs*) both from the Balkans and the Russian Empire. In doing this, they irreversibly altered the population composition of Anatolia. Second, the Unionists decimated the Armenian population through the massacres, traumatized and dispersed them in such a manner that it made it virtually impossible for them to reunite against the Turks as a coherent political and military entity. And finally, the Unionists capitalized on the property and goods left behind by the deported Armenians and utilized these resources to mobilize and finance an army and a populace that were supportive of the nationalist cause.

When the Unionists emerged victorious in the subsequent War of Independence under the leadership of Mustafa Kemal, they started to justify their anti-Armenian measures as a tragic but necessary move for the preservation of the Turkish state. Contrary to the Sèvres treaty, which awarded the Armenians a homeland and was tantamount to a death warrant on the Ottoman Empire, the subsequent Lausanne treaty signed by the Turkish nationalists guaranteed them a new state and a homeland. That very homeland was established in significant measure at the expense of a projected homeland the Allied Powers had set aside for the Armenians. In signing the Lausanne treaty, the Allied Powers allowed their immediate interests to take precedence over their pledges to the Armenians. The Armenians themselves were sapped of the strength required to realize their claims. As a consequence, the Lausanne treaty now brought political death to the Armenians.

Hence, the Sèvres and Lausanne treaties offer totally contradictory solutions to the Armenians and the Turks, also reflected in the subsequent narratives that the two sides formulate. Discussion of the Sèvres treaty psychologically unnerved the Turkish nation-state and brought back memories of the insecurity and impending doom felt before and during the War of Independence. The Lausanne treaty, on the other hand, was for the Turkish nation-state one of birth, celebration, and joyousness. It was a reminder of the pride and glory felt when Turkish envoys went to the very Europe that had shamed the Turks through frequent political intervention and the ultimate shame of occupation of their core lands after World War I, a shame experienced for the first time in their six-hundred-year history. This was then linked with the increasingly nationalist contention that the Turks were the only people who could claim possession of this last vestige of the Ottoman Empire as their own. As the victorious Turks signed the Lausanne treaty, they finally declared as theirs what they now imagined had been their national homeland since the beginning of time.

Yet the Armenians had exactly the opposite experience. The contemplation of the same Sèvres treaty kindled hope and joy among the Armenians, brought back memories of when they almost gained a homeland of their own on lands they had inhabited from time immemorial. This treaty took them back to an era when they had flourished financially and intellectually, when they had produced a new generation educated with the European ideals of freedom and liberty. They stood to inherit a homeland where they could create a brand new, advanced, civilized nation-state, one that would have brought back their proud ancient civilization that had been a cradle of Christianity. The Lausanne treaty produced the opposite effect on the Armenians, however, as it reminded them of the final destruction of their dreams of that ideal homeland where they could have brought out the best in their culture and civilization and created a collective future for their sons and daughters. The possibility of such a homeland is categorically denied by the Turks who instead established for themselves the nation-state desired by the Armenians. The Turks succeeded at the expense of the Armenians, with the wealth that had been confiscated from them and from the energy sapped out of the lives of the Armenian children who instead of growing to flourish in their homeland were tragically destroyed.

Both of these narratives contain much sorrow, for each has been constructed at the expense of those who lost their lives. Many scholars have noted how Western imperialism aggravated this suffering. I would argue that the role of another social actor, that of nationalism, needs to be emphasized time and again in contextualizing the Turkish and Armenian narratives. I contend that nationalism caused the Armenians and the Turks to polarize and challenge each others' existence, instilled in them the idea that they each had a primordial right to create a homeland filled with compatriots in pursuit of the same dreams, and decreed that these ideals could only be accomplished by them alone and to the exclusion of others.

Even though I find it morally unproductive to discuss who suffered more—because I think that posing the degree of human suffering to establish rights only increases the tendency to cause more suffering—let me note that nationalism caused much more physical, social, and psychological damage and eventual death to Armenians than to Turks. Because the CUP members, who espoused the concept of an imagined community of Turks, had the support of the state machinery to actualize their goals, they were able to impose death and destruction on the Armenians, who ironically and tragically were also members of the same state.

Let me now turn to the question of why it has been so difficult to sustain scholarly analyses of the tragic events of 1915. I would identify the transition from the political form of an empire to that of the nation-state as the main cause. During this transition, there briefly existed two concurrent narratives, one formulated by the same officials of the Ottoman Empire who still attempted to interpret the events swirling around them within an imperial framework, and the other by select groups, like some CUP members, who formulated a new exclusionary nationalist framework and forcefully strove to shape events by any means necessary to achieve their envisioned homeland. Their ideology also produced a new sense of empowerment and entitlement, preyed on deep-felt resentment among the populace, and enabled them to follow their objectives with intense zeal.

From the standpoint of the present, I think it is unfortunate that the latter nationalist vision prevailed. While both Armenians and Muslims of the Ottoman Empire had coexisted in relative peace in an imperial system that did not treat them equally, this inequality had been part and parcel of the social system for so long that most groups that challenged this inequality did so within the imperial framework. But the concepts of the Enlightenment and the French Revolution helped spark an alternate vision of society, that of nationalism, and an alternate political structure, the nation-state. The Ottoman Empire became one of the many testing grounds of both this nationalist outlook and the political structure it sought to create. This test brought with it a strong sense of empowerment and entitlement to transform everything in order to realize a so promising and so liberating alternate vision. It came to appear almost natural to exclude, remove, or destroy anything or anybody not fitting into this construct. The world had to fight and suffer through two very bloody world wars in the twentieth century to comprehend clearly the destructiveness embedded in this way of thinking.

How were these two concurrent narratives during the transition from Ottoman Empire to Turkish nation-state reconciled to produce the Republican narrative? The emergence of a Turkish "nation-state" on the ashes of the Ottoman Empire precluded discussion of any claims of the homeland the Turks now identified as their own. It was no accident that Mustafa Kemal declared, and the Turks constantly reiterate, that there is not "a hand-span of the soil of the motherland"[12] to be relinquished. What Mustafa Kemal had forcefully articulated was shared by those who had no qualms then or have none now "to fight for the motherland until the last drop of blood."[13] The willingness of people to sacrifice themselves for a vision demonstrates both the ideological strength of nationalism and its incredibly destructive power. As those willing to chance self-destruction have no intention of taking that risk alone, they beckon their compatriots to join them, and they define a target, a clearly specified group of human beings who differ from them according to their own definition, to annihilate in the process.

This nationalist tone dominates the Republican defensive narrative. In this regard, a significant historical occurrence has colored the Republican narrative. After the Armenian massacres and deaths in 1915, the period of Russian and Allied occupation of parts of the central Ottoman lands, both directly and also through the Greeks, was marked by massacres committed by Armenian armed groups. These groups were joined by their coreligionists who had become polarized by atrocities committed against their people, so they sided with the occupying forces, took up arms, and perpetrated new atrocities against the Muslim Turkish populace in some locations. Armenian massacres of Turks in the eastern provinces in 1918 are central to the Republican narrative.

The other defensive element on which the Republican narrative has capitalized was provided by the murders of Turkish diplomats around the world in the late 1970s into the 1980s by the Armenian Secret Army for the Liberation of Armenia (ASALA). This attempt to draw attention to the Armenian Genocide, when combined with

the Turkish nationalist rhetoric, pol
only against ASALA and Armenian
all Armenians. The only liability o
were representatives of the Republic
connection to the Armenian deaths
cials of the Turkish nation-state foun
the Armenian homeland. I think that t
harmful effect that nationalism had o
The violence presented Republican Tu
include, in a nationalist move, the ave
narrative. The murders only strengthene ... resolve to
resist the Armenian claims and further strengthened the resolve to
continue a total denial of the organized Armenian massacres of 1915.

The Republican Defensive Narrative on the Events of 1915

The works in this category emerge largely as clusters of analyses within the nationalist paradigm. Two works in 1953 that comprehensively cover the previous material on the Armenians[14] are then selectively drawn on by the second cluster of works written with direct or indirect state support in the 1970s and 1980s in reaction to the ASALA murders.[15] The third cluster since the 1990s either reproduces the same arguments that were made in the 1970s and 1980s or attempts to offer a new perspective while remaining within the nationalist paradigm.[16] Among these perspectives are efforts to provide oral histories of Turkish survivors of Armenian massacres in the east,[17] to locate the Armenian Question within Western diplomatic history,[18] or to identify and exclude from Turkish politics everyone of minority origin.[19] Two recent works must be cited separately. The first emerges out of an Islamist critique of the secular Republican thesis,[20] but fails to escape the nationalist paradigm with the exception of two articles which inadvertently provide new historical information on the failure of the Ottoman state in undertaking reforms.[21] The other work provides a psychoanalytical approach to the contemporary trauma of the Armenians but does so at their expense and without bringing in the role of the Turks.[22]

The Republican nationalist narrative on the Armenian deaths of 1915 traces the origins of the tragedy to the intervention of the Western powers in the affairs of the Ottoman Empire and justifies the Armenian relocations and subsequent massacres as the result of the sub-

Armenian revolutionary committees. This narra- recognize, on the one hand, the significance of the structural divide in Ottoman society among the social o-religious groups and its institutionalized Muslim superi- and, on the other hand, the fact that Turkish nationalism was ne of the many nationalisms that emerged and was no more just than any other but just happened to triumph at the expense of all others.

This non-recognition cloaked by a Turkish nationalism identifying the preservation of the Turkish state at all costs has led the Republican state to assign the entire moral responsibility for the Armenian massacres and deaths to everyone other than the actual perpetrators. As a consequence of this non-recognition, in the Republican narrative the Armenian victims themselves have tragically and ironically emerged alongside the guilty Western powers as the main culprits. Any feeble attempt to assign blame to the Turkish perpetrators is immediately dismissed in this narrative with the defense that what happened was an unfortunate but necessary act for the preservation of the "state."

If one reviews these works chronologically to depict patterns of meaning, no significant studies on the Armenian deaths and massacres appear until the two works by Esat Uras and Y. G. Çark in 1953, and when they appear they do so with declarations of loyalty to the Turkish nation-state at every opportunity.[23] There is then another gap until 1976 when the scholarship that does appear is even more strongly dominated by Turkish nationalism. Its authors not only pledge allegiance to the Turkish nation-state as loyal citizens, but also employ historical knowledge selectively to preserve Turkish state interests at all costs, including that of critical scholarship. These two significant chronological gaps in the scholarship on the Armenian massacres and deaths of 1915 warrant further examination.

Why were there no works during the first thirty years of the Turkish Republic on the important social and moral issue of the Armenian massacres? I think the first thirty-year gap after the foundation of the Turkish Republic in relation to an event that was so crucial and central to the period immediately preceding it was caused by several factors. In addition to the general trauma and devastation of the war years that everyone in Turkey must have wanted to put aside, it is likely that the close link between the Unionist leadership, which not only funded the War of Independence but in large measure also staffed it,[24] and the connection of the same leadership to the Armenian deaths, prompted the founders of the Turkish nation-state to employ a nationalist Republican rhetoric to silence discussion of the Armenian issue.

Another reason was that by 1926 Mustafa Kemal had effectively eliminated those CUP leaders he regarded as a potential threat to his rule. The only ones who managed to survive were those who declared and proved their personal loyalty to the person of Mustafa Kemal by turning against their former comrades. Some Unionists who were labeled as particularly dangerous were executed following the 1926 trials to expose and punish those implicated in an assassination attempt against Kemal. Although there was insufficient evidence, Kemal first accused all those who criticized his regime and then, with the help of those Unionists who had declared their personal allegiance to him, had them executed. Others had to go into voluntary exile to survive and were unable to return to Turkey until after Mustafa Kemal's death in 1938, and still others who remained in Turkey did so at the risk of their lives and survived so long as they retired from political life and maintained strict silence. The series of the traumatic social reforms the young Turkish Republic underwent during Kemal's reign within the format of single-party rule also precluded public discussion of significant social and historical issues. The subsequent promulgation of the laws regarding treason against the Turkish state and against the person of Mustafa Kemal rendered any discussion of the events that countered the official version subversive as well.

After Mustafa Kemal's death, the same political framework prevailed during the rule of his successor and close friend, İsmet İnönü. Even though some opponents of Kemal were now able to return to Turkey, they maintained their silence and self-censorship in tacit support of the existing regime. Both the Kemal and İnönü periods were also marked by strong Turkish nationalism that informally defined citizenship in terms of religion and ethnicity, whereby the Turkish Muslim citizens, like their Ottoman Muslim predecessors, were ascendant and all other social groups were either co-opted, marginalized, or silenced.

The transition to the multi-party system in 1948, after twenty-five years of the single-party system, and the subsequent sweeping electoral victory of the Democrat Party formed in opposition to the ruling Republican People's Party (RPP) of Kemal and İnönü, initially liberalized censorship of the media. This transition also gave some RPP members like Esat Uras who retired from active politics time to write. Many memoirs of former Unionists such as Rauf Orbay also began to emerge during this period. The particular reason for the two authors, Uras and Çark, to elect to write on the Armenians in 1953 may also be a consequence of the concern felt about the strong populist and Islamic elements that had become more visible with the ascendance of the Democrat Party. The organized riots of September 6-7, 1955, accompanied by widespread looting and incidents of death against the Greek minority in particular and all minorities in general, showed that such concerns were not ill-founded.

Why was there another gap of twenty-three years until 1976? This most likely is ascribable to the 1960 purge from power of the Democrat Party by the Turkish military and the re-imposition of censorship and government control over scholarship. Yet, this state of affairs changed once again in the late 1970s because of the assassination of Turkish diplomats by the radical Armenian group ASALA in an attempt to draw international attention to the Armenian Genocide. The defensive Republican narrative became even more polarized during this period as it drew selectively on Ottoman documents and the works of early Republican writers to maintain its ascendance down to the present.

I have criticized this Republican defensive narrative for its inherent Turkish nationalism, which makes self-reflective, critical scholarship impossible. The nationalist cloak over this narrative creates the following shortcomings: the use of archival material is highly selective in that the nationalist scholars almost unanimously overlook, for instance, the records of the Ottoman military tribunals and the accounts in the contemporary Ottoman newspapers that document the massacres and deaths beginning in 1915. These scholars also assume that the pre-nineteenth century Ottoman communal relations were peaceful until the intervention of Western powers subverted the Ottoman Armenians. They fail to note that these communal relations institutionalized Muslim dominance over the minorities and the rhetoric reflected the Muslim view of those relations, not the non-Muslim ones. Even though the Western powers did indeed play a destructive role, one also needs to recognize another equally, if not more devastating force, that of nationalism. Yet the Republican defensive narrative also makes no reference to the effect of Turkish nationalism, because this narrative is itself a product of the same nationalism and therefore lacks a critical distance from it.

The French Revolution and the social transformations it envisioned altered the expectations of all social groups, including those of the Ottoman Muslims. The frustrations of the Muslims created the social group of Young Turks and their Muslim followers who assumed power in 1908 and ultimately carried out the massacres of 1915. The frustrations, in turn, of the Ottoman minorities first generated demands for reform and, upon their failure and also upon increased Muslim aggression, escalated the communal support for Armenian revolutionary activities and ultimately the taking up of arms against the Muslim elements. While both the Ottoman Muslims and the minorities nurtured nationalist visions, the Turkish actualization of these objectives occurred at the expense of the others.

Since the Muslims had the support of the Ottoman state and the advantage of a social structure that protected their privileged position, they eventually triumphed over the minorities. Their victory was couched within the ideology of nationalism that condoned all actions undertaken in the name of the imagined community and for the sake of the nation-state. This ideology enabled the nationalists within the Ottoman state first to justify the Armenian massacres and then to join the Turkish Independence movement to create such an imagined community. The emergent Turkish nation-state in turn disclaimed its Ottoman past and the massacres in which its leaders had been implicated. The Republican scholars themselves who started to research the Armenian massacres on behalf of the Turkish state absorbed its inherent nationalism. As a consequence, they could only identify as the culprits of the Armenian tragedy the two "others" of Turkish nationalism, namely the Western powers and the Ottoman Armenians themselves.

Their interpretations of the actions of these two "others" were so colored by Turkish nationalism that they refused to see the destructiveness of the Ottoman Turks. Hence, they defended their view of the events and not only dismissed the claims of massacres but even argued that the Turks were the victims rather than the perpetrators. Only within the current post-nationalist phase has it become possible to have a more critical and self-reflective reading in a new

Turkish historiography that places blame on all social groups, including the Turks. A brief survey of the post-nationalist critical narrative of the 1915 events that has started to emerge in contemporary Turkey may point the way toward the future.

The Post-Nationalist Critical Narrative on the Events of 1915

The works in this category emerge in three disparate clusters in terms of the knowledge they demonstrate of both the Ottoman Armenians and Turkish Armenians. The first cluster is either written specifically on the events of 1915, with the intent both to understand the historical context within which the events occurred and to analyze critically the persistent Turkish denial of these events,[25] or to inform the contemporary Turkish reader about the historical transformation of the Armenians from the past to the immediate present.[26]

The second cluster comprises works that are written on topics of recent Turkish history that do not focus directly on the Armenians but nonetheless provide ample new information on the historical background of the events of 1915 because, unlike the Republican narrative, they do not mute the role of the Ottoman minorities in their accounts. One scholar undertakes a meticulous historical analysis of the Young Turks to reveal how, in spite of their formal public rhetoric of Ottomanism, the CUP leaders had informally formulated very early a proto-nationalist, exclusionary stand toward the Armenians.[27] Another work presents a history of the first seventy-five years of the Turkish Republic that contextualizes the Armenian deportations within that formal history.[28] Still another work studies the activities of the Committee of Union and Progress through the records of the Ottoman military tribunals and the investigations of the Fifth Chamber of the Ottoman Parliament, which also contain much information on the Armenian massacres.[29] Finally, another scholar examines the CUP's relocation and resettlement policy of Muslim refugees to reveal in the process how these newcomers were resettled on lands and properties left behind by the deported Ottoman Armenians.[30]

The third cluster includes literary works that reveal the worlds of meaning the Armenians created within both the Ottoman and the Republican periods. The Armenians emerge as cultural actors as the literature produced by them is presented by one scholar,[31] and as the literary works of Ottoman and Turkish Armenians themselves are translated from the original Armenian to the Turkish language.[32] Another interesting recent work is a memoir by a Turkish author who recounts how his childhood memories of the Armenians in his neighborhood disappeared with their relocation.[33]

The most significant factor that unites the works in this category is that none is written to defend a particular thesis or is supported for publication, in one capacity or another, by the Turkish state. They are also not colored by the Turkish nationalism that pervades the official narrative discussed in the preceding section but assume instead a post-nationalist stance. As such, these works are the products of the emerging civil society in contemporary Turkey. They are, as stated, divided into three broad categories: those specifically on the Armenian issue; those penned on various aspects of Turkish history that indirectly illuminate and contextualize the Armenian massacres and deaths within Turkish history at large; and those that are literary works, mostly novels, by Turkish-Armenian writers that are being translated into Turkish after a silence of more than seven decades.

The most significant dimension of the post-nationalist critical narrative that begins to emerge in Turkey is its willingness to recognize Turkish society, not as an imagined community of nationalist compatriots of Turks, but rather as a cultural mosaic that includes many diverse groups, such as Kurds and Alevis, as well as the much atrophied former minority groups such as Armenians, Greeks, and Jews. Turkish society at large is now involved in an exploration of these ethno-religious and social groups through the literature and historical narrative of these groups. Some societal segments have started to engage further in critical self-reflection. Islamists have begun to challenge the dominant secular nationalist writing of history through publications of many memoirs that highlight the agency of religion in Turkish history. Liberal Turkish intellectuals have, on their part, taken on the challenge of critical self-reflection about what constitutes and ought to constitute Turkish identity. These groups are willing to move beyond the narrow bounds of the nationalist cloak that places the blame for all actions on others, on imagined and fabricated threats. Some are also ready to recognize how Turkish nationalism caused great pain and suffering to the Armenians. If these evolving groups transform into a movement associated with human rights, and if they are able to overcome the resistance of the nationalist elements embedded in society and especially in the military, then the depth of the Armenian calamity of 1915 would be recognized in contemporary Turkey.

Conclusion

Why are the world in general and Turkey in particular still not fully able to make the transition from the nationalist phase to a post-nationalist one? I believe the problem originates in the periodization of the War of Independence. It is extremely significant that the current Turkish nationalist rhetoric identifies the passage of Mustafa Kemal from Istanbul to Anatolia on May 19, 1919 as the starting point of the nationalist struggle that culminated in the establishment of the Turkish nation-state. This dating dismisses entirely the significance of the preceding historical events and interprets the nationalist movement as a spontaneous development predicated solely on the agency of a single person, Mustafa Kemal.

I would argue that discussion and recognition of the Armenian massacres and deaths of 1915 in particular, and demystification of nationalism that still cloaks contemporary Turkey in general, can only take place through the adoption of an alternate periodization. The emergence of Turkish nationalism as a significant historical force needs to be traced as far back as 1839 when the Ottoman state officially recognized the need to undertake the first in a series of political and social reforms. These *Tanzimat* reforms, initiated in 1839 and then continued in 1856 and 1876, all mark the unsuccessful attempts to incorporate the Ottoman minorities into the empire's structure on equal terms. It is my thesis that they also give rise to the first stage of "nascent nationalism" within the Ottoman Empire.

The suppression of the counterrevolution of traditionalist elements around Sultan Abdul-Hamid by the Action Army on April 25, 1909 signals the beginning of the second stage of "proto-nationalism." It is then that the CUP military officials take control of the emerging political structure in the name of state and nation. These officials assume formal control of the Ottoman Empire in a coup d'état in January 1913, thereby reaching the apex of the proto-nationalist stage. It is during this pernicious period of proto-nationalism, between 1913 and 1918, that the atrocities against the Armenians are committed and justified in the name of the new imagined state and nation. The ebb of this proto-nationalist phase comes with the escape of the CUP leaders to Germany in November 1918 after the defeat of the Ottoman Empire in World War I.

The third stage of "official nationalism" commences, not on May 19, 1919 when Mustafa Kemal initiates the Turkish War of Independence, but rather on May 15, 1919 with the Allied-backed Greek occupation of Smyrna. It is then that many Turkish Muslim groups begin to mobilize throughout Anatolia with the arms, military personnel, and financial capital that the leadership of the Committee of Union and Progress had stored there for a possible future resistance movement. This third stage reaches its pinnacle not, as the Republican state argues, at the signing of the Treaty of Lausanne or the establishment of the Republic of Turkey, but rather with the Greek-Turkish population exchange of 1923-24. That exchange marks the final mass deportation of surviving Ottoman Armenians from Anatolia with the goal of achieving the imagined Turkish Muslim nation. This highpoint of nationalism is sustained until 1983, in spite of repeated political attempts in 1924 with the Progressive Republican Party and in 1946 with the Democrat Party to sever the connection between the military, which assumed the guardianship of Turkish nationalism, and the transforming nation-state. I believe that the demise of the third stage of "official nationalism" commences with the establishment of political organizations that seek support, not from the Turkish nation-state, but rather from the emergent civil society, as witnessed in the creation in 1983 of the Motherland Party, the emergence of the New Democracy movement in 1995, and the formation of the liberal Islamist party in 2001. These all attempt to withstand the state- and military-centered Turkish nationalism with differing degrees of success.

Turkey is currently at a turning point. I contend that the third stage, that of "official nationalism," is slowly coming to an end. The first sparks of the fourth stage, that of "post-nationalism," are in the making by a new generation that has come of age not during the foundation of the Republic but rather during its contestation and critique by the currents of opposition. This new generation will determine what becomes of these post-nationalist sparks. If it fails to sever the connection between the Turkish military and the nation-state, "official nationalism" will probably sustain itself for a time longer. If, however, it does break this connection and also supports, strives for, and achieves the integration of the Republic of Turkey into the European Union, this would open the way to the post-nationalist period in Turkey. The Armenian massacres and deaths of 1915 may be finally, formally, and officially acknowledged and find a place in Turkish historiography if and when contemporary Turkey enters that post-nationalist stage.

Notes

1. Pars Tuğlacı, *Ermeni edebiyatından seçkiler* [Selections from Armenian Literature] (Istanbul: Cem Press, 1982), p. 164 [translation mine].
2. Hagop Mintzuri, *Atina, tuzun var mı*?[Athena, Have You Got Some Salt?] (Istanbul: Aras Press, 2000).
3. Antan Özer, *Yaşamı beklerken* [While Awaiting Life] (Istanbul: Aras Press, 1997).
4. Yervant Sırmakeşliyan, *Balıkçı sevdası* [Fisherman's Passion] (Istanbul: Aras Press, 2000).
5. Krikor Zohrab, *Hayat, olduğu gibi* [Life, As It Is] (Ankara: Ayraç Press, 2000).
6. See Mehmed Asaf, *1909 Adana Ermeni olayları ve anılarım* [The Adana Armenian Incidents of 1909 and My Memoirs] (Ankara: Turkish Historical Society, 1982); Gül Çağalı-Güven, ed., *Kamil Paşa ve Said Paşanın anıları: polemikleri* [Memoirs of Kamil Pasha and Sait Pasha: The Polemics] (Istanbul: Arba Press, 1991); Mehmet Kasım, *Talat Paşa'nın anilari* [Memoirs of Talaat Pasha] (Istanbul: Say Press, 1986); Ahmet Mehmedefendioğlu *Sürgünden intihara: Dr. Reşid Bey'in hatıraları* [From Deportation to Suicide: Memoirs of Dr. Reshid Bey] (Izmir: Belge Press, 1982); Sait Paşa, *Anılar* [Memoirs of (Grand Vezir) Sait Pasha] (Istanbul: Hürriyet Press, 1977).
7. See *8 Mart sene 335 tarihinde irade-i seniye-i hazret-i padişahiye iktiran eden kararname ile müteşekkıl divan-ı harb-i örfi muhakematı zabıt ceridesi* [Turkish Military Tribunal Records] (Istanbul: Takvim-i Vekayi Press, 1919-1920).
8. See Hüseyin Nazım Paşa, *Ermeni olayları tarihi* [History of the Armenian Incidents] (Ankara: Prime Minister's Press, 1994); Erdoğan Cengiz, ed., *Ermeni Komitelerinin a'mal ve hareket-i ihtilaliyesi* [The Actions and Revolutionary Movements of the Armenian Committees] (Ankara: Prime Ministry Press, 1983).
9. See National Congress of Turkey, *The Turco-Armenian Question: The Turkish Point of View* (Constantinople: Societe Anonyme de Papeterie et d'Imprimerie, 1919).
10. See Cemil Birsel, *Lozan* [Lausanne] (Istanbul: Sosyal Press, 1933); Bilal Şimşir, *Lozan telgrafları: Türk diplomatik belgelerinde Lozan Barış Konferansı* [The Lausanne Telegraphs: Lausanne Peace Conference through Turkish Diplomatic Documents] (Ankara: Turkish Historical Society, 1990).
11. See Prime Ministry Directorate General of Press and Information, *Documents* (Ankara: Prime Ministry Press, 1989); Prime Ministry Directorate of State Archives, *Osmanlı belgelerinde Ermeniler (1915-1920)* [Armenians in Ottoman Documents] (Ankara: Prime Ministry Press, 1994).
12. The Turkish term is "*bir karış vatan toprağı*."
13. The Turkish term is "*kanımızın son damlasına kadar*."
14. Y. G. Çark, *Türk devleti hizmetinde Ermeniler (1453-1953)* [Armenians in the Service of the Turkish State] (Istanbul: Yeni Press, 1953); Esat Uras, *Tarihte Ermeniler ve Ermeni meselesi* [Armenians in History and the Armenian Question] (Istanbul: Belge Press, 1953).

15. See Neşide Kerem Demir, *Bir şehid anasına tarihin söyledikleri: Türkiye'nin Ermeni meselesi* [What History Told a Martyr's Mother: The Armenian Question in Turkey] (Ankara: Hülbe Press, 1976); Atatürk Üniversitesi yirminci yıl armağanı, *Ermeniler hakkında makaleler derlemeler* [Articles and Selections on the Armenians] (Ankara: Kalite Press, 1978); Jamanak, *Facts from the Turkish Armenians* (*Réalités exprimees par les arménien turcs/Türk Ermenilerinden gerçekler*) (Istanbul: Jamanak Press, 1980); Dokuz Eylül Üniversitesi rektörlüğü, *Türk tarihinde Ermeniler sempozyumu* [Symposium on the Armenians in Turkish History] (Manisa: Şafak Press, 1983); Nejat Göyünç, *Osmanlı idaresinde Ermeniler* [Armenians under Ottoman Administration] (Istanbul: Gültepe Press, 1983); Nurettin Gülmez, *Türkiye Büyük Millet Meclisi zabıtlarından doğu ve güneydoğu meselesi* [Eastern and Southeastern Question from the Proceedings of the Turkish Grand National Assembly] (Istanbul: Hamle Press, 1983); Kamuran Gürün, *Ermeni dosyası* [The Armenian File] (Ankara: Turkish Historical Society, 1983); Şinasi Orel and Süreyya Yuca, *Ermenilerce Talat Paşa'ya atfedilen telgrafların gerçek yüzü* [The Truth about the Telegrams Attributed to Talaat Pasha by the Armenians] (Ankara: Turkish Historical Society, 1983); Cevdet Küçük, *Osmanli diplomasisinde Ermeni meselesinin ortaya çikışi (1878-1897)* [The Emergence of the Armenian Question in Ottoman Diplomacy (1878-1897)] (Istanbul: Istanbul University Press, 1984); Anadolu Basin Birliği, *Katliam efsanesi* [The Myth of Massacre] (Ankara: Anatolian Press, 1987); Kinyas Kartal, *Van'dan Erivan'a hatıralarım* [My Memoirs from Van to Erevan] (Ankara: Anatolian Press, 1987); and the following by Bilal Şimşir, all published in Ankara in 1983 by the Turkish Historical Society: *The Deportees of Malta and the Armenian Question*; *British Documents on the Ottoman Armenians (1856-1880)*; *The Genesis of the Armenian Question*; and *British Documents on the Ottoman Armenians (1880-1890)*.
16. See Bilal Eryılmaz, *Osmanlı devletinde gayrımüslim teb'anın yönetimi* [The Administration of the Non-Muslim Subjects in the Ottoman State] (Istanbul: Risale Press, 1990); Azmi Süslü, *Ermeniler ve 1915 tehcır olayi* [Armenians and the 1915 Population Transfer Incident] (Ankara: Sistem Press, 1990); Salahi Sonyel, *The Great War and the Tragedy of Anatolia* (Ankara: Turkish Historical Society, 2000), and *Minorities and the Destruction of the Ottoman Empire* (Ankara: Turkish Historical Society, 1983); Türkkaya Ataöv, *The Armenians in the Late Ottoman Period* (Ankara: Turkish Historical Society, 2001), and *The "Armenian Question": Conflict, Trauma and Objectivity* (Ankara: Strategic Research Center, 1997).
17. See Hüseyin Çelik, *Görenlerin gözüyle Van'da Ermeni mezalimi* [Armenian Atrocities in Van through Eyewitness Accounts] (Ankara: Turkish Historical Society, 1995); Gürsoy Solmaz, *Yasayanlqrin dilinden Erzurum-Sarikamiş-Kars'ta Ermeni zulmü* [Armenian Cruelties in Erzurum, Sarikamish, and Kars from Accounts of Those Who Lived Through Them] (Van: New Hundredth Year University Press, 1995).
18. See Mim Kemal Öke, *Ermeni sorunu 1914-1923* [The Armenian Question, 1914-1923] (Ankara: Turkish Historical Society, 1991).
19. See Süleyman Yeşilyurt, *Atatürk, İnönü, Menderes, Gürsel dönemlerinin Ermeni Yahudi, Rum asıllı milletvekilleri* [Parliamentary Deputies of Armenian, Jewish, and Greek Origin during the Atatürk, İnönü, Menderes, Gürsel Eras] (Ankara: Zine Press, 1995).
20. Hasan Celal Güzel, *Osmanlıdan günümüze Ermeni sorunu* [The Armenian Question from the Ottomans to Our Time] (Ankara: Yeni Türkiye Press, 2000).
21. These articles, by Nuri Adıyeke, "Islahat fermanı öncesinde Osmanlı İmparatorluğunda millet sistemi ve gayrımüslimlerin yaşantılarına dair" [Concerning the Millet System and the Lives of Non-Muslims in the Ottoman Empire before

the Reform Edict of 1856], pp. 183-92, and by Musa Şaşmaz, "Ermeniler hakkındaki reformların uygulanması (1895-1987)" [The Application of the Reforms Concerning the Armenians (1895-1897)], pp. 93-104, demonstrate how unsuccessful the Ottoman state was in carrying out the promised reforms in the eastern provinces.

22. Erol Göka, "'Ermeni sorunu'nun' (gözden kaçan) psikolojik boyutu" [The "Overlooked" Psychological Dimension of the "Armenian Question"], *Ermeni Araştırmaları/Armenian Studies* 1:1 (2001): 128-36.
23. Refer to note 14 for a full citation of these works.
24. For a full discussion, see Erik Jan Zürcher, *Milli mücadelede İttihatçılık* [The Unionist Factor: The Role of the Committee of Union and Progress in the Turkish National Movement, 1905-1926] (Istanbul: Bağlam Press, 1987).
25. See Taner Akçam, *İnsan hakları ve Ermeni sorunu* [Human Rights and the Armenian Question] (Istanbul: İmge Press, 1999), and Taner Timur, *Türkler ve Ermeniler: 1915 ve sonrası* [Turks and Armenians: 1915 and Its Aftermath] (Ankara: Imge Press, 2001).
26. See Hüdavendigar Onur, *Ermeni portreleri: milet-i* [sic] *sadıkadan hayk'ın çocuklarına* [Armenian Portraits: From the Loyal Community to the Children of Hayk] (Istanbul: Burak Press, 1999).
27. M. Şükrü Hanioğlu, *Preparation for a Revolution: The Young Turks, 1902-1908* (New York: Oxford University Press, 2001), and *The Young Turks in Opposition* (New York: Oxford University Press, 1995).
28. Türk Tarih Vakfı, *75 yılda tebaa'dan yurttaş'a doğru* [From Subject to Citizen in 75 Years] (Istanbul: History Foundation, 1999).
29. Osman Selim Kocahanoğlu, *İttihat-Terakki'nin sorgulanması ve yargılanması: meclis-i mebusan zabıtları* [The Interrogation and Trial of the Union and Progress: Proceedings of the Ottoman Assembly] (Istanbul: Temel Press, 1998).
30. Fuat Dündar, *İttihat ve Terakki'nin Müslümanları iskan politikası (1913-1918)* [The Muslim Settlement Policy of the Union and Progress Party] (İstanbul: Iletişim Press, 2001).
31. Pars Tuğlacı, *Ermeni edebiyatından seçkiler* [Selections from Armenian Literature] (Istanbul: Cem Press, 1982).
32. See, for instance, the works cited in notes 2 through 5 above: Hagop Mintzuri, *Atina, tuzun var mı?*); Antan Özer, *Yaşamı beklerken*; Yervant Sırmakeşliyan, *Balıkçı sevdası;* Krikor Zohrab, *Hayat, olduğu gibi.*
33. İsmail Arıkan, *Mahallemizdeki Ermeniler* [Armenians in Our Neighborhood] (Istanbul: İletişim Press, 2001).

12

Denial and Free Speech: The Case of the Armenian Genocide

Henry C. Theriault

Denial of the Armenian Genocide is a well-coordinated, well-funded, and comprehensive assault on the collective memory of the Armenian people and a major obstacle to widespread knowledge of this important part of universal human history.[1] Armenians experience denial as a painful denigration that recalls the horrors of the genocide and as a reassertion of the same prejudice and hatred that motivated it.

In recent decades, the international denial campaign has intensified in reaction to growing calls for acknowledgment of and restitution for the genocide. Beyond activities by diplomatic leaders and staff, the Turkish government since the 1960s has spent millions of dollars in the United States on denialist public relations and political lobbying.[2] The Turkish government and its supporters have also funded chairs at prestigious United States universities awarded to prominent deniers.[3] Typical denial arguments contend that documentation of the genocide is inconclusive, biased, or falsified;[4] that the genocide was actually a civil war or mutual conflict in which Turks were also killed and for which Armenians likewise bear responsibility;[5] that Armenians instigated any Turkish violence;[6] and that Armenian deaths in 1915 and after were not the result of a deliberate, centrally-coordinated extermination program.[7]

In the United States and elsewhere, Armenian organizations and activists as well as comparative genocide, Holocaust, and Armenian Studies scholars have done much to teach the public about this tragedy. Yet, active denial backed by political blackmail has blocked general recognition and restitution. Deniers have repeatedly thwarted passage of Congressional resolutions commemorating the genocide. In recent administrations, the Department of State and the Pentagon have routinely joined in Turkey's cover-up.[8] Moreover, the negationist campaign has minimized inclusion of this significant event in modern world history curricula and enforced full exclusion from Turkish history courses.

In a number of countries, laws have been passed banning public dissemination of Holocaust denial. No laws similarly protect the truth of the Armenian Genocide, and laws regarding Holocaust denial cannot be stretched for this purpose. For instance, in 1994 the Committee for the Defense of the Armenian Cause filed a suit attempting to apply a French law forbidding denial of Nazi crimes against humanity to negationist statements by Bernard Lewis published in *Le Monde*. The 17th Division of the Parisian Magistrate Court heard the case and, although sympathetic, rejected this use of the Gayssot Law.[9] The United States has no law barring denial of the Holocaust or any other genocide.

The thesis of this chapter is that restriction of public speech denying the Armenian Genocide is consistent with free speech protections in the liberal tradition and is warranted by the extreme harm done by denial.[10] Three points follow from this. First, denial of the Armenian Genocide should be illegal in the United States. Second, Holocaust denial prohibitions already enacted in other liberal democracies should be extended to cover the Armenian Genocide or supplementary laws should be passed. The crucial role of scholastic deniers draws special attention to college campuses. Third, educational institutions justifiably can and should proscribe denial.

The Textuality of the Genocide

Two elements of present-day engagement with the Armenian Genocide dramatically increase denial's effectiveness. The first is the transformation of the genocide from an immediate to a "textualized" event. During World War I and in the years that followed, the genocide was as well known to a British, French, or American audience as mass violence in the Balkans was in the 1990s. As CNN and other major news outlets provided ongoing coverage of the Balkans, so did the *New York Times* and other newspapers cover the Armenian Genocide in detail.[11] There was no question of whether it was happening or had happened: it was implicitly known, embedded in the consciousnesses of people in the United States and many other countries. It was present in the ordinary routines of daily life, for instance, through widespread dinnertime admonitions about remembering "the starving Armenians."

As time has passed and public discourse on the genocide has decreased, what was once immediate awareness is today the infrequent and often chance outcome of encounters with textual representations. The genocide is no longer experienced as a directly accessible and unquestionable occurrence firmly rooted in our world and history but rather as a function of the particular texts that portray it. In effect, the genocide has become the books, articles, poems, speeches, and films that are written or made about it; the museums, religious services, and memorials that commemorate it; and the words of educators, family members, and friends that tell of it. The genocide's textuality is sometimes overtly emphasized, as when survivor memoirs are treated as narratives to be studied from literary or psychological perspectives rather than straightforward reports of events.[12]

Textualization does not mark a change in the genocide itself. It is an absolute historical reality, no matter how much time passes. Textuality does not reduce the Armenian Genocide to a false object created by discursive reference but means that it has come to be treated as a construction despite the fact that it will always be a real historical event. It is our relationship to the genocide, not the event itself, that is altered.

Textualization can be a positive shift. In literature, music, visual art, film, museums, monuments, and scholarship, Armenians can determine at least to some extent what the genocide signifies for them and how it will affect them individually and as a community. In a just world, this increasing Armenian agency relative to the genocide would mark the ultimate resolution of the issue, an advanced stage in coming to terms with the genocide and overcoming its power. The recession of this catastrophe from the immediate world would be a healthy distancing, decreasing its contemporary impact on Armenians and allowing reverential rather than despairing remembrance.

But, the world for Armenians has been anything but just. As the genocide has been enclosed within the realm of texts, the range of what is written and presented about the relevant period determines what people believe to have happened. The nature of false representations qua texts is identical to that of faithful ones. Distinguishing truth from fiction requires comparison to the events that actually occurred, but access to these is possible only via other representations subject to the same equivalence. When all representations are treated simply as texts without further analysis, negationist propaganda seems to have as much legitimacy as reliable depiction. Deniers have exploited this opening by flooding the world with books, essays, newspaper articles and editorials, public lectures and discussions, and Internet web sites that deny the genocide. Their influence has eroded previously widespread knowledge of the genocide.

Academic Relativism

According to the prevalent liberal-utilitarian conception of public discourse, dissemination of correct information about the Armenian Genocide should be mitigating the effects of denial. The current "debate" about it should, indeed, be leading to an increasingly better understanding of the genocide, as pointed critical assessment sorts out the accurate facts and superior analyses from the false and weak.[13] Denial is an acceptable and even desirable part of the process. In this vein, Jonathan Rauch contends that public expression of Holocaust denial, such as the claim that gas chambers were not used to kill Jews, has spurred research in refutation that has greatly added to our knowledge of the Holocaust in ways that otherwise would not have occurred.[14]

Terrence Des Pres rejects the liberal-utilitarian tenet that open debate on a topic eventually leads to general acceptance of the correct understanding of it.[15] In a far-reaching essay that takes denial of the Armenian Genocide as its motivating problem and central example, he argues that underlying the increasing credibility of genocide denial is the Enlightenment principle that "there is another side to every story" which should be taken into account. Although this principle originally functioned to validate alternative viewpoints against the tyrannical grip of religious and political orthodoxies in early modern Europe, "the other side" is now quite frequently a propagandistic version of history and politics buttressing the power of a government or political elite. Where once "the other side" represented truth struggling against power, it is now typically power subverting truth. What is more, because states and dominant elites have the resources to insist more vigorously on "their side of the story," they overwhelm honest voices in the competition for public attention and acceptance.[16] Thus, the contemporary Turkish state and its supporters exploit intellectual openness to create a "debate" that calls the Armenian Genocide into question. They then use their significant political and economic advantages to get their deceptions taken more seriously than the truth.

The central problem for Des Pres is abuse of the university to promulgate a falsified "other side." Because of its relationship to modern states and their international order, the Western academy has been corrupted by political agendas and ideologies. Scholars promote denial of the Armenian Genocide not as the result of research and reflection, but out of national chauvinism, cynical political interests, or petty careerism served by obedience to the state.[17] They manipulate otherwise honest colleagues by playing on their well-intentioned embrace of "the other side of the story."[18] Des Pres entreats these victims to resist and rescue the academy from its present corruptors.[19]

Terrence Des Pres perceives the average impartial professor who accepts genocide denial to be a casualty of the "age of information," overwhelmed by "so many sides to so many issues."[20] But the evidence is that the openness often greeting different sides of the dispute over the Armenian Genocide is not always or even usually an innocent position. Bystanders who confirm the legitimacy of denial are not simply passive victims of manipulation. Despite possibly good intentions, they are partners in the cover-up. A milieu containing a critical mass of supportive bystanders is the key factor in the success of denial. Though of course corrupt scholars are culpable for their mendacity, their presence is inevitable in any educational environment. What gives them an impact is acceptance by bystanders.[21]

This professorial complicity is not the result of naïveté, but of an active commitment to neutrality in the face of controversy. Against Des Pres' hope, just pointing out the collusion of these bystanders is insufficient to break their tacit support of denial. After all, to them such criticism is merely another element of the conflict in which they refuse to take sides.

This commitment to neutrality is grounded on a distortion of "academic freedom," the collegiate form of liberty of expression. When challenged for not intervening against denial, apparently disinterested scholars and institutions frequently cite this principle on behalf of deniers.[22] Academic freedom properly understood guarantees a professor the right to arrive at any conclusion toward which his or her work leads. Without such protection, it is feared that theories and findings that diverge from public norms or the views of the political or academic powers-that-be will be squelched.

Invocation of academic freedom in defense of genocide denial, however, runs far afoul of its rightful use and devolves into what might be termed "academic relativism."[23] Academic relativism is the belief that any viewpoint held by a scholar declaring expertise is automatically a credible perspective. In practice, this stretches the two-sides principle into a mechanical neutrality with respect to even the most important issues on which there is overwhelming evidentiary support for one position over another.

Academic relativism is widely practiced, greatly inhibiting universal recognition of the Armenian Genocide.[24] Instead of applying careful analysis to adjudicate the apparent debate created by the presence of denial, academic relativists retreat into a neutrality that accepts all parties to the "debate" as equally worthy simply by their status as academics. As a consequence, they avoid the Armenian Question in teaching and writing because they believe the history to be uncertain, or they promote in classrooms and other forums a two-sided approach that validates denial.[25] They also contribute to a climate of academic relativism that influences other researchers and educators. This is reflected in media coverage and political decision-making. Toleration of denial in the academic realm invites journalists to take the same position in their articles, while political leaders with geopolitical agendas against genocide recognition have a ready rationale in the dissent of seemingly credible experts. Academic relativists sometimes go as far as publicly affirming the legitimacy of denialist stances.

Academic relativism is not even the balanced approach its proponents hold it to be. They are so eager to embrace noncommittal negationist assertions that not all the relevant data on the Armenian issue have been examined or that the existing data are inconclusive, they fail to consider the ample evidence at hand.[26] There is a wealth of material showing unequivocally that the Turkish government carried out a premeditated, centrally planned, systematic program to exterminate its Armenian subjects.[27] A properly critical attitude would distinguish between the failure to be aware of compelling evidence because one has not investigated the question adequately and a genuine shortfall of decisive evidence. Moreover, academic relativists usually exempt deniers from scrutiny when a rudimentary evaluation of their attempted documentation, rejection of credible data, and lines of argument would reveal indefensible omissions, distortions, and outright falsehoods, as well as fallacious logic and inconsistencies.[28]

Academic relativism is attractive because it appears to embody central principles of Western intellectual discourse, for instance, that a conscientious assessment of any position requires fanning the flames of doubt. In many circumstances, this is a productive method that supports deeper and better insights into the topic at hand. But, deniers play on this otherwise healthy skepticism.[29] The inevitable bare logical possibility that evidence disproving the genocide exists is exaggerated into the basis of a reasonable doubt.[30] Given that there are no serious grounds for believing that radically divergent data will emerge, a perfunctory and indeterminate logical doubt should not counterbalance the extensive and compelling evidence already assembled.[31]

At its most extreme, academic relativism takes the form of historical relativism. Historical relativists believe that, where there are competing versions of historical periods or events, there is no ultimate fact of the matter. Each perspective or side is as accurate as the other. Historical relativists fail to distinguish between situations in which the indeterminacies of a historical event allow more than one legitimate interpretation and those in which a participant group or other party maintains a stance inconsistent with the actual facts. They do not recognize, that is, that some views are subterfuges, while some others, if perhaps sincerely held, are a function of the propaganda and manipulation to which members of a given group have been subjected. Denial and correct representation of the genocide are not two discrete perspectives marking isolated or distinct realities, but the single world of Turkish oppression of Armenians.[32]

At its core, academic relativism turns on the conflation of *neutrality* and *objectivity*. Academic relativists believe that objectivity is guaranteed by neutrality. Where accurate history and deception collide, however, objectivity requires affirming truth over falsity. It does not mean rising above all particular standpoints but choosing the correct position or synthesis of positions. With regard to genocide denial, a purportedly neutral position is not actually neutral. The decision to accept two views as equally legitimate obscures the truth when it is contained exclusively in one of them.

Beyond Debate

The usual counter to denial is refutation of the spurious arguments and alleged evidence.[33] Researchers sometimes take a different tact, analyzing the general phenomenon of denial as an immoral, pathological, and politically objectionable activity and exposing the dishonest self-promotion of deniers pretending to be sincere knowledge-seekers, victims of Armenian fraud and intellectual aggression, and anti-racist political progressives.[34]

Both of these approaches are crucial in combating denial but by themselves are not sufficient to defeat it. Each time a negationist contention is decisively countered by well-supported critiques, deniers construct new arguments or reconfigure old ones. Unfettered by the facts or a commitment to historical accuracy, they have a free hand to fabricate data. What is more, investigations of the pathological and ideological nature of denial are turned back on their sources through assertions that those who promote knowledge of the Armenian Genocide are motivated by ethnic hatred or obsessive resentment.[35] Even in cases where deniers simply ignore the evidence or re-deploy an already discredited argument without addressing the evidence against it, their counterclaims are still taken seriously in an environment of textuality and academic relativism.[36]

Because deniers are well funded and government backed, they can continue in this way indefinitely. The upshot is a stalemate that functions as a de facto victory for deniers. The Young Turk and the Kemalist governments that committed the genocide as well as the subsequent Turkish regimes that have colluded by covering up the original crime continue to escape moral condemnation and responsibility.[37]

This situation calls into serious question John Stuart Mill's tenet that unregulated open debate inevitably establishes the truth. Though researchers have amassed compelling evidence of the details of the genocide and refuted negationist contentions, the prevalence of incorrect and misleading versions of the history has led academic consensus, political discourse, and public opinion away from the truth, toward uncertainty, skepticism, and sometimes outright disbelief.[38] Indeed, deniers seem to be relying on the probability that the longer the impasse holds, the more distant the events of the genocide will become, until, even for many Armenians, a point will be reached at which pursuit of acknowledgment will no longer seem worth the effort of wading through the manufactured complexities of the issue and confronting pro-Turkish intransigence and hostility.

If critique of denial alone will not lead to broad recognition of the historical facts, then it can be achieved only by precluding manipulation and exploitation of the textuality of the genocide and the openness of the university. And this is possible only if public dissemination of genocide denial is prohibited. It is important to emphasize that proscription will not foreclose or prevent a full discussion and fact-finding process, because they have already occurred. After decades, it is clear that no denial argument has contained evidence or reasoning that successfully refutes the genocide. That deniers frequently repackage previously disproved contentions and routinely ignore or reject reliable data confirms that a continuation of the denialist-fabricated debate over the genocide will add nothing to the understanding already developed. Even the mere claim that there is a debate about whether the genocide happened ignores the long and comprehensive research process that established its veracity.

That limits on speech are necessary to stop genocide denial does not mean that they are justified, only that they *might* be. A proposal for restricting speech must offer a positive case.

The Threshold for Restriction

Genocide denial is not a problem simply because it presents erroneous history or covers up a great tragedy. Although denial of the Armenian Genocide is regularly couched in professional-sounding and seemingly disinterested language, it is a form of "hate speech." Hate speech demeans members of an identity group, usually a group based on race, nationality, ethnicity, religion, gender, or sexuality. As Israel Charny explains, inherent in denial is the "humiliation and mocking of the sensibilities and memorial [needs] of the survivors" and "an attack on the collective identity, peoplehood and national and cultural continuity of the victim people."[39] Many deniers disparagingly mischaracterize Armenians of the Ottoman Empire as disloyal, deceitful, exploitative, and violently aggressive.[40] Some deniers also vilify Armenians and others who raise the genocide issue today as aggressors, liars, conspirators, fanatics, ultra-nationalists, or terrorists who are advancing an agenda of ethnic hatred against Turks.[41] In certain cases, deniers have publicly made nakedly denigrating remarks about Armenians.[42]

Many arguments have been advanced to justify banning hate speech. Charny has offered one specifically targeting denial of any known genocide.[43] Opponents of restriction characteristically test the arguments against the strictest standard available, the "harm principle." This principle states that a right can be limited only when its exercise substantially injures another person or other people.[44] The formulation of the principle can be utilitarian, requiring that the sum of the damage done by a type of speech clearly outweighs the great benefits of unbounded speech for societal and individual well being and offsets the negative consequences of barring it, or it can be rights-based, requiring that a type of speech directly violate a right that has precedence over the very important right to freedom of expression.

Arguments for restriction of hate speech sometimes reject the harm principle. One reason cited is that it fails to take account of relationships of dominance that typically exist between hate speech perpetrators and their targets. According to these arguments, barring hate speech is justified not only when it causes direct material injury, but in any case where the power of a group's speech is increased by and is part of an overarching system of oppression.

Though it is quite defensible to hold that the harm principle is too extreme a standard for determining whether prohibition of hate speech is permissible, it is granted here for the sake of argument. If a case for restriction succeeds when tested against the harm principle, it can be assumed to succeed relative to all less exacting standards. What is more, such a case must meet the criteria in order to convince the large number of judges, political leaders, professors, and members of the public who are opposed to speech limits and thus have a chance of being enacted into law.

Charny's innovative approach likens denial to dishonest advertising and "a variety of other failures to provide accurate and accountable information that democratic societies insist upon." As there are laws against these, there should be laws against the lies of genocide denial.[45] This is a powerful challenge to the widely held position that denial cannot be limited because it merely expresses an undesirable point of view. Charny's analysis indicates that denial speech should not be considered a point of view but a form of deception. It is wrong because it falsifies verifiable facts, not because people find it disagreeable. At a minimum, this argument offers a basis for firing deniers based on codes of professional ethics and performance standards. At the same time, while it does advance the present argument substantially, it does not itself meet the harm principle requirement. A consumer pays money in exchange for a product under the impression that it will operate a certain way, that it is made of certain things, that it is safe, and so forth. If false advertising has misled the consumer, then a culpable act has clearly been done—money has been taken by deception. The falsehoods of genocide denial, however, do not occur in relation to an implied contract: denial is advanced in the realm of intellectual or public discourse in which it is understood that people might intentionally or unwittingly present inaccurate information. The burden is on those presented with denial to evaluate it critically.

Charny also characterizes denial as incitement to "renewed discrimination and persecutory behaviors," coinciding with a general case for barring hate speech that is often made.[46] Hate speech incites discrimination and violence, either by whipping up listeners or readers against a target group or in a subtler way, by fostering an environment in which members of a target group are increasingly degraded and seen as approved targets of discrimination and violence. In the first instance, speech directly motivates violence, and in the second, speech is part of a continuum on which the distinction between speech and action is blurred and words sooner or later give way to violence.

Opponents of restriction normally respond that the connection between hate speech and violence is not a necessary causal relationship.[47] Although it might be possible that, say, a public articulation of anti-Semitism had motivated a listener to commit violence against a Jew, it could not have compelled this behavior, because listeners have the power to accept or reject such statements. The connection between unsaid words and possible subsequent violence is even more speculative. How can one predict ahead if violence will result at all from a discursive act? On this objection, only speech that openly calls for violence against a target group can be prohibited. By its very nature, genocide denial, far from overt incitement to violence, asserts that the Turkish government did not commit systematic violence against Armenians in the past and does not condone violence against them now.

The Four Harms of Denial

The foregoing objection to the incitement argument assumes that speech precedes act. Yet, in the case of genocide denial, there is no need to speculate about subsequent acts, given that associated violence has already occurred. Negationist discourse is fundamentally linked to the violence of the genocide, because this violence is its implicit if disavowed referent. Moreover, this relationship is causal, from speech to violence. At first glance, the reversal of the assumed sequence of speech and act—that speech occurring after violence is its cause—seems absurd, but it is not. As Charny explains, denial is not a distinct act; rather, it is part of the genocide. "Deniers in later years are, in effect, 'one' with the Talaats and Eichmanns who originally issued the administrative orders to deport the victims on forced marches and torture-chamber trains; they are one with the bayonet and machete-bearing killers, and the soldiers who indifferently executed their victims."[48] Deniers join the initial perpetrators by reviving the overall injury that the genocide represents for Armenians. Denial thus functions as a retroactive partial cause of the genocide. While denial might be meaningless if the Armenian Genocide had not already occurred, still, in the absence of denial, the total damage done by the genocide would be markedly less.

The following sections describe four ways in which deniers increase the material injury done by the Armenian Genocide. Together, they more than constitute the level of injury that the harm principle requires. Even the first or second taken alone is probably sufficient to satisfy the principle.

Accessories after the Fact

Deniers help the original perpetrators get away with the crime. At stake is more than just the perpetrators' status in history, although this has an important role in contemporary Turkish self-conceptualization and resultant political relations with non-Turkish groups. Deniers are "accessories after the fact of genocide," who have so far prevented an international political and legal process affirming the genocide, requiring appropriate restitution, and curbing further Turkish mistreatment of Armenians. As a consequence, Turkish individuals and society continue to enjoy the spoils of their predecessors' bloody deed. The most obvious fruits are land depopulated by the Armenian Genocide and the immense amount of money and other property pilfered by the Turkish government and by private individuals through arrangement with the government. Major benefits also include greater regional power guaranteed in part by the absence of a significantly larger and stronger neighboring Armenian state than now exists and long-consolidated ethnic-Turkish domestic political dominance. Other benefits with substantial material consequences are a significantly less tarnished international image and continuing availability of Turkism and pan-Turkism as apparently legitimate political ideologies. Finally, in the absence of universal recognition of the Armenian Genocide, Turkish citizens and their government are able to oppress and denigrate Armenians at home and abroad without guilt or international scrutiny and outrage. This allows ongoing discrimination against the small residual Armenian community in Turkey, powerful Turkish military and diplomatic support to Azerbaijan in its attempted "ethnic cleansing" of more than 100,000 Armenians from the Karabagh region, and Turkish participation in a related devastating prolonged blockade of the landlocked Armenian republic.

What is more, the wealth and land taken, the approximately 1.5 million dead, the social and political networks fragmented, and the cultural processes cut off were not merely static losses. They were the foundation of the subsequent Armenian development that would have occurred if the genocide had not. Not only have these things been lost; so have all the gains that would have been based on them. The original damage continually accrues interest. As long as deniers obstruct reparation of the original losses, they are principally responsible for this steady increase.

Psychological Harm

A key component of many hate speech prohibition arguments is attention to the emotional suffering hate speech produces.[49] Opponents usually counter this approach by asserting that psychological pain is not a proper form of material damage.[50] Words are inherently incorporeal, as our mental reactions to them must also be. Furthermore, emotional pain is subjective, a function of the psychology of a person claiming or judging it, not the objective features of what has been said. While emotional duress might be a real experience, it is impossible to quantify relative to a consistent standard. If it were the criterion for proscription, a great deal of speech could be prevented based on the variable sentiments of specific individuals, strangling free expression. Emotional pain at being exposed to opinions different from our own and possibly hostile to us is unfortunate, but it is the price citizens must pay for living in a free society.[51]

Not all emotional pain is immaterial, however. When a person is the victim of a violent deed or loses a family member to murder, the traumatic event produces psychological pain. This pain is the expected, normal, and reasonable mental registry of concrete violence. It is an inevitable consequence, inseparable from the experience of violence. Indeed, it is possible to contend that without it violence would not be truly experienced or considered as significant as it is. Though the precise constellation of emotions might vary somewhat by individual, and there are valid differences over the exact bounds of psychological normalcy, certain types and levels of emotional reaction to violence are typical. Thus, pain that is a response to actual violence is objective, not subjectively arbitrary. Furthermore, since this kind of emotional harm is imposed by external force, it is not volitional. To say that it is means wrongly holding victims responsible for damage done by violence against them.[52]

Denial of the Armenian Genocide causes this second mode of psychological suffering.[53] This is especially clear for survivors. Most, if not all, were directly brutalized, through beating, rape, torture, forced starvation, enslavement, death marches, and other kinds of violence and deprivation. All inevitably lost loved ones, often with their own eyes seeing them similarly tormented as well as immolated, bayoneted, hacked up, impaled, decapitated, or drowned. The consequences of these traumas can never be overcome, but their severity can be mitigated somewhat in time. Denial blocks this, on the contrary expanding the genocide's impact by increasing the longevity and intensity of the emotional pain. The psychological distress caused by denial is not an emotional response to incorporeal words; instead, the words reactivate and deepen the original material trauma. The actual violence of the genocide is what gives the words their material power. Deniers thrust the genocide back onto its victims, so they must recall the violence done to and witnessed by them and experience renewed psychological pain. Denial re-imposes the power of the genocide and emphasizes the impunity of its authors and executors.[54] Deniers operate as agents of the original perpetrators, pursuing and hounding victims through time. Through these agents, the perpetrators reach once again into the lives of the victims long after their escape from the perpetrators' physical grasp.

The material psychological harm of denial is not limited to survivors, extending as well to subsequent generations of Armenians.[55] The genocide was a collective attack on Armenians. This includes members of succeeding generations, both those later born and those preemptively eliminated by the murders of the people who would have been their parents, grandparents, or great-grandparents. Even for those who consider a group simply an aggregate of individuals and concede a collective injury only when most or all constituents have been injured specifically, the genocide must be seen as an assault on Armenians as a group. Its authors aimed to annihilate the group by murder of individual members, yet also by means of an intertwined obliteration of the very foundations of their lives—familial, cultural, political, economic, and religious institutions, relations, and identity. Even though later generations of Armenians did not suffer the violence of the genocide firsthand, they have lived with the full consequences of its disruption and devastation of Armenian families, communities, and nationality in general. In a sense, Armenians can never escape the consequences of the genocide: no matter how much time passes, how heroic the efforts to reconstitute the community, how much external support is received, and how impressive the success of rebuilding, the heights achieved will always be less than would be the case had no genocide occurred.

In addition to the genocide's material legacy, the psychological trauma of survivors affects later generations as well. The overwhelming blow could not be absorbed by Armenian survivors and overflowed into successive generations. The great excess of immediate emotional trauma became embedded in the social relations and institutions developed or reconstructed in the genocide's aftermath. Internalized in Armenian culture, family dynamics, and social structures, the shared trauma has dramatically affected and even shaped the psychologies of later generations, as recent work on the intergenerational transmission of genocidal trauma describes.[56] These effects, too, are the inevitable and objective long-term product of the genocide. Under the best conditions, with survivors supported in rebuilding their group and universal recognition of their suffering, the shock of these losses would have strongly reverberated in the Armenian world for decades.

Genocide denial exacerbates these two modes of material psychological reaction in later generations in much the same way it does with survivors. In a sense, it drags post-survivor Armenians back to the genocide, despite their distance in time and the fact that they did not live through it. The suffering of later generations, then, is not just a function of the persistence of residual pain from the genocide. Denial continually drives the genocide back into a central role in the lives of the children, grandchildren, and great-grandchildren of survivors.

A certain inconsistency might be perceived between the contentions made in this section and in that of the textualization of the genocide. If the calamity is becoming less immediate even for Armenians, then presumably its psychological impact is weakening. If this is the case, deniers need only persist until the emotional pain diminishes enough to justify the rejection of any speech restrictions. Textuality does not, however, refer to a change in the power of the genocide, but in the way in which people relate or have access to it. It signals a shift from an immediate apprehension of the genocide to a mediated one. That its emotive force acts via an intermediary text does not necessarily mean it is weaker. On the contrary, it is textuality itself that allows the genocide an emotional impact well after its passing into history. Moreover, for many Armenians, the struggle against denial actually tends to reverse the effects of textualization, increasing the immediacy of the genocide.

Destruction of Armenian Identity

It is possible to object that the psychological harm of denial to second and later generations depends on two contingencies: their awareness of and concern about their history. However unlikely it is that indifference to the genocide would become universal among Armenians, the chance of at least a critical mass of apathy can be admitted for the sake of discussion. The pain of confronting an intensive and hurtful denial campaign merely for affirming the genocide, in conjunction with the sense of futility the genocide and wide acceptance of its denial have engendered, might well drive some Armenians to abandon this issue. This could be the motive behind recent denialist attempts to foster a "forget and forgive" attitude among Armenians, on the grounds that the genocide happened long ago and Turks and Armenians should focus on building a positive future relationship rather than on the past. Affected individuals would no longer feel psychological pain at denial and might even be disquieted by continued Armenian efforts toward genocide recognition. As opposed to the trend described in the foregoing section, highly successful denial could eventually eliminate Armenian pain at denial.

To the degree that Armenian disinterest would depend on denial, on the other hand, it would be a distinct kind of damage. As opposed to a liberation from suffering, it would be a coerced and unnatural alienation from the experience of the genocide. Certainly, Armenian identity depends on much more than the genocide and its continuing aftermath, but the genocide is just as surely a central part of modern Armenian history and as such an essential part of contemporary Armenian identity. Manipulation of Armenian identity and culture through denial is an assault on both and might properly be considered an extension of the annihilative program of the original genocide. Even partial success must be seen as harm to the individual Armenians succumbing to it.

Grave Desecration

The discussion so far has concerned damage done only to living Armenians. This might seem to suggest that, though the acts of the genocide did great harm to the Armenians killed in the genocide, in death they are untouched by denial. Death appears to be the ultimate and final injury, beyond which no further harm can occur. Yet, it is possible to harm the dead. In many societies, including the United States, grave desecration is a crime. If it is not as serious as murder, it is still a significant violation and punishable.

How does this apply to genocide denial? After all, most casualties of the Armenian Genocide died anonymously, thrown into pits along desert paths to rot; burned alive en masse in caves, churches, or town squares; drowned in rivers; and so forth. Those permanently enslaved died beyond the knowledge of and proper mourning by other Armenians. There would seem to be few or no graves to be defiled.

Important surrogate grave markers exist, however, in the books and articles written about the genocide, such as survivor memoirs and testimonies, other descriptions identifying particular people killed, and accounts referencing the dead through fatality figures, documentary films, genocide museums and memorials, commemoration events, and stories of the dead passed orally within families and communities. The lack of actual tombs presses these texts into the role of cenotaphs.

Because denial specifically attacks them, it is a form of grave desecration. Though denial is made through speech, the surrogate markers are vulnerable to discursive onslaughts because they themselves are likewise constructed by speech. Most obvious are denial assertions that reduce the number of Armenian dead.[57] With a few deft keyboard strokes, demographic manipulators destroy the main markers—statistical counts and demographic studies—of the deaths and lives of hundreds of thousands of people. Other denial arguments and the denial campaign as a whole undermine and negate the substitute memorials in similar ways.

A Captive Audience

Advocates of absolute freedom of expression frequently add a further requirement for prohibition. The target of hate speech must be unable to avoid it or its consequences.[58] There is no escape from denial. Deniers actively seek out and counter public mention of the genocide by politicians, professors, journalists, and community members. In addition, they often disrupt programs of discussion and remembrance with denialist statements. Simply engaging the genocide elicits an encounter with denial. Avoiding negationist discourse seems to necessitate giving up the genocide issue all together, with the adverse effects on Armenian identity. Yet, even this does not end its impact. When Armenians ignore denial, it helps consolidate the material gains of the genocide and despoils the cenotaphs to the dead all the better.

The Concrete Proposal

Legal restriction of public dissemination of denial of the Armenian Genocide would entail a law barring denial and setting penalties for it or authorizing civil suits against deniers. The law need not determine particular statements to be counted as denial but rather offer general guidelines for determining this. Because universities, colleges, scholarly associations, and sometimes school systems have greater latitude in setting limits on hate speech than Congress or a lower-level legislature, they could ban denial in the absence of laws doing so.

There are a variety of possible penalties. Crucial for anyone found guilty of or responsible for denial would be an order to cease and desist. A just remedy would in addition require a statement affirming the genocide as a historical fact. Other penalties might include punitive cash awards to support genocide education and awareness; exclusion from federal or state research grants, depending on the level of the law violated; and, for violation of a university rule, loss of rank or job.

Laws and regulations should target statements that falsify the basic fact that the Armenian Genocide occurred or that the events in the Ottoman Empire in 1915 and after constitute genocide according to the United Nations Genocide Convention and other generally accepted standards.[59] They should also target narratives omitting the genocide, when any reasonably accurate treatment of the topic under consideration should include it.

The motives behind an instance of denial are important in determining whether a proscribing law or rule should be applied to it. At one end of the continuum are intentional deniers. They are aware of the essential evidence of the genocide but choose to negate it nonetheless. Heath Lowry is a good example. As Roger Smith, Eric Markusen, and Robert Jay Lifton show, he has worked with the Turkish government to deny the genocide that he indirectly appears to accept as a historical fact in a memorandum submitted in 1990 to then-Turkish Ambassador to the United States, Nuzhet Kandemir.[60] Circumstantial evidence indicates that most other major deniers also know that the genocide occurred and deliberately deny it.

At the same time, presumably all deniers, including Lowry, "deny being deniers."[61] Even if some of them really have come to believe their lies, because of, say, a psychological mechanism of rationalization, they are fully culpable. An Aristotelian distinction between voluntary and involuntary acts in assessing moral responsibility clarifies the reason for this. In the case of involuntary ignorance, a person is genuinely unaware of information necessary to a good decision and thus inadvertently does harm. Under the given circumstances, he or she could not fairly have been expected to know the facts and, when they are pointed out, immediately admits the error and expresses regret for it.[62] An active genocide denier, however, cannot rightly claim involuntary ignorance. Putative experts on the relevant history who omit the genocide from their writings or deny it outright deliberately disregard evidence they are or should be aware of in accordance with elementary historiographic principles. Furthermore, when the evidence is presented to them, major deniers without exception redouble their negationist efforts instead of acknowledging the truth.

Voluntary ignorance does not require an explicit decision to lie about the genocide. Minor deniers might be unaware of the available evidence, but the choice to take a public position on as important an issue as the Armenian Genocide without adequately researching it makes them blameworthy nonetheless. Many who signed a 1985 denialist advertisement placed in the *New York Times* are examples of this type of denier.[63] Others in this category include individuals of Turkish descent who, challenged with evidence of the genocide, refuse to evaluate critically the propaganda of the Turkish government and instead publicly continue to support it. Presented with the opportunity to learn the real facts, they are culpable for failing to overcome ideological or psychological commitments to fabrication.

In cases where a person is genuinely ignorant of the facts and has not had adequate opportunity to become acquainted with them, public denial or omission of the genocide is most likely inadvertent and involuntary. He or she is not properly categorized as a denier but rather as a victim of the Turkish denial campaign. Sanctions are not warranted. Education as opposed to legal action is the appropriate remedy. On the one hand, a truly inadvertent denier will recognize the veracity of the genocide when confronted by the evidence. Indeed, this approach is a dependable test of whether an individual is really a denier. On the other hand, as the mechanisms described above are employed, academic relativism and other elements of the current climate of falsely credible denial will be tempered. As fewer people are manipulated into inadvertent denial, it will become less of a problem in need of remedy.

Practical Concerns

Opponents of restriction buttress their case by asserting that any curtailment of freedom of expression might eventually lead far beyond those engaging in hate speech. They offer a "slippery slope" argument, according to which any move away from nearly absolute freedom of expression sets a precedent that makes further infringement easier. Small step by small step, significant constraints on speech and other basic rights can evolve. Even apparently trivial limitations start a society down the path toward tyranny.[64]

Slippery slope arguments and related concerns about the abuse of speech restrictions should not be taken lightly. At the same time, this objection might be met by a slippery slope argument in the reverse direction. Permitting genocide denial despite the damage it does not only reinforces deniers in their destructive activities but also opens an ethical loophole that will potentially allow a range of harms, including violence, in various circumstances. At the extreme, successful genocide denial begets genocide. For instance, awareness of the impunity of the perpetrators of the Armenian Genocide appears to have been one of the factors that emboldened Hitler to commit the Holocaust.[65]

A brake on abuse of denial proscription is that restrictions under the present proposal are not automatic. As Lamar University philosopher Kevin Dodson has pointed out, the prohibition under discussion is not censorship.[66] It does not entail a preemptive screening of statements before publication or public presentation. Rather, individuals and groups will be held responsible for the actual material harm their words have already produced. Just as important, the proposal calls for a judicial process that will guarantee that alleged deniers have ample opportunity to defend themselves.

The real dangers here, on the contrary, are that a denier will be found innocent or not responsible and that trials and university judicial proceedings will provide public stages to the accused and other deniers called as expert witnesses. Still, these risks should not be overestimated. The forces of denial already make themselves strongly felt in intellectual, journalistic, and political circles. Furthermore, unlike what now transpires in the "court of public opinion" and the "marketplace of ideas," judicial processes will almost always have definite results. They will lead not to a stalemate but, quite the opposite, conclude with a judgment as to whether the defendant did deny the genocide. Moreover, the judgment will be based on the evidence, which decisively proves the genocide and can bear the greatest scrutiny, while negationist claims cannot. If a juridical proceeding offers deniers an opportunity to publicize their views further and possibly to have them judged legitimate, it also offers those filing suit a rare opportunity to interrogate publicly deniers and expose the weaknesses of their positions in front of an authority that can officially affirm the occurrence of the genocide and the falsity of denial. Finally, this process will shift the focus from whether or not the genocide occurred to whether or not an individual or group has denied the crime. Instead of the veracity of the genocide being constantly assailed by deniers, it will be the deniers who will be put on the defensive.

There is the additional danger that prohibitions will be turned against Armenians. Some deniers avow that during World War I Armenians murdered large numbers of Turks and others. Justin McCarthy makes this claim frequently.[67] On the fringes of the denial campaign, these erroneous assertions are sometimes elevated to the status of genocide.[68] Based on a wealth of evidence, Armenian Genocide and comparative genocide scholars reject any possibility that Armenians committed largescale atrocities against Turks and others, especially in any way that could be interpreted as genocide. Could cases be filed against them? Yes, but this would be a positive development. So far, these suggestions of mass murder and genocide by Armenians have escaped direct critical evaluation in the popular press and political sphere but are trotted out when the Turkish government or its proxies believe them useful. For instance, "Key Facts to Consider Regarding H.Res.398," which was distributed to Members of Congress in 2000 by former Speaker Robert Livingston's lobbying organization "on behalf of The Republic of Turkey" to convince them to vote against the pending resolution recognizing the genocide, claims that "Russians and their Armenian allies murdered up to 3 million Ottoman Muslim citizens" and "killed upwards of 200,000 Jews."[69] If those who rightly reject this kind of bogus accusation against Armenians are charged with genocide denial, a minimally fair court or university proceeding cannot but expose the lie. Such a process is the perfect opportunity to expose this fabrication publicly and to put it to rest permanently.

The mere attempt to enact a law or rule barring denial carries risks. Foremost among these is the possibility that deniers will mischaracterize Armenians generally as "enemies of free speech" just because a few are challenging their abuse of it. Many outsiders relatively unconcerned with the Armenian Genocide might well get involved, and some will likely rally against what they will misconstrue as an assault on freedom of expression. Some might inappropriately go so far as to glorify denial activity as resistance to an assault on a basic liberty.

But, this is not the dramatic problem it might appear to be. First, the Turkish government already complains that Armenian Americans devote "vast energy" to these pursuits, seeking to deny freedom of speech, as demonstrated by passage of commemorative resolutions at the federal and state levels and lobbying for inclusion of the genocide in public school curricula.[70] That these activities do not in any way limit the liberty of expression of deniers and that the Turkish government's statement does not refer to an actual call for a ban of denial indicate that this charge will be made whether or not there is a drive for restriction.[71] Second, increasing these vilifications of Armenians will place speech rights squarely in the center of discussion. This will provide an excellent opportunity to call attention to the contradiction between the Turkish government's concern for the rights of deniers in the United States and its use of censorship, intimidation, imprisonment, physical violence, and even torture and assassination to prevent the voicing of unsanctioned views in Turkey.[72]

Pressure for restriction of denial speech might in addition produce at least a form of support among third-party opponents. Similar to other types of hate speech, some advocates of absolute freedom of speech are likely to reject denial publicly and call attention to harm it does at the same time that they uphold what they perceive to be the right of those issuing false statements to do so. In order to render proscription of genocide denial less appealing, or out of a commitment against hate speech, some might actively participate in the push for universal genocide recognition via other avenues.[73]

There is a reasonable question as to whether laws or rules against denial would ever be passed. It is an uphill battle in Congress, where recent resolutions commemorating the genocide have not succeeded. Yet, lower-level laws could be enacted. Passage in just one locality will have a tremendous symbolic value, helping to ameliorate Armenian suffering and aiding in public education efforts. Universities and colleges that support denial activities will be unlikely to adopt rules against dissemination of denial, and so their deniers will probably remain untouched. Still, passage by other institutions and associations will help stop the spread of denial and will also have great symbolic importance. A good starting point would be universities and colleges that already have campus hate speech codes, which could be revised to include specific provisions regarding genocide denial. Finally, in both political and intellectual circles, working with other victim groups is morally required from a conscientious comparative genocide perspective, and for ethical consistency.

Notes

1. I wish to express appreciation to Israel Charny and Richard Hovannisian for their helpful comments on drafts of this paper and to George Aghjayan and Greg Arzoomanian for their research support.
2. On the role of Turkish government officials in denial efforts, see Roger W. Smith, Eric Markusen, and Robert Jay Lifton, "Professional Ethics and the Denial of the Armenian Genocide," *Holocaust and Genocide Studies* 9:1 (1995): 1-22; Richard G. Hovannisian, "The Armenian Genocide and Patterns of Denial," in *The Armenian Genocide in Perspective*, ed. Richard G. Hovannisian (New Brunswick, NJ: Transaction Publishers, 1986), pp. 113-14, 121-24, 126-31; Dennis R. Papazian, "Misplaced Credulity: Contemporary Turkish Attempts to Refute the Armenian Genocide," *Genocide & Human Rights: Lessons from the Armenian Experience*, special issue of *Journal of Armenian Studies* 4:1-2 (1992): 227-56; Vigen Guroian, "Collective Responsibility and Official Excuse Making: The Case of the Turkish Genocide of the Armenians," in Hovannisian, *Armenian Genocide in Perspective*, pp. 135-52.

   Speros Vryonis, Jr., *The Turkish State and History: Clio Meets the Grey Wolf*, 2d ed. (New Rochelle, NY: Aristide D. Caratzas, 1993), pp. 79-118, discusses financial details of Turkish lobbying in the United States, while "Turkey Signs Up Big Guns in D.C.," *Congress Daily*, February 2, 2000, covers the Turkish government's award of a $1.8 million lobbying contract to former House Appropriations Committee Chairman Robert Livingston, retired House Rules Committee Chairman Gerald Solomon, and former New York Congressman Stephen Solarz, all of whom had been active opponents of commemorative resolutions while serving in Congress.
3. The best-known case is the appointment in 1993 of major denier Heath Lowry to an endowed Turkish Studies chair at Princeton University. Lowry's scholarly accomplishments are quite limited, and he appears to be unqualified for such a position. The chair was created largely through $750,000 provided by the Turkish government. See William H. Honan, "Princeton Is Accused of Fronting for the Turkish Government," *New York Times*, May 22, 1996, pp. B1, B8, and Amy Magaro Rubin, "Critics Accuse Turkish Government of Manipulating Scholarship," *The Chronicle of Higher Education*, Oct. 27, 1995, p. A44. As Roger Smith, Eric Markusen, and Robert Jay Lifton expose, during his tenure as Director of the Institute for Turkish Studies prior to the Princeton appointment, Lowry was actively working with the Turkish government in its genocide denial efforts.

4. Examples are discussed in Ara Sarafian, "The Archival Trail: Authentication of *The Treatment of Armenians in the Ottoman Empire, 1915-16*," in *Remembrance and Denial: The Case of the Armenian Genocide*, ed. Richard G. Hovannisian (Detroit: Wayne State University Press, 1999), pp. 52-54; George M. Aghjayan, "Genocide Denial: The Armenian and Jewish Experiences Compared" (Worcester: Armenian National Committee of Central Massachusetts, 1998), pp. 5-9; Israel W. Charny and Daphna Fromer, "Denying the Armenian Genocide: Patterns of Thinking as Defense-Mechanisms," *Patterns of Prejudice* 32:1 (1998): 39-49.
5. Instances of this approach are examined by Aghjayan, "Genocide Denial," pp. 2-4, and Henry Theriault, "Universal Social Theory and the Denial of Genocide: Norman Itzkowitz Revisited," *Journal of Genocide Research* 3:2 (2001): 241-56.
6. See Robert Melson, "Provocation or Nationalism: A Critical Inquiry into the Armenian Genocide of 1915," in Hovannisian, *Armenian Genocide in Perspective*, pp. 61-84; Richard G. Hovannisian, "Denial of the Armenian Genocide in Comparison with Holocaust Denial," in Hovannisian, *Remembrance and Denial*, pp. 207-11, 214; Aghjayan, "Genocide Denial," pp. 2-4.
7. See Charny and Fromer, "Denying the Armenian Genocide," p. 47; Hovannisian, "Denial of the Armenian Genocide," pp. 27-29.
8. See Guroian, "Collective Responsibility," p. 150; Hovannisian, "Patterns of Denial," pp. 120-21. In this regard, it is significant that no incumbent U.S. President has referred specifically to the annihilation of Armenians as "genocide" in April 24 annual commemoration statements.
9. Yves Ternon, "Freedom and Responsibility of the Historian: The 'Lewis Affair'," in Hovannisian, *Remembrance and Denial*, pp. 237-48.
10. While some points in this chapter are specific to the Armenian Genocide and its denial, the overall line of reasoning concerns elements and issues common to denials of many other genocides as well. Any effort to prohibit public dissemination of denial of the Armenian Genocide would presumably be part of a broader initiative seeking laws and regulations applicable to any known genocide. In this regard, I have developed a generalized schematic of the main argument that applies to denials of a range of genocides, which will be published under the title "Freedom of Speech and the Intentional Denial of Genocide," in *Values in an Age of Globalization: The Selected Proceedings of the 28th Conference on Value Inquiry*, ed. Kevin Dodson (forthcoming).
11. Richard D. Kloian, *The Armenian Genocide: News Accounts from the American Press, 1915-1922* (Berkeley: Anto Printing, 1988), reproduces hundreds of articles appearing in American newspapers, especially the *New York Times*.
12. This interesting path is taken by Lorne Shirinian, "Survivor Memoirs of the Armenian Genocide as Cultural History," and Rubina Peroomian, "Problematic Aspects of Reading Genocide Literature: A Search for a Guideline or a Canon," both in Hovannisian, *Remembrance and Denial*, pp. 165-73, 175-86.
13. The classic articulation of this position is by John Stuart Mill, in *On Liberty*, ed. Elizabeth Rapaport (Indianapolis: Hackett, 1978), pp. 15-52.
14. Jonathan Rauch, "In Defense of Prejudice: Why Incendiary Speech Must Be Protected," *Contemporary Moral Problems*, 6th ed., ed. James E. White (Belmont, CA: Wadsworth, 2000), p. 401. Rauch follows Mill, who argues that, even in cases where a false idea (such as denial of the Armenian Genocide) is presented against a true idea (the fact of the genocide), the challenge is crucial both for keeping proponents of the truth alert and the idea fresh and for supporting an overall climate of open discussion that is absolutely essential to intellectual, scientific, cultural, and social progress.

15. Terrence Des Pres, "On Governing Narratives: The Turkish-Armenian Case," *Yale Review* 75:4 (1986): 517-31.
16. Ibid., pp. 517-21.
17. A denier might be, say, pro-United States and deny out of a belief that strong ties to Turkey are in the U.S. national interest.
18. This account is similar to that of Ternon, in "The 'Lewis Affair'," pp. 237-38.
19. Des Pres, "On Governing Narratives," p. 530.
20. Ibid., pp. 520-21.
21. This follows Ervin Staub's emphasis on bystander participation in genocide. See Ervin Staub, *The Roots of Evil: The Origins of Genocide and Other Group Violence* (Cambridge and New York: Cambridge University Press, 1989).
22. The defense of denier Heath Lowry is a case in point. See, for instance, statements by Professor Abraham Udovitch, who served on the search committee that selected Lowry for the Turkish Studies position at Princeton, in Rubin, "Critics Accuse Turkish Government of Manipulating Scholarship," p. A44. Hovannisian, in "Denial of the Armenian Genocide," pp. 225-27, provides an incisive treatment of the manner in which academic freedom is exploited.
23. The concept of "academic relativism" is inspired in part by Stephen Satris' description of "student relativism." Student relativism is the attitude among some students in philosophy courses that there is no absolute truth. Right and wrong, truth and falsity, and so forth are relative to each individual and depend on what he or she "feels" to be true and right. Student relativists hold that any position on a philosophical topic is automatically legitimate and should not be subject to critical evaluation. According to Satris, student relativism functions as a protective charm or suit of armor, shielding its bearer from external challenge and engagement of difficult philosophical issues. Though it appears the height of open-mindedness and tolerance, it functions in reality to shut down discussion and debate and to reinforce the prejudices of its bearers. See Stephen A. Satris, "Student Relativism," *Teaching Philosophy* 9:3 (1986): 193-200.
24. For an important instance, see the memorandum of May 30, 1996 from Princeton University's Dean of the Faculty, Amy Gutmann, to Princeton professors. In it, she encourages academic relativism in response to the criticisms of Heath Lowry's hiring in the *New York Times*, presumably in Honan, "Princeton Is Accused of Fronting for the Turkish Government."
25. Joyce Apsel, "Official Denial: The Armenian Genocide, Genocide Studies and the Internet," paper presented at the fourth international conference of the Association of Genocide Scholars, University of Minnesota-Minneapolis, June 10, 2001.
26. See Charny and Fromer, "Denying the Armenian Genocide," p. 46.
27. Ara Sarafian, comp., *United States Official Documents on the Armenian Genocide*, vols. 1-3 (Watertown, MA: Armenian Review, 1993-1995), presents a selection of the eyewitness accounts submitted by U.S. diplomatic personnel in genocide execution zones. A comprehensive description of the genocide that collates these and other eyewitness reports from American sources is provided in *The Treatment of Armenians in the Ottoman Empire, 1915-16: Documents Presented to Viscount Grey of Fallodon by Viscount Bryce*, Arnold Toynbee, ed. (London: Sir Joseph Causton & Sons, 1916; new ed., Princeton, NJ: Gomidas Institute, 2000). For 1913-16, see the account of U.S. Ambassador Henry Morgenthau, including discussions and attempted intercession with Talaat and other Young Turk leaders, in *Ambassador Morgenthau's Story* (Garden City, NY: Doubleday, Page, 1918; reprint, Princeton, NJ: Gomidas Institute, 2000), pp. 182-255. Vahakn Dadrian examines Turkish primary sources in "The Armenian Genocide in Official Turkish Records:

Collected Essays by Vahakn N. Dadrian," *Journal of Political and Military Sociology* 22:1 (Summer 1994; reprinted with corrections, Spring 1995). For an analysis of the German documentation, see Vahakn N. Dadrian, *German Responsibility in the Armenian Genocide: A Review of the Historical Evidence of German Complicity* (Watertown, MA: Blue Crane Books, 1996); Hilmar Kaiser, "The Baghdad Railway and the Armenian Genocide, 1915-1916: A Case Study in German Resistance and Complicity," in Hovannisian, *Remembrance and Denial*, pp. 67-112. For survivor testimony, see Donald E. Miller and Lorna Touryan Miller, *Survivors: An Oral History of the Armenian Genocide* (Berkeley, Los Angeles, London: University of California Press, 1993).

For some of the important work based on these and other sources, including consideration of the perpetrators' premeditation and responsibility, see Robert Melson, "Provocation or Nationalism," pp. 61-84; Vahakn N. Dadrian, *The History of the Armenian Genocide: Ethnic Conflict from the Balkans to Anatolia to the Causasus*, 3d rev. ed. (Providence, RI: Berghahn Books, 1997); Richard G. Hovannisian "The Historical Dimensions of the Armenian Question, 1878-1923," in Hovannisian, *Armenian Genocide in Perspective*, pp. 19-41; Stephan H. Astourian, "Modern Turkish Identity and the Armenian Genocide: From Prejudice to Racist Nationalism," in Hovannisian, *Remembrance and Denial*, pp. 23-49; Levon Marashlian, "Finishing the Genocide: Cleansing Turkey of Armenian Survivors, 1920-1923," in Hovannisian, *Remembrance and Denial*, pp. 113-45.

28. Many of the articles on denial and some of the works on the genocide itself cited in prior notes expose these types of problems in a range of denial arguments.
29. For an example, see Justin McCarthy, "Let Historians Decide on So-Called Genocide," *Turkish Daily News*, April 10-12, 2001, http://www.turkishdailynews.com/old_editions/04_10_01/feature.htm (Jan. 25, 2002), http://www.turkishdailynews.com/old_editions/04_11_01/feature.htm (Jan. 25, 2002), and http://www.turkishdailynews.com/old_editions/04_12_01/feature.htm (Jan. 25, 2002).
30. Exculpatory evidence appears especially unlikely to emerge, given the implications of the long-standing ban of non-deniers from access to the relevant archival records in the Ottoman Archives. See Sarafian, *United States Official Documents*, vol. 1: *The Lower Euphrates*, p. ix. As part of a panel discussion on the Armenian Genocide at Brown University on April 17, 1999, Hilmar Kaiser described his attempt to use the archives in the early 1990s. He explained the ways in which archive officials, who had become aware of the nature of his research, consistently prevented his access to the documents he sought.
31. Cf. Ternon, "The 'Lewis Affair'," p. 237.
32. Norman Itzkowitz's approach of relativistic denial appeals especially to historical relativists. See Theriault, "Universal Social Theory and Denial," pp. 241-56.
33. This "evidence" is typically fabricated, misquoted so as to alter the meaning and even reverse it, or substantially misused. See Hovannisian, "Patterns of Denial," pp. 122-23; Sarafian, *United States Official Documents*, vol. 1, pp. 161ff.
34. Examplars of this approach are Des Pres, "On Governing Narratives," pp. 517-31; Israel W. Charny, "A Contribution to the Psychology of Denial of Genocide," in *Genocide and Human Rights*, pp. 289-306; Charny and Fromer, "Denying the Armenian Genocide," p. 47.
35. Norman Itzkowitz has pioneered this technique. See Theriault, "Universal Social Theory and Denial," pp. 241-56.
36. For illustrations, see Sarafian, "The Archival Trail," pp. 52-54.
37. On the extension of the genocide to 1923 by the Kemalist revolutionaries, see Marashlian, "Finishing the Genocide," pp. 113-45.

38. See the works cited in note 27 above.
39. Charny, "A Contribution," pp. 299-301.
40. For discussions of this point, see Aghjayan, "Genocide Denial," pp. 2-4; Melson, "Provocation or Nationalism," pp. 61-84; Charny and Fromer, "Denying the Armenian Genocide," pp. 47-48; Hovannisian, "Denial of the Armenian Genocide," pp. 207-11, 214; Roger W. Smith, "Genocide and Denial: The Armenian Case and Its Implications," *Armenian Review* 42:1 (1989): 11-14; Israel W. Charny, "The Psychology of Denial of Known Genocides," *Genocide: A Critical Bibliographic Review*, ed. Israel W. Charny, vol. 2 (New York: Facts on File, 1991), pp. 14 (4th denial strategy), 15 (10th denial strategy).
41. For two of the seemingly countless examples of this kind of attack on Armenians, intertwined with denial of the genocide, see Mahmut Esat Ozan, "A Glance at Year 2000," and M. Orhan Tarhan, "The Enemies of Turkey," both in *The Turkish Times*, May 1, 2000, http://www.ataa.org/times/news/html (May 3, 2000). Ozan's article presents a series of observations about issues in the year 2000, from domestic health care and crime to irrigation and the natural disasters that struck in Asia, Africa, and the Americas. But, by far the greatest amount of space is reserved for a diatribe against the Armenian republic and diasporan Armenians, particularly in relation to the genocide. "Every year around April 24, [American Armenians] leave behind their false facades of civilized citizens of [the United States] and are transformed into sub-human species, attacking mercilessly every known Turkish institution around, also inundating the American and the international media with their distorted version of fictional sob stories." The first enemy Tarhan lists is the Armenian republic, whose falsified "Armenian Genocide" is a plot to get land and money from Turkey.
42. An obvious instance is Norman Itzkowitz's 1997 public recitation of a personal anecdote belittling a survivor grandmother of the Armenian Genocide and her concerned grandson. See Theriault, "Universal Social Theory and Denial," pp. 243ff.
43. Charny, "A Contribution," p. 302.
44. Mill, *On Liberty*, p. 9, and Introduction by Elizabeth Rapaport, pp. xv-xvii; Joel Feinberg, "The Harm Principle," in *Ethical Theory and Moral Problems*, ed. Howard J. Curzer (Belmont, CA: Wadsworth, 1999), pp. 396-405.
45. Charny, "A Contribution," p. 302.
46. For two versions of such arguments, see Mari J. Matsuda, "Public Response to Racist Speech: Considering the Victim's Story," in *Moral Issues in Global Perspective*, ed. Christine M. Koggel (Ontario: Broadview, 1999), pp. 688-89, and Thomas W. Peard, "Hate Speech on Campus: Exploring the Limits of Free Speech," in *Taking Sides: Clashing Views on Controversial Moral Issues*, 7th ed., ed. Stephen Satris (Guilford, CT: Dushkin/McGraw-Hill, 2000), p. 118.
47. For one instance of this argument, see John Arthur, "Sticks and Stones," in Satris, *Taking Sides*, pp. 114-15.
48. Charny, "A Contribution," p. 299.
49. Matsuda, "Public Response to Racist Speech," pp. 690-91; Peard, "Hate Speech on Campus," pp. 118-20.
50. See, for example, Arthur, "Sticks and Stones," pp. 112-15; Nadine Strossen (President of the American Civil Liberties Union since 1991), "Balancing Rights to Freedom of Expression and Equality: A Civil Liberties Approach to Hate Speech on Campus," in *Ethical Theory and Social Issues: Historical Texts and Contemporary Readings*, ed. David Theo Goldberg, 2d ed. (Orlando, FL: Harcourt Brace, 1995), pp. 337, 341. Even Andrew Altman, in arguing for restriction, rejects emotional harm as a justification. See his "Liberalism and Campus Hate Speech: A Philosophical Examination," in Goldberg, *Ethical Theory*, pp. 353-65.

51. Strossen, "Balancing Rights," p. 337.
52. This is the approach of Norman Itzkowitz. See Theriault, "Universal Social Theory and Denial," pp. 241-56. On the other hand, in a case in which a person or the person's group has not suffered an injury that he or she firmly believes to have occurred, any emotional pain felt as a consequence of this false belief is clearly subjective. Genuine Armenian psychological harm resulting from the genocide or its denial is not balanced by the distress felt by some Turkish people because they have been convinced of denialist claims of great Turkish suffering at the hands of Armenians.
53. The following theory of the psychological effects of denial on survivors and other Armenians primarily concerns their metaphysical (causal) nature and ethical implications. That survivors experience serious and continuing psychological pain from the genocide and its denial is perhaps obvious, but various sources confirm this fact, including 1) three clinical studies: Anie Kalayjian and Siroon P. Shahinian, "Recollections of Aged Armenian Survivors of the Ottoman Turkish Genocide: Resilience Through Endurance, Coping, and Life Accomplishments," *Psychoanalytic Review* 85:4 (1998): 489-504; Anie Kalayjian, Siroon P. Shahinian, E.L. Gergerian, and L. Saraydian, "Coping with Ottoman Turkish Genocide: An Exploration of the Experience of Armenian Survivors," *Journal of Traumatic Stress* 9 (1996): 87-97; Levon Boyajian and Haigaz Grigorian, "Psychosocial Sequelae of the Armenian Genocide," in Hovannisian, *Armenian Genocide in Perspective*, pp. 177-85; 2) statements by survivors in genocide commemorative programs, newspaper articles, and documentary films as well as my own small interactions with survivors; and 3) accounts from children and grandchildren of survivors conveyed in private conversations, public settings, or published works, such as Peter Balakian, *Black Dog of Fate* (New York: Bantam Doubleday Dell-Broadway Books, 1997).
54. Charny, "The Psychology of Denial," pp. 22-23.
55. This treatment of the psychological pain the genocide and its denial cause for members of post-survivor generations is based on personal discussions with hundreds of individuals in this category and their speeches and writings, genocide commemoration addresses, letters to the editor, full-length memoirs, such as Michael J. Arlen's *Passage to Ararat*, and comments made at public discussions of and educational programs on the genocide. It is consistent with the findings in Boyajian and Grigorian, "Psychosocial Sequelae of the Armenian Genocide" pp. 181ff. It is also consistent in broad terms with the observations presented in Boyajian and Grigorian, "Reflections on the Denial of the Armenian Genocide," *Psychoanalytic Review* 85:4 (1998): 505-16, but differs on certain particular interpretative points.
56. Boyajian and Grigorian, "Psychosocial Sequelae," pp. 181ff. and "Reflections on Denial," pp. 505-16, are two such studies dealing specifically with the Armenian Genocide.
57. See Hovannisian, "Denial of the Armenian Genocide," pp. 217-19; Aghjayan, "Genocide Denial," pp. 10-14.
58. Strossen, "Balancing Rights," p. 337; Feinberg, "The Harm Principle," p. 404.
59. The United Nations definition of genocide includes five methods of genocide. As Richard Hovannisian points out, the Armenian Genocide is a rare instance in which all five were employed. See his introduction to Hovannisian, *Remembrance and Denial*, p. 14.
60. Smith, Markusen, and Lifton, "Professional Ethics and Denial," pp. 1-22.
61. This is Steven Jacobs' fitting phrase, in reference to Holocaust denier David Irving. See Steven L. Jacobs, "Holocaust/Shoah Revisionists," in *Encyclopedia of Genocide*, ed. Israel Charny, vol. 1 (Santa Barbara, CA: ABC-CLIO, 1999), p. 184. For

the related concept of "the deniability of denial," the degree to which features of a denial argument undermine charges of denial, see Theriault, "Universal Social Theory and Denial," p. 244.

62. For the basis of this distinction, see Aristotle, *Nicomachean Ethics*, trans. W. D. Ross, revised, J. O. Urmson, in *The Complete Works of Aristotle*, ed. Jonathan Barnes, vol. 2 (Princeton, NJ: Princeton University Press, 1984), pp. 1729-1867.
63. See Charny and Fromer, "Denying the Armenian Genocide," pp. 39-49.
64. See Strossen, "Balancing Rights," pp. 342-43; Arthur, "Sticks and Stones," pp. 109-10.
65. The most widely cited evidence of this feeling of impunity is a statement Hitler made before the 1939 invasion of Poland. Some generals were concerned that Hitler's order to maximize civilian death and suffering would open them up to punishment for war crimes. Dismissing this possibility, he responded: "Who, after all, speaks today of the annihilation of the Armenians?" See Kevork Bardakjian, *Hitler and the Armenian Genocide* (Cambridge, MA: Zoryan Institute, 1985): pp. 1-2, 25-42.
66. Statement of Kevin Dodson in comments on Henry Theriault, "Freedom of Speech and the Intentional Denial of Genocide," presentation, 28th Conference on Value Inquiry, Lamar University, Beaumont, Texas, April 14, 2000.
67. Justin McCarthy, "Let Historians Decide on So-Called Genocide," and his "Anatolia 1915: Turks Died, Too," *Boston Globe*, April 25, 1998, p. 17.
68. See, for instance, "Declaration by the Turkish Academicians on the Turkish-Armenian Problem, April 23, 2001," *The Turkish Times*, May 15, 2001, http://www.ataa.org/times/news/html (May 19, 2001). It is telling that the vast majority of the more than 100 "Turkish Academician" signatories of this statement are in physical sciences, engineering, biotechnical, and professional disciplines unrelated to study of Turkish history.
69. The Livingston Group, LLC, "Key Facts to Consider Regarding H.Res. 398," (no date).
70. Embassy of the Turkish Republic, "The Armenian Allegation of Genocide: The Issue and the Facts," under "Politics & Policy," http://www.turkey.org (Aug. 4, 2001).
71. Deniers often complain that their free speech rights are suppressed when their views do not appear alongside published statements about the genocide or if in public forums these statements are given more attention than denialist claims. Such protests distort the meaning of freedom of speech. The right does not guarantee access to the podium during a discussion of the genocide or publication of a response to a newspaper or scholarly article on the genocide, or automatic inclusion of denial sources next to information on the genocide in school curricula. It does not require that deniers receive equal attention from politicians, professors, journalists, or private citizens. And it especially does not oblige the government or any other group (especially Armenians) to help deniers disseminate their propaganda. It is a "negative" freedom from interference. It means only that, say, if a Turkish group organizes a discussion, neither the U.S. government nor any other group or individual has the right to stop it.
72. A variety of reports document the Turkish government's antagonism toward freedom of expression within Turkey. Examples include the United States, Department of State, Bureau of Democracy, Human Rights, and Labor, "Country Report on Human Rights Practices—2000: Turkey," Feb. 2001, http://www.state.gov/g/drl/rls/hrrpt/2000/eur/index.cfm?docid=844 (Aug. 4, 2001), as well as reports of previous years; Human Rights Watch, "Turkey," in *World Report 2001*, http://www.hrw.org/wr2k1/Europe/turkey.html; Human Rights Watch, *Violations of Free*

Expression in Turkey, Feb. 1999, http//:www.hrw.org/press/1999/apr/turkey1504.htm (July 27, 2000); the Committee to Protect Journalists, "Country Report: Turkey," 2000, http://www.cpj.org/attacks00/mideast00/Turkey.html (Aug. 4, 2001); Committee to Protect Journalists, "Journalists in Prison in 2000," in *Attacks on the Press in 2000*, March 2001, http://www.cpj.org/attacks00/pages_att00/attacks00.html (Aug. 4, 2001).

73. Cf. Strossen, "Balancing Rights," pp. 344, 347-50.

13

Healing and Reconciliation

Ervin Staub

I have been studying the origins of genocide and mass killing for many years, trying to understand how people are capable of such violence and how it comes about that a society engages in the horrible acts involved. My concern with roots or origins comes from a deep desire to find out what we can do to prevent such violence.[1]

While prevention has always been part of my work, in recent years it has become the central focus.[2] Here, I shall consider primarily healing by victimized groups and reconciliation between groups as elements of prevention. There are many other aspects as well. The behavior of bystanders, especially the passivity of the international community, contributes to genocide. Actions by bystander nations can be very important in preventing genocide.[3] Even actions by a small but committed group can make a difference in inhibiting violence. The efforts of the Baha'i community around the world led the United Nations and some individual countries to protest the executions of Baha'i in Iran in the 1970s, which led to their discontinuation[4]—although they resumed on a much smaller scale in the early 1990s.

The Impact of Genocidal Violence on Survivors

Members of groups that have been victimized by the horrors of genocide or mass killing and who have survived are deeply affected in many and varied ways. What are some of these effects? One effect that has limited direct relevance to Armenians alive today is post-traumatic stress disorder (PTSD). Post-traumatic stress disorder includes anxiety, hyper-vigilance, arousal, as well as numbness and avoidance of remembering and thinking about painful events, together with intrusive imagery and nightmares.[5] It is relevant to Armenians today because trauma can be transmitted by survivors to children and grandchildren and on to later generations.

Another important effect is on the sense of self.[6] If a group has been victimized in horrible ways, almost invariably, in a really deep sense, the question is present for its members: who am I, and who are we, that something like this would have been done to us? This usually is not conscious. Consciously, people may know and believe that they were innocent victims, but in a very deep part of themselves there is likely to be a feeling that something is wrong with them, with their group. This creates a deep sense of vulnerability in the world. If they could be victimized as they were, it can be done again. This vulnerability is also because of another effect of genocidal violence, an orientation that survivors develop toward the outside world, a sense of mistrust, of danger, of seeing people and the world as dangerous.[7] I have come to think more and more in terms of profound, universal human needs that are involved both in the perpetration of genocide and in the "woundedness" of survivors. The intense frustration of these needs can in fact be a starting point leading to the perpetration of genocide.[8] Genocide, in turn, painfully frustrates the vital human needs in survivors.

Human beings have fundamental psychological needs to feel secure from physical and psychological harm, to have a positive view of self or identity, to feel effective in the world and have a sense of control over important events in their lives, to be connected to other human beings. These instincts are severely weakened by intense victimization. People also have a need for understanding the world, of how life is lived, which is thwarted by the overthrow of normal ways of life that genocide represents.[9] Finally, when these needs are reasonably satisfied, another important urge emerges, the need for spirituality, for transcendence, for going beyond the self. Severe trauma results in a focus on basic needs and on the self and thereby limits spirituality and transcendence. In this way it interferes with growth and fulfillment.

These needs are not only undermined for people who are direct survivors, who were present, with their lives in danger, but also for those members of the group who have lived in safety, in some distant place. Because our identity is deeply rooted in racial, ethnic, or religious groups, members of the group who were not present still carry many of the burdens of the collective experience.

Even the later generations, the unborn children, are affected. This happens in part through emotional reactions of and communications by parents in the course of everyday life. Insecurity, anxiety, mistrust in people are all transmitted to children. They are also conveyed through parental practices in raising children. Past history can lead parents to be afraid all the time that something will happen to their child. Being overprotective of children, keeping them very close to parents, confining them to "safe" places and activities, can limit their growth.

The research findings on "representative" (rather than clinical) samples of children of Holocaust survivors, who have been studied to a fair extent, indicate that the trauma of the parents does not usually result in psychopathology in the children. However, some of the children, especially those whose parents do not talk about their own suffering, are affected in their interpersonal relationships. They have difficulty trusting people, avoid intimacy, perceive other people in negative terms, and also describe themselves as cold, vindictive, and socially aloof.[10] Children who are less affected are normally those whose parents have talked about their experiences in the genocide, such as being in camps, rather than concealing the past in order to protect the children or themselves. They have discussed these events in a factual manner, without overwhelming the children with their feelings.

Wounded people can also be harsh and punitive. Thinking about Jews and Armenians, for example, in both groups families tend to be close, with much love. Children in both groups may be especially cherished because so much was lost. One would think that there should be no harshness. In spite of that, some children of survivors do mention sternness and unpredictability by their parents. While this may not be common, it is a psychologically understandable effect of trauma that makes living a normal life more difficult.

Growthful Effects of Trauma and Survival

The effects of trauma are not all negative. Research with individuals who have suffered physical or sexual abuse, injurious accidents, life-threatening illnesses, or other trauma-causing experiences shows that in addition to the problematic and negative impact there are also some positive, "growthful" effects.[11] People can gain an intense appreciation of life and come to cherish every single day.

It is also the case that people who survive group violence, while they have usually benefited from an element of luck, often have taken action to save themselves. In threatening circumstances they may sometimes make difficult, courageous decisions. They step forward and put themselves into a new situation that may turn out to be even more dangerous than the previous one in the hope of protecting their families and themselves. So, often survivors have learned to act when action is needed.

Young children who are part of this environment see this behavior. They observe the actions of their parents or others who did things to save them. I am a child survivor of the Holocaust. I was six years old in Budapest, Hungary, in 1944, the year when about 450 thousand Hungarian Jews were killed, most of them transported to Auschwitz and gassed. My own parents engaged in incredibly resourceful measures that contributed to our survival. This made me learn, I believe, that it is possible to take effective action in life and that what one does can make a difference. On the negative side, all this also taught me that those who could not or would not take the initiative were doomed. One cannot just wait and see how things turn out.

Another growthful aspect is that frequently people who have survived have gotten help from some source. Sometimes, Armenians and other survivors of genocide received assistance for which they had to pay, but at other times they were helped by caring, altruistic people. This experience can facilitate later healing by showing that in the midst of evil there is also the reality of human goodness. Unfortunately, when I was in Rwanda interviewing Tutsi survivors who were saved by Hutus, I found that amid extreme evil it can be difficult to see goodness even in those of the other group who have taken risks to shield and help.[12]

Children and later generations are also affected by the way the group remembers and memorializes the terrible events. This can either help with healing or create severe problems for the group. I will later return to constructive and destructive ways of carrying the memories of past victimization.

From Trauma to Perpetration

A potential effect of victimization of a group has been of special concern to me. Groups of people who have been so horribly treated and have not healed from the inflicted psychological wounds can under certain conditions become perpetrators themselves.[13] Feeling vulnerable and seeing other people, especially those outside the group, as dangerous and threatening is a source of this behavior. When there is conflict, it becomes more difficult to take the perspective of the other side and to negotiate in constructive ways. More likely, the insecure group will strike out, its members believing that they are defending themselves but actually becoming perpetrators of new violence.

Healing is essential to allow people to have satisfying and fulfilling lives and to improve conditions for their children and future generations. Healing is also critical to make it less likely that there will be a continuing cycle of violence. The danger of a victimized group with open wounds becoming a perpetrator is especially present under menacing conditions. For example, neither the Armenian community nor the Jewish community in the United States faces serious threat or danger. However, the Armenian people in Armenia and the Jewish people in Israel do face danger. Under conditions of threat, the external danger and the internal sense of danger growing out of past history tend to merge.

Healing by Victimized Groups

What is required for healing? Empathy, support, and acknowledgment of the group's suffering by the rest of the world can make a major difference. What does this do? World acknowledgement of the horrible violence and suffering tells survivors that what they have experienced is not normal, that the world does not view it as tolerable or acceptable. This can help survivors feel that they were not at fault, that nothing was wrong with them, and allow them to believe that it is not likely to happen again. In addition, receiving empathy from others has a healing effect, especially as it enables people to feel empathy with themselves.

Ideally, one should receive acknowledgment of the suffering from the perpetrators as well. This almost never happens. But sometimes, rarely enough, the rest of the world will give recognition and reach out. Even if this is done to a limited extent, it makes a great difference to survivors. For example, after abandonment by the world, the people in Rwanda reacted very strongly to President Clinton stopping at the airport in Kigali and expressing his regret for his own nation's passivity, which was a contributor to the genocide in Rwanda. The United States was not only a passive bystander, but at some point its reluctance to get involved thwarted attempts of the United Nations to send peacekeepers back into Rwanda.[14] Whatever the reason for Bill Clinton's apology, it was mentioned by people again and again while I was in Rwanda. It had special meaning for them.

While acknowledgment has a positive effect, not surprisingly, denial of victimization and suffering has the opposite impact. Denial intensifies pain. It interferes with the healing process, generates anger, and redoubles efforts to establish the truth about what was done. Even when the victimization of a group is not denied, it is often ignored. It becomes important, therefore, for groups that have suffered to minimize their dependence on the outside world and to deal with their pain and suffering by engaging in healing processes internally.

Not relying on perpetrators or the world in general for healing but finding trustworthy others who show empathy is also important in individual victimization such as sexual or physical abuse. Very often neither the perpetrators nor their family members who were passive bystanders acknowledge what has been done.[15] They deny the occurrence or refuse to talk about it or show remorse. Since such relatives withhold support, the victims must turn to other people to affirm the truth and gain empathy and encouragement.

Not much knowledge has accumulated about group healing. There are no good examples of efforts to help groups of people close their wounds or of natural healing. Most of the knowledge is derived from research and therapy with traumatized individuals rather than groups. It also comes from research and therapy with Holocaust survivors and with members of victimized groups in Bosnia.[16] A certain degree of experience and knowledge has been gained through work in Rwanda.[17] A part of what follows is based on these sources and on theory derived from them.

What are some of the processes that can help with healing? One is engagement with the past. It is extremely important to face what has happened, to confront painful experiences. It is also essential for this to happen under supportive conditions, when people can join together and receive as well as give encouragement to each other. For Armenians, this may mean confronting both what occurred at the time of the genocide and also what may have happened in their families and communities since then, as the result of genocide, flight, starting new lives in new places, denial of the genocide, and other experiences.

People may talk with each other and inquire about how their families were affected at the time; how did people live; what was lost; what has happened since; how were grandparents, parents, children, and the current generation impacted. There is great value at looking at all this, feeling it, grieving over it, supporting each other. Many questions can be asked about loss, suffering, and sadness. Doing this also opens the way to talk about the good things that have developed over time. All this can be done within small groups of people.

Ceremonies, memorials, and testimonials are also helpful. They can happen on a larger scale, with many people, and can involve outsiders. What kind of ceremonies are useful? On the one hand, ceremonies can focus singularly on pain and sorrow in a way that maintains woundedness and a sense of endangerment. They can enhance isolation, generate the desire for revenge, and feed unhealthy nationalism. Seemingly, the Serbs focused on their woundedness in grieving their defeat by the Turkish army in Kosovo in the fourteenth century. Of course, in the case of the Serbs this focus was reinforced by centuries of Turkish domination. Nonetheless, the way Kosovo was memorialized may have contributed to harmful manifestations of nationalism. Alternatively, testimonials and ceremonies can grieve the past but also open the group to connections with the outside world, generate hope, and show possibilities for constructive rebuilding of lives.

Between 1998 and 2000, my associate, Dr. Laurie Anne Pearlman, and I were engaged in a project in Rwanda on healing, forgiveness, and reconciliation. What motivated this project was my hope that any degree of healing from the genocide of 1994 might reduce the likelihood of a continuing cycle of violence between Hutus and Tutsis. The way we tried to promote healing was partly experiential, getting people to talk about what has happened to them. We asked them to write, to draw something, or simply to think about their experiences. Then they discussed these in small groups. In Rwanda, it was not only strangers who killed. In mixed families, Hutus would give up Tutsi family members or sometimes killed them themselves. Neighbors would come into the house to kill. Talking about these incredible things, combined with a sympathetic response and support of others, seemed to have a genuinely healing effect for people.

We also provided psychological education. One element seemed extremely powerful for people: hearing talks on and then discussing the origins of genocide. How does such violence come about? Gaining some understanding of how genocide originates seemed to lead people to feel more human, to be humanized in their own eyes. Our participants did not know much about other genocides. Information about other victims in the course of talking about the origins of genocide was very meaningful to people. They came to feel that if these terrible things were done to others as well and are the result of understandable human processes, then they themselves were not placed outside the realm of humanity by what happened in Rwanda.

Another element in healing is establishing the truth. People respond powerfully to an affirmation of what has actually happened. Truth is important for justice, but even by itself it contributes to healing. A number of countries, from Argentina to South Africa, have established truth commissions.[18] Unfortunately, the truth is often complicated, and groups with different involvement in violence maintain and assert their own truths. An international truth commission that is unbiased except for its goal to establish what has actually happened would be extremely valuable. Establishing the truth not only helps victims but makes it less likely that members of the former perpetrator group feel victimized by the punishment of guilty and convicted persons from among them.

Assuming the role of positive bystanders in the world also contributes to healing, whereas becoming a passive bystander contributes to the conditions for genocide. Persons whose group has been victimized can do much good in the world. It has been found in work with individual trauma survivors that part of healing is to give some kind of meaning to their suffering. But how can one make genocide meaningful? The same question applies to other traumas as well. How can one create meaning, for example, out of being severely abused as a child? One answer may be: "Because I suffered and because I understand this, I can make a difference in the world. I can use my own suffering to inform others, to tell the world, and to be a positive influence." This kind of response, I believe, strongly facilitates healing.

The Need to Reconcile

When two groups continue to live together after a genocide or mass killing, as in Rwanda or Bosnia, reconciliation becomes very important. There can be no reconciliation without some degree of healing. But it is difficult to proceed with healing if groups refuse to begin the process. Without some movement toward reconciliation, members of the victim group will continue to feel tremendously endangered. They will justifiably feel that if the people who did horrible things to them continue to live next to them, they will have to be alert and watch out all the time. Feeling unsafe is a major hindrance to healing.

Reconciliation involves a real acceptance of each other. It is a mutual process involving both victims and perpetrators. There can be no reconciliation without the two groups engaging with each other: talking about what has happened, accepting responsibility for what has been done, participating in joint activities for shared goals, and so on. Perpetrators are often not open to this. They are also intensely wounded—wounded by their own violence. They cannot commit the kind of deeds that are involved in genocide without being affected by their own actions. Perpetrators tend to protect themselves from this pain by surrounding themselves with a shell. They continue to devalue the other group and blame it for instigating the measures taken against it. And as long as perpetrators do this, their own ability to live freely and open up to the world is stymied.

Imagine what Germany would be like today without the Nuremberg trials. This goes back to the issue of truth, in that an important effect of the Nuremberg trials and its millions of pages of documents was that it showed incontrovertibly—incontrovertibly at the time, because Holocaust deniers have appeared since—to many Germans what their own country had done. Most Germans, albeit tentatively and reluctantly, opened up to some reasonable degree to seeing the truth. Gunter Grass may have become a writer about genocide and German culpability because he was one of those persons whom the American forces made to march around a concentration camp to see what such treatment was like.

Healing for the perpetrators is important both for themselves and for the rest of the world. But it is difficult to engage unwilling perpetrators in the process. As long as there is no officially established international truth commission set up by the United Nations or other international organizations, it might be possible to create truth commissions composed of important public persons, for example, eminent Nobel Peace Prize winners. It is a critical challenge to find ways to promote acceptance of the truth and self-awareness in perpetrators.

I have come to feel some empathy with perpetrators of past violence or at least members of the perpetrator group and their descendants. The frozen state in which they find themselves because of denial of the group's guilt and their continued blaming of others are quite tragic. I feel a lot of anger with passive bystanders. These are people who do not engage and who are not actively part of the psychological and social processes that lead to genocide, but rather who stand on the side, see what is happening, have an opportunity to take action, yet go on with business as usual. I do not mean primarily internal bystanders, members of the population in a country that is moving toward genocide, for they are shaped by their culture. Rather, I mean the external bystanders, the international community, which can take varied actions without substantial risk to itself but usually does not.[19]

One may ask what forms of healing are appropriate and acceptable to Armenians. What would reconciliation mean and what does it require, especially in Armenia, the place where circumstances make it relevant and important, where relations with Turkey make it most significant? What I have learned in Rwanda is that each group has to work out for itself in what way any ideas, anything in the realm of healing and reconciliation, are useful. The act of engaging in this effort has great value.

A Note on Forgiveness

Our project in Rwanda has been supported by the John Templeton Foundation's program on the scientific study of forgiveness. The project's title is "Healing, Forgiveness, and Reconciliation in Rwanda." When I first considered applying for this grant, I thought, how can one think about forgiveness only three or four years after the genocide? Is it possible or even appropriate?

As it turned out, people in Rwanda began themselves to talk about forgiveness. They were saying the very things that we know from the limited research that exists on forgiveness as imperative for reconciliation: "I cannot forgive them until they admit what they have done," and "I cannot forgive them until they apologize for their actions." There is also the question of whom to forgive, with whom to reconcile. Forgiveness, as well as reconciliation, when they involve relationships between groups, may involve members of the other group who have not been perpetrators. Or they may involve or be aimed at descendants of perpetrators or other members of the group.

Groups that have survived genocide tend to keep the notion of forgiveness distant from themselves. I dare to talk about it in the context of genocide only because I am a Holocaust survivor. An important point is that forgiveness is not primarily for the benefit of the perpetrator. Forgiveness is to the benefit of those who have been harmed. Research shows that when victims of physical abuse, for example, begin to be able to forgive, which may not even involve any contact with the perpetrator, there is psychological relief, a letting go, a giving up of a burden. Forgiveness is not a practical act. It is a spiritual act. And in my view it does not release perpetrators from their responsibility.

Notes

1. See the following studies of Ervin Staub: *The Roots of Evil: The Origins of Genocide and Other Group Violence* (New York: Cambridge University Press, 1989); "The Psychology of Bystanders, Perpetrators and Heroic Helpers," *International Journal of Intercultural Relations* 17 (1993): 315-41; "Cultural-Societal Roots of Violence: The Examples of Genocidal Violence and of Contemporary Youth Violence in the United States," *American Psychologist* 51 (1996): 117-32; *A Brighter Future: The Development of Caring and Nonviolent Children*, forthcoming, Oxford University Press.
2. See the following: "Breaking the Cycle of Genocide Violence: Healing and Reconciliation," in J. Harvey, ed., *Perspective on Loss: A Source Book* (Washington DC: Taylor and Francis, 1998), pp. 221-38; *A Brighter Future*; "Mass Murder: Origins, Prevention and U.S. Involvement," in Ronald Gottesman and Richard M. Brown, eds., *Encyclopedia of Violence in America* (New York: Scribner, 1999); Ervin Staub and Laurie Anne Pearlman, "Healing, Forgiveness and Reconciliation after Genocide and Other Collective Violence," in *Forgiveness and Reconciliation: Religious Contributions to Conflict Resolution* (Radnor, PA: Templeton Foundation Press, 2001), pp. 205-29.
3. Philip Gourevich, *We Wish to Inform You That Tomorrow We Will Be Killed with Our Families* (New York: Farrar, Strauss, Giroux, 1998); Staub, *Roots of Evil*, and *A Brighter Future*.

4. K. R. Bigelow, "A Campaign to Deter Genocide: The Baha'i Experience," in Helen Fein, ed., *Genocide Watch* (New Haven: Yale University Press, 1999), 189-97.
5. Judith L. Herman, *Trauma and Recovery* (New York: Basic Books, 1992); I. Lisa McCann and Laurie Anne Pearlman, *Psychological Trauma and the Adult Survivor: Theory, Therapy, and Transformation* (New York: Bruner/Mazel, 1990).
6. Laurie Anne Pearlman and Karen W. Saakvitne, *Trauma and the Therapist* (New York: Norton, 1995).
7. Staub, *Roots of Evil*; Staub and Pearlman, "Healing, Forgiveness and Reconciliation."
8. Staub, *Roots of Evil.*
9. Staub, "Cultural-Societal Roots of Violence," and *Roots of Evil.*
10. H. Wiseman et al., "Parental Communication of Holocaust Experiences and Interpersonal Patterns of Offspring of Holocaust Survivors" (Haifa: University of Haifa, 2000), manuscript in the School of Education.
11. Ronnie Janoff-Bulman and Michael Berg, "Disillusionment and the Creation of Values: From Traumatic Losses to Existential Gains," in John H. Harvey, ed., *Perspectives on Loss: A Source Book* (Washington, DC: Taylor and Francis, 1998), pp. 35-39.
12. Staub and Pearlman, "Healing, Forgiveness and Reconciliation."
13. Staub, "Breaking the Cycle of Genocide Violence."
14. Alison Des Forges, *Leave None to Tell the Story: Genocide in Rwanda* (New York: Human Rights Watch, 1999); Gourevich, *We Wish to Inform You*; Staub, *A Brighter Future*.
15. Herman, *Trauma and Recovery*.
16. Inger Agger and Soren Buss Jensen, *Trauma and Recovery under State Terrorism* (London: Zed, 1996); Stevan M. Weine, *When History Is a Nightmare: Lives and Memories of Ethnic Cleansing in Bosnia-Herzegovina* (New Brunswick, NJ: Rutgers University Press, 1999).
17. Staub, "Mass Murder"; Staub and Pearlman, "Healing, Forgiveness and Reconciliation."
18. Nunca Mas, *The Report of the Argentine National Commission on the Disappeared* (New York: Farrar, Straus, Giroux, 1986); Ervin Staub, and Daniel Bar-Tal, "Genocide and Intractable Conflict: Roots, Evolution, Prevention, and Reconciliation," in David Sears, Leonie Huddy, and Robert Jervis, eds., *Handbook of Political Psychology* (New York: Oxford University Press, forthcoming).
19. Staub, *Roots of Evil,* and *A Brighter Future*.

14

State and Nation: Their Roles after Independence

Raffi K. Hovannisian

The decades separating us from the Armenian Genocide—the prototype of modern-day nation-killings—have fundamentally changed the political composition of the region. Virtually no Armenians remain on their historic territories in what is today eastern Turkey. The Armenian people have been scattered about the world. And a small independent republic has come to replace the Armenian Soviet Socialist Republic, which was all that was left of the homeland as the result of Turkish invasion and Bolshevik collusion in 1920.

But one thing has stayed the same. Notwithstanding the eloquent, compelling evidence housed in the United States National Archives and repositories around the world, successive Turkish governments have denied that the predecessor Young Turk regime committed genocide. Making facially plausible but essentially empty arguments of an Armenian "rebellion," a mutually deadly civil war, and Armenian collaboration with the Allied Powers in World War I, the Turkish authorities have flouted the worldwide testimony, rejected the charge of genocide, and—like the Nazis who followed—sought aggressively to deflect blame by accusing the victims themselves.

What is more, Turkish officialdom, far from educating new generations about the crimes of their predecessors, has attempted to cover up the evidence and has gone to great lengths to entice American and other apologists of some repute to assist in this effort. Perhaps the time has come for Turkey to reassess the propriety of its approach, to take Germany and its road to redemption as an exemplary precedent, and to begin the process that will allow it to move into a post-genocide era.

Turkey and the now sovereign Republic of Armenia are neighbors. Since its declaration of independence in September 1991, Armenia has integrated into its foreign policy the desire to regulate relations with all neighboring countries, including Turkey, hoping in this case that initiation of consular and economic links would prepare in due course a climate in which political normalization would be possible. Ironically, it has been official Ankara, citing a variety of domestic and international considerations, that has not reciprocated in kind or intent, instead refusing to establish diplomatic ties with Erevan and closing the border to commercial traffic, passenger land crossings, and humanitarian shipments, thereby completing an Azerbaijani blockade of landlocked Armenia. Skirting the watershed issue of genocide and its legacy, then, has only compounded the mutual relationship, which remains strained to this day.

In short, Turkey has not acted in good faith—to the detriment of both nations. Just as Armenia needs access to Turkish roads and ports to reach European destinations, so, too, could Turkey profit from unhindered transit over the Armenian roads and railways to points in the rest of the former Soviet Union. More important, at a time when Turkey faces a full internal, external, and Euro-integration agenda, both in political and economic terms, its interests should indeed dictate that it come out once and for all of its "genocide closet," just as Armenia's interests demand peace on its western frontier.

The Turkish-Armenian knot that history has bequeathed to both peoples can be loosened only by the normalization of relations. And the record of the past years demonstrates that normalization can result, not from a puerile fiction that nothing has happened in their history, but rather from a brave, fact-anchored reexamination of the issues dividing them, the definition of a program for negotiations, and the conclusion of a comprehensive, lasting solution achieved by direct dialogue and hard, honest exchanges of views.

Entering into political discourse with Armenia, rather than avoiding it, will enable Turkey to free itself and its generations from constantly having to look back defensively over the shoulder of their past. The Turkish youth will be able to learn the lessons associated with recognizing the excesses of the Ottoman state, as well as the stories of individual Turks who saved many Armenians from certain death. And the Turkish state will send a signal to countries near and far that it is prepared to take the high road in advancing bilateral relationships, enhancing regional security, and finally grasping the connection between its image-robbing refusal to communicate on the Armenian Genocide and its ongoing affront to its own people's openness and freedom of expression.

The proposed process will be easy neither for Turks nor for Armenians. In fact, governments on both sides of the border may offer resistance to this approach, arguing that it is not pragmatic or sensitive to the existing political landscape. Domestic opinion, for its part, may be unleashed to block development of discussions. But there is no escape. If Turkey and Armenia want to attain the heights of true normalization—window dressing excluded—then they must start facing the central questions of their common inheritance. These no doubt hold the keys to more peaceful, prosperous, and harmonious horizons. Turks and Armenians will have to defy the odds of history, grapple with their thorny issues, and ultimately give resolution to them. They owe it to the children of their children, who are destined to live side by side in the same geopolitical neighborhood.

Against this backdrop, the Armenian people and their republic face in the twenty-first century a complex challenge of defining identity and formulating policy in a way that responds at once to the imperatives of historical remembrance, the pursuit of vital state interests, and the controlling context of national security both in Armenia and abroad. Achievement of a broad-based consensus among the politically and geographically disparate components of the Armenian polity will require strategic vision, tactical flexibility, and a distinguished assumption and performance of roles.

At bottom, however, both nation and state, in contemplating their approaches in the new era to the Armenian Genocide, must coordinate and master a spectrum of activities between ensuring historical memory and pressing legal redemption, from defense of human rights to expression of collective aspirations. This critical equilibrium of ways and means accepts the genocide, its domestic and foreign instruction, and its universal affirmation as a necessary point of departure, and it views the physical and spiritual integrity of the Republic of Armenia, the Armenian Diaspora, and their history as national values to be protected at all cost.

The Armenian republic's ambivalent policy since 1992 begs the question of state responsibility to remember national calamity. A variety of officials, both former and current, have joined a selection of foreign representatives in making the caveat that "politicizing" memory and thus preventing development of good-neighborly relations would resubmit Armenia to its all-too-frequent cruel fate in history. They posit the need to save subsequent generations from their genocide-driven shackles in order to take on a forward-looking modern identity that can keep stride with the growing demands and attractions of globalization.

The first years of the new Republic of Armenia were marked by fruitless Armenian initiatives and standard Turkish responses, including but not limited to demanding as a precondition Erevan's relinquishment of "genocide claims," relative to the policy objective of the normalization of relations. Witness as evidentiary examples:

a) Armenian diplomacy's first major challenge at the January 1992 meeting in Prague of the foreign ministers of the Conference on Security and Cooperation in Europe (CSCE), where Armenia was granted membership in the organization only after its principled position compelled withdrawal of a threatened Turkish veto intended, among other things, to force Armenia to renounce any genocide-related claims.

b) Turkey's active lobbying of the Council of Europe to deprive Armenia of special guest status and ultimate membership, eliciting the Armenian foreign minister's critique of Turkish policies at the ministerial meeting of the Council at Istanbul in September 1992.

This record, in a fundamental sense, has provided conceptual depth to and practical evidence of the following theses:

1) The entire range of positions taken by the Armenian nation and its constituent parts, in the first instance the Republic of Armenia, cannot but be founded on historical memory. There indeed do exist room and reason for diversity of substantive approaches between state and nation, homeland and Diaspora, political associations and non-governmental rights groups. But the fundamental policy source, from which flows the immutable procedural right of the Armenian people to seek recognition, demand redress, and obtain some degree of closure, is one and the same. This axiom applies equally to activity in the executive, judicial, legislative, and educational realms.

2) Recognition, resolution, and reconciliation are in the interest of the Armenian and Turkish peoples and states but will

require positive external impulses. This encompassing statement underscores the pressing need for a qualitative differentiation between past and present, for personal cleansing and an ethical recasting of expedient politics, for unified defense against recurrence, and for creation of a new security architecture in the region. A first step in this long process of normalization requires the international community to bring the matter of genocide affirmation above board by renewing official recognition and encouraging Turkey to do so as well. In this process, the United States should play a leading role. Official American recognition of the Armenian Genocide is among the most important contributions Washington can make to the long-term interests of Armenia and Turkey, to stability along Armenia's border with Turkey, and therefore to development of a crucial new system of regional security in which the two states are true partners. In view of its own complicity in the Armenian Genocide, Germany also has a special responsibility to support Armenia and Turkey toward this end.

3) There can be no comprehensive normalization of relations without such resolution and the attendant mutual respect, although confidence-building measures in advance might under certain circumstances facilitate attainment of that objective. Joint economic, scientific, cultural, and academic endeavors can be helpful in creating a favorable atmosphere if they demonstrate historical regard, not state-sponsored revisionism. Yet such initiatives alone will not be deep or broad enough to surmount the genocide-founded wall of distrust. While certain Turkish scholarly circles recently have taken commendable steps in this direction, they remain far from representing the academic mainstream, let alone the ever-potent political-military establishment. Similarly, trade and commercial contacts between the countries, expressive as they are of natural economic propensities, still are indirect, intermediate, and perforce of episodic character. In this connection, the Armenian authorities have sometimes taken a tactically conciliatory position on the genocide issue in the belief that Turkey could move beyond its irrational defense mechanisms and, in shared trust, normalize relations in these and all other spheres. In each case, however, they have been disappointed. Tactical compromise of the genocide, it has been repeatedly shown, can never achieve real long-range results.

4) The underlying national bedrock, for the state as for the people, entails full settlement of the matter but never at the expense of the security of either. Vital state interests and Armenian security dimensions draw on the national genocide experience as policy lesson and guide—the imperative to defend Armenian rights, individual and collective, around the world and simultaneously to deal flexibly and effectively in a geostrategically charged environment. Armenia's administration and the Armenian people must steer clear of serving the shifting interests of external forces or of embracing without warranty the enticing pledges proffered by others. Rather, it behooves them to forge a strong, secure, and legitimate state structure, which is an essential prerequisite for the cultivation of political conditions for recognition of the Armenian Genocide.

5) The Armenians and, for that matter, the Turks of the twenty-first century, whether on an official level or as ordinary citizens, at home and in dispersion, can become constructive, modern contributors to peace and progress, culture and civilization. This engagement envisages a self-confident tete-à-tete with their history, drawing lessons from it and finding their roles relating to it, not seeking the hatch to a false modernity that is devoid of memory and hence of meaning, conscience, and identity. Identity depends on the possibility of communication; truth sets it free, while untruth empties it. Just as an imprisoned individual loses his liberty and thus himself, so too has the Armenian Genocide deprived Turkey of its self-esteem and self-recognition. The state guards against and fights away even involuntary revelations and consequently disparages freedom of thought and expression to this very day. Turkey's coming to terms with itself would be tantamount to discovering a path between its past and present culpability—a discovery based on integrity and dialogue with its own citizenry, the Armenian people, and the world. In this vein, the declaration of the Stockholm International Forum on the Holocaust in January 2000 testifies to the currency and capacity of concerted, recognition-oriented governmental and public action and forcefully rejects ulteriorly-motivated pronouncements about "politicizing memory" and "legislating history."

As they now stand, however, Armenia and Turkey are very much prisoners of the past. Without attempts to address that past, they will continue to find themselves in opposite camps in the Caucasus and elsewhere and thereby allow opportunities for fomenting regional conflict and division. Mutual mistrust between Turkey and Armenia stemming from the genocide thus attains contemporary context and remains a threat to local, regional, and overall Eurasian security. The legacy of the genocide, for instance, has loomed large over the Mountainous Karabagh conflict. The Karabagh Armenians, unable to exorcise the ghost of the past and fearing total annihilation, have forged an independent republic. Meanwhile, Turkey, haunted by its past as well as future ramifications, has looked on with consternation as Armenians restore lands once arbitrarily placed under Azerbaijani dominion. In this sense, the Karabagh-Azerbaijani conflict has become the vehicle through which both Turks and Armenians continue to live out their worst fears of each other, fears rooted in the inheritance of genocide.

With this legacy unresolved and unrequited, Turkey will remain ever wary that a politically, diplomatically, and economically effective Armenia may someday raise the issue of the genocide and make derivative claims for reparations and restitution. Armenia's concerns are existential and self-evident. Until Turkey makes the long-awaited breakthrough to European benchmarks, rule of law, and self-deliverance, therefore, we can expect that Ankara will do all it can to prevent the emergence of a sound and stable Armenian state. It is nevertheless clear that unless both Turkey and Armenia confront the genocide head-on, it will hold their relations, and thus relevant security interests, hostage. Like Germany or Japan in this respect, Turkey is unlikely without international encouragement and pressure to face an inconvenient past on its own. And while the importance of normalization has not been lost on European and American policymakers, their efforts have thus far failed because they have tried to ignore the Armenian Genocide, its causes and consequences, as the source of reciprocal suspicion. They have not, therefore, exerted their influence with clear-cut purpose and sharp focus.

The primary argument for international recognition and tangible measures toward resolution is overwhelming. Renewed affirmation will provide Turkey and Armenia with a foundation for understanding and accepting their history, eliminating their mutual lack of confidence, exploring their combined comparative advantages, and rendering their relations meet and right. Honesty on the genocide issue is also one of the principal avenues for helping Turkey move on to create frontiers of peace and harmony, not only with Armenia but also with all of its neighbors.

Because of the changing map of Europe, Turkey can no longer persuasively threaten that universal recognition of the Armenian Genocide would seriously affect its ability to serve as NATO's southern bulwark against communism (a long-standing claim) and other undesirable ideologies. Among the less serious Turkish arguments against recognition have been that it would encourage Armenian political violence and that the historical record is unclear. Armenian terrorism, which was born of Turkish state terror and denial, effectively wrapped up years ago, and the documentation in the archives of Germany alone, an ally of Turkey at the time of the Armenian Genocide, is enough to put to rest the Turkish professions of innocence.

Sadly, Turkey's inability to date to deal with the genocide translates into no normalization of relations with Armenia, and its failure to "assume history" (French: *il faut assumer l'histoire*) incarcerates both Turkey and Armenia in the past. That state of affairs means that the two countries necessarily become surrogates in a larger power game over which neither has any real control, and their bilateral relations continue to play a major destabilizing role in the region. The results for both sides are unpredictable. Neither one can be sure that it will come out ahead. And there are grave implications for regional stability and global security.

Moreover, the absence of a multifunctional Armenian strategy also does disservice to the special role Armenia and the Armenian people should be undertaking in the struggle for human rights. Recognition of the genocide goes beyond both parochial concerns and regional and world security interests. It is a question of universal ethical dimensions affecting all humanity. The official, political, juridical, and thorough multidisciplinary recognition of the Jewish Holocaust, as renewed in the declaration of the Stockholm international forum on the subject, and the correspondingly striking non-recognition of the Armenian Genocide send the message that some genocides are impermissible while others are tolerated and that this duality has more to do with power politics than with the uniform application of international law and principles of human rights. This may be the case in the real world, but in fact with no clear message on genocide, that crime of crimes in its various forms continues to constitute an increasingly important instrument for preserving arbitrarily drawn borders or dealing with minority constituencies.

It is beyond doubt that history and morality, government action and political puissance, precept and practicality, right and might, are all intertwined factors in the battle still being waged between meaningful remembrance and interest-based denial. The Armenian state and nation need to take full stock of this mix and strive toward their lawful goal with endurance and coordinated efforts.

In sum, the international community should have an interest in promoting a fresh, new approach to the relationship of the NATO member-state of Turkey with the friendly, strategically placed country of Armenia. For reasons of regional security, economic development, and increased cooperation in a potentially volatile area of the world, individual governments might consider reviewing their own policies and weighing in on the side of creative, contemporary solutions that address, not evade, the problem at hand. In order that the twenty-first century will not proceed like the blood-drenched start of its predecessor, Ankara as the senior government ought to be persuaded to take the initiative in creating a good-faith, confidence-building environment free of the past rigid policies and conducive to open and frank communications. And while annual commemorations of the Armenian Genocide may come and go without much perceptible change, it is incumbent on Armenians to continue in their quest for justice and on Turks to search their souls for who they were, who they are, and, if they take the right turn, who they can be in regional and international affairs.

Turkey and its people might properly assume this higher mission by looking truth in the face and daring to turn a new page in Turkish-Armenian relations. We wish them every success and self-confidence in bridging this most monumental divide of their modern history. Apart and together, but always in balance, independent Armenia and its people the world over must be strong and steady enough to stay the course, shed their light all about, and attain the redemptive day of the triumph of truth—with distinction, determination, and dignity.

About the Contributors

Joyce Apsel is master teacher in the General Studies Program at New York University and has taught courses on twentieth-century genocide, genocide and human rights, and the Armenian Genocide and politics of denial at various universities. She is founder and director of Rights Works, an international human rights education project, and conducts student, teacher, and public education workshops on genocide and human rights. She is president of the International Association of Genocide Scholars (2001-03) and former director of education at the Anne Frank Center USA. She is coeditor with Helen Fein of *Teaching about Genocide*. Her award-winning public education series, "Anne Frank: Lessons in Human Rights and Dignity," is available on the *St. Petersburg Times* web site at www.sptimes.com and includes three articles on the Armenian Genocide.

Donald Bloxham is lecturer in Twentieth Century History at Edinburgh University. His research centers on the Armenian Genocide, the Holocaust, war crimes trials, and the comparative study of genocide. His chapter in this volume was written while he was holding a Leverhulme Special Research Fellowship at Southampton University. He is the author of *Genocide on Trial: War Crimes Trials in the Formation of Holocaust History and Memory*.

Fatma Müge Göçek is associate professor of sociology and women's studies at the University of Michigan. Her contribution in this volume is a summary of a larger manuscript she has recently completed. Her previous books, *Rise of the Bourgeoisie, Demise of Empire: Ottoman Westernization and Social Change*, and *East Encounters West: France and the Ottoman Empire in the Eighteenth Century*, reflect her interest in social change in the context of the Middle East. The next project she intends to undertake will focus on what she calls "other silences" in Turkish history.

Raffi K. Hovannisian is executive director of the Armenian Center for National and International Studies in Erevan, Armenia. A graduate of UCLA, Fletcher School of Law and Diplomacy, and Georgetown Law Center, he was employed in international law firms and founded the Armenian Bar Association before moving to Armenia as the regional director of the Armenian Assembly of America. In 1991-92 he served as the first foreign minister of the newly independent Republic of Armenia. During his tenure, Armenia was recognized by more than 150 countries and was admitted into a number of international organizations, including the United Nations and the Conference on Security and Cooperation in Europe (CSCE). In 2002 he organized the National Citizens' Initiative, a broad-based coalition for public empowerment and the rule of law in Armenia.

Richard G. Hovannisian is holder of the Armenian Educational Foundation Chair in Modern Armenian History at the University of California, Los Angeles. His publications include *Armenia on the Road to Independence*; the four-volume *Republic of Armenia*; *The Armenian Genocide in Perspective*; *The Armenian Genocide: History, Politics, Ethics*; *Remembrance and Denial: The Case of the Armenian Genocide*, and ten other volumes relating to Armenian and Middle Eastern history and culture. A Guggenheim Fellow, he was elected Academician of the National Academy of Sciences of Armenia in 1990 and has been awarded state medals by the Republic of Armenia and the Nagorno-Karabagh Republic and honorary doctoral degrees by Erevan State University and Artsakh State University. He has also received encyclicals and medals for distinguished scholarship from the Holy See of the Armenian Church in Echmiadzin, Armenia, and the Holy See of the Great House of Cilicia, now located in Lebanon.

Steven L. Jacobs is holder of the Aaron Aronov Chair of Judaic Studies and associate professor in the Department of Religious Studies at the University of Alabama, Tuscaloosa. His books include *Shirot Bialik: A New and Annotated Translation of Chaim Nachman Bialik's Epic Poems*; *Raphael Lemkin's Thoughts on Nazi Genocide: Not Guilty?*; *Contemporary Christian and Contemporary Jewish Religious Responses to the Shoah*; *Rethinking Jewish Faith: The Child of a Survivor Responds*; *The Holocaust Now: Contemporary Christian and Jewish Thought*; *The Meaning of Persons and Things Jewish*; *The Biblical Masorah and the Temple Scroll*; *Encyclopedia of Genocide*, associate editor; and *Pioneers of Genocide Studies,* co-editor.

Simon Payaslian is Kaloosdian-Mugar Professor of Modern Armenian History and Armenian Genocide Studies at Clark University, Worcester, Massachusetts. He holds a Ph.D. in political science (Wayne State University, 1992) and is completing his second Ph.D. in Armenian history at UCLA. He is the author of *The Armenian Genocide, 1915-1923: A Handbook for Students and Teachers*; *International Political Economy: Conflict and Cooperation in the Global System* (co-authored with Frederic S. Pearson); and *U.S. Foreign Economic and Military Aid: The Reagan and Bush Administrations*, as well as articles and book chapters on the United Nations, international law and human rights, peace studies, the Kurdish Question, and U.S. foreign policy. He is currently preparing a study on U.S. policy toward the Armenian Question and the Armenian Genocide.

Rubina Peroomian is research associate at the University of California, Los Angeles. She has taught Armenian Studies courses at UCLA, Glendale Community College, and the University of La Verne. Her publications include *Literary Responses to Catastrophe: A Comparison of the Armenian and the Jewish Experience* and, in the Armenian language, *Armenia in the Context of Relations between the Armenian Revolutionary Federation and the Bolsheviks, 1917-1921*(also in Russian), three secondary-school textbooks titled *The Armenian Question*, and several research articles on the Armenian Genocide and diasporan literature. She is the recipient of the Mesrop Mashots Medal from the Holy See of Cilicia and a lifetime achievement award from the Armenian Educational Foundation.

Vahram L. Shemmassian is principal of the Merdinian Armenian Evangelical School in Sherman Oaks, California. He has conducted extensive archival research and written about the villages of the Musa Dagh district near Antioch and the Armenian refugees in the Middle East in the post-genocide period. A frequent participant in conferences and programs on modern Armenian history, he is currently preparing for publication the history of the life of the villages and villagers of Musa Dagh from 1840 to 1915.

Ervin Staub is professor of psychology at the University of Massachusetts, Amherst, and director of the Ph.D. specialization "The Psychology of Peace and the Prevention of Violence." He has published on helping behavior and altruism and the passivity of bystanders as well as on violence, especially by groups. His works include *The Roots of Evil: The Origins of Genocide and Other Group Violence* and two forthcoming books, *The Psychology of Good and Evil* and *A Brighter Future: Raising Caring and Nonviolent Children.* He is currently engaged in a project in Rwanda on healing and reconciliation. Among his awards is the Otto Klineberg Intercultural and International Prize of the Society for the Psychological Study of Social Issues. He is past president of the Society for the Study of Peace, Conflict, and Violence: Peace Psychology Division of the American Psychological Association and of the International Society for Political Psychology.

Henry C. Theriault is assistant professor of philosophy at Worcester State College, where he serves as coordinator of the College's Center for the Study of Human Rights. His research focuses on genocide as well as mass violence and oppression more generally, with particular emphasis on issues of denial. His model course syllabus on the Armenian Genocide is forthcoming in the third edition of *Teaching about Genocide*, published by the American Sociological Association. His most recent research article is "Universal Social Theory and Genocide Denial," *Journal of Genocide Research* (June 2001).

Joe Verhoeven is a specialist in public international law and in European Union law. He now serves as professor at the Université de Paris II (Panthéon-Assas), after having taught at the Catholic University of Louvain for thirty years. Author of numerous papers, articles, and books in the field, his most recent publication is a manual on international law, *Droit international public*. He is member of the Institute of International Law and ad hoc judge at the International Court of Justice in the case *Uganda versus Congo.*

Gijs M. de Vries is former State Secretary of the Interior in the Government of the Netherlands. From 1984 to 1998, he was a member of the European Parliament, leading his party twice in the European elections, and between 1994 and 1998 he served as leader of the Liberal and Democratic Group in that body. He is co-founder of the Transatlantic Policy Network, bringing together politicians and companies from the United States and the European Union. The World Economic Forum (Geneva/Davos) selected him in 1998 as one of its Global Leaders for Tomorrow.

Index

VERMONT STATE COLLEGES
0 0003 0749103 5

VCTC Library
DISCARD
Hartness Library
Vermont Technical College
Randolph Center, VT 05061